June 4, 1907 - Aug. 18, 1944

(p. 225)

*A Knot
in the Thread*

A Knot in the Thread

THE LIFE AND WORK OF JACQUES ROUMAIN

CAROLYN FOWLER

HOWARD UNIVERSITY PRESS
Washington, D.C.
1980

Library of Congress Cataloging in Publication Data

Fowler, Carolyn.
    A knot in the thread.

    Bibliography: p.
    Includes index.
    1. Roumain, Jacques 1907–1944. 2. Authors, Haitian—Biography. I. Title.
PQ3949.R73Z66   841   76–53817
ISBN 0–88258–057–4

Grateful acknowledgment is made to the following:

George Bass and the curator of The Langston Hughes Papers in the James Weldon Johnson Memorial Collection of Negro Arts and Letters Founded by Carl Van Vechten, Collection of American Literature, The Beinecke Rare Book and Manuscript Library, Yale University, for permission to reprint excerpts from "A Poem for Jacques Roumain" by Langston Hughes. Reprinted by permission of Harold Ober Assoc.

George Bass and Mercer Cook for permission to reprint passages from *Masters of the Dew,* translated by Langston Hughes and Mercer Cook and published by Macmillan Co. in 1971.

Editions Gallimard, Hutchinson Publishing Group and Rosica Colin for permission to reprint a passage from "Black Orpheus" by Jean-Paul Sartre. First published by Editions Gallimard, 1949.

International Publishers for permission to reprint a passage from Joseph Freeman's "Introduction" to *Proletarian Literature in the United States: An Anthology* edited by Granville Hicks, Joseph North, et al. Copyright © 1935 by International Publishers.

New Directions Publishing Corp. for permission to reprint "Quand Bat le Tam-Tam" and "Guinée" from *American Anthology of Contemporary Latin American Poetry,* edited by Dudley Fitts, translated by Langston Hughes. Copyright © 1942 by New Directions. Reprinted by Permission of New Directions.

Joseph North for permission to reprint excerpts from "Is Poetry Dead?" by Jacques Roumain from the January 7, 1941, issue of *New Masses.*

Librarie Plon for permission to reprint passages from "Grievances of the Black Man" by Jacques Roumain, in *L'Homme de couleur* edited by Cardinal Verdier in 1939.

Presses Universitaires de France for permission to reprint "Madrid" from *Anthologie de la Nouvelle Poesie Nègre et Malgache de Langue Française* edited by Léopold Sédar Senghor.

The U.S. Naval Institute for permission to reprint a passage from *La Garde d'Haïti: Twenty Years of Organization and Training by the United States Marine Corps,* by James McCrocklin. Copyright © 1956, United States Naval Institute.

Appreciation is also due to the Alain Locke Collection, Moorland-Spingarn Research Center, Howard University and to the Schomburg Center for Research in Black Culture, The New York Public Library, Astor, Lenox and Tilden Foundations.

Contents

Preface   ix

INTRODUCTION

Early Youth: The Emergence of
Personality   1
Study and Growth: The First
European Period   3
Homecoming: The American
Occupation   6

CHAPTER I   *La Trouée* and *La Revue Indigène:*
Recasting an Image through Poetry   13

CHAPTER II   A Time to Act: Nationalism   43

CHAPTER III   Bourgeois Nonauthenticity   73
La Proie et L'Ombre   73
Les Fantoches   91

CHAPTER IV   From Port-au-Prince to the Haitian
Hills   109
La Montagne Ensorcelée   109
The Middle Poetry   131

CHAPTER V   Mobilizing the Haitian Masses and
a New Use for Literature   139
Le Champ du Potier   156

CHAPTER VI   Exile   175
The Second European Period   175
The United States and Cuba   205

Chapter VII   The Second Homecoming   213
                   Ethnology and Debate   213
                   Diplomacy and Death   223

Chapter VIII   *Gouverneurs de la Rosée:* Song of Hu-
                   man Solidarity   229
                   Conclusion   251

Appendix   Translations of French and
                   Spanish Passages in Text   255

Bibliography   345

Index   365

Preface

The Haitian poet and journalist Roussan Camille, writing in 1942, observed:

> Jacques Roumain réalise en sa personnalité attachante une chose fort rare: l'harmonie complète entre la vie et l'idée, entre l'homme et l'écrivain.[1]

Never having met the man, knowing little of his life, the contemporary reader nonetheless senses the truth of these words as he reads Jacques Roumain's fiction and poetry. The feeling deepens into conviction if he turns to Roumain's journalism and speeches, is not broken even by an examination of the ethnographic and sociological writings, and is confirmed, finally, by his letters and the recollections, such as the sentence quoted above, of those who knew him.

The study presented here is the outgrowth of my own efforts to understand to their fullest the literary works of Jacques Roumain through an investigation of his life in all of its aspects. Roumain, in his brief thirty-seven years, was a journalist, politician, revolutionary, diplomat, professor, and ethnographer as well as a poet and novelist. He crowded a lot of activity into those years and, especially in the early part of his adult life, seems to have gone rapidly and successively through several definable periods. His literary works consistently reflect the rest of his preoccupations at any given period, but yet a basic underlying concern with human betterment is discernible in the romantic youth of nineteen, as it is in the matured and cosmopolitan diplomat of thirty-seven. Upon analysis, Roumain's writings yield an undercurrent through which a constant need or ideal is symbolically transmitted.

---

[1] *Le Nouvelliste*, October 27, 1942.

ix

Often he transposes into literary terms the same idea or incident expressed elsewhere in his writings or in other aspects of his life.

An understanding of the literary production of such a personality becomes inseparable from a knowledge of the totality of his life. As Roussan Camille's words suggest, Jacques Roumain presents the phenomenon of the integrated personality. Moreover, he eagerly exposed himself to all the currents of humanist endeavor which were available to him. This tendency and the fact of his many years in Europe, in Anglo-Saxon and Latin America led, as one might expect, to the result that his conscience and activities reflect the major philosophical, literary and political currents at work in the era through which he lived. Because he was endowed with a capacity to seek honestly into the heart of issues, whether his own character, social conditions or man's ultimate relation to the universe, Jacques Roumain's life reflects successive and maturer *prises de conscience* and a reorienting of his activities in accordance with them, all of which is illuminated through his literature. Thus, his life and literature illuminate each other for us. But at the same time, they can provide us with a fruitful perception of the New Man of modern humanism, which is what Roumain's literature, in the final analysis, attempts to generate.

For this reason I have felt it best to present Jacques Roumain's life in a chronological order as undisturbed as possible by the exigencies of literary analysis hoping to show the interplay between his life and his literary activities, between the historical movements to which he was exposed and their influence on his life and work. Such an approach necessarily sacrifices some smoothness in the presentation and analysis of the literature, as it makes presentation by genres impossible and interrupts discussions of style, theme and symbolism. However, it does allow for the study of marginal areas never before treated in studies of Roumain, such as his journalism and his speeches.

Where it is necessary to deal with topics important to Roumain's life and work, such as vodun, dialectical materialism or the American Occupation and Haitian politics, I have given as clear and detailed an account of the material as sources available to me permitted, with a minimum of commentary except insofar as these para-literary activities turn up in literary transposition. I do not call the resulting biography "critical" for the simple reason that it attempts to be critical only in respect to the literature studied.

In my efforts to fill in gaps in the story of Roumain's life, I interviewed many people. I spoke with those who knew Jacques Roumain personally and were associated with him either socially or professionally or both. These persons are referred to throughout the work as "Group I Interviews." I also had a number of interviews with Haitian scholars in the various fields upon which Roumain touched, and with critics and writers familiar with Haitian literature and with Roumain's work and that of his generation. This group I refer to as "Group II Interviews." Several people in both categories have asked to remain anonymous. In order to preserve the identity of some, it has been necessary to preserve the anonymity of all.[2] For the same reasons, I have refrained in most cases from giving the location of private manuscript sources. The sources of the few manuscripts cited which are available in public repositories have, of course, been indicated.

When this study was originally presented as a Ph.D. dissertation, Roumain's work was available almost exclusively in first editions and not easily accessible. I therefore made liberal use of quotations. Since that time, most of his imaginative work has become available in inexpensive paperback editions. However, I have retained the wealth of quotations, as Roumain's works are still not widely circulated in this country, and most of the periodicals in which he published are largely inaccessible in the United States.

My indebtedness to the considerable number of people who have helped me realize this project is far too great to find

---

[2] Common courtesy demanded, however, that I make an exception and identify Group II interviews in instances where I use critical observations or factual information supplied to me to develop an argument of my own.

complete expression here. Particularly valuable have been the recollection of many of those who knew Jacques Roumain and who graciously allowed me to interview them and peruse relevant materials in their possession. A special note of appreciation is also due my Haitian colleagues who initially led me to sources which proved helpful beyond my hopes, and to the Haitian scholars whose stimulating discussions with me about currents in black literature in general and Haitian literature in particular, and about Jacques Roumain's place in this scheme, provided me with a number of ideas and clarifications. I wish also to thank Professor Gerald Prince of the University of Pennsylvania and Professors Léon Damas and Jacques Antoine of Howard University for their careful reading of the manuscript and their valuable suggestions, and Brother Lucien, librarian at the Institution Saint Louis de Gonzague, for the graciousness with which he received my many requests.

A Knot
in the Thread

Introduction

EARLY YOUTH: THE EMERGENCE OF A PERSONALITY

In the first decade of the twentieth century, the Bois Verna section of Port-au-Prince, along with neighboring Turgeau, consisted of peaceful streets lined with tall, imposing houses and lovely gardens. These residential areas set the tone of relaxed and gracious living enjoyed by the upper classes of Haitian society, primarily of mulatto origin at that period. These were the old families of Haiti, whose members had often been presidents and statesmen, lawyers, doctors, and writers, who passed on to their children a long tradition of meticulous education, much of it through the schools of France. Jacques Roumain was born into this environment on June 4, 1907, first of the eleven children of Auguste Roumain. Jacques's father was a large landowner, of considerable stature in the community; his maternal grandfather, Tancrède Auguste, had served as president of the republic in the period 1912–13. These circumstances of his background were to have important consequences in the life Jacques Roumain found waiting for him in Haiti, and the life he chose to live.

Roumain's early boyhood must, in most respects, have resembled that of other Haitian youths of his class and condition. He took trips into the countryside with his family, a customary practice, especially in prewar years when urban distractions were fewer. Because the family owned lands in the countryside, their visits often extended to several weeks. In this way Jacques Roumain while still a small boy became acquainted with the Haitian countryside and with the Haitian

1

peasant. In Port-au-Prince, he ordinarily spent his days in classes at the Institution Saint Louis de Gonzague. Run by the Frères de l'Instruction Chrétienne, an order of French monks long established in Haiti, the Institution enjoyed a reputation for quality. Witnesses[1] remember Jacques Roumain as being about like other boys of his age, but more exuberant, more *"bruyant"* and aggressive than the average. At eight or nine years, he was *"turbulent."*

By Roumain's own admission, he was an *enfant terrible*. In a 1927 interview he recalled: "Je trouvais plaisir à déchirer mes fonds de culotte avec toutes les mauvaises têtes du quartier."[2] One witness recounts how Roumain organized the Bois Verna boys in games of battle against the Turgeau boys. Another recalls a game they used to play that Jacques invented, called *venceremos*, and which, as the name implies, represented the victory of the oppressed over those who wronged them. The same person says:

> Ever since he was young, he . . . rebelled against any wrongs toward the weak and the poor. He has always been a champion of a cause. Of course, the cause was not well-defined at the beginning. . . . He was always some sort of leader.

Another witness relates an incident which occurred when Roumain was perhaps ten years old. He had learned that a cousin, a girl a few years older than himself, had been replaced in the affections of her "boy friend" by another. The witness states:

> Et Jacques nous a fait annoncer qu'il viendrait—il savait que nous étions toujours ensemble à tel jour, telle heure—et de l'attendre . . . qu'il viendrait . . . donner un coup de pied à

---

[1] The people interviewed for the purposes of this study fall into two groups: those who knew Jacques Roumain and were in a position to give first-hand information (designated here as "Group I interviews"); and scholars who are familiar with literature or other disciplines relevant to the study and with Jacques Roumain's life and work (designated as "Group II interviews"). The material in this chapter was compiled from information supplied by Group I interviews.

[2] Antonio Vieux, "Entre Nous: Jacques Roumain," *La Revue Indigène*, no. 3 (September 1927), p. 105.

l'autre. . . . Effectivement, il est venu, il m'a donné la main—
Comment vas-tu? Comment vas-tu?—et un coup de pied à
l'autre. . . . Et pour vous dire comment il était aventureux.
Un enfant de son âge ne serait pas allé attaquer un autre de
deux ans plus âgé et assez fort.

Most people remember the turbulent side of the boy
Jacques—full of life, aggressive, a leader, possessed of a sense
of social justice. But there is another, reverse side to Roumain's
character. He was reflective, introspective, melancholy. According to one witness, this side of him goes back to earliest
youth. With adolescence, this quiet side of his nature was to
display itself more fully, perhaps aided by the inevitable
longings which accompany a long absence from home.

STUDY AND GROWTH: THE FIRST EUROPEAN PERIOD

Roumain's absence from home began some time in 1920 or
1921, when he left Haiti for Switzerland, where he was to
continue his education at the Institut Grünau in Berne. It is
clearly the melancholy romanticism of a sensitive youth that
we see in some of the letters he wrote from Grünau. One such
letter mentions nocturnal walks in the park: "Je suis nerveux,
regarde toujours dans le vague, me promène seul, parle peu
et mange peu." He apparently took the Institut's director into
his confidence, for he mentions the director's reassurances that
such feelings would pass. The letter goes on: "La seule chose
que je fasse avec passion est la lecture: Schopenhauer,
Nietzsche, Darwin et les vers de Heine et de Lenau."[3] Roumain's readings were quite varied, in fact. In addition to
nineteenth-century German letters, he was quite taken with
Near Eastern philosophy and art: the Rissalvat al Tarohid, the
Koran, the Upanishads, Hafiz, Omar Khayyam.[4] It is probable
also that his readings in pre-Columbian archeology—the Aztec
and Mayan cultures in particular—date back as far as these
years in Switzerland (Group I interviews). But in other moods,
Roumain was also capable of lines such as these:

> . . . laisse toute conversation à propos de philosophie de
> côté. Que chacun cherche la vérité où il la trouve. A quoi

---

[3] Letter written from Grünau in 1922.
[4] Vieux, p. 103.

bon discuter? Tout doit passer, tout doit rentrer dans le néant.
. . .[5]

The anti-intellectualism of these nihilistic lines betrays very
real intellectual pursuits; their philosophizing is based on a
voracious reading in a certain type of philosophy. But they
also allow us to see how deep was the affective life of the
adolescent Roumain.

It was during the time in Switzerland that Roumain began
to write poetry, a very Romantic poetry, heavily influenced by
Heine and to a lesser extent perhaps by Hafiz and Omar
Khayyam (Group I interviews). Witnesses do not seem to
remember him having written poems or stories before leaving
Port-au-Prince, but poems do begin to appear in letters written
by him from Europe, such as the following one, included in
a letter dated April 10, 1923, from Grünau:

"Violettes fanées"

Je vous contemple et une sourde tristesse m'envahit
En voyant vos pauvres pétales défraîchies.
Pareilles à des lèvres de morte, des lèvres à jamais fermées
Vous penchez vos têtes pensives où peut-être une bouche mig-
   nonne
Posa un baiser en songeant à l'être aimé.
Pensez-vous, o fleurettes, à la main inconsciente
Qui devait vous perdre et se fit caressante?
Songez-vous à l'heure où encore parées de vos charmes
Vous [. . .][6] quand d'un baiser on vous faisait l'aumône?
      Ou bien vous rappelez-vous la minute
      où un malheureux amant
Confia à vos corolles une larme
Que pareille à la rosée y scintilla un moment?!

The synesthetic imagery of Romantic correspondences, the
structure of the poem, which is divided into statement and
resolution—beginning at line six, the poet brings in the human
experience, for which the elaborate description of nature in
the first five has served as setting and metaphor—and the use
of the flower as a symbol of the fleeting delicacy of love all
show the young poet to be operating entirely within the

---

[5] Letter from Grünau dated October 23, 1922.
[6] Manuscript is illegible here.

Romantic tradition and its borrowings from the Renaissance. We can be more readily impressed with the polish of the poem and what it reveals of Roumain's knowledge of European literature than with its intrinsic value.

It would be a mistake to picture the Jacques Roumain of the 1922–23 Grünau period as simply a sensitive, melancholy youth given over to the private pleasures of reading. While some photographs show Jacques Roumain at Grünau dressed for a costume ball as a wistful Arabian prince in jeweled robes and turban, others portray him in boxing trunks and sparing stance. He enjoyed sports, particularly track, tennis, football, and boxing (Group I interviews). Roumain himself was to reflect several years later on what was clearly a dual nature:

> Qui donc affirme . . . qu'il y a deux hommes en chacun de nous? Auprès du sportsman . . . exubérant de vie, il y a en moi un côté mélancolique, l'élégant ennui de Byron. Ces deux hommes, dans mes actes, je les sens se heurter. En Suisse, nous étions de joyeux étudiants, aimant le plaisir et ne reculant pas, certains jours, devant la rixe joyeuse.[7]

So it is that the essential traits of Roumain's character appear from the earliest youth. That they are so evident from the start points to the excessiveness of his personality. The searching and sensitive poet, the robust and aggressive leader are nonetheless two extremes which never neutralize each other; nor does one ever submerge the other for very long. These essential traits profoundly impress those who come to know Roumain throughout his life, and will mark all of his work.

From Grünau, where he had completed his secondary schooling, Jacques Roumain went to Zurich, where he studied a year at the Ecole Polytechnique, in preparation for advanced studies in engineering. These years in Switzerland were rich in study and intellectual growth. Roumain came to speak German fluently. Apart from the reading, he profited too by exposure to the meeting of French and German cultures (for which his reading of Heine had probably prepared him), and from the coming together of various nationalities in the cosmopolitan atmosphere of Zurich.

---

[7] Vieux, p. 107.

Roumain changed his mind as to the profession he wished to pursue, and in 1926 he left Zurich for Spain, where he was to study agronomy, intending to use his knowledge in that field to develop land left by his grandfather. It seems likely, however, that he was attracted to Spain just as much by Montherlant—who had just published *Les Bestiares*[8]—as by any professional aspirations. The time spent in Spain also gave him the opportunity to gain fluency in Spanish. Roumain has explained the attraction of Spain in the 1927 interview with Antonio Vieux:

> En fait de Zootechnie, je m'intéressais surtout aux courses de taureaux. J'aimais surtout le plein soleil des corridas. Cela correspondait à cet excès de vie que je porte. Ce fut aussi à cette époque que je connus Montherlant. Ses "Bestiaires" m'ont frappé à un point que vous ne pourrez supposer. J'y sentais un poète avec lequel j'avais de certaines affinités. (Vieux, p. 105)

The poem "Corrida,"[9] written in this period in Spain, provides a good record of the *mélange* of Roumain's readings on pre-Columbian American culture and his interest in active sports. Roumain purposely emphasizes in the poem that aspect of sports activity which symbolizes or ritualizes heroic deeds. The poem also shows that Roumain had put aside—at least tentatively—the Romantics for the Surrealists.

HOMECOMING: THE AMERICAN OCCUPATION

Jacques Roumain left Spain within the year, thus interrupting his formal education. But he came back to Haiti, as one writer puts it, "avec tout un bagage de connaissances variées."[10]

---

[8] Roumain's arrival in Spain and publication of *Les Bestiaries* both occurred in 1926. That the latter event predates the former is based on statements from among Group I interviews. The same statements leave the impression that Roumain had read *Les Bestiaires* before leaving for Spain.

[9] This poem was later published in the *Revue Indigène;* it is discussed along with the other poems published in the 1927–28 period.

[10] Louis Garoute, "Portrait: Jacques Roumain," *Le Nouvelliste,* 19 Décembre 1941. It would be erroneous to give the impression that

Now he was back in Haiti prepared to fight in the cause of Haitian Nationalism, in the movement which was gaining momentum to free Haiti from the foreign domination that had gripped it since 1915. In that year, Roumain had been eight years old. When he left Haiti in 1920 or 1921, he had been a boy no older than fourteen. He had observed with the growing political consciousness of oncoming maturity the events in Haiti from Switzerland and from Spain. He had been at times impatient to be home and active in the struggle. This feeling was well crystallized by 1925, the year in which he addressed a letter to Joseph Jolibois Fils, director of the Opposition newspaper *Courrier Haïtien* and acknowledged Nationalist leader. The letter begins:

Monsieur le Directeur,

Vous excuserez l'audace que j'ai prise en vous écrivant, car personnellement je vous suis tout à fait inconnu. Vous me pardonnerez sûrement quand je vous dirai que je me vante d'être Haïtien . . . forcé à cause de mes études d'ingénieur, de m'exiler encore quelque temps en Europe, l'inaction m'est de jour en jour plus insupportable. J'ai hâte de retourner en Haiti, afin d'aider à relever le courage des masses et à soulager le peuple.

Roumain alone had visited or studied in Europe or that he alone had been exposed to the intellectual currents there. Some European education was typical of his class. Others of his generation had been in Paris at roughly the same time, among them Emile Roumer, whose *Poèmes d'Haïti et de France* were published in Paris in 1925, and Philippe Thoby-Marcelin, who, along with Roumain, appears to have influenced Haitian art by some of the concepts he brought back from Europe. Pétion Savain, a prominent painter and indigenist novelist, has said: "Tandis que se déclenchait le mouvement littéraire de la jeunesse actuelle, la peinture me fut révélée par Jacques Roumain et Philippe Thoby-Marcelin. Quelle explosion de joie quand je parcourus les bouquins qui'ils me passaient! Je vis s'annoncer une aube nouvelle. (Pétion Savain, "De l'avenir et de l'intégration de la Peinture Haïtienne dans la Peinture Moderne," in *La Voix de la génération de l'occupation* (Port-au-Prince: Editions de l'Assaut, no. 2 [mars 1936]), p. 47. Antonio Vieux's article leaves the impression that all the young men of Roumain's group had read and been impressed by Nietzsche. It is nonetheless true that in the years in Europe, Roumain had absorbed an unusually rich variety of doctrines, disciplines, and skills.

> Je vous paraîtrai peut-être extrêmement présompteux si je vous dis que je n'ai que dix-huit ans; mais le patriotisme, aussi bien que la valeur, n'attend pas le nombre des années, et vous me combleriez si vous vouliez me faire l'honneur de me considérer au nombre de vos alliés les plus fidèles.[11]

In order to follow Roumain's activities and writings with any degree of understanding for the next eight years and the movements in which he took part, it is necessary now to take a rather long parenthetical look at the Haitian situation generally in these years when Roumain was growing up in Bois Verna and maturing in Europe.[12]

During the years 1908–15, Haiti had gone through a period of continuous political and financial upheaval. In seven years, seven men acceded to the presidency largely through a series of revolutionary uprisings begun in the North with the support of the *cacos*, revolutionary armies comprised primarily of peasants in the pay of the presidential aspirant. American intervention had been intermittent for a number of years but became more pronounced in 1914–15 when the United States on occasion landed small contingents of marines for the purposes of protecting foreign monetary and business interests, partly out of fear of intervention by other foreign powers— Germany notably—and in accordance with the Monroe Doctrine. In June and July 1915, Rosalvo Bobo began massing *cacos* for a revolutionary march against the recently formed government of Vilbrun Guillaume Sam. Bobo's first goal was the taking of the northern city of Cap-Haïtien.

---

[11] Letter from Zurich dated January 15, 1925, in Georges Sylvain, ed., *Dix Années de Lutte pour la Liberté: 1915–1925* (Port-au-Prince: H. Deschamps, n.d.) 2:134–35.

[12] Historical information in this chapter has been synthesized from the following sources: Dantès Bellegarde, *Histoire du Peuple Haitien (1492–1952)* (Port-au-Prince: Collection du Tricenquantenaire de l'Indépendance d'Haïti, 1953); Harold Davis, *Black Democracy: The Story of Haiti* (New York: Lincoln MacVeagh-The Dial Press, 1928); Roger Gaillard, *Les Cent-Jours de Rosalvo Bobo* (Port-au-Prince: Presses Nationales, 1973); James H. McCrocklin, *La Garde D'Haïti* (Annapolis, Md: U.S. Naval Institute [1956?]); Arthur Chester Millspaugh, *Haiti Under American Control, 1915–1930* (Boston: World Peace Foundation, 1931).

Admiral Caperton of the U.S. Navy hastily stationed himself off Cap-Haïtien and tried personally to conduct the hostilities. Caperton sent communiqués to Probus Blot, commander of the government forces, and to Rosalvo Bobo, that no fighting should occur within the city of Cap-Haïtien itself. The American commander made it a point to appear neutral. But since Blot's troops now held the city, while Bobo's forces were camped some distance outside of town, Caperton was, in effect, favoring the government's cause.

But while Caperton was busy watching Blot and Bobo in the North, the center of revolutionary activity switched, unexpectedly, to Port-au-Prince, where prominent Haitians, former statesmen and politicians, adherents of the government preceding Guillaume Sam's or of Bobo, had taken refuge in various embassies. From these sanctuaries, a group of them mapped out a plan, in collusion with *cacos* within the palace in the pay of Guillaume Sam. On the night of July 27, 1915, these men, reinforced by *caco* troops massing in town, attacked the National Palace. Guillaume Sam fled with his family to the French legation, which was directly behind the palace.

Meanwhile, in the National Prison, some 167 political prisoners, mostly from prominent Haitian families, were massacred in their cells by officers of the government. The following day, an angry mob, led by young men of the Haitian elite on the way from burying their slain relatives, pulled Guillaume Sam from the French legation, killed him and paraded his dismembered body through the streets.

The American chargé d'affaires had sent an urgent wire to Caperton in the North immediately after the attack on the National Palace. Caperton arrived in the aftermath of Guillaume Sam's death, and after sending scouts ashore and inviting the English and French ministers to confer with him aboard ship, he concluded that the moment for full-scale intervention had arrived. He sent word to the *Comité Révolutionnaire* which had been hastily formed for the purposes of maintaining governmental machinery that he was occupying the capital in order to protect American lives and interests. This done, Caperton notified Washington of his actions and received approval to land the marines.

Within two weeks, the Haitian legislature had elected Sudre Dartiguenave (instead of Rosalvo Bobo) to the presidency. Although the election was to all evidence conducted autonomously by the Haitian people, there can be little doubt that the United States' open support of Dartiguenave and the advance quizzing to which Caperton had subjected both candidates influenced the outcome. A treaty was eventually signed, with the United States agreeing to float a new loan consolidating the existing national debt, and giving the United States full control over customs revenue and all final say in affairs of government and finance. This authority was exercised by a General Receiver and High Commissioner, nominated by the president of the United States and appointed by the president of Haiti. The United States was also mandated to disband the existing army and police and to institute and administer a constabulary for the nation as a whole. This constabulary—called the *Gendarmerie d'Haïti* until 1928, when its name was changed to *Garde d'Haïti*—was officered and manned by the United States Marine Corps, with Haitians in the ranks. The plan called for the training of Haitian officers for their eventual take-over of the *Garde*. In addition to its police functions, the *Gendarmerie* also had responsibility for public works and sanitation until the late 1920s, but much of its work in this area involved the building of *Gendarmerie* garrisons.

The marines' reactivation of the *corvée*—a kind of forced labor by which peasant workers were employed to rebuild roads—and their practice of having the peasants work longer than the prescribed time and at distances from their homes greater than the law allowed, were the immediate causes of *caco* resistance. The marines erroneously saw the *cacos* as simple bandits. They were determined to rid the countryside of them. During the period 1915–19, the *Gendarmerie* and the *cacos* were engaged in frequent skirmishes. The most successful of the *caco* chiefs was Charlemagne Péralte who in 1918–19 mobilized perhaps as many as five thousand men, made frequent raids on *Gendarmerie* outposts and finally marched on Port-au-Prince. His men were repelled and in October 1919 *Gendarmerie* agents infiltrated his camp and shot him. Charlemagne Péralte had become a popular hero. With his death, the *caco* uprisings were soon suppressed.

Dartiguenave's government, though it did not openly challenge the Occupation, nevertheless managed in devious ways to delay and frustrate American orders and wishes. The Legislature showed itself more openly hostile by refusing to put through a new Constitution, needed to legalize the recently signed treaty. Particularly odious was a clause allowing for ownership of land by foreigners. Such ownership had been banned in each of Haiti's constitutions since independence. When the Legislature attempted to put through a Constitution of its own making and showed signs of its intention to impeach Dartiguenave for accepting stipulations in the treaty which, by the existing Constituion, were illegal, the American High Commissioner required Dartiguenave to sign an order dissolving the Legislature and himself walked into the Legislature in session and forcibly disbanded it.

A new, pro-American Constitution was ratified by plebiscite. According to its terms, new legislative elections were to be called at the discretion of the president. Between 1917 and 1930, no such elections were called and functions of the legislative branch were taken over by ministers appointed by the president (the *Conseil d'Etat*).

With the election of Louis Borno to the office of president, a more conciliatory government came into being in May of 1922, one which gradually became more pro-American and Haitian opposition to Borno's collaborationist politics began to gather momentum. By 1930, in anticipation of the expiration of Borno's second term of office, Nationalist groups such as the *Union Patriotique*, the *Ligue de la Jeunesse Patriote Haïtienne*, and the *Ligue d'Action Constitutionnelle*[13] had begun to close ranks and were demanding new legislative elections and an end to the Borno era. The United States sent a commission to study the situation (the Forbes Commission) and through its offices a plan was worked out whereby Eugène Roy was agreed upon jointly by the Borno ministers and by the Nationalist

---

[13] This last group was composed primarily of candidates for the presidency and therefore of men whose motives were perhaps less disinterested than those of the two other groups.

groups as provisional president. His express duty was to call for and oversee the long-postponed legislative elections.

On November 18, 1930, a newly elected Legislature elected Sténio Vincent, well-known Nationalist leader, as president.[14] General Russell, a naval officer associated with the unpleasant memories of the Borno government, was replaced by a career diplomat, Dana Munro, in pursuance of the recommendation of the Forbes Commission and the post of high commissioner was dissolved. This series of events marked the turning point in the Occupation. Thenceforth, the administration of government was gradually returned into Haitian hands and in August 1934 the last contingent of marines departed. The American Occupation was formally at an end.

The events back to 1915 must certainly have been well-known to those who had come of age in the years following. And the Haiti to which Jacques Roumain returned in 1927, in the middle of the Borno era, had been shaped by those events.

---

[14] The Haitian president was formerly elected by the joint House of Deputies and the Senate.

CHAPTER I

La Trouée *and* La Revue Indigène: *Recasting an Image Through Poetry*

The year 1927 is an important one in the literary history of Haiti, for it marks a definite stage in a literary movement which was attempting to formulate and, through its journals, exemplify an ideology inspired on the esthetic level by the same anti-American Nationalist sentiments as the snowballing political movement. The occupying forces, mostly marines, many of whom were from the South, in their missionary zeal equated efficiency, progress, and justice with their own way of life and in many cases treated the Haitians as inferiors. Unable or unwilling to understand cultural differences, the marines seemed intent—consciously or otherwise—on transforming Haiti into a country patterned on the United States model.[1]

---

[1] An incident reported by James McCrocklin reveals an attitude, to judge by all other accounts, typical of the Marine Corps vis à vis the Haitian masses:

"A man had killed his ward, a girl of twelve years. Brought to trial, the murderer's defense was that he obeyed a force stronger than himself. The jury, under the impression that they were finding the man guilty with extenuating circumstances, acquitted him, thus freeing what was undoubtedly a homicidal maniac. The Gendarmerie took the only action possible in the circumstances and confined the man as insane." (McCrocklin, p. 132).

The suppression of Haitian life-styles and concepts inevitably followed, under such circumstances, the suppression of Haitian autonomy. As early as 1916, reactions to the Occupation had begun to materialize in the literary milieu. The first journal to grow out of this reaction was *La Revue de la Ligue de la Jeunesse Haïtienne*, in which men such as Fernand Hibbert (1873–1929) and Léon Laleau (1892–1979) figured prominently. Their intention was to preserve, in the face of foreign intrusion, Haiti's intellectual and spiritual heritage.[2]

In 1925, a group of young men—Max Hudicourt, Antonio Vieux, André Liautaud, Philippe Thoby-Marcelin, Etienne Charlier—came together to form *La Nouvelle Ronde*. The name of the review implied a wish to perpetuate a tradition of Haitian letters,[3] but it looked more to the future than the past in that it sought to renovate rather than preserve Haitian literary culture. The journal criticized the work of the previous generation, apparently seeing in it an evasion into the past which could not take into account present realities, and a style which seemed stilted and outmoded. *La Nouvelle Ronde* gave much of its efforts to negative criticism; there were, however, attempts to formulate a basis for Haitian literature of the present and future:

> Il aurait fallu, pour que la littérature haïtienne existât, que
> les oeuvres réfléchissent davantage les aspirations, les tend-

---

[2] In speaking of reactions to the Occupation, it becomes necessary to take generational differences into account. One scholar has written: "Tous les Haïtiens ont vivement ressenti cette secousse, mais ses répercussions sur les oeuvres littéraires ont été variables. L'équipe dont les membres étaient déjà formés à l'arrivée de l'occupant a réagi par un retour à la poésie patriotique: ils se sont lamentés sur le sort du pays (*Thrène pour Haïti*, de Edmond Laforest [1876–1915]) ou bien ils se sont mis à exalter le geste de 1804 [i.e., the Haitian war of Independence] (Christian Werleigh [1895–1947], *Le Palmiste dans la lumière* [1938]); d'autres ont choisi d'évoquer des légendes et paysages quisquéyens [Indian] (*Poèmes quisquéyens* [1926], de Frédéric Burr-Reynaud), quand ils ne se répandaient pas en anathèmes vengeurs contre l'occupant et ses collaborateurs [i.e., Burr-Reynaud's *Anathèmes*, 1930]. . . ." (Franck Fouché, *Guide pour l'étude de la littérature haïtienne* [Port-au-Prince: Editions Panorama, 1964], p. 95).

[3] The literary review *La Ronde* had, at the turn of the century, been the organ with which Nationalist writers had been associated.

ances, l'âme même du pays. . . . Nos aînés ont pu faire des oeuvres de valeur. Ils n'ont pas fait des oeuvres assez profondément nôtres. Il faudrait . . . analyser l'âme haïtienne, la mettre à nue et la disséquer. Par là et par là seulement peut se produire cette originalité dont le souci fut une obsession et qu'on allait chercher si loin, sauf où elle pouvait se trouver.[4]

To a great extent, this emphasis on the psychological and the esthetic was influenced by the phases through which the Occupation was passing. Direct resistance, as practiced during the *caco* movement, had proven futile. The possibility of a Nationalist government coming to power was still remote. Self-interest in the military and governing classes had brought morale to a low pitch. It became increasingly important to wage the battle on the persuasive level of ideas and writing.[5] Those Haitians who reasoned in this way conceived the problem as a confrontation of values and reacted in defense of Haitian modes of being. They proposed to reflect the image of those modes of being in a literature which would no longer imitate European models, but would look to Haiti and things Haitian for its inspiration. Now, since man acquires his image, his sense of self, through his art forms, it is imperative that those art forms reflect what is truly him. This general philosophy, implicit in *La Nouvelle Ronde*, was also the basis of the two reviews in which Jacques Roumain collaborated in 1927–28: *La Trouée: Revue d'Intérêt Général* and, more especially, *La Revue Indigène: Les Arts et La Vie*.

Both journals appeared in July 1927, *La Trouée* considerably earlier in the month. The first issue carried the names of Richard Salnave and Jacques Roumain as co-editors, with Daniel Heurtelou as secretary and Max Hudicourt as business manager. André Liautaud, who had figured among the founders of *La Nouvelle Ronde*, also figured prominently among contributors to *La Trouée*. As the name implies, *La Trouée*

---

[4] Antonio Vieux and Philippe Thoby-Marcelin, *La Nouvelle Ronde*, 1er Juillet, 1925, p. 30 (cited in Fouché, pp. 97–98).

[5] Fouché: "Comment s'opposer à l'envahisseur tout puissant, si ce n'est que par une résistance morale, pour la sauvegarde de l'héritage ancestral et du patrimoine culturel, intellectuel de la nation." (p. 105).

sought to "percer la ligne d'ignorance et d'apathie qui nous étouffe."[6] The "ligne d'ignorance et d'apathie" was, in the minds of the collaborators, contiguous with the Occupation. The founders enunciate in the first issue their position with respect to literature:

> La littérature n'est pas ce qu'on pense en Haïti. Elle n'est pas une occupation de pédants et de désoeuvrés. Nous bannirons les uns et les autres. C'est le cri d'un peuple qui veut dire ce qui bout en lui. Ce n'est pas ce pastiche agréablement "couleur localisée" de certains, non plus que cette pâle mignardise de certains autres. C'est l'expression des Idées, de nos idées, à nous Haïtiens. (p. 1)

Literary renovation, however, was seen as only one aspect of the work the founders of *La Trouée* cut out for themselves:

> Nous étudierons les grands problèmes. Ceux qui se posent à la génération haïtienne actuelle et qu'elle fait semblant d'ignorer, alors qu'ils lui crèvent les yeux. . . . nous nous attaquerons à eux et le faisceau de nos bonnes volontés réunies en arrivera à bout. (p. 1)

In the following paragraph of the article, considerable admiration is expressed for Italian Fascism (the word *"faisceau"* above is an allusion to it), and it is held up as a model for Haiti.[7]

In this first issue Jacques Roumain's presence is very much in evidence; he contributed two poems and a short story and also had a share in framing the editorial statement (Group I interviews). His contributions grow fewer in subsequent issues.[8] Roumain's name had disappeared from the editorial board with the appearance of the second issue. It seems that he had been displeased by the first issue, feeling that the magazine lacked sufficient unity from a political as well as literary point of view. The preparation of the second issue had

---

[6] From the statement of purpose, which opens the first issue, signed "La Direction," p. 1.

[7] One of the members of this generation has explained that Fascism attracted them because it was a nationalist movement. They became disenchanted with Mussolini when he aligned himself with Hitler, who was a racist (Group I interviews).

[8] One poem each in the second, third, fourth, and seventh issues.

brought into the open divergences of viewpoint between the editors, Roumain apparently feeling that some of the manuscripts were low in literary merit or expressed political views not in accord with what he felt should be the thrust of the journal. His differences with Salnave resulted in Roumain's withdrawing from the administration of the journal (Group I interviews).

Leafing through the issues of *La Trouée*, one notes among the contributors the frequent presence of authors and poets born in the 1880s and 1890s, whose poetry projects a patriotic and Neo-Romantic aura onto the journal. Many of the articles deal with phases of the Haitian War of Independence. Side by side with this older current, one finds works of more 'indigenist' character.[9] Many of the writers of *La Revue Indigène*—

---

[9] The terms *patriotic, nationalist,* and *'indigenist'* characterize different periods in Haitian literary history. Poetry of the Patriotic school sings the exploits of the heroes of the Independence, of Haiti's beauty and grandeur, and cries out in anguish at her problems. It arose in the 1860s in reaction against the European and American detractors of the Black Republic, as well as in patriotic defense of Haiti in her disputes with Spain and Santo Domingo. The Nationalist school of the turn of the century, weary of the grandiose exaltation of the Patriotic school, sought to infuse local color and customs, a sense of nature and of the Haitian mentality into its literature. (See Ghislain Gouraige, *Histoire de la Littérature Haïtienne,* pp. 41–85, 100–104, 151–61). The poets associated with the *Revue Indigène* sought to develop in a less stilted style a more intimate poetry, that is, one which should reveal the Haitian soul. Objection to the term 'indigenism' has been raised from among the group of the *Revue Indigène* as misleading with respect to their intentions. The sense of the journal's title is clearly stated in Normil Sylvain's "Chronique-Programme" in the first issue. It has nonetheless been used by some literary historians to identify any poetry with the same thrust as the movement seen through the pages of the *Revue Indigène*. Other historians use the term even more generally to designate any literature in any period which celebrates or derives its inspiration from the indigenous landscape or culture. (See particularly Hénock Trouillot, *Les Origines sociales de la littérature haïtienne* [Port-au-Prince: N.A. Théodore, 1962] pp. 122–ff.) The members of *La Revue Indigène* were not always in agreement as to who might fall within the definitions of their movement. Jacques Roumain said of Oswald Durand: "Oswald Durand est un précurseur. Il est indigène." Antonio Vieux did not agree. (Vieux, pp. 108–9).

Philippe Thoby-Marcelin, Normil Sylvain, Carl Brouard, Daniel Heurtelou—were, as well as Jacques Roumain, contributors to *La Trouée*.

Late in July 1927, the first issue of *La Revue Indigène* appeared, founded by Emile Roumer, Normil Sylvain, Jacques Roumain, Antonio Vieux, Philippe Thoby-Marcelin, Daniel Heurtelou, and Carl Brouard. (Several of these men had launched *La Nouvelle Ronde* two years earlier.) That *La Trouée* and *La Revue Indigène* could have appeared almost simultaneously and with an overlapping list of contributors is indicative that their aims were somewhat different: *La Revue Indigène* was to be purely literary (Group I interviews). Indeed, what distinguished *La Revue Indigène* from *La Trouée* was not the newness of the ideas (some had already been enunciated in *La Nouvelle Ronde*) but the fact that they were more clearly elaborated, more succinctly put, and more genuinely illustrated in the poetry and fiction published in its pages. Perhaps the greater clarity in its doctrine can be attributed to the fact that the review concerned itself solely with literature. It is probably also important that almost all of the contributors to *La Revue Indigène* were of the same generation, aged twenty to twenty-five, fired by the same impatience with the comparative resignation of their elders and dreaming the young man's dream of greatness and heroism. In its opening statement *La Trouée* had appealed to the youth of Haiti but did not discount the contribution of the more mature:

> . . . nous faisons appel à tous ceux qui ont des aspirations: Jeunes ou Vieux. . . . Aux vieux, que l'expérience des hommes et des choses a muris et qui ont le mot de la sagesse; aux jeunes, pour que le lecteur découvre, d'entre les talents qui se cherchent, le talent qui s'affirme. (p. 2)

The invitation of *La Revue Indigène* was less moderate:

> Le lecteur que nous choisissons, celui qui nous est le plus cher, c'est le jeune homme de vingt ans qu'un noble et généreux enthousiasme transporte, qui a encore une âme héroïque et folle . . . qui rêve d'absolu. . . .[10]

---

[10] Normil G. Sylvain, "Chronique-Programme," *La Revue Indigène* no. 1 (July 1927), p. 4.

Of course, the lines drawn were not precisely held. Aside from the inclusion of excerpts from Jean Price-Mars's *Ainsi parla l'oncle* (in the first issue, and before it was published as a book), the *Revue Indigène* published Léon Laleau's poem "Discrétion" and a brief poem by Paul Valéry. Dominique Hippolyte's name appears also under a brief introduction to three of Countee Cullen's poems. Normil Sylvain saw the group's mission as the creation of indigenous literature, and he defended the journal's exlusively esthetic preoccupations in the socially troubled times:

> Les idées vraies ou fausses qu'on a d'un pays sont celles qu'en donnent les poètes, les romanciers, les peintres, les sculpteurs, image fidèle ou tableau trompeur. . . .
>
> La littérature donne l'expression infaillible de l'âme d'un peuple. (Sylvain, p. 3)

It was possible to create an indigenous literature, however, through the lesson of others. The *Revue Indigène* proposed to expose its public to the ideas being expounded in France and to currents in Latin American literature, in short, proposed to widen the consciousness and reduce the isolation of the Haitian intellectual by exposing the similarity of impetus behind apparent racial and cultural divergencies, by showing that all peoples shared the goal of self-realization as human beings.

In its brief existence, *La Revue Indigène* adhered faithfully to these objectives. But at the same time that the group sought to expose Haitians to a diversity of cultures, it stated its intention to uphold and clarify the cultural integrity of Haiti:

> *Ce que nous tâcherons de faire de notre revue.* Un tableau fidèle et vivant des diverses manifestations de la vie et de la pensée haïtienne contemporaine.
>
> Vie intellectuelle et artistique, vie économique et commerciale. Le point de vue haïtien des questions . . . et comme on fait une manière d'insulte du mot *indigène* nous le revendiquons comme un titre, le point de vue de l'indigène. Un retour à la sincerité et au naturel, au modèle vivant, à la description directe, un parfum plus accentué d'haïtienneté voilà qui semble caractériser notre jeune poésie. (Sylvain, p. 9–10)

In the second issue of *La Revue Indigène*, Normil Sylvain continued to study the question of a truly Haitian literature.

He criticized the use of local color by so many earlier poets as somewhat insincere, a pretext in imitation of the French muse. This time he went more boldly along the indigenous path charted in the first issue:

> La vraie poésie, je la trouve dans les refrains que nous chantaient le soir les nourrices noires, qui bercèrent notre enfance, "Dodo dodo pitite moin, crabe nan calalou. . . ."
> Les chansons des "reines-chanterelles" qui mènent les danses champêtres. . . .
> Notre folklore est riche de chansons pareilles. C'est le bruit des tams-tams . . . l'appel des lambis. . . . c'est le rythme trépidant et sensuel d'une meringue avec sa mélancolie lascive, qui doit passer dans notre poésie.[11]

It was in such things that one discovered the authentic Haitian soul.

In their use of free verse and unregimented rhythms, the poets of La Revue Indigène introduced a mode into Haiti which had been recently practiced in Europe but which was new in Haitian literature. Although their actual poetry does not depart drastically from the European production of the period in form and imagery, and though it by no means confines itself to indigenous themes, it does nonetheless introduce a less stylized, more intimate vision of Haiti than any Haitian poetry before it.

Through these journals, Haitian poetry began to set itself apart from what it had been before 1915 (Fouché, p. 100). The pages of La Trouée and of La Revue Indigène allow us to glimpse, however fleetingly, the âme haïtienne of which Antonio Vieux, Philippe Thoby-Marcelin, and Normil Sylvain had spoken.

Jacques Roumain's contributions to La Revue Indigène are mostly in the form of poetry. (One short story—"La Veste"—appeared in the October 1927 issue.) However, that he was an integral member of its movement is seen in the fact that he is featured in the September 1927 issue. In that issue, his translations of two poems by Rafael García Barcena appeared ("Vision d'outre-tombe" and "Mirage"), as well as his trans-

---

[11] Sylvain, "La Jeune Littérature Haïtienne," La Revue Indigène, 2 (August 1927), p. 52. cf. Fouché, pp. 98–99.

lation of Franck Braun's "Le Héros Caché." An extensive interview with him, conducted by Antonio Vieux, is also printed. This issue also contains four of his poems ("Insomnie," "Orage," "Le Chant de l'homme," "Calme") grouped under the title *Le Buvard*, a title under which Roumain apparently intended eventually to publish a collection of his poetry.[12]

The twenty-four poems which Jacques Roumain published in *La Trouée* and *La Revue Indigène*, and in the *Anthologie de la poésie haïtienne "indigène*," which the collaborators of *La Revue Indigène* published in 1928 before disbanding, as well as those published in *La Presse* in September 1929, constitute a group more or less consistent in tone and can be taken as a unit and studied together.[13] The most curious thing about them, given the context in which they appear to have been written, is their relative lack of "indigenousness." Few poems of this period can actually be said to reflect the Haitian soul, however obliquely. In this respect, Roumain's early poetry differs somewhat from that of other young poets of his group. Jacques Roumain's quest is in most cases more personal.

We do not know the order in which these poems were composed. Internal evidence as well as the theoretical position taken by Roumain in the Vieux interviews suggest that the dates of publication do not reflect the dates of composition. It is possible to view the four poems published in the September 1927 issue of *La Revue Indigène* under the general title *Le Buvard* as an organic unit, each poem representing a progression in the poet's affective state. The titles alone would give this impression: "Insomnie" (the poet's anxiety or anguish); "Orage" (the anguish bursting forth); "Le Chant de l'homme" (a return after the Orphic descent-into-hell of "Orage" and a profession of renewed faith); "Calme" (the dissipating of the

---

[12] Vieux, p. 110; cf. Naomi Garret, *The Renaissance of Haitian Poetry*, (Paris: Presence Africaine [1963]) p. 112.

[13] The poems are: "Absence," "Angoisse," "Appel," "Après-Midi," "Attente," "L'Aube," "Calme," "Cent mètres," "Le Chant de l'homme," "Corrida," "La Danse du poète-clown," "Echappée," "Horizon . . . soleil," "Insomnie," "A Jouer aux billes," "Midi," "Mirage," "Miragôane," "Noir," "Nungesser et Coli," "Orage," "Pluie," "Je rêve que je rêve," "Surgi d'une natte de paille peinte."

storm, which leaves the poet spent and released of desire). But then one wonders why Roumain would have chosen to publish only one of the four—"Orage"—among the nine poems he contributed to the *Anthologie . . . "indigène,"* published just a few months afterward.[14]

It is possible that many of these poems, given their style and themes, were written before Roumain returned to Haiti. Two poems that are definitely dated—the very early "Violettes fanées" and "Corrida"—show a very wide range in Roumain's poetic development before leaving Europe, the style and technique of "Corrida" comparing favorably with the bulk of the poems published in Haiti in the period 1927–29. However, according to testimony of those close to him, it is far more likely that the poems published in the period 1927–29 were written after Roumain's return to Haiti (Group I interviews). A close study of the poems of this period does reveal several different styles and the influences of various European schools and poets: Romanticism, symbolism, Surrealism, probably Baudelaire and Eluard as well. Some poems show considerably more sophistication in their imagery and structure than others. But most of them reveal the same esthetic universe through their treatment of images and themes. These aspects embody an unstated belief in what the function of poetry must be and allow us to treat these poems as a corpus, distinct from the poetry of later years.

The first issue of *La Trouée* (July 1927) carries on the same page two poems by Jacques Roumain, "Pluie" and "Midi" (p. 22):

"Pluie"

La pluie, monotone dactylo, tapote
aux fenêtres closes.
Des lumières tremblotent
roses
dans l'obscurité dense.
Des éclairs, serpentins géants,
dansent
Tordus à des pans

---

[14] "Orage" was also republished in the January 20, 1932, issue of *Haïti-Journal.*

de ciel noir.
La nuit
déploie ses voiles de moire
sur les lointains
jardins
où pleure sans bruit
le deuil
des roses qui s'éffeuillent.

"Midi"

Les palmiers veillent sur le paysage
las. Les orangers portent des grappes de soleil
d'or mûris au midi vermeil.
Un latanier balaie solitaire
des nuages dans l'azur
où fulgurent
des insectes, étincelles
subitement
nées dans d'incandescents
rayons. J'écoute le rythme du silence
embaumé de l'encens
des fleurs irréelles.
Mon âme est attirée vers la tangente
des désirs lourds que hantent
divinement insaisissables
l'ombre des fantômes implacables.

These very first poems published after Roumain's return to
Haiti are striking in their preoccupation with form and in their
plasticity. They are carefully wrought miniatures, portraits of
nature and natural phenomena. "Pluie" shows a kind of near-
animism which seems to incorporate both Romantic and
symbolist images. Natural phenomena take on the attitudes
and gestures of animals, and nature seems to be the emotive
reflection of man's own state of mind or mood. The distance
between the garden of the "Violettes fanées" and the "jardins/
où pleure . . . /le deuil/ des roses qui s'effeuillent" ("Pluie")
is not great. "Pluie" retains the theme of the poet wandering
in the garden, projecting his own sensitivities onto nature,
but the imagery is more plastic, and the natural landscape
begins to breathe in its own right. The same development is
more apparent in "Midi," where the palm trees *veillent*, where
the latania *balaie des nuages*, where insects change sponta-

neously from a chemical to an animal state. But the last lines
of "Midi" still reveal the troubled poet and his pathetic fallacy.

While these two poems contain nothing specifically indigenous, "Midi" does have a tropical atmosphere, and a few
other poems published in this period also reflect the tropics.
"Après-Midi" (*La Trouée*, September 1927) represents the still,
hanging atmosphere of a tropical afternoon, but without the
romantic intrusion of the poet. The poem "Miragôane" (*La
Trouée*, October 1927), named after a town situated on the bay
about ninety-four kilometers west of Port-au-Prince, describes
the automobile ride over rough country roads and through
scenes of peasant life. It is only the title, however, which ties
the poem to the land; the scenes might be that of any peasant
tropical community. The images describing the experience are
very animistic, and this is the most noticeable feature of the
poem:

> Sur la route sournoise de crevasses,
> la voiture comme un béquillard
> soubresaute. . . .
> . . . Très basses,
> accroupies sur la butte,
> des cahutes
> regardent avec indifférence.
> Puis soudain: Rouges,
> Les yeux du monstre tapi dans l'ombre
> La chaleur de mille vies intenses
> Monte brutale vers moi.

The poem "Echappée" (*La Trouée*, March, 1928), which seems
intended to recall scenes from boyhood play, allows a glimpse
of the countryside:

> Se croire solitaire et joyeux
> dans la savanne. . . .
> . . . .
> Courir dans les champs de canne
> parmi
> le hérissement des sabres d'argent
> au soleil. . . .

These four poems ("Midi," "Après-Midi," "Miragôane,"
"Echappée") are the only ones published by Roumain in these
first years of Indigenism which reflect in any way the Haitian

spirit and climate. Curiously enough, it is to the pages of *La Trouée* and not *La Revue Indigène* that we must go to find all four of them.

Running through the different styles and themes of the 1927–29 poetry there is a system of motifs whose symbolism is consistent. It is these motifs which more than anything else tie together the various tendencies of the early poetry. The same or similar images and metaphors may occur in a poem which seems inspired by the tropical countryside, in another which displays traces of Romanticism or the influence of Surrealism. The most general and pervasive are those which paint a tableau against the backdrop of the sky. Broad infinite expanses in which vivid phenomena unfold create a cosmic tone in most of the poetry. This feature is apparent in the poetry already cited; "Orage" provides an even better example:

> Le vent chassa un troupeau de bisons blancs
> dans la vaste prairie
> du ciel. Silencieux et puissants ils écraserent
> le soleil; le soleil s'éteignit.
> Le vent hurla telle une femme en mal
> d'enfant:
> la pluie accourut, . . .
>
> . . . .
>
> et tira sur le monde des rideaux de brume,
>
> . . . .
>
> vint le tonnerre
> et applaudit. Alors tout se tut pour laisser
> applaudir le tonnerre; . . .
> Un troupeau de bisons noirs émigra de l'orient à
> l'occident, et la nuit arriva comme une femme en deuil.

The tableau combines the mythic consciousness of prophets and poets with the child's unspoiled vision of how one part of the universe relates to another, which the Surrealists took as an indication of the child's intuitive, preintellectual knowledge of correspondences in the world. "A Jouer aux billes" (*La Revue Indigène*, January 1928, p. 208) provides the same impression:

> Le ciel est trop vaste pour qu'un enfant puisse le saisir dans ses
> petits bras. Mais dis-lui: Ciel, chapeau melon; alors il tendra ses

menottes vers le firmament accroché à la patère du palmier,
cueillira la lune et la mettra dans sa poche.
O poète enfant!

Within this cosmic setting, impressions of light and dark
seem to polarize around the images of the sky; *ciel* and *soleil*
are contrasted with *nuit:*

Clarté indécise.
La nuit
entre dans la chambre, sombre voile
brodé l'étoiles.
La lune est un gros fruit
se balançant à mon insomnie.

("Insomnie")

Light is sometimes represented as streaking through or standing out against a backdrop of darkness, as in these lines,
already quoted, from "Pluie":

Des lumières tremblotent
roses
dans l'obscurité dense.
Des éclairs, serpentins géants,
dansent
Tordus à des pans
de ciel noir.

or in this image, from "Surgi d'une natte de paille peinte"
(Anthologie . . . "indigène," p. 40):

Nuit opaque à peine trouée par le vol des lucioles

An important image in the light-dark motif represents darkness
as encircling a spot of light:

Le soleil de minuit
de ma lampe. Le temps qui fuit
n'atteint pas ma quiétude.

. . . .
Ma table est une île lumineuse
dans la ouate noire de la silencieuse
nuit.

("Calme")

Here, the poet is in intimate contact with cosmic nature. He
becomes part of it and merges with that within it which is

bright. Human endeavor is thus calculated against the back-drop of infinity.

Other poems are illuminated at their beginning, but by the end, light has given way to darkness, as in "Orage" or "Horizon . . . soleil" (*La Presse*, September 7, 1929, p. 3):

> Fil tendu tout au long
> Des pierres, il ne rompt.
> Seul l'éclat blanc d'une aile
> Un instant l'interrompt
>
> Le repos est la chute
> Vers la nuit. . .
>
> .   .   .   .
> Soleil à la dérive
> Ton arc dessus la rive
> Lance au ciel l'éventail
> Dont la nuit, tôt nous prive.
>
> .   .   .   .
> Le filet de la nuit
> Nous soustrait à l'ennui
> De tout plaisir qui dure.
>
> O paix, au fond du puits.

This spiraling of the light into darkness seems to suggest a similar spiritual descent on the part of the poet. Darkness here (as in Western poetry generally) is associated with gloom and despair. The association surfaces more clearly in "Midi" where the nighttime sky, the pervasive mesh of gloom, is submerged under the image of the soul spiraling downward ("Mon âme est attirée vers la tangente/des désirs lourds").

The spiral is all the more striking, since the soul's course is downward instead of upward, as Neo-Platonic imagery has taught us to expect, and since (again counter to Neo-Platonic descriptions) the soul here is heavy, weighted down rather than weightless. Although the soul is not a frequent motif in Roumain's poetry, its mention in the poem "Angoisse" (*Anthologie . . . "indigène,"* p. 36) intensifies the impression that this poetry reverses the Neo-Platonic concept of soul:

> L'âme
> est trop lourde pour monter
> au miroir des yeux

The title in this case would seem to tie the soul motif to the theme of *douleur*. *Pluie, âme, nuit* in fact all merge in this theme. The impression of heaviness, carried through the weighty impenetrability of night, through the gloomy descent of the soul, is achieved also through the images of rain, as in "Pluie," and in the first line of "Attente" (*Anthologie . . . "indigène,"* p. 37):

> Le plomb de la nuit s'égoutte dans le silence.

Subsequent images in the same poem set up metaphoric resonance:

> O les yeux douloureux d'épier le ruisseau d'or
> que verse sur l'asphalte le réverbère borgne
> et par où tu viendras miraculeusement pâle
> et douce et les yeux pleins de pétales.
>
> Voici la pluie
> qui tombe, tombe, tombe, tombe.
> Le ruisseau rie et roule
> d'imaginaires pépites, mais tu ne viendras plus,
> La pluie
>   tombe, tombe, tombe, tombe.

The "pluie/qui tombe" recalls the verb *s'égoutter* of the first line. But there is also some suggestion that the *ruisseau*, the golden ray of light associated with the lover's presence, becomes confused with the *ruisseau* which drains off the leaden rain, so that the antithetical light and darkness—hope and despair—merge in the end in this poem also. Despair is by implication cosmic, since it is nearly always accompanied by cosmic imagery.

The poet's hope, carried on bright images of sun and sky, is painted in these poems against a backdrop of infinite space. It is surrounded by or must give way to night and despair. The poet seems lost in space, surrounded by it, and therefore seems bound on a cosmic quest destined to failure. It is not surprising to find also in this poetry images of still, suspended time, impatience, and ennui:

> . . . Sagaies fines,
> des palmiers—éventails
> immobiles dans le Temps figé.

.   .   .   .
Chaque minute comme un siècle d'ennui
baille.

("Après-Midi")

The passing of time is equated with the still, suspended, impotent absence of activity. The motif of suspension in time joins that of oncoming darkness in symbolizing failure:

Le repos est la chute
Vers la nuit, des minutes.
Silence, un doigt aux lèvres

("Horizon . . . soleil")

Le plomb de la nuit s'égoutte dans le silence,
La souffrance d'être limité et la tentation puérile
d'avancer la pendule qui grignotte le temps avec des
dents dérisoires.

("Attente")

Still, the poet cannot avoid his journey, cannot stop searching. Certain verbs explain the source of anguish by aptly describing the cosmic quest:

Je me penche hors de moi
pour écouter une voix
ténue, et triste comme un parfum.

("Insomnie")

O se pencher
    cueillir des étoiles
    et un morceau du ciel.

("Mirage," Anthologie . . . "indigène," p. 39)

The poet remains a cosmic, if ineffectual, being, suspended or floating in infinity, yet unable to make contact with that infinity.

Making contact of some sort is a major need. The motif of the hands, usually outstretched, seems to represent the human need for love, reassurance, for contact. Often the loved one, absent or nearby, is invoked in moments of empty dark despair. Sometimes there is contact:

. . . Je veux entendre ma douleur
sangloter. Puis pose ta main, o
très doucement sur mon coeur;

("Noir," La Revue Indigène, August 1927, p. 62)

but more often not:

> Je tends les mains
> vers toi et j'étreins
> le ciel
> —et le vide.

("Insomnie")

> Fermer la porte,
> l'ouvrir:
> Le bonheur demeure toujours dehors.
> Si tu étais là
> tes mains prolongeraient ma vie.

("Mirage")

The outstretched hands provide an illuminated bride of contact for the lover, enveloped in darkness, with the reassuring warmth of the beloved.

The motif of the hands searching out the reassuring contact of another functions on a human level. A similar motif, that of the outstretched arms, seems to represent a kind of sustaining power, the only support available to the poet, extended forth to carry the burden of the universe, or projecting the hero into it by the posture he assumes:[15]

> La mort se tient devant toi avec des cornes pointues. Tes bras prolongés par les banderilles, tu avances; tu es un jeune dieu aztéque nourri du soleil, et du coeur des vaincus.
> ("Corrida," *La Revue Indigène*, September 1927, pp 115–16)

In "Mirage" (the title signifying perhaps a glimpse of the unattainable), the human creature fails in his efforts to establish human contact and he also fails to reach beyond himself into

---

[15] The sole exception may be the poem "Echappée":

> les mains qui saignent
> d'avoir halé jusqu'au coeur
> le vide amer
>
> . . . .
>
> sentir la caresse des bras multipliés
> y mêler ses bras multipliés;

Here, the desire for contact is expressed in the images both of the *mains* and of the *bras;* but the proliferation of *bras* may also symbolize strength.

infinity. The quest is nonetheless heroic for the effort, and the effort is carried in the arms:

Je regarde
  trembler la Voie lactée.
O se pencher
  cueillir des étoiles
  et un morceau de ciel.
Adieu
  adieu
mes bras sont une croix trop lourde.

Running through this group of seemingly lyric poems, there is an undeniable heroic quest. That quest is a sublime one, for the hero is set in a cosmic ambience. The recurrent theme is that of the hero reaching beyond himself to make contact with something greater, something unknown. Through a steady progression from hope to despair, with frequent pleas for the succor of reassuring human contact, the lonely figure of the hero lost in space and in darkness prevails. It is this pervasive hero-quest which links these poems directly to those for which Roumain is most well known: the later poetry of revolution and freedom, "Bois d'ébène" and "Sales nègres." The concept of the hero is one of the most constant features of all Roumain's writing. Roumain will carry on the quest of the true hero figure through all the portrayals of the protagonists of his fiction. The hero thus becomes in Roumain's creative writing a metaphor for what in his essays and polemics is expressed as commitment to the cause of human betterment, and the exhortation to others to commit themselves to that cause. The early poetry, superbly idealistic in all its celestial imagery, still very much romantic in all its stress on *douleur*, *âme*, and *pleurs*, showing marked influences of certain surrealist images, techniques, and probably certain poets, is thus seen to be in direct lineage with the more rugged poetry—far less cosmic and more involved with the lot of man in society—which is to follow.

Nowhere is the meeting point more apparent than in "Le Chant de l'homme":

J'ai voulu à ma détresse
des rues étroites, la caresse

à mes epaules des bons murs durs.
Mais vous les avez, o hommes
élargis de vos pas,
de vos désirs,
de relents de rhum,
de sexe et de "draught-beer."
J'erre dans vos labyrinthes
multicolores et je suis las
de ma plainte.

II

Ainsi:
vers vous je suis venu
avec mon grand coeur nu
et rouge, et mes bras lourds
de brassées d'amour
Et vos bras vers
moi se sont tendus très ouverts
et vos poings durs
durement ont frappé ma face.
Alors je vis:
vos basses grimaces
et vos yeux baveux
d'injures.
Alors j'entendis
autour de moi croasser, pustuleux,
les crapauds—Ainsi:
solitaire, sombre,
maintenant fort en mon ombre
mon seul compagnon fidèle,
je projette l'arc de mon bras
par dessus le ciel.

The poem depicts the lonely, sensitive hero, with his clearer vision of the ugliness of man's present petty state, trying to bring salvation. But he is not heeded. We will find essentially the same theme repeated in "La Danse du poète-clown" and in "Appel." But in "Le Chant de l'homme," the hero's effort spirals into a dark and gloomy ending; here, the hero still floats in cosmic detachment from his fellows. Even the title (with *homme* in the singular, indicating the generic entity) suggests an aloofness willed by fate.

The hero-figure is obliquely present in the group of poems of primarily lyric intensity, just discussed. However, he is the overt subject of another group, fewer in number and stylistically quite different from those studied above. The two groups seem to represent more or less distinct cycles. Those which we now take up celebrate the hero for what he symbolizes of man. The poet himself, when present, is a reflection of the whole race. The intent of these poems, if not their form, is therefore epic.

The poem "Corrida" is a narrative depicting the bullfighter-Aztec hero Armillita in the ring, with the Spanish queen and the crowd watching as the moment of truth approaches.[16] But on this spectacle is superimposed the image of the Aztec priest in the moment of sacrifice, and perhaps there is also a vague reminiscence of the Roman arena in which the Christians were sacrificed to the lions. There is a marked surrealistic quality in the imagery:

> Sur le sable le sang éparpille de petits drapeaux espagnoles pourpre et or;

The fluidity of forms, one image transforming dreamlike into another, one entity acquiring the essence of another, is also seen in the way in which the Aztec hero becomes the bull. The image of the bull is implicit in the metaphor: "La mort se tient devant toi avec des cornes pointues." One can almost see the bull stamping. Four lines later, it is the hero who stamps before the flashing flags:

> . . . mais toi tu vas piétinant les drapeaux et tu montes un escalier invisible au-dessus de la foule, au-dessus des mains enthousiastes, au-dessus des femmes évanouies, avec un sourire ambigu au coin des lèvres.

The surrealism and motif symbolism and the slow, proselike sweep of the rhythm set "Corrida" apart from the other poems of epic intent. It differs significantly also in that the hero appears to emerge from the ordeal the victor. But his victory is only apparent, not real. His gesture is at once a mark of

---

[16] Florence White ("Poesía Negra" in Latin America [Ph.D. Diss., U. of Wisconsin, 1951], p. 411) states that this poem is about the Mexican torero Armillita l'Azteque. If Roumain is alluding to a historical and contemporary figure, as Miss White indicates, the poem acquires added levels of meaning.

victory and homage paid to those who, looking on from above, control his fate:

> Alors toi, Armillita l'Aztèque, tu présentes avec le geste hiératique du prêtre de Huitzilopochtli l'oreille de la victime à l'adoration de la foule espagnole.

It is significant that in the end, in the epic as in the lyric cycles, the hero's superb gesture ends in magnificent failure. The poem "Nungesser et Coli" (*La Trouée*, August 1927, p. 49), to the memory of the World War I fliers who disappeared over the Atlantic in May 1927, bears the same message:

> Nungesser et Coli, je pense à votre mort,
> —splendeur du vol vers l'infini
> volupté sidérale d'être fort—
> Nungesser et Coli, je pense à vos poings hors
> de l'eau glauque, s'agrippant encore
> de leurs doigts calcinés à la cruelle
> immensité du ciel.

The images portray the magnificence of the effort to reach beyond oneself; the human failure is part of that magnificence.

"Cent mètres" (*La Revue Indigène*, July 1927, pp. 14–15) presents the hero as sportsman. The will to win, to prevail, to reach beyond, contrasted with the human failure at the end, is portrayed through the rather banal situation of the hundred-yard dash. But it becomes under Roumain's pen, a life-and-death struggle. Four men start out at the signal:

> Bras, hélices brusquement
> déclanchées par le pistolet
> tournant éperdument
> en quart de cercle. Vingt mètres.
> Tous de front. Bien-être;
> volupté du vent
> entre les dents.
> Cinquante mètres: deux lâchent
> pieds. Hâchent
> l'air. Bûcherons
> de la fatigue qui colle
> les muscles au sol.
> Désespoir.
> Les deux autres de front.
> Quatre-vingt mètres. L'un pense:
> "Passerai-je? Oh

passerai-je?
Souffrance,
Souffrance du petit marteau
contre l'enclume de ma tempe
Souffrance du trou noir
entre la misère de mes jambes
et l'arrivée. Je veux.
Je passe. Non.
Je veux. Je passe"
L'autre: "Ha! Mon corps las
Ha! Mes poumons
carburateurs douleureux
dans ma poitrine en feu."
Dernier effort du corps projeté
contre le fil. Rictus de Prométhée
délivré. Trombe.
Enfin.
(Journaux du lendemain:
Un tel, gagné d'une poitrine).
L'herbe est une verte et fraîche tombe.

"La Danse du poète-clown" (*La Revue Indigène*, August 1927, p. 62) represents the hero in another of his guises: that of savior-martyr. The poet is an apt figure, for it is he who sees beyond with the eyes of a visionary. His sensitivities are acutely open to the needs and possibilities in human experience. This poem has but one image, sustained and accumulated the length of the poem: that of the dance of the poet-clown. As is often the case in Roumain's poetry, a quotation directly under the title contributes to the imagery:

O Agni! toi qui flambes
dans le sang du
danseur éperdu!

Amarou

The lines recall the sacrificial lamb of the Old Testament and the epithet given, by extension, to Christ. The poet, like Christ, is portrayed in the poem as a sacrificial victim, and he seems to become his own sacrificial pyre. Repetition of the verb *tourne* evokes, in the Eastern setting of the poem, the whirling dervish who builds up to a prophetic frenzy:

. . . Tourne sur toi-même, ô pur
à réchauffer ton désespoir

tourne à ne plus les voir
tourne, déjà ils ne sont plus
que brume. Entends-tu
maintenant vivre la blessure
de ton coeur, ils furent,
ils furent! à mort, tourne
danse, tourne, ô poète, ô flamme, ô clown.

The poem "Appel," lone expression of Nationalism within the corpus of the 1927–29 poetry, seems, when viewed in context, to prolong several of its pronounced tendencies. The striking metaphors and the constant presence of the sky join the will to rise beyond and the celebration of the heroic figure. The abruptness, rudeness, hardiness of the style of "La Danse du poète-clown" and of "Cent mètres" is translated into the ruthless commitment of "Appel." In this poem we again encounter the hero-martyr of "Le Chant de l'homme," the sacrificial victim of "Corrida" and of "La Danse du poète-clown." In "Appel," the poet is a martyr-messenger:

Ceci et cela ont fait éclater
ma douleur,
et ma douleur a grandi

· · · · · · · · · ·
et une grande clameur de rage
est devenue

· · · · · · ·
j'irai à vous

As in "La Danse du poète-clown," he is associated with raging sacrificial fires:

Alors je hurlerai
et vous accourrez
car, à la mort
j'aurai hurlé
et la mort
attire
par ses bras longs

Vous accourrez
avec les yeux hagards
des fauves poursuivis
par l'incendie et la brousse

The symbolism of the fire joins the symbolism of spilled blood:

> écoutez ma clameur;
> Je veux
> que flamme
> elle vous pénètre
> . . . .
> Je veux qu'en sang rouge
> dans les veines des vieillards
> elle allume:

The bleeding heart, and blood in general, denote courage and vital force, as they do traditionally. But vital force is also communicated through stylistic devices, as in the following segment:

> Ha lâches, ha chiens
> Ha, hommes-aux-yeux baissés
> Faut-il que la mort
> hurle
> faut-il que le feu
> brûle,
> faut-il que la bouche
> crache
> pour qu'en foule vous accourrez?

By isolating the three verbs on lines by themselves the poet intensifies the action and movement of the poem; using verbs of one syllable, in positions of stress, he creates a rugged rhythmic pattern, which underscores the brutal, rugged survival nature of the situation depicted. Several other parts of speech fall together in groups of three. The poet uses this device to sustain the rhythmic pattern. Since it never varies, the rhythm continues to transmit the same message. This rhythmic segment culminates with the recurrence of the same three verbs, but in a context which now enlarges their original meaning (italics added):

> Et vos yeux sont-ils *crevés*
> et vos coeurs
> *desséchés*
> et vos poings *mutilés*
> pour que point vous ne sachiez
> *en* vous

autour de vous
parmi vous
la mort venue d'au delà des murs
qui *hurle* des insultes
brûle votre patrimoine
et *crache*
son mépris blanc
sur vos fronts noirs?

Roumain's experiments with form result here in a style which seems distinctly his own, marked by abbreviated staccato rhythms and a paring down in the range of the imagery. These two aspects combine to create the *drame* of which he had spoken in *La Revue Indigène* interview:

> Pour moi, le poème contient un drame. Et ce côté dramatique, lui seul peut dégager une émotion. Ce qu'on appelle l'émotion artistique et qui n'est que la satisfaction de la chose bien dite, ne me suffit pas. Je suis plus exigeant. Je veux au poème la force vibrante qui secoue. Le moteur. Dans "Cent Mètres" je n'ai pas voulu brosser un tableau. Je ne suis pas peintre. J'ai voulu faire vivre ce que j'avais couru. La fièvre. Les impressions délirantes. Et l'Angoisse. Montrer la profondeur douleureuse de cette chose banale, extraire son âme. Le drame de la piste. Le drame dans les nerfs et les muscles. Depuis qu'ils se sont courbés, les coureurs, prêts à la détente, jusqu'à la minute où le fil blanc fera, à l'un d'eux, une fine écharpe. (Vieux, p. 106)

By 1927, then, to judge from his own comments, Roumain had formulated a theory of literature and had in his own writing advanced beyond the point of experimenting with literary tradition and with form, beyond the stage of manipulating imagery. However, his conception of the poem is not exactly borne out by the poems he had published up to the time of the interview, nor by those which follow. It is true that poems such as "Cent mètres," "La Danse du poète-clown," and "Appel" exhibit pared-down imagery and an abbreviated rhythm, but poems such as "Orage" and "A Jouer aux billes," on the other hand, belie his assertion that he is not a painter.

His words seem on the other hand to suggest that a Baudelairian esthetic quest and a preoccupation with images have been earlier phases through which he has passed, and which are now internalized as part of his poetic vision. He also says that the poem is not, as the naïve believe, a "jeu d'images." "Elle [the image] vient seule. Ell s'impose même. On souffrirait de ne pas le mettre" (Vieux, p. 106). Craftsmanship and imagery are important, but the true poem contains "la force vibrante qui secoue." The poem is the tension of forces unleashed; the unleashing does something to the person experiencing the poem. The distance to go between this conception of the poem and the position of *poésie engagée* is not very great. Roumain's terms, devoid as they are here of social content, contain nevertheless the germ of later, more concise formulations on the significance of poetry.

Yet, some poems show a preoccupation with form which verges at times on literary virtuosity, while others show a blatant disregard for form and tradition. Within the former group can be placed two of the three poems published two years after the ideas quoted above. One of them, "L'Aube" (*La Presse*, September 14, 1929, p. 3) yields a twelve-syllable scansion and can be looked at as a possible modernized Alexandrine (modernized because it is only possible to read twelve syllables to the line if one consistently disregards mute *e*'s). Moreover, the theme, title and dialogue form conspire to bring the poem under suspicion as an exercise in traditional lyric poetry: Was Roumain imitating the medieval lyric genre, the *aube*, a dialogue poem in which two lovers separate as the town crier announces the break of day?

> . . . Adieu, voici l'aube; la froide lumière du réveil
> —Demeure encore, les bagues d'un rayon de soleil
> Jouent dans tes boucles et ton corps est doux à mes lèvres!
> . . . Adieu, ami, voici l'aube, à chaque temps ses fièvres.

In "Horizon . . . soleil" the poet experiments with six-foot lines, and his rhythm scheme is quite rigid: aaba ccdc eefe. These exercises are strange in that they do not really reproduce any of the traditional forms, but they come close enough at times to appear intentional. Rhyme patterns are a case in point. Roumain rhymes inconsistently, and the handling of rhyme seems to bear no relation to the order of publication. In "Pluie," for example, the rhyme pattern suggests an exercise in traditional forms. If we group the lines not as written but

in stanzas, the rhyme pattern *abba cddc efe ggf hh* emerges as
a form very close to the sonnet, but submerged under the final
doublet. Roumain seems to be making an appeal to the reader's
esthetic sensibilities, and one does, in effect, get an uneasiness
as one approaches the end, an uneasiness which cannot be
immediately explained until the submerged pattern is perceived. If rhyme patterns such as *aaba ccdc eefe gghg iiji*
("Horizon . . . soleil") or *aabbccdde* ("Orage") are compared
to rhyme patterns such as *abccbdaefdgghifjkklm* ("Insomnie")
or *abba ccde fdgdhgdiejjke* ("Miragôane"), the question arises
as to why some poems establish a rhyme pattern in the first
few lines only to trail off indeterminately. Experimentation or
affectation is also in evidence in the use of voiced and voiceless
stops: *quiétude/minute* ("Calme"); *étroite/roide* ("Miragôane");
cordes/fortes ("Cent mètres").

Some of Roumain's poetry of this period is entirely free of
rhyme, which is what one would expect given the currents of
the time. In fact, it is somewhat amazing to find such a wealth
of rhymed poetry in an era absorbing the Surrealist shock.
Roumain's poetry certainly does come under Surrealist influences, and rhyme is significantly absent in those of his poems
so influenced. The poem "Je rêve que je rêve" (*La Presse*,
September 14, 1929, p. 3) suggests in its title the concentric
box effect of surrealist imagery and is the kind of image
triggered by a play on words which had currency with the
Surrealists. The same poem contains, in the line: "Désir qui
ni est, la paix qui naît," a device which neither an Apollinaire
nor an Eluard were above using.[17]

Two years after the *La Revue Indigène* interview, Roumain
found the occasion to write in one of his articles in *La Presse*:

> . . . le poète en général est un instinctif qui saisit la vie
> puissamment par tous les sens. Son esprit n'intervient dans
> la conquête poétique que pour le butin délicat, pour les plus
> subtiles jouissances de l'arrangement prosodique. Cette sen-
> sualité se traduit dans le vers, par des sons, des images, des
> assonances qui sont à la réalité ce que l'onomatopée est au

---

[17] E.g., "la scène se passe à Zanzibar autant que la Seine passe à
Paris" in Apollinaire's *Les Mamelles de Tirésias*; "ô tour de mon
amour autour de mon amour" in Eluard's "Giorgio de Chirico,"
Mourir de ne pas Mourir, in *Capitale de la Douleur.*

sens du mot qu'elle veut exprimer. Nul, comme Baudelaire, ne me donnera autant raison que par ce vers immense:

Descendez, descendez, lamentables victimes . . .

Remarquez l'extraordinaire progression du d de "descendez" aux t de "lamentables" et de "victimes": on croit percevoir visuellement les "Femmes damnées" descendant lentement des marches: on croit entendre leurs pas!
    Cette sensualité ainsi extériorisée est la marque de tous les écrivains éminents.[18]

It is precisely this close attention to details of prosody and of form which we have seen in many of the poems published in this period. And it may be no coincidence that some of the poems most marked by this preoccupation appeared also in *La Presse* during the two weeks prior to this article.

The notions expressed in this article differ from those of the September 1927 *Revue Indigène* interview primarily in their emphasis on the value of esthetic devices. In *La Revue Indigène*, Roumain seemed to be deemphasizing the *émotion artistique*, whereas now he evokes the imposing figure of Baudelaire in support of it. The line he quotes (from *Les Epaves*, "Pièces Condamnées Tirées des Fleurs du Mal") celebrates sensuous lesbianism, but it is the techical skill of the poet which he is pointing to. The two passages express essentially the same attitude toward poetry, however, in that Roumain seems in both to put his faith in the supremely affective nature of poetry; he seems to be arguing that art makes contact with the very source of man's emotive and sensory nature. Such appears to be the sense of terms such as "la force vibrante qui secoue" (*Revue Indigène*) and the notion of the poet as "un instinctif qui saisit la vie puissament par tous les sens." ("Mon Carnet")

At the time of the *Revue Indigène* interview, Roumain can have been known only as a poet. However, he does not seem to have conceived of his life as being centered around literature. He had told Vieux:

—Ce que je compte faire je ne sais pas encore. Je n'ai pas, vous savez, d'ambition littéraire, ni n'envisage de publication avant trois ans. Mon volume de vers sera intitulé: Le Buvard.

[18] [Jacques Roumain] "Mon Carnet," *La Presse*, September 21, 1929.

Je prends des notes pour un roman.
Mais quelle que soit mon oeuvre, c'est à mon sol que je
la dédierai. . . . (p. 110)

It would be erroneous to give the impression that all was
unmitigated work and gravity for him in this stage of his life.
If he demonstrated the zeal typical of his years, he also shared
its love of fun and pleasure. Jacques Roumain in his first years
back home must have seemed a very elegant and romantic
figure. Tall, slender, charming and witty, handsome, and with
a penchant for stylishly cut clothes, he was from "the smartest
Houbigant scented aristocracy" and rode around "in one of
the finest automobiles in Port-au-Prince."[19]

The well-loved—even spoiled—child of an affluent family,
it was hardly necessary for him to devote much time or energy
to self-support (Group I interviews). He tried his hand for a
while at selling eyeglass lenses manufactured by an optician
he had met in Spain. Next he tried selling *tafia* (a Haitian
whiskey made from sugar cane) produced on his family's
lands. (Group I interviews). But these ventures were short-
lived, and Roumain was often with huge crowds of his friends,
with other members of the *Revue Indigène* group avidly discussing the new Haitian literature. One of their favored
meeting places was the second floor of the shop owned by
Carl Brouard's father, where Carl had a huge collection of
books brought back from Europe, and which all the *Revue
Indigène* group were at liberty to borrow. Later, during the high
point of his collaboration with *Le Petit Impartial*, Roumain
could be found again with a group of friends radiating around
the offices of *Le Petit Impartial*, waging their campaign against
the Borno government.

In the first year or two back home, Jacques Roumain was
indeed living the life of a *"grand bourgeois"* (Group I interviews). There were those at first who doubted his sincerity
(Jacques Antoine, p. 108), but as his commitment grew, as he
began to take risks, to undergo periods in prison, his emergence as leader of the youth of Haiti became patently clear.

---

[19] Jacques C. Antoine, "Literature—From Toussaint Louverture to
Jacques Roumain," ed. Mercer Cook, *Introduction to Haiti* (Washington, D.C.: Pan American Union, 1951) p. 108.

CHAPTER II

A Time to Act: Nationalism

At the time of *La Trouée* and *La Revue Indigène* Roumain had been known primarily as a poet. But in early 1928, he began turning toward a more direct involvement in the Nationalist struggle against the American Occupation. There is evidence that he was beginning to feel that the esthetic avenue might be too indirect (Group I interviews). His association with *Le Petit Impartial* marks the decisive step in his Nationalist activities.

Le Petit Impartial, Journal de la Masse had been established December 5, 1927, by George J. Petit, who was listed as *directeur propriétaire*. From the beginning, the newspaper sought to appeal to all Haitians and took an uncompromisingly anti-Borno anticollaborationist position. Many issues carried notices urging a boycott of certain businesses which treated Haitians improperly or insulted the Haitian flag. There were many articles reviving the glories of the War of Independence and of Toussaint Louverture. These were complemented by articles reviving the more recent glories of the *caco* resistance during the first years of the Occupation. Charlemagne Péralte was treated as a true national hero (Emile Roumer contributed a poem in honor of his memory). The sensitive nature of French culture was opposed to the vulgar utilitarianism of American culture and the latter was rejected while the former was lauded. *Le Petit Impartial,* though of manifestly political orientation, recognized that it had common goals with the

43

literary efforts of the group of the *Revue Indigène*. The February 15, 1928, issue observes:

> Par ce temps, où il est dit qu'un vil mercantilisme vient souiller les meilleures intentions, où il se répète que toutes les activités tendent vers un matérialisme régressif, l'on ne saurait trop louer le noble effort de cette belle pléiade d'intellectuels de la "Revue Indigène" qui consacrent béné-volement leurs jeunes ardeurs à l'entreprise méritoire de continuer—tout en renouvelant les cadres—nos traditions de forte et pure culture française, en dépit des contingences ambiantes.

With the February 22, 1928, issue of *Le Petit Impartial* Jacques Roumain became *gérant-responsable* of the newspaper. This position put Roumain effectively in charge of the paper's operation; the title carried with it full responsiblity for opinions expressed and accuracy of facts presented in its pages.[1] On the surface it would appear that Jacques Roumain had come to feel that poetry alone would not spur the Haitian heart to reassert its Haitianity. But the assumption is valid only if we define poetry in a narrow sense. Roumain in a sense continues to write poetry. That is to say, his message is still to a large degree carried on impassioned metaphors and rhythmic buildup. Many articles in *Le Petit Impartial,* clothed in prose format, are examples of Haitian epic poetry in the tradition laid down from the beginning of Haitian literature in Boisrond Tonnerre's Declaration of Independence and exemplified best by the patriotic poetry of Alcibaides Fleury-Battier and Massillon Coicou. Two themes only slightly developed in "Appel"—that of the dead heroes serving as inspiration to those who must now do battle, and that of the legacy to be left to the children—are repeated over and over in the impassioned lines printed by Roumain in the pages of *Le Petit Impartial.*

The February 22, 1928, issue bears a lengthy article by

---

[1] In February 1928, Jacques Roumain was still a minor. This meant of course that any responsibilities he assumed fell legally on his parents. His father was understandably displeased, and with the March 7 issue, Jacques Roumain became *rédacteur en chef* and the initial title was dropped. It was added again in the June 13 issue (after Roumain's twenty-first birthday).

Roumain, "Le Peuple et l'Elite." This first of many articles reveals a bent of mind that leads Roumain to view the solution to Haiti's problems in terms of human solidarity across distinctions of caste or class. Roumain makes a characteristically bold and unmitigated statement of position and displays clearly enough that his poetic vision had adapted itself, perhaps unconsciously, to the needs of survival propaganda:

> Nous sommes aujourd'hui en face de l'américain comme nos Ancêtres en face des armées du Premier Consul.
> Et y avait-il à la Crête-à-Pierrot, à la Ravine-à-Couleuvres,[2] une "Elite" et un "vil peuple"? Non. Il y avait des hommes décidés à mourir plutôt que de vivre esclaves. Des hommes qui savaient que la mort aveugle fauche indifféremment riches et pauvres, lettrés et illetrés.
> Nous tous souffrons. La Souffrance nous a égalisés. Durement. Au-dessus de toutes mesquines querelles. Il y a la Patrie meurtrie à sauver.
> Ainsi voyez ce paysan. Mettez votre main dans sa rude main caleuse et belle de toucher, de peiner chaque jour dans la Sainte Terre.
> Soyons des frères unis—Sans cela une mort plus cruelle que la mort physique nous attend.
> Brisons les barrières! Etreignons-nous!

It is obvious from this article that Roumain's political consciousness had been steadily maturing through the period when his literary production was overwhelmingly in the form of lyric poetry. There is a subterranean continuity of intent between the youthful letter of 1925 to the Nationalist leader Jolibois and the period of Roumain's direct action in the Nationalist struggle, ushered in by this article. This statement of position remains rather general and abstract, even philosophical. But its major thrust is crusading, and it is this crusading intent which inspires the kind of poetry (we might call is "manifesto poetry") which Roumain now turns to writing, very often in collaboration with Georges Petit. Neither original nor of much intrinsic value, the lines they published were meant to inspire their readers to action.

---

[2] Sites of battles during the Haitian War of Independence in which the Haitian army performed heroically.

In a special issue dedicated to Charlemagne Péralte and the *caco* heroes, Roumain wrote:

> Montrez donc, spectres de Péralte et de Battraville[3] et vous soldats inconnus des plaines de Nord surgissez du gouffre avec vos pauvres membres convulsés et déchirés, vos po-itrines trouées par la mitraille américaine et précédez-nous dans les chemins par où marchent les guerriers. ("Péralte Crucifié," November 1, 1928)

The evocation of heroic ancestors need not be so specific. Haitian youth from their earliest schooling learn the exploits of the heroes and the battles of the Revolution. A general allusion therefore suffices to set off a whole series of associations in the mind of the reader.

The very strong sentiment in Haiti for ownership of the land and closeness to it can be explained on the basis that land tilled and worked for a master had been won for one's own. This feeling for the land takes on a quasi-religious symbolism when viewed in the context of African beliefs which endure in Haiti, where typically the souls of the ancestors are bound to the ancestral soil. This complex of associations is exploited by Roumain in lines such as the following:

> Cette terre ne saurait mourir: ce magnifique champ saccagé par les mains sacrilèges.
> Dévasté mais en surface. Et ses profondeurs sont gonflées et riches en sang et en cadavres d'hommes noblement tombés: nos pères.
> Ces hommes passèrent. Mais après eux demeura cette chose vivante, cette flamme: leurs sacrifices. . . . .
> Les Ancêtres sont cet arbre aux profondes racines dont parlait Louverture et sa sève puissante est montée jusqu' à nous, et nous a fortifiés.
> Nous avons entendu la Voix des Héros morts. Leur appel a sonné sur nos coeurs comme sur les cloches sonnant le tocsin. ("La Terre et les Morts," February 25, 1928)

Writings of this tone and style are addressed almost without exception to the youth of the nation, and in most cases, the intended audience is evident from the title. The generation of

---

[3] Péralte's lieutenant, who continued for a time the *caco* struggle after Péralte's death.

1927, like other revolutionary generations, felt itself to be alienated from its immediate predecessors, those who had sold out to the Americans, or so it seemed, those who had forgotten Haiti's tradition of independence. The notion that it is up to the youth to deliver the homeland recurs in their writings. Thus, the generation of 1927 equated Nationalism and idealism to a large extent with youth. Although there is no reason to doubt the sincerity of their concerns, there is evidence that the generation gap may have been more rhetorical than real. The *Revue Indigène* could publish in large part because of the financial generosity of Carl Brouard's father. Normil Sylvain states the ideological position of the *Revue Indigène* under the title "Un Rêve de Georges Sylvain" (his father, a writer who had translated La Fontaine's fables into Creole); his article is a testimonial to the continuity of efforts to Haitianize Haitian letters. And as legislative elections became eminent in late 1929, the various Nationalist groups, younger men and older, closed ranks.

Roumain shares with his contemporaries this disillusionment with the preceding generation and their sense of alienation from it. It seems more in a spirit of pain and reluctance than bitterness that he feels obliged to call the youth of the nation away from their fathers in defense of their homeland:

> Cela est dur à dire.
> Dure à dénoncer cette cause de notre nourriture: la génération qui nous précède.
> N'est-ce pas elle, la vaincue, qui patauge dans la boue gouvernementale? . . .
> Embourbés dans le fossé ils ne nous virent pas au-dessus d'eux prêts à les enjamber d'un bond, le coeur douleureux par la volonté du sacrifice, mais les jambes légères et les yeux tournés vers les Ancêtres. ("Jeune Haïti," March 3, 1928)

Articles such as the following formulate a more direct call to arms and stress the need for unity and solidarity, if the battle is to have any hope of success:

> Jeunesse, où êtes-vous? . . .
> Douze ans durant, nous avons assisté, indifférents pour la plupart, au dépécement de la Nation, à la trahison de ceux appelés à nous défendre, aux capitulations des uns et des

autres, à la mise aux enchères de l'Héritage de[s] Aieux par
une faction minoritaire à la fois servile et cynique.

Comme des dégénérés, nous avons accepté en guise
"d'Honneur et de Bonheur" et en laissant tern[i]r la gloire
des Ancêtres, à vivre dans la plus abjecte servitude, corrom-
pus par le dollar américain et lâches à être incapables de
produire aucune réaction salutaire. . . .

Jeunesse, vous êtes éparpillée! Cela ne doit pas être.
Groupez-vous! (Petit and Roumain, "A la Jeunesse," March
7, 1928)

Manifesto poetry, as evidenced in the passages quoted
above, is by no means Roumain's only journalistic style. Other
articles in the pages of Le Petit Impartial show Roumain in
search of more specific, practical, or immediate avenues of
liberation. Two series in particular deserve mention, as they
are extensive: the seven articles on Mahatma Gandhi and his
strategy of nonviolent resistance, and the running battle with
the clergy.

In "Un homme Contre un Empire—Mahatma Gandhi,"
Roumain examines India's Nationalist struggle against a capitalist invader to determine whether India's tactics might be
applicable to the Haitian situation. But pragmatic analysis was
not Roumain's only motivation. The Eastern point of view, so
different from that of the West, had attracted him as far back
as his years in Grünau. At the same time that Roumain had
been absorbing Nietzsche, he had been profoundly affected
by the exemplary life of Hindu leaders such as Ramakrishna
and his desciple Vivekananda and their abiding faith in the
spiritual nature of man. It was these same qualities in Gandhi
which struck Roumain, and to which, above all else, he laid
Gandhi's success. The first article in the series is prefaced by
a quotation from Gandhi's writings which stresses the need
for stoic acceptance of the misery accompanying nonviolent
resistance and the moral obligation to withdraw cooperation
from all levels of unjust leadership. Heroism patterned on
Nietzsche's concepts struggles to a signficant degree with the
quieter, less ego-oriented and sustained heroism of the Eastern
tradition, exemplified in this case by Gandhi. Yet, Roumain's
ideal remains the exceptional man, set apart (here, by his
infinite altruism) from his fellows. The terms chosen by

Roumain to express the ideal show no real willingness to abandon the image of the superior being:

> Je ne l'appellerai pas surhumain.
> Ce mot a pris un sens Nietzschien presqu'exclusivement, un sens trop rude pour celui qui recommande l'Ahîmsa, la Non-Violence.
> Nous pouvons saisir directement l'essence du surhomme.
> Pour cela, il nous faut, nous intensifiant, lever les yeux, regarder vers plus haut.
> Tel Gandhi tellement hors de l'humanité commune, que pour le comprendre il faille se purifier, pour le saisir, regarder hors de soi.
> Je l'appellerai extra-humain. . . . (March 3, 1928)

It seems above all to have been the sincerity of absolute commitment, bordering on mysticism, which attracted Roumain to Gandhi. Tactical questions must however be answered as well: Will nonviolence rid Haiti of the American occupation forces? Implicit behind that question is another: Did it rid India of the English? Roumain implies, in his subsequent sketch of Gandhi's life, that it will. In subsequent articles in the series, Roumain is at pains to distinguish nonviolent resistance from passive resistance, perhaps because he sees as one of the weak points of Haitian character a tendency to passivity:[4]

> "La Non-Violence"
>
> A entendre ces mots, on pourrait croire à un lâche pacifisme issu de quelque fatalisme oriental.
> On se tromperait. La Non-Violence de Gandhi est une RESISTANCE ACTIVE sans violence. Il en a tellement exclu l'idée de pusillanimité qu'il l'appelle EPEE du sacrifice de soi. Il exige à ses côtés des Non-Violents braves. . . .

---

[4] An article entitled "Réflexions" and signed "JR" in the March 20, 1928, issue of *Le Petit Impartial* compares the Muslim, who acts, then assigns whatever results from his acts to the will of God, and the Haitian who says: "A quoi bon s'agiter? Tout s'arrangera Bon Dié Bon." The Muslim is "un actif résigné," but the Haitian is "un apathique." (It is fairly safe to assume that "JR" would stand for Jacques Roumain; none of the other regular collaborators to the journals under study have names to which these initials could be assigned.)

> Et quelle fine lame il a en main. Souple, flexible, fluide,
> dirais-je. Ne s'engageant pas, mais blessant immédiatement
> qui la veut saisir. . . .
> Contre un tel ennemi le gouvernement anglais s'essouffla.
> (March 7, 1928)

Roumain was greatly impressed with the national solidarity
of India's diverse elements, which Gandhi was able to achieve
largely through the personal appeal of his moral character.
Roumain implies that such national solidarity was a prereq-
uisite to the actual confrontation of the Indian with the British,
and that national unity led quite naturally to self-assertion:

> Il travaille à unir fortement par des aspirations communes
> tous les Indiens: les Bramanes qui sont en majorité, les
> Musulmanes, qui sont 80 millions, les Bouddhistes très
> nombreux et enfin les faibles minorités Parsis, Juives et
> Chrétiennes.
> Il les appelle ses "chers amis," leur préscrit leurs devoirs
> d'INDIENS AVANT TOUT el ils l'écoutent pieusement et lui
> obéissent. (March 10, 1928)

The object lesson of Hindus and Moslems united in demonstrating throngs, forcing the British to acquiesce to their
demands, cannot have been lost on Roumain's audience. And
while he held up to view the glory of Gandhi's successive
victories, Roumain did not hide the risks and the misery, the
carnage and loss of life, trial and imprisonment. Gandhi's
imprisonment becomes a glory, and the last article in the series
ends in a kind of apotheosis:

> Dans sa sombre prison, je le vois le Mahatma, la grande
> Ame, qui a fait siennes toutes les souffrances, toutes les
> misères de sa patrie. Je le vois, faible, petit, laid, mais les
> yeux débordant d'amour et tissant pour l'Inde régénérée le
> Khaddar[5] de la liberté. (March 28, 1928)

The series about Gandhi shows that Roumain was able to
put his wide excursions into other cultures in the service of

---

[5] An allusion to Gandhi's 1920 order to all castes of Indians to
weave their own cloth for native garments (Khaddar), an order
designed to boycott the British system of exporting raw material
(cotton) for manufacture in England and resale to the colonies (as
calico).

Nationalism. There were times, however, when Nationalism required a clear-cut delineation between Own and Other. Now when the Other had over a period of time cleared for itself a domain in the Haitian landscape, the demoralizing effect on Haitian self-image and on Haitian autonomy could be neither clearly seen nor felt. The desire to neutralize the effect and eradicate the image rather than antireligious motives as such, seems to have been the motivating force behind Roumain's articles of this period attacking the church. The Catholic church had enjoyed official status since 1860, when the Haitian government had signed a Concordat with the Holy See in Rome. Although there were Haitians in the clergy, the upper ranks were regularly filled by French priests. The Haitian clergy was thus white, with a few blacks at the bottom. The dispute began in June 1928 when *Le Petit Impartial*, incensed by what it labeled "Un article Tendencieux" in the Port-au-Prince newspaper *Le Matin*, accused that newspaper of Borno-pleasing collaborationism because of its pro-clergy position. An article, signed by both Petit and Roumain, affirms:

> . . . nous protestons contre le clergé français séculier qui particulièrement depuis l'occupation yankee s'immiscie dans notre politique de la façon la plus malheureuse, la plus anti-haïtenne . . . (June 13, 1928)

Le Petit Impartial states further that the French clergy, by making an alliance with the Borno government, had in effect allied itself with the Occupation. The paper felt therefore called upon to fight the clergy. But the authors go even further in their expression of Haitianism:

> Ce que nous réclamons, c'est le respect du Concordat dont les termes veulent l'ascension des prêtres haïtiens aux dignités écclésiastiques. (June 13, 1928)

Roumain and Petit reasoned that the loyalty of the French clergy in Haiti could not suffice. The church must show its Haitianism—its patriotism—by becoming truly Haitian, that is, by changing its composition from a predominantly foreign to a predominantly Haitian clergy. Jacques Roumain and Georges Petit are here concerned with the political liberation of Haiti and an end to social injustice. They dare to attack, even to ridicule, the most venerated of institutions—the Church—to achieve it. They write:

> Nous savions bien qu'avec la déformation civique et mentale opérée dans notre milieu par les prêtres et congréganistes français, nous allions à compter avec une coalition de gens infâmes et interlopes qui ne peuvent pas vivre en dehors des intrigues des côteries et des orgies que procurent [sic] la sacristie desservie par les embusqués en quête de jouissances, se faisant ignoblement passer pour des chrétiens, voire même ministres de Dieu; quand on n'a qua'à leur enlever leurs robes souillées pour y découvrir l'antéchrist grimaçant, ricanant sur la tête des "sales nègres" qu'ils disent que nous sommes! (July 24, 1928)

An incident around which LePetit Impartial could rally was the alleged mistreatment of a Haitian priest because, we are told by Roumain, he did not bow sufficiently to the American Occupation forces. Roumain defends the Haitian clergyman's right to fight for his country, and in support of his argument he cites numerous cases from history where priests have fought valiantly for their country ("Un Prêtre a le droit d'être un soldat quand sa patrie est en danger," June 29, 1928).

It is clear that these debates bypass completely the question of dogma. It is purely as an antipatriotic, anti-Haitian political force that Roumain was seeing the church. Consequently, he considered as misguided attacks against religious bodies, which would result not in Haitian unity but in dissension and disunity within the ranks. In the heat of his battle with the clergy, he could still take time to admonish the author of an article appearing in the newspaper *Le Nouvelliste* for having accused various religious sects of methodic infiltration into Haiti in order to undermine Catholicism:

> Ce passage [containing the accusation] est un péché de lèse patrie, car son auteur a oublié qu'au-dessus des catholiques et des protestants, il y a l'HAITIEN et il les arme d'une rancoeur bête et inutile l'un contre l'autre. ("Le 'Nouvelliste' Inconscient," June 16, 1928)

Although the germs of Africanism as the basis of a Haitian race consciousness are implicit in the controversy, *Le Petit*

Impartial does not exploit them. It would probably be an error to read true race consciousness into these anticlerical tirades. Jacques Roumain at this period, like his colleagues of *La Trouée, La Revue Indigène, La Presse,* and *Le Petit Impartial,* had uppermost in view the liberation of the nation of Haiti; national consciousness and race consciousness were concepts which perhaps overlapped but were by no means fused into a complete and self-contained vision of Haitian man. The racial antitheses, the play on black and white word imagery which developed, were logical corollaries to the dominant Nationalist theme. But they were only corollaries. This explains the sporadic nature of their appearance.

When the race theme appears in Roumain's poetry of 1927–28, as in "Appel" ("la mort . . . /qui . . . crache/son mépris blanc/sur vos fronts noirs"), it polarises and makes clear just where the lines of battle are to be drawn. But the device is only a preliminary to the essential goal of group solidarity. When the race theme appears in the articles of *Le Petit Impartial,* here too it serves to mobilize Haitians for the Nationalist struggle. Roumain and Petit, in an article entitled "Manifeste à la Jeunesse des écoles," caution: "Il vous faut garder une position nettement défensive de vos professeurs blancs," for it is they who seek to brainwash the youth just as they did a previous generation. But the same article ends: "Vive le Clergé national naissant! . . . A bas le Clergé français!" (October 7, 1928).

Roumain speaks briefly of psychological reasons for feelings of racial inferiority in two articles entitled "Défense de Paul Morand." The articles deal with Morand's *Tsar Noir* and the indignant reaction of many Haitians to it. Roumain dismisses this reaction as misguided:

> C'est de notre faute si nous sommes laids et cela n'est pas tellement paradoxal qu'il paraît tout d'abord: il n'existe point d'étalon de beauté ou plutôt chaque race à son étalon de beauté. Ainsi ce sentiment esthétique ne peut être que relatif et limité à chaque groupement ethnique. Or nous nous sommes habitués à considérer comme étalon de beauté la race blanche. Lui étant opposés nous nous sommes *créés laids.* (May 16, 1928; italics in text)

What matters to Roumain is that Morand defends the Nationalists and lays blame on the Americans, and with them, inevitably, the collaborationists:

> certains passages . . . ont l'allure d'un Appel aux Armes: "Le peuple noir vaincra, se jurait Occide à lui-même. Il ne verra jamais pire que le passé. Mais il ne se contentera plus d'une courte vengeance." (May 19, 1928)

Roumain and Petit, using *Le Petit Impartial* as their propaganda organ, were able to mobilize large numbers of Haitian youth in the Nationalist cause. (We have already seen some examples of their propaganda in Roumain's poetic articles.) Their appeals became increasingly to the point. It was probably in early April 1928 that they organized the Ligue de la Jeunesse Patriote Haïtienne, with Jacques Roumain as president, Georges Petit as vice president, and Philéas Lemaire as secretary. On April 18, 1928, *Le Petit Impartial* added a second subtitle: *Organe officiel de la Ligue de la Jeunesse Patriote Haïtenne.* The Ligue united all social levels of Haitian youth in its drive to expulse the Americans and return to national self-determination. Its immediate tactics were unification and education. Unification could be achieved, first of all, by a proliferation of units of the Ligue. Branches were organized in the provincial capitals. Unification could also be achieved through cooperative efforts among Haitians in times of crisis. In August, the Ligue sent out an appeal to Port-au-Prince residents for material help for cyclone-ravaged provincial areas in the southwest (*Le Petit Impartial*, August 18, 1928). The Ligue educated its members by holding meetings and forums.

On December 13, 1928, Jacques Roumain, Georges Petit, and Elie Guérin were arrested for "délit de presse." Specifically, their arrest appears to have been caused by an article written by Elie Guérin, a regular collaborator of their paper (*Le Petit Impartial*, February 5, 1929). His articles attacking the French clergy and his burning Nationalism put him well within the philosophical context of the newspaper. It is not clear whether Roumain was arrested on this occasion because of his position as *gérant-responsable* for *Le Petit Impartial,* or for a more direct involvement. According to the February 5, 1929, issue of the paper, Guérin's article had been "en faveur de la défense des droits du peuple Haïtien." The statement is vague enough to mean almost anything. According to Roger Gaillard, the arrest was made "à la suite d'un manifeste signé par eux [Guérin, Petit, and Roumain] contre le 'sacre illégal des évêques blancs Juliot et Lebinhin' au lieu des 'honorables prêtres haïtiens' Mondésir, Qualo et Codada."[6] The case finally came to court on April 1, 1929. It caused quite a sensation, due in part to the exuberant nature of the three prisoners and their firm determination to seize the opportunity for an anti-Borno, pro-Nationalist forum. For example, when the judge asked Roumain to speak in his own defense, Roumain responded:

> Si pour me défendre de l'accusation portée contre moi, je remontais aux événements de 1922,[7] il me serait aisé de prouver comment Louis Borno . . . ("Le Jugement de M.M.E. Guérin, Georges J. Petit et Jacques Roumain," *Le Petit Impartial*, April 4, 1929.)

The judge objected, the audience applauded. When things quieted down again, Roumain continued:

> M. le Substitut Lanoue se trompe volontairement quand il insinue que seule une minorité d'hommes mécontents de ne pas participer au pouvoir, hait le gouvernement de Louis Borno. Non, c'est là le sentiment de tous les Haïtiens si l'on excepte le faible pourcentage des fonctionnaires se nourissant aux poubelles de la Coopération. ("Le Jugement . . .," April 4, 1929)

The judge, reacting to the growing emotion of the audience, ordered the courtroom evacuated. According to the account in *Le Petit Impartial*, Roumain, indignant, promptly turned to those present in the courtroom, exclaiming: "Peuple, ne vous laissez pas faire!" ("Le Jugement de MM. Elie Guérin, Georges J. Petit et Jacques Roumain," April 4, 1929) The next session proved even more tumultuous. The judge read a prepared statement in which he termed Roumain's words at the previous session a "cri de sédition." Petit rose to protest. Guérin accused

---

[6] Roger Gaillard, *La Destinée de Carl Brouard* (Port-au-Prince: Henri Deschamps, 1966, hereinafter referred to as *Carl Brouard*) pp. 70–71.

[7] The year in which Borno entered office.

the court of having made a farce of the judicial process. He went on to say:

> Vous n'êtes pas notre juge. C'est vous qui auriez dû être à notre place. Condamnez-nous, assassinez-nous la trahison vous écrasera.
> Vous vous nourissez de la crasse du blanc. Il vous étouffera, c'est elle qui vous tuera.

Again the courtroom was thrown into a state of uproar. Their lawyers finally got the three to agree to leaving the courtroom. *Le Petit Impartial* gives the following account of what happened next:

> . . . les prévenus se laissent conduire au sous sol, sous la garde d'un sergent de la gendarmerie. Tandis qu'ils s'y trouvent et recevaient les encouragements bruyants et les vivats d'une foule de jeunes gens campés dans la rue, le Substitut Lanoue insulta à haute voix M. Jacques Roumain.
> Celui-ci, en deux bonds, échappa au sergent qui voulait le saisir, se précipita dans l'escalier, et fit une irruption violente dans la salle.
> On le contint pour qu'il ne se précipita pas sur le Substitut Lanoue, qui esquissa un geste suspect vers sa serviette dans laquelle il avait placé un revolver.
> Le tumulte atteint son maximum et on a conduit les prévenus en prison aux acclamations d'une foule qui les accompagna jusqu'a la porte du pénitencier. ("Le Jugement de M.M.E. Guérin, Georges J. Petit et Jacques Roumain," April 6, 1929)

Although this account makes no mention of direct physical contact, there is reason to believe that blows were exchanged. Some brief accounts state: "son [Roumain's] sang coula en plein prétoire."[8] Persons who were at the trial state that as Roumain was leaving the courtroom, he heard someone shout out an insult, a political allusion, presumably to his grandfather, former President Tancrède Auguste. This was insupportable to Roumain. He managed to get free of the police and rushed at the insulter, who pulled out a revolver. The police

---

[8] These words appear in the anonymous introduction to *Gouverneurs de la rosée* (p. viii in the 1944 edition, p. 246 in the 1964 edition) and are repeated in Daniel Guérin, *Les Antilles décolonisées* (Paris: Présence Africaine, 1956), p. 144.

intervened, but Roumain had been wounded in the struggle (Group I interviews). It is probable that Roumain had not been shot but clubbed (Group II interviews). Roger Gaillard has written of these events:

> A la fin de cette première audience, au moment des salutations habituelles, Jacques Roumain, croyant que sa soeur, se dirigeant vers lui, va être molestée par un garde, se précipite dans sa direction; il est matraqué et blessé. (Gaillard, *Carl Brouard*, p. 72)

When the trial ended on April 29, 1929, Jacques Roumain and Georges Petit were given sentences of a year in prison and fines of 5,000 gourdes each. The verdict was appealed. On June 19, the court of appeals reduced the sentence to six months and ordered a joint fine of 2,5000 gourdes. Roumain and Petit were released from custody on August 2, 1929, after a confinement of over seven months.[9]

Roumain's collaboration with *Le Petit Impartial* was interrupted by his arrest, with its publisher, in April 1929 and his last articles appeared in that month. After several additional issues, the newspaper ceased publication, reappearing in 1930 under the direction of Louis Diaquoi. Jacques Roumain's name was carried through the first four issues of the new series as *directeur littéraire* (with Antonio Vieux), but he published no articles or literary pieces in it, and although the tone of references made to him in the paper leaves no doubt that he was highly regarded by the new directors, there is little evidence that he had much to do with the publication of *Le Petit Impartial* after April 1929. It was through other organs that his voice was now to be heard.

In August 1929, just after his release from prison, Roumain began a period of collaboration—this one a brief two months—with the newspaper *La Presse*. Although a Nationalist paper, its tone was much more sober, its content more conventional than that of the *Le Petit Impartial*. Roumain's contributions to *La Presse*, though they came in the thick of his militant political activism, show almost no trace of it. To the literary supplement,

---

[9] See Gaillard, *Carl Brouard*, pp. 70–72. The gourde is the Haitian monetary unit; its value is based on the United States dollar at 5:1.

"La Vie Littéraire," he contributed poetry, reviews, and translations. The three poems "L'Aube," "Je rêve que je rêve," "Horizon . . . soleil," which appear in the September 7 and 14 issues, recall the personal lyric poetry published in *La Revue Indigène* and the *"Anthologie . . . indigène"* of the previous two years and have already been discussed. Translations from the German of Roni Amberger de Osa ("Monte Carlo, Palace Hotel," August 13 and September 7, 1929) also appear over Roumain's signature.

The writings appearing regularly in the newspaper under the rubric "Mon Carnet" are more interesting; they reveal yet another facet of Jacques Roumain's personality. Those articles, all signed "Ibrahim," a pseudonym affected by Roumain specifically for this column (Group I interviews), offered amused commentary on life in general and life in Haiti in particular. Perhaps Roumain had in mind as models the decadent poets of Persia, Omar Khayyam and Hafiz, with whose work he was familiar and whose philosophies of life are reflected in the column. Roumain's tongue-in-cheek observations on carnal love and man's incompleteness without woman, and his linking these concepts with Pascalian thought ("Mon Carnet," August 22, 1929) provoked immediate responses in the form of letters from scandalized readers, some of whom called the column "mi-pornographique, mi-vénéneux, mi-prétentieux" ("Mon Carnet," August 24, 1929). Roumain blithely countered his detractors with reasoning linking the sensuous with the esthetic impulses, and it was in response to such reactions that Roumain set down, perhaps not in a completely serious mood, the ideas on poets and poetry which we have already examined in our discussion of his poetry of these first years back home.

The "Mon Carnet" articles go capriciously from light to serious, from innocuous to controversial topics; they give the air of being written on the spur of the moment and according to the mood of the commentator. We can pick up the newspaper one day and read a passage such as the following:

> Aujourd'hui, je me sens morose: que suis-je au fond? Une sorte de clown juché au haut d'une colonne de journal et qui fait des cabrioles d'un sujet à l'autre pour distraire les

lecteurs. Un salarié qui débite sa pensée et parfois son coeur, au détail, dans une chronique quotidienne. (September 21, 1929)

In the next issue we may be confronted with an entirely different mood:

Voici: ce matin en ouvrant ma fenêtre je vis qu'il faisait beau.
. . .

Non décidément, aujourd'hui, il fait trop beau, pour la cueillette des paradoxes: en toute tranquillité, je vous déclare, lecteurs, qu'en ce moment vous m'ennuyez considérablement et que je n'ai nulle intention de vous entretenir avec de petits commentaires sur le mariage, l'amitié ou l'ennui. (September 23, 1929)

The collaboration with *La Presse* ended abruptly. Roumain left the paper due to personal differences with the management, and nothing by him appears after September 1929. In June Georges J. Petit had established *L'Action, Journal de la Masse, Organe de la Ligue de la Jeunesse Patriote Haïtienne.*[10] Although this newspaper was as militant as Petit's first, its format was less elaborate, and it carried few articles that did not deal with present-day Haitian political realities. *L'Action* carried no signatures on editorials. In fact, only the most innocuous articles were signed at all. It can only be inferred that Roumain had a hand in the writing of any of them; his name appears as *gérant-responsable* and as *rédacteur en chef* only in the last quarter of 1929.[11] The headquarters of *L'Action,* like those of *Le Petit Impartial* before it, served as meeting place for the Ligue de la Jeunesse Patriote Haïtienne.

Toward the middle of October, Roumain, as president of the Ligue, began to formulate plans for a joint meeting with the Union Patriotique to discuss legislative elections. The

---

[10] Frère Lucien Jean (*Catalogue de la Bibliothèque haïtienne des frères de l'instruction chrétienne* [Port-au-Prince: Institution Saint Louis de Gonzague, 1958], p. 382) gives June 1 as the date of the first issue. According to accounts in *Le Petit Impartial* of April 1929 and Gaillard's chronological tables in *Carl Brouard,* Petit would have been incarcerated at the time *L'Action* first appeared.

[11] Roumain held these positions with the paper at least during the month of October 1929, but his name had disappeared by January 1930.

meeting, scheduled for the twentieth of the month, was to include speeches by Victor Cauvin (secretary of the Union Patriotique), Jacques Roumain, Y. Chatelain, and A. Pierre Paul ("Union Patriotique," *La Presse*, October 18, 1929). There were to be "manifestations publiques" after the meeting, apparently in the form of a mammoth march ("Le Meeting Se Tiendra Dimanche Matin," *L'Action*, October 13 [sic], 1929). The meeting was apparently an important one and was announced several times by both organizations in the Nationalist press. A few days before the meeting, Roumain was called into the Garde d'Haïti headquarters by the American commander, F. E. Evans, apparently at the request of the Haitian government, for questioning regarding the Ligue's membership and activities. ("Mr. Jacques Roumain au Quartier-Général de la G.d'H.," *L'Action*, October 17, 1929).

On October 17, Evans directed a letter to Roumain in which he advised him that meetings in public places must be authorized by the police. (The October 20 meeting was to be held at the offices of *L'Action*.) After a lengthy and detailed exposition of laws dating back to 1889, 1918, and 1925, Evans concluded:

> En vue de ce qui précède, je vous avise que la formation de votre Ligue paraît être en contravention avec les lois existantes relatives aux associations de 20 personnes ou plus.

The Ligue membership, according to Evans, was now at 23; the Ligue was therefore operating illegally ("Correspondance," *L'Action*, October 22, 1929). This reasoning seems to have formed the basis for Roumain's arrest, along with that of Victor Cauvin and Antoine Pierre Paul, on October 19, the day before the meeting at which all three were scheduled to speak. They were charged with having sent out an "appel sédicieux" (according to Seymour Pradel in *La Presse*, October 22), were jailed without a preliminary hearing, and held incommunicado at least until October 22 ("MM Roumain, Pierre Paul, Cauvin sont-ils des assassins ou des conspirateurs?" *L'Action*, October 22, 1929). Nationalist groups objected strongly. [12]

---

[12] See *La Presse*, October 21 and 22, 1929; *L'Action*, October 26, 1929.

Cauvin and Pierre Paul were released on October 28, but Roumain's incarceration continued until December 17, 1929.[13]

Roumain had become by now a very prominent political figure. As the Borno term drew to its end, and it began to be apparent that a new, Nationalist government might be constituted, Roumain in the nature of things passed from the outside to the inside in the machinery of government. Thus he campaigned for the election of his co-worker Georges J. Petit as magistrate in the communal elections scheduled for January 10, 1930 ("Bulletin de la Ligue de la Jeunesse . . . ," *L'Action*, January 7, 1930).

Sometime between February 11, 1930, and February 25, presidency of the Ligue de la Jeunesse Patriote Haïtienne passed from Roumain's hands.[14] Roumain continued to be recognized as leader of the nation's youth, as attested by his being named honorary president of the newly formed Fédération des Jeunesses Haïtiennes and his heading of the anti-Occupation Comité de Grève. An outgrowth of the student strike of Damiens (which had been staged by agricultural students in protest against the Occupation), the strike soon spread to other sectors—employees at the Agricultural School at Damiens and other Haitian workers soon joined in. The Comité de Grève attempted to organize, support, and educate these sectors. The Federation named Roumain as delegate to the Comité Fédératif des Associations Patriotiques, which worked out in conjunction with the Forbes Commission the plan whereby a provisional president might be chosen.

In mid-March, Roumain was elected by a committee representing various Nationalist groups as one of the three

---

[13] "M. Victor Cauvin et Antoine Pierre Paul en Liberté," *La Presse*, October 29, 1929. I am indebted to Professor Roger Gaillard for providing the date of Roumain's release.

[14] The February 11, 1930, issue of *L'Action* bears a communiqué from the Ligue signed Jacques Roumain, president. The February 25, issue of the same paper bears an "Appel à la Jeunesse" from the Ligue, signed J. D. Sam, president, and Jean Brierre, secretary. An article entitled "Interview de M. Jacques Roumain" in the March 18, 1930, issue of *Le Nouvelliste* mentions that Roumain is honorary president of the Ligue.

delegates from Port-au-Prince to the Assemblée des Délégués des Arrondissements de la République. On March 20, 1930, the Assembly chose Eugène Roy as provisional president, according to plan. Jacques Roumain's name appears as second secretary of that body on the decree officially naming Roy, under the signatures of Etzer Vilaire (president of the Assembly) and Jean Price-Mars (first secretary). The youngest member of the Assembly, Roumain accepted the compromise plan in the spirit of political realism, stating that the current crisis "ne peut s'accomoder de romantisme politique."[15]

On June 1, 1930, Eugène Roy called Roumain to the post of *chef de division* in the Department of the Interior.[16] To all appearances, a new, quieter period in Roumain's life had begun. He held the position until September 24, 1930, when he resigned so that he might campaign for Sténio Vincent (Group I interviews). Within a matter of months, he was recalled to the post by Vincent, the newly elected president (see *Le Petit Impartial*, February 12, 1931). The appointment was applauded by *Le Petit Impartial*, which stated that Roumain's proven sincerity made a marked contrast to the self-seeking of individuals who frequently filled such positions. Jacques Roumain seemed destined to the life of a functionary and politician.

His private life had also changed. On December 29, 1929, he had married Nicole Hibbert (see *La Presse*, December 30, 1929). She was the daughter of Fernand Hibbert, a well-known novelist of the Nationalist school of the first decade of the century. Sensitive and intelligent, knowledgeable about literature, she had received a better education than most Haitian women and seems to have been aware of her husband's gifts (Group I interviews).

In addition to his new role as government functionary and

---

[15] "Interview de M. Jacques Roumain," *Le Nouvelliste*, March 18, 1930.

[16] The *chef de Division* ("Under Secretary") is the second in command at the ministry where he holds the title. Since the Département de l'Intérieur is the most important ministry, Roumain's position was an important beginning.

his still newer one as family man, Roumain continued for a time his more familiar occupation of journalist. During the first half of 1930, several articles by Roumain appeared in a newly established newspaper, *Haïti-Journal*. Quite varied in tone and subject matter, these articles are of interest for the light they shed on the development of Roumain's thought during this transitional period in his life. The article "Agissons!"[17] reveals a conviction that national self-determination was now possible within the framework of government. Reactions such as the *grève de Damiens* to the occupying forces had brought Haiti to the attention of the American public and had caused Washington, prompted by several Americans working in the cause of Haitian liberation, to reevaluate its position. This turn of events had in large measure been responsible for the defeat of Borno's bid for a third term. Clearly, Roumain reasoned, the next step was the reestablishment of the legislative branch:

> C'est à cette proposition que doit se rattacher actuellment toute la campagne nationaliste. D'elle seule peut nous venir le salut. La Commission d'Enquete, à part ses pouvoirs restrients, arrivera trop tard en Haïti pour que son rapport puisse être un obstacle à l'élection d'un président par le Conseil d'Etat.
>
> Il faut que se soient les Chambres législatives, c'est-à-dire le peuple qui choississe l'arbitre patriote et consciencieux de ses destinées, car, pour citer le grand nationaliste hindou Mahatma Gandhi: "Un gouvernement n'est un instrument de service qu'autant qu'il est fondé sur la volonté du peuple. In n'est qu'un instrument d'oppression lorsqu'il obtient l'obéissance à la pointe des baïonnettes."

Roumain further calls for Haitians to respond to the efforts of Americans working in their behalf "en créant ici le parallèle du formidable mouvement d'opinion qui aux Etats-Unis, concentra l'attention publique sur nous."

One sees in the article the continued influence of Gandhi, but the faith in public opinion is strongly reminiscent of a

---

[17] Jacques Roumain, "Idées et Opinions—Agissons!" *Haïti-Journal*, January 25, 1930, p. 1.

position taken by Jean Price-Mars in the same column of *Haïti-Journal* several days earlier.[18]

Roumain had obviously been greatly influenced by Gandhi and his philosophy of nonviolence, as attested by the series of articles in *Le Petit Impartial*. In March of 1930, Gandhi had come out of political retirement and begun a new campaign of noncooperation in the continuing Nationalist struggle against Britain. That spring, the struggle reached its climactic stages, and widescale violence finally broke out. The efficacy of Gandhi's philosophy continued to occupy Roumain, and he went back to it in an article in May 1930.[19] Roumain began by voicing considerable doubts about political movements that base themselves on "une mystique" and listed several cases in history in support of his position. Thus, one might doubt the efficacy of Gandhism, since "les dernières émeutes nous apportent des témoignages formels d'une transgression de la nonviolence." However, despite these "atteintes partielles," Roumain feels that the events prove the excellence of Gandhi's doctrine. He stresses the fact that Gandhi is a practical idealist, not a visionary, and that his doctrine is, above all, one of moral courage, not of weakness. He quotes Gandhi as having said: "Notre âme entière doit résister à la volonté du tyran." Thus, Gandhism is a "sorte de Non-Violence violente qui exige plus de bravoure que la violence proprement dite." Roumain notes further that the concept of nonviolence can be fitted rather easily into traditional Indian morality:

> Gandhi greffe la question politique sur le sentiment religieux. On n'ignore pas le caractère extraordinairement religieux de l'Hindou. . . . du lever au coucher du soleil ses actes sont contrôlés par des préceptes pieux.

---

[18] Price-Mars had said: "Qu'on ne se le dissimule pas. Les Etats-Unis sont un pays d'opinion. Plus la cause haïtienne fera appeal à la souveraine puissance de l'opinion publique, plus elle aura la chance d'être entendue, comprise et traitée selon la justice et l'équité." (Jean Price-Mars, "Idées et Opinions—Un aspect du problème haïtien," *Haïti-Journal*, January 21 and 22, 1930, p. 1.

[19] Jacques Roumain, "Idées et Opinions—Mahatma Gandhi," *Haïti-Journal*, May 14, 1930, p. 1.

But despite Roumain's admiration for Gandhi and his interest in nonviolence and noncooperation as techniques in national liberation struggles, he concludes that such techniques are not applicable in the West:

> Pour ma part je crois que la Non-Violence est irréalisable dans les pays de civilisation occidentale justement parce qu'elle no pourrait être basée sur le même terrain religieux.

Roumain implies that Haitians should sympathize readily with India's struggle on the basis of their own, similar experience. As for Gandhi himself, "le tribut d'une admiration universelle lui est dû." When we compare this article with those of *Le Petit Impartial*, we see that here there is no fiery language, no attempt to use images in such a way that they mobilize readers to acts of heroic emulation. Roumain stresses, rather, the meaning of the title given Gandhi—Mahatma ("great-souled")—and ends with a quotation from the Bhagavad-Gîtâ: " 'dans l'homme victorieux et pacifié l'-Ame suprême demeure recueillie au milieu du froid et du chaud, du plaisir et de la douleur, des honneurs et de l'opprobe.' "

A brief article, "Notes pour servir à un manuel de parfait arriviste,"[20] displays some of Roumain's incisive wit. Roumain seems to be attempting to shame (or shock) certain sectors of Haitian society into a reassessment of their values. He starts out:

> Je connais un homme sincère qui pense que tous les défauts sont des possibilités de qualités; qu'ils demandent seulement à être surmontés et qu'ils sont susceptibles en quelque sorte de transmutation: la vérité peut devenir fierté; l'envie, volonté de supériorité; la grossièreté, sensualité, raffinement, et cétéra, et cétéra.
>
> Toi, ne t'embarrasse pas de ces préoccupations. Simplement appelle ta couardise, prudence; ton avidité, noble ambition; ta bassesse, modestie; ta répugnance à la vérite, tolérance; ton cynisme, franchise; et ton manque de franchise, modération.

---

[20] Jacques Roumain, "Notes pour servir à un manuel de parfait arriviste," *Haïti-Journal*, January 30, 1930, p. 1.

The "manual" continues in the same vein, and the last "note" provides the student with a rationale for his behavior:

> XI Pour ton excuse et pour étouffer tes scrupules et apaiser tes remords, dis-toi que la vie est un combat à mort.

These "notes" are curious in that they provide an example of Roumain's tendency to insert the same phrase or concept into different contexts. Roumain's explorations of the "transmutation" of values, with its corollary notion that qualities are neutral and can be activated negatively or positively, put forward in very tongue-in-cheek manner here, will be more seriously explored several years later in an unpublished work, Roumain's most doctrinaire novel, "Le Champ du potier." The notion that life is a fight to the death is implicit in much of the early poetry (see especially "Cent mètres") and in the prose soon to follow. And Roumain will repeat the same concept in essays and speeches written in the beginning years of World War II.

In an article appearing in a May issue of Haïti-Journal, Roumain explores the character of one of Haiti's founding fathers, Henri Christophe, from the point of view of his famous cruelty.[21] The article begins:

> La cruauté est un des attributs les plus remarquables de l'homme fort. . . .
> Toute grande oeuvre demande le total mépris des scrupules: il est peut-être regrettable pour la sensiblerie de certaines bonnes âmes que le mortier des vastes édifices politiques soient quelque peu mélangés de sang, mais rien ne prouve pour cela qu'ils soient moins solides.
> Et n'est-il pas singulier que tels historiens qui acceptent sans sourciller les grands crimes collectifs que sont les guerres frémissent d'horreur devant de petites exécutions capitales, bien moins importantes par leurs conséquences, et surtout bien moins stupides!
> La cruauté est une qualité constructive. . . .

Roumain goes on to apply these forceful generalizations to the

---

[21] Jacques Roumain, "Idées et Opinions—Eloge à la 'Cruauté' de Christophe," Haïti-Journal, May 7, 1930, p. 1.

case of Christophe, forger of the Haitian nation, and builds up a strong apology for the cruelty of the Haitian king:

> Et peut-on appeler cruauté cette discipline intelligente à laquelle il courbait son royaume? Christophe avait compris avec la plus grande netteté qu'un peuple surgi par la violence de l'esclavage le plus abjecte ne saurait faire usage de sa neuve indépendance qu'avec excès.
>
> L'Haitian après 1804 était un peuple improvisé et comme tel, prêt à toutes les turbulences des nations jeunes grisées par la liberté. Christophe se dévoua à l'éducation politique du Nord en lui imposant la routine de la paix et du travail. Il importe peu qu'il restreignit à d'étroites limites et sévèrement une liberté qui été mal comprise. Se moquant royalement de la Déclaration des Droits de l'Homme et du Citoyen, il mit fin à l'intolérable sans culottisme qui sévissait encore dans l'Ouest et dans le Sud et commença son labeur de chef clairvoyant en construisant des écoles, des académies, des instituts d'art et métiers, et en accordant à l'agriculture la protection intelligente qu'exigeait la prosperité du Pays.
>
> Sa cruauté fut un facteur de civilisation dans l'accomplissement de son oeuvre forte et grande.

Such praise may seem to contradict the humanistic values which Roumain's writings, and his life, overwhelmingly reflect. One must not overlook, however, his penchant for shock effect. The article is indeed an equivocal element in Roumain's writings, but it does share some aspects in common with the bulk of his work. War, for instance, is condemned as being totally destructive, and it is a collective *crime*. Thus, in Roumain's value system, there is no grandeur in wide-scale destruction, nor does the anonymity afforded to each executioner by the nature of war allow individual members of the collectivity to escape responsibility for participating in the events of their history. Grandeur lies in *constructive* acts; whether or not such constructive acts lead to "petites exécutions capitales" is incidental and irrelevant. Cruelty is inherent in the forcefulness and determination of the individual will.

The priorities established in the article lead at times to valuation of the same qualities for which Roumain will praise Gandhi one week later in the article "Mahatma Gandhi," discussed previously. Gandhi's *Satyagraha* also represents forceful determination, is an act of will. And Gandhi, like

Christophe, was able, by an act of will, to mould his followers
into an army of nation builders. The following paragraph of
the article on Christophe might apply to Gandhi as well, if one
deleted the adverb "durement" from the metaphor:

> Christophe fut le forgeron d'une nation. Il savait qu'une
> idée vaut mieux qu'une vie: c'est là de l'excellente psychologie
> de grand homme politique. Et il martela durement, comme
> sur une enclume, le peuple soumis, qu'il façonnait à sa
> grandeur.

Roumain's "Eloge à la cruauté de Christophe", which on the
surface appears so different in its values to the "éloge" to
Mahatma Gandhi, shares with it Roumain's continued admiration for the hero figure. Roumain has discovered and explored
a moral fortitude and a grandeur, in the two men, of a quite
different quality. Both men, in their own way, are heroes. But
in addition, the article on Christophe, like the "Notes pour
servir à un manuel de parfaite arriviste," takes up a theme
which will be explored elsewhere. It is quite likely that
Roumain was at work on *Les Fantoches* at the time this article
was published, for a somewhat shorter version of it is inserted
in that novel.

An article entitled "Port-au-Prince—Cap-Haïtien"[22] gives
the account of a trip to Cap-Haïtien apparently made by
Roumain and one or more others for the purpose of visiting
Charlemagne Péralte's home. The article is noteworthy not so
much for what is said (briefly, and in the final lines) about
Péralte, but rather for the descriptions of the Haitian countryside, of a peasant girl Roumain may have seen along the way,
and of Péralte's mother. Under the subheadings "Savane
désolée," "Puilboreau" (a place name), "Portrait d'une paysanne rencontrée", and "Pélerinage," Roumain describes his
reactions to what he witnesses in a style more that of the
personal essay than the newspaper article. His descriptions of
the countryside emphasize its barrenness and stillness:

> La chaleur et la monotonie sans cesse renouvelées des
> bayahondes et des cactus accablent l'esprit.

---

[22] Jacques Roumain, "Port-au-Prince—Cap Haïtien," *Haïti-Journal*,
April 3, 1930, p. 1.

Pourtant je me suis laissé prendre au pathétique d'un petit cimetière endormi au bord de la route luisante, dans un calme immatériel. Des corbeaux traçaient un vol noir comme une auréole funèbre autour d'une croix tragique, couverte de haillons. . . .

. . . La Savane est morte; et ses arbres ont les chevelures blanches de poussières; ces arbres que nul sève ne redresse droit et qui s'appuient sur leurs troncs tordus.

We will find similar descriptions among the writings in Paris and in the novel *Gouverneurs de la rosée*.

The "Portrait d'une paysanne rencontrée" seems to correspond to an inner vision:

Je la rêvai dans un paysage de Gauguin, paradis recréé par l'enchantement des couleurs; au milieu d'arbres torturés de lianes et de lichens gluants autour de leur tronc monstreux et de leurs branches, cédant au jaillissement irrésistible de la vie qui brise l'écorce et fait couler un sang d'ambre; au milieu de feuilles larges et de fruits gorgés de parfum. Au milieu des fruits, des feuilles, des arbres, dans le glauque d'une lumière jade qui résiste à l'éclat des fleurs épanouies: elle-même, couchée nue, belle et restituée enfin à la nature primitive; les bras au hasard de l'herbe, le buste haut, odorant et rond, soulevé au rythme violent de la volupté, les hanches, mouvante corbeille et douces, se prolongeaient subtilement par le jet des jambes fines et fortes—en toute animale innocence, couchée nue, et doucement offerte comme un beau fruit aux secrets délices.

This is indeed a curious passage. It will be seen that, aside from the mothers, the women in Roumain's fiction will be passive projections of Roumain's ideas or of his mythology. They will be symbols of earth's fecundity, of simplicity, of serenity, of the unseen powers of emotive nature, or they will be mirrors of society's values. But nowhere else in his work does Roumain paint the exotic, lush, and frank sensuality which we encounter here.

On the other hand, the portrait of Péralte's mother is like a study for the portraits of mothers in *La Montagne ensorcelée*, *Gouverneurs de la rosée*, and the short story "Gouverneurs de la rosée":

La voici dans le cadre de la porte, toute menue en son austère robe noire. . . .

Ses mains longues et fragiles sont de celles qui doivent bien se joindre pour la prière. Toute à l'heure, elle nous dira combien elles furent meurtries par l'effroyable labeur des corvées et quelle souffrance elles savent quand elles se portent tremblantes sur son coeur brisé, comme pour le protéger contre une trop grande souffrance.

Ce sont des mains longues et fragiles; des mains de Mater dolorosa: les mains de la mère de Charlemagne Péralte.

. . .

Elle nous conte son long calvaire à travers le pays, suivant son fils partout, de bourg en bourg et chacune des prisons où on l'enfermait marquait une station de son chemin de croix.

Et quand, les yeux levés au-delà de nous, vers la vision de Péralte en casaque de forçat, elle dit:

Ay, pitite à mouin! Elle a le geste émouvant qui nous met de brulantes larmes aux yeux, de bercer un tout petit enfant.

Nous baisons ces mains vénérables et prenons congé d'elle, pour ne pas prolonger dans la plaie vive du souvenir, sa douleur de mère martyr.

The portrait of Péralte's mother may be somewhat overdrawn here. Nevertheless, it heralds the treatment of mothers in Roumain's fiction. Aside from those hero-protagonists whose inner life reflects Roumain's own, the mothers in his fiction are his most three-dimensional characters. They reveal an uncanny intuition on Roumain's part of the pain of a mother for her sacrificed son. Through his mother figures, Roumain will, in later works, probe the inner reaches of human emotion.

The articles of *Haïti-Journal* are varied in tone and theme. Yet they all seem somehow to blend two factors uppermost in Roumain's mind: the Haitian reality of the early thirties and an ongoing private struggle to infuse meaning and purpose into the life of the individual self in its relationship with the outer world. With Nationalism very near to the point of triumph in Haiti, Roumain sought to focus attention on the concerns of rebuilding the nation after the departure of the foreign element. All these articles, directly or indirectly, address the question of national self-discipline in preparation for that day. The articles are also very much concerned with the concept of heroism and with several historical figures whose involvement in Nationalist struggles changed the course of history and who are thus models of heroism.

The years 1930 and 1931, years of association with the established government,[23] represent a period of comparative calm in a typically turbulent life. The quiet was only apparent, however, and the turbulence would soon erupt again. Moreover, these two years are of particular importance in a literary sense, for during them Roumain published his first extensive fiction, *La Proie et l'ombre*, *Les Fantoches*, and the very first of the long line of *romans paysans* to come out of Haiti, *La Montagne ensorcelée*.

---

[23] Roumain's articles in *Haïti-Journal* were further acts of association with the government, since the newspaper had been founded in 1930 by Sténio Vincent.

CHAPTER III

Bourgeois Nonauthenticity

LA PROIE ET L'OMBRE

Of all the periodical literature turned out during the years in question, very little was concerned with social inequities or the inadequacies of Haitian life before the Occupation. Jacques Roumain's portrayal of the aimlessness of bourgeois existence in *La Proie et l'ombre*, and the implications in his *Les Fantoches* that the "boue gouvernementale" of Haitian politics will remain a real problem after the departure of the marines, were appreciated by his contemporaries, but these works are not typical of the prose literature of the period. *La Proie et l'ombre*, a collection of short stories, appeared in late 1930. It is first advertised in the August 25–26 issue of *Le Petit Impartial*. The small, ninety-five-page volume contains four short stories, of which two had previously appeared.[1]

The first story, "Propos Sans Suite," opens on nighttime street scenes of Port-au-Prince. Two friends, Jean and Daniel, are conversing:

> La place était petite, sordidement éclairée par un réverbère solitaire. La foule s'écoulait d'elle par une ruelle étroite, et des chiens faméliques, chassés, s'enfuyaient en aboyant hargneusement.

[1] "La Veste," *La Revue Indigène*, no. 4 (October 1927), pp. 167–71; "Préface à la vie d'un bureaucrate," *Haïti-Journal*, pp. 19–22, February 24–25, 1930. Another short story, "Mon Ami Alcibiades" had been published in *La Trouée*, no 1 (July 1927), pp. 26–28, but is not included in *La Proie et l'ombre*.

> Mais derrière la masse écrasée des maisons, quelque part dans la nuit, on entendait la voix sinistre et joyeuse d'un tambour, la voix de mille dieux africains, hilares et obscènes, qui trouait le silence à petits coups frénétiques.
> — Pourquoi disiez-vous, Daniel, que cette foule est triste?
> . . .
> — Parce qu'elle va vers le plaisir. La joie n'attire pas la joie. Vous semblez croire que je prête à tout, mon propre découragement. . . . Non. Nous pourrions aller sous cette tonnelle où l'on débite un pauvre bonheur: danse et tafia. Je vous montrerais ces hommes et ces femmes, leurs visages, et vous sauriez alors qu'une foule gaie se compose d'hommes tristes. Vous verriez le désespoir du plaisir. (p. 4)[2]

In response to Jean's suggestion that he perhaps is asking too much out of life, Daniel says:

> — Vous voulez dire que ma volonté n'est pas à la mesure de mes forces et que ce déséquilibre ne me porte qu'à de vaines tentatives, à de stériles convulsions. Et encore, qu'il faut savoir se résigner, se plier à une vie mesquine: se contenter de peu. Cela jamais; je me refuse à ce piteux stoïcisme. (p. 13)

He wishes his life to be "grande, belle, telle que toujours je la rêvai" (p. 12). Through the Port-au-Prince night, the tom-toms throbbing in the background, the two friends make their way to the teeming Wharf-aux-Herbes, with its street merchants, prostitutes and crowds of people. There they encounter the poet Emilio, singing the beauty of the peasant woman. When Daniel asks him why he no longer writes:

> — La poésie, la poésie. . . . On n'en fait pac avec la vie; en tout cas, pas avec la nôtre. Pourtant, l'oeuvre est là, mûrit, grandit—se dessèche. . . . Ah, réaliser un livre, un poème, si parfaits qu'en leur donnant naissance, on s'allègerait du même coup d'une vie achevée dans la grandeur.
> — Pardonnez-moi, Emilio, dit Daniel d'une voix étouffée; je pensais que vous étiez heureux.
> — Heureux? Vous l'avez cru parce que je saisis mon existence passionnément comme on étreint une femme. Mais après l'amour, Daniel, que les yeux deviennent lucides, quelle affreuse clarté soudain! . . . (pp. 21–22)

---

[2] Page references to all of Roumain's works are to the original editions.

As a bleak drizzly day breaks, the three friends separate and go their several ways.

"La Veste" is also set in nighttime Port-au-Prince. Sitting at a bar, the gloomy and irritable Saivre is told by the man next to him that Saivre's jacket, hanging on a peg facing them, reminds him of the young student, a boarder in his home, who had hanged himself in his room. The image enrages and obsesses Saivre. He rushes out into the night, to the hovel he shares with a woman, whether in marriage or common-law is not specified. Hiding her face against the wall, she hears him muttering: "La veste, Ex-ac-te-ment. Ah démon! Tout à fait comme la veste" (p. 40). A chair falls over, then silence. When she musters enough courage to turn and look: "A la flamme de la bougie, elle vit le corps qui pendait" (p. 41).

In "Fragment d'une confession," Benoît Carrère, alone in a room at night, soliloquizes on his life, with its deceptions and failures:

> Médiocre: je pronoçai déjà ce mot qui est la chute douleureuse de l'homme oscillant sur la corde tendue entre le désire et la volonté. Si loin que je rebrousse chemin vers mes jeunes années, je me heurte à cette image de l'acrobate tendant les bras vers le but, mais toujours perdant l'équilibre, et qui fut mon impuissance à réaliser.
>
> Et je me demande aujourd'hui, si l'ardeur même de mon désir ne fut pas l'insurmontable, le desséchant obstacle, car plus il grandissait, plus il éloignait une satisfaction dès lors devenue incomplète et que je cherchais à atteindre en la dépassant. (p. 47).

The emotional effort finally exhausts him, and as day breaks, we see him

> dormant, la tête entre ses bras, contre la table, et le vent frais porté par les éventails des palmiers baignait son front, mais ne le réveillait point. (p. 47)

The last story in the collection, "Préface à la vie d'un bureaucrate," takes us through a day in the life of Michel Rey, writer of unfinished manuscripts. Michel Rey awakes rather late to a gloomy Port-au-Prince morning and wanders downstairs, where he encounters Mme Ballin, his mother-in-law. He manages to insult her and send her off in a pique, after which, contemplating the seascape from his bedroom window, he dresses for his afternoon's activities:

> Michel Rey pense que désormais sa vie se déroulera semblable à ce va-et-vient aquatique, amer et monotone: sans belles tempêtes. . . .
> Pour tromper l'attente de cet apaisement final, il lui reste à injurier sa belle-mère, à rendre sa femme malheureuse et à boire des cocktails multicolores.
> — Continuons donc notre intéressante journée, soupira-t-il. . . . (pp. 73–74)

He visits a rich leisured friend. They drink, talk, and listen to music. When he returns home, his wife, Jeanne, is waiting for him in tears. She entreats him to come to his senses, to bring the family out of its unnecessary financial misery by accepting the position in the Department of the Interior being offered him through Mme Ballin's influence. Michel is finally defeated by his wife's incessant pleadings and by his own despair. Upstairs, he sits contemplating his writing desk:

> Voici des feuillets blancs entassés sur la table, et puis d'autres couverts de son écriture, jaunis par le temps, et l'encre déjà pâlie.
> Toute sa vie manquée est là. (p. 91)

In a protracted moment of soul-searching, Michel Rey confronts himself. He opens a drawer, sees the gun lying there, and longs for deliverance:

> Mais il se sentit lâche.
> Il ne referma pas le titoir, mais saisissant soudain une feuille blanche, il commença lourdement, lentement:
> Monsieur le Secrétaire d'Etat,
> J'ai bien l'avantage . . . (pp. 94–95)

"Mon Ami Alcibiades," not included in the collection but contemporary with at least one of the stories ("La Veste"), is likewise set in the nighttime streets of Port-au-Prince. The narrator encounters his friend Alcibiades in front of the Bar Terminus. Alcibiades is a "charmant garçon" delightfully full of wit, but his life and family ties are a complete mystery:

> . . . on ne sait exactement où il loge, on ne lui connaît aucune sorte d'occupation; il arrive souvent qu'il disparaisse une

quinzaine, puis un beau jour on le revoit flottant dans un complet trop large immanquablement verte-pré et "chapeauté d'un panama" que la vieillesse n'a point blanchi.

On ne peut affirmer avec sécurité qu'une chose de lui: sa régularité à s'enivrer. (*La Trouée*, July 1927, p. 27)

All four stories show essentially the same thematic preoccupations. The protagonists are all young urban intellectuals roaming aimlessly about Port-au-Prince, caught in the empty monotonous pettiness of their existence. Their despair stems from their sense that there is something missing in their lives. They should be capable of more. They are inadequate heroes, incapable of reaching beyond their lives. They realize this in a sudden moment of truth. Emilio's "affreuse clarté soudain" has close affinities with Saivre's flash of insight as he recognizes himself fully in his threadbare jacket, hanging defeated on a peg in the bar. And Michel Rey, contemplating the yellowing sheets of manuscript and the gun in the desk drawer, can recognize the vanity and pretension of all his activities. Incapable of changing his destiny, he sees that suicide and the writing of a letter of application for a government post are equally futile acts. The clear perception of this reality is what seals his doom. Alcibiades, the first of these heroes to appear in print, is a rootless drunken wanderer. Having no past and no future, he lives in a void. He is unlike the more introspective heroees whom Roumain subsequently reveals in that he has not as yet become honest with himself; he is not yet a hero, with the moral courage to look squarely and honestly into the dead center of his life.

The theme of these five stories is therefore none other than that already encountered in most of Roumain's poetry of 1927–29. His poetry reflected the hero in various settings: the romantic hero, sensitive, lonely and unhappy; the cosmic hero, just as lonely but reaching beyond himself into the vastness of space, the only bright spot in a universe shrouded in darkness; the valiant hero, fighting for rightful control of his destiny in the society of his compatriots. The hero now, in the early prose, becomes spokesman for a kind of Lost Generation, unable to find fulfillment in the old values and unable to find any new ones, and so existing in a vacuum. It is not the vacuum which ultimately destroys these heroes, but their lucidity about their condition.

But it is not only in the theme that this first prose seems closely related to the early poetry. Certain motifs recur, some of which have appeared in the poetry. Rhythmic buildups into lyric tirades at the moment of lucidity and a use of the self very reminiscent of the lyric or the epic *moi* of Roumain's poetry are also evidence that Roumain's mind is still functioning to a great extent in the poetic mode.

The most impressive of the motifs is the light-darkness antithesis already seen in so much of the poetry. Darkness is announced in the collection's title and enshrouds most of the stories. Occasionally, an image will recall a similar one depicted in the poetry. In "La Veste":

> Saivre . . . regarda par la fenêtre. La pluie faisait fondre la lumière du réverbère. De fines aiguilles d'or tombaient. Derrière, la grande nuit vague, le grand silence noir. (pp. 29–30)

We are reminded of the image of the beloved in "Attente":

> O les yeux douloureux d'épier le ruisseau d'or
> Que verse sur l'asphalte le réverbère borgne.

In both passages night, darkness and rain represent vast unending gloom and eternal unfulfilled waiting but are accompanied by the one contrasting spot of light.

Other images found in the poetry seem to repeat themselves with great insistence in the early prose. In reading "Fragment d'une confession," one finds oneself immersed in the same poetic universe as in "Calme," where the lonely hero, after attempting to reach beyond, finally succumbs:

> Me voici plus seul d'être dans cette chambre obscure; la fenêtre ne laisse pénétrer que la nuit, effarouchée à peine par la lampe timide autour de laquelle elle remue comme un sombre papillon.
> Me voici dans mon île deserte: ce plat, pâle rocher de la table, tout entouré des remous du silence et de l'ombre.
> Heure paisible et médiocre. Tout bruit s'en va sur la pointe des pieds, et s'approche doucement la rêverie aux yeux mi-clos.

C'est tenter encore une fois la décevante expérience d'être courbé sur le passé comme sur un fleuve agité des cris et des froissements d'aile de ces mouettes furtives: les souvenirs. (pp. 45–46)

The passage offers the image of the poet alone at a lighted desk surrounded by silence and darkness, as in "Calme":

Ma table est une île lumineuse
dans la ouate noire de la silencieuse nuit. . . .

The passage also associates silence and space with suspension in time, an association found in much of the early poetry. Expressions such as "courbé sur le passé" suggest the body's futile efforts to escape its contingencies and recall other expressions such as "un homme courbé sur ses désirs morts" ("Calme"). The past participate "courbé" recalls other verbs: "je me penche hors de moi" ("Insomnie"). The image of the "acrobate tendant les bras vers le but" in this story strongly recalls the images in the early poetry of the outstretched arms, symbolizing the effort sustained, the source of strength called upon to reach the goal. When the arm motif recurs a few paragraphs later, it reveals the failure of the poet's individual effort. And it is at this juncture that the comforting presence of the beloved is invoked:

. . . Ah, que s'ouvre cette porte et entre une femme aux pas hésitants; qu'elle vienne avec ce mystérieux sourire que je ne connus jamais jusqu'à mon front pesant et mes bras inutiles. . . . (p. 52)

Again, we are reminded of certain of Roumain's early poems, which also invoke the comforting presence of the beloved. In the paragraph following, the motif of the hands also appears, symbolizing, as in the poetry, human contact in love:

Mon Dieu, que s'ouvre cette porte et entre un tout petit enfant et vienne jusqu'à mes genoux et que j'entende sa douce voix malhabile et qu'il mette ses mains puériles sur mon vieux visage. Mon Dieu, peut-être m'aimera-t-il? (p. 53)

The story from beginning to end involves the reader in Benoît Carrère's nocturnal quest, up to the moment of final exhaustion at daybreak, when the reader is suddenly catapulted out of the character's private emotional universe by the sudden shift into third-person narrative. The effect is very much like the rhythmic buildup in poems like "Cent mètres" and "Appel," which implicates the reader in the internal drama of the protagonist and releases him suddenly at the end from involvement in the hero's destiny. "Fragment d'une confession" is short, broken up into short stanzaic paragraphs. Given all these considerations, it is perhaps valid to raise the question whether "Fragment d'une confession" is not really, after all, a poem.

"Préface à la vie d'un bureaucrate," on the other hand, presents an entirely different case. It has a plot, which, however tenuous, functions toward the resolution of a central "problem" announced by the title. It contains as well the usual dialogue and narrative passages and the characterization associated with prose fiction. Yet a lyric interlude interrupts the action toward the end of the story, and at that point the same motif, conveying the same message as in "Fragment d'une confession," reappears. Michel Rey angrily leaves his wife, goes upstairs, sits at his desk, pulls open his drawer, contemplates the gun, reaches instead for paper and pen, and writes a letter. These are his successive acts. But in between the act of sitting and the act of opening the drawer:

> Toute sa vie manquée est là.
> La tête entre les mains, il la récapitule:
> — Suis-je limité par ma faiblesse ou bien est-ce un désir inhumain qui dépasse les frontières d'un but que je ne veux, que je ne puis me proposer, que lointain!
> Au fond, il est possible que tout ceci revienne aux "raisins verts" que je me persuade dédaigner, tangner [sic], tandis qu'en réalité je ne suis point capable du bond qui les mettrait à ma portée.
> La question est simple: je suis un raté aux dents agacés par la vie, cette grappe de fruits acides, à laquelle je ne puis mordre.
> Mais à quoi me sert cette piteuse analyse? Tout interrogatoire que l'on fait subir à sa vie, laisse subsister la question: Pourquoi? et toute vérité acquise péniblement continent la simplicité de son explication ridiculement, en elle-même.

Ou bien, tout se résume à dire:
A quoi bon? et justement 'A quoi bon?' n'est pas une
question; mais une réponse.[3] (pp. 91–92)

In this interlude, Michel Rey is hardly distinguishable from
Benoît Carrère, and it is the author's technique that makes it
so.

The image of the man bent over his writing desk, with a
lighted lamp and surrounded by darkness, is almost an ob-
sessive metaphor, and we will encounter it again. It is noteworthy perhaps that in the fully developed short story the
meaning is carried more by discursive speech, and is put more
explicitly, is less a reverie with a dreamlike succession of
images. Michel Rey's soul-searching is much closer to self-
analysis, a term he uses himself. The lyric introspective rhythm
is broken up by a narrative style which did not exist at all in
"Calme" and which existed only as a kind of coda at the end
of "Fragment d'une confession." The play on light and dark
has been entirely lost. (One might argue that since we have
followed Michel Rey from the beginning to the end of his day,
the darkness outside the house and the room is implied; but
it is not seen, and in this instance the author has not under-
scored the internal drama by any visual contrasts.)

The stories of *La Proie et l'ombre* often evoke gloom and
monotony, not solely through surrounding darkness but also
through tableaux of an overcast sky and of the sea. Light has
an altogether different meaning when it is the diffuse light of
day rather than a concentrated spot of light generated by or
associated with the solitary, searching hero. In these stories,
night typically fades into day, and the day is gloomy, a different
form of monotony, as in the opening lines of "Préface à la vie
d'un bureaucrate": "Michel Rey, en se réveillant, vit un jour
sale se glisser à travers les persiennes" (p. 57). Almost immediately, he thinks of this daylight as "lumière morte." It is
not the sunny tropics and the warm, blue-fringed beaches

---

[3] Roger Gaillard has singled out this last sentence for special
attention in his study *L'Univers romanesque de Jacques Roumain* (Port-
au-Prince: Henri Deschamps [1965?] pp. 8–9.

which we see in these stories, but the overcast sky, the murky grey water, the thin, drizzly rain:

> Le jour s'annonçait; la nuit glissait comme un masque, et des lueurs s'élançaient déjà comme des doigts pâles et laissaient des traces sales au-dessus des mornes.
> Ils se sentirent pleins de tristesse et délaissés et inutiles comme ces caisses défoncées, ces débris de poteries, éparpillés sur le sol, autour d'eux.
> Jean partit le premier.
> Daniel prit le bras de son compangon. . . .
> Ils marchèrent jusqu'au quai.
> La mer avait des reflets métalliques.
> Ils restaient là, sans plus rien dire, écoutant le bruissement de soie des vagues contre les pilotis.
> A la fin, ils se séparèrent, car une petite pluie froide commençait à tomber dans le matin blême. ("Propos sans suite," pp. 23–25)

If some of the motifs of *La Proie et l'ombre* repeat those of the poetry, others are new. We find over and over in these stories the lonely nocturnal walks through deserted streets contrasted with (sometimes immediately followed by) sudden immersion in a crowd of common folk. The noctambulation represents alienation, whereas the crowds of Creole-speaking blacks represent the Haitian identity which the alienated, intellectual, bourgeois heroes go out nightly in search of. A prostitute's sad cry reaches Daniel's ears as he stands discoursing in a deserted square on the general futility of his existence. "Allons là-bas," he says. "Ça doit être une belle et forte négresse." (p. 6)

> Ils quittèrent la place déserte, s'engagèrent dans un dédale de ruelles noires bordées de cabanes mi-effondrées et malodorantes comme des tas d'ordures, s'égarèrent un instant jusqu'à un cul-de-sac, mais Daniel qui connaissait les lieux assez bien retrouva le chemin en traversant quelques courettes endormies et ils arrivèrent au Wharf-aux-Herbes.
> L'endroit présentait son visage familier rongé de nuit et d'une lèpre de crasse. Ça et là au-dessus des étalages des marchandes de frites et de *pois et riz* vacillait la lueur fumeuse des chandelles. ("Propos sans suite," pp. 14–15)

In "Préface à la vie d'un bureaucrate," Michel, on waking, sees his raincoat still dripping from the night's rain, and it reminds him of the moment of his return home:

> Il y avait cinq ans . . . il se rappelait le jour de son retour en Haïti. Le soleil de midi domptait une mer silencieuse remuée de vagues douces et sans écume. Une joie profonde le possédait; dans la foule anonyme qui montait sur le pont en se bousculant sur l'échelle étroite: visiteurs, porte-faix, parents, il se reconnaissait enfin, se sentait l'écho heureux de ce monde noir, écoutait fondre en lui la gace [sic] amassée en Europe, disparaître de son coeur ce qu'il nommait avec amertume "le grand silence blanc," et qui était l'abîme racial que là-bas ses amitiés, ses amours, ses relations n'avaient pu combler. Maintenant il était parmi ses frères et son peuple. Il aurait voulu s'agenouiller, baiser cette terre chère. . . .
> Ses parents qui l'entrainaient vers la ville l'accablaient de questions. Il essayait de répondre, mais il aurait voulu se séparer d'eux, marcher seul, dans une extase solenelle, et étreindre cette marchande de mangues qui passait, portant ses fruits sur la tête comme une reine sa couronne, les reins cambrés, crevant l'étoffe bleue de sa robe grossière, oui, l'étreindre fortement et lui dire: "Soeur!"; prendre dans ses bras cet enfant déguenillé qui tendait la main à un touriste américain, le presser sur son coeur: "Frère, petit frère! . . ."
> (pp. 58–60)

We are not told why the dripping raincoat should remind Michel of his homecoming day, but the fact that the memory directly follows an allusion to nocturnal wanderings is perhaps significant, for it is the same juxtaposition of loneliness followed by sudden immersion in a crowd that we find in other passages in the prose of this period.

Less elaborate but more frequent is the recurrence of the forced smile or laugh. In almost every instance, laughter is hollow, the smile is a sneer or a pose, behind which bitter emptiness is discernible:

Daniel, in "Propos sans suite":

> . . . il éclata de rire. La voix était blanche, tremblait et se brisa avec une sorte de rage. (p. 6)

> Le rire fêlé recommençait. (p. 9)

Emilio, in "Propos sans suite":

> Emilio fit une curieuse grimace: on eut dit que son rire s'était
> réfugié dans une ride subite qui tirait ses lèvres, amèrement.
> . . . (p. 20)

Michel, in "Préface à la vie d'un bureaucrate":

> Il sourit de ce sourire qui lui était particulier: une sorte de
> rictus douleureux, qui tirait ses lèvres, d'un côté par deux
> rides divergents. (p. 57)

> Un ricanement intérieur le déchire. (p. 85)

Each succeeding image recalls the ones before it, establishing
a kind of metaphoric resonance. The message of empty helplessness in the lives of these young men is transmitted as in
Roumain's early poetry by the indirect means of motif symbolism.

Within the sordidness of the urban setting, here and there
images and metaphors allude to the native fruits of Haiti. Such
allusions are not usually gratuitous; they give the impression
of lush growth and productiveness, of the overabundance
resulting from natural, uninhibited growth. These metaphors
seem to refocus on that which is indigenous, as contrasted
with the gloomy artificiality of intellectualized urban life.
Significantly, allusions to fruit occur in passages dealing with
women, who themselves are symbols of hope and regenerative
power. Sometimes that power is depleted, as in the case of the
old peasant woman whom Michel, in "Préface à la vie d'un
bureaucrate," had glimpsed the day of his return. But more
often, fruit and women still hold the promise of future growth.
Crowds of common folk, women, and fruit all seem to represent
the essence of Haiti and the source of Haitian life. This
symbolism becomes more important as we go from *La Proie
et l'ombre* to *Les Fantoches*, where it becomes more closely
associated with certain characters and not with others, and
more will need to be said of it later.

The meaning of the title Roumain chose for his first
collection is revealed in Benoît Carrère's soliloquy, previously
quoted in part:

> Et je me demande aujourd'hui, si l'ardeur même de mon
> désir ne fut pas l'insurmontable, le desséchant obstacles, car

plus il grandissait, plus il éloignait une satisfaction dès lors devenue incomplète et que je cherchais à atteindre en la dépassant.

Dans cette lutte avec une ombre toute ma vie, je fus distancé. (p. 47)

These heroes stalk a prey in the darkness of night, where shadows are thrown by an occasional lighted spot. Indeed, they are themselves the lone bright spot projecting shadows, for the source of greatness, as they rightly perceive, lies within themselves.

Professor Mercer Cook has spoken of the influence of the French Decadents of the turn of the century in *La Proie et l'ombre*.[4] Although Roumain does not speak of such an influence in any of his writings now available to us, certain parallels do exist between his early prose and the Decadents. In their nighttime wanderings, Roumain's young heroes often show a propensity for seeking out the dives and hovels of the city. Amid the stale smells of alcohol and cooking grease, the painted prostitutes and flotsam thrown in the sea and washed back up, they comment on man's dismal spiritual state. The heroes of *La Proie et l'ombre* share in common with the Parisians of the turn of the century a feeling that they are witnessing the empty culmination of a civilization. But it is doubtful that the *fin-de-siècle* ethic goes very deeply into the matrix of these stories. The young men of *La Proie et l'ombre* do not seek out depravity because of some genetic degeneracy; they do not seek it as a means of purification or of control over their destinies as do the heroes of the Marquis de Sade and their literary descendants.[5] These young bourgeois of Port-au-Prince are far more humanitarian in their idealism. One is reminded by certain passages more of Baudelarian decadence and fallen angels. Daniel's remark—

J'aime les prostituées. Elles ont des baisers douloureux: c'est d'avoir meurtri la chair de leurs bouches à tant de lèvres

---

[4] Mercer Cook, Introduction to Jacques Roumain, *Masters of the Dew*, trans. Langston Hughes and Mercer Cook (New York: Collier Books [The MacMillan Company], 1971), p. 19.

[5] See especially A. E. Carter, *The Idea of Decadence in French Literature: 1830–1900* (Toronto: University of Toronto Press, 1958).

étrangères, à tant de caresses infâmes. Auprès d'elles je suis
apaisé. Je suis leur pareil. . . . Pareil à elles par la souffrance
et le dégoût quotidien. Prostitué aussi: à moi-même, à mon
impuissance, à ma lâcheté devant la vie. (pp. 7–8)

—echoes more the compassion of Baudelaire's lines:

Vous que dans votre enfer mon âme a poursuivies,
Pauvres soeurs, je vous aime autant que je vous plains,
Pour vos mornes douleurs, vos soifs inassouvies,
Et les urnes d'amour dont vos grands coeurs sont pleins.
("Femmes Damnées" (CXI), *Fleurs du Mal*)

than the self-willed perversion of an Almani, a character in
the Marquis de Sade's *Justine:*

Le mal seul m'émeut; je ne respire qu'en le commetant; mon
organisme n'est délecté que par lui seul. . . . J'aime à voir
périr une créature dans quelques-unes de mes expériences.
. . . Je suis bestialitaire et meurtrier.

Undoubtedly, decadent writers—Eastern and Western alike—
had an attraction for Roumain; the "Mon Carnet" series alone
shows it quite amply. And there are traces in the early poetry
as well. (In, for example, "Le Chant de l'homme," where the
poet says of the streets and walls: ". . . vous les avez, o
hommes/élargis de vos pas,/de vos désirs,/ de relents de rhum,/
de sexe et de "draught-beer"/ J'erre dans vos labyrinthes/
multicolores. . . ."). Certain of the ideas spread by the Decadents at the end of the nineteenth century, certain of the scenes
in their novels and the major traits of the characters they
created, no doubt find a hospitable milieu in these early
stories.

In the heroes of *La Proie et l'ombre,* Jacques Roumain's
contemporaries immediately recognized themselves and the
author. Almost immediately, the obvious question was posed:
Were these stories autobiographical? Antonio Vieux had gone
straight to the heart of the matter in the opening words of his
preface:

Je n'irai pas jusqu'à dire de cette oeuvre, la première que
M. J. Roumain nous donne, que c'est une confession. C'est
plutôt un témoignage—et je le préfère. La confession se
limite à un seul homme, à une seule âme. . . . Le témoignage

est plus large. . . . Le témoignage sert à l'histoire de l'âme collective. . . .

Analyse profonde et impitoyable de nous-mêmes, je le crois. . . . Ce livre? Un témoignage, je vous dis. (pp. i–iv)

Another of Roumain's associates has recently stated:

> I would go so far as to say a full confession. Jacques' noctambulism was a *prise de contact* with the people as well as a means of escape from the élite to which he belonged but soon despised. (Group I interviews)

The manner in which Roumain's friends and associates chose to put the problem has special implications. Quite apart from any examination of its literary merits, young Haitians embraced *La Proie et l'ombre* as a kind of solace. The stories were an esthetization of an inner life which they could recognize as their own.

Carl Brouard avowed that even though only one of the stories was known to him, all of them *seemed* familiar. He agreed with Antonio Vieux that the collection was a "témoignage." But at the same time he implied that that testimonial, the result of Roumain's ability to analyse deep into human motivations, was also the result of Roumain's own analysis of himself:

> Il n'est pas bon que l'homme soit trop avec soi-même. Le monde extérieur n'existe pas assez pour ROUMAIN. Ce monde extérieur qui dilate les coeurs et les rend optimistes. . . . Il ne faut pas qu'il prête *ses propres* reflexes, ses propres sensations aux paysans qui évolueront dans le roman annoncé.[6]

Another review praises Roumain's trenchant portrayal of the milieu and ends by proclaiming: "Le succès de 'La Proie et l'ombre' n'est plus à augurer. C'est déjà un fait."[7]

Several years later, and at great psychological remove from

---

[6] Carl Brouard, review of *La Proie et l'ombre, Le Petit Impartial,* September 8–9, 1930. Italics added. The novel alluded to is *La Montagne ensorcelée.*

[7] G.J.P. [Georges J. Petit?], *Le Petit Impartial,* September 10–11, 1930.

the matter, the question of autobiography is still pertinent.
Edner Brutus brings it up:

> Beaucoup y voient une pure autobiographie et n'y découvrent
> guère le résultat d'une enquête menée à travers les méandres
> de l'âme des désaxés de notre génération. Ce livre est, tout
> ensemble un témoignage et un aveu. L'auteur, tant en lui
> qu'en nous, a ramassé ses observations.[8]

Elsewhere in his article, Brutus corroborates the suggestion in
these words that *La Proie et l'ombre* is a revelation of Roumain's
inner life. When he speaks of Roumain's poetry he shifts
almost imperceptibly into a discussion of Roumain's *character*.

> Sa poésie traduit un état de fatigue du coeur et la sensation
> de repos donnée par l'acceptation de cet accablement. Elle
> rend ce silence intérieur d'un homme recueilli pour mieux
> capter ses impressions.(p. 9)

> M. Roumain m'a toujours paru un élégant ennuyé qui par
> l'une de ces contradictions bizarres, intensément, vit. (p. 10)

> Son mal, en certaines occasions, lui apporte des instants
> de calme alternant avec des périodes de dépression amères.
> (p. 11)

> En s'etudiant, il prend du plaisir à poser le doigt sur la fêlure
> de son coeur. (p. 11)

The description would fit most of the heroes of *La Proie et
l'ombre*.

All of these contemporary judgments seem to be making
the same basic assumption. They all see Jacques Roumain the
man as a repository for the feelings and aspirations of his
generation. The inner life of Jacques Roumain, analyzed and
revealed to his peers, reflects the inner life of all of them.

The impulsion of the poet to use himself as model, to effect
an esthetic reworking from the specific to the generic, is at the
basis of these stories, as it was of the early poetry, and
illustrates again their transitional nature. Unlike the poetry,
however, these stories have specific characters who move about
in more or less well-defined environments (and in the case of

---

[8] Edner Brutus, "Jacques Roumain," *La Relève*, October 1933, pp.
12–13.

"Preface à la vie d'un bureaucrate", must resolve certain problems). This explains why most readers have perceived and drawn meaning from La Proie et l'ombre on two levels.

While it seems safe to conclude that the individual soul's journey of the poet-prophet is also a testimony of the anguish of his contemporaries, the relationship between events in the life of the man, Jacques Roumain and those of certain of his characters is by no means as clear. There is strong evidence that certain of the actions and circumstances of some of the characters in La Proie et l'ombre parallel those of Jacques Roumain or certain of his associates. The poet Emilio recites the verses of Emile Roumer and has much of the latter's special type of wit. Carl Brouard wrote of La Proie et l'ombre: "on est tenté à chaque instant de mettre des noms sur certains per- sonnages, l'inoubliable Madame Ballin, par example." (Le Petit Impartial, September 8–9, 1930) Although Brouard states that he will not indulge in this game, the bait has already been laid: Is Roumain speaking of historical persons close to him in real life? Roger Gaillard tells us that Jacques Roumain never knew his mother-in-law and was not even married when the story was written (Gaillard, L'Univers romanesque de Jacques Roumain, p. 71, n. 1).

If we compare Mme Ballin not with possible historical prototypes but with the other women in Roumain's work, it becomes apparent that the women in his work are more than anything else projections of his own feelings, his reactions, his needs. The author had very definite feelings about the Haitian bourgeois woman. She was a repository of all the useless pretensions of the class, exhibited all its prejudices. The younger women lack true vision, lack ambition to go beyond their material existence, and the heroes alternately long for and reject them. But the dowagers are all perfectly empty-headed, vain, assimilationist women bent on pushing those nearest them to getting ahead in society. It is upon this class, age, and sex that Roumain's satire dwells most linger- ingly. When viewed in this fictional context, Mme Ballin emerges as the first in a line of bourgeois dowagers, and it is in this light that she seems to have most meaning.

Michel Rey, like Jacques Roumain, has returned home after

years of study in Europe. He is a writer; he becomes a functionary in the Department of the Interior. The scene in which Michel, standing once again on Haitian soil and contemplating the Haitian folk, thinks back to the "grand silence blanc" of Europe and wishes to embrace the peasant woman and the ragged boy, might reasonably cause us to suspect that Jacques Roumain is borrowing from his own actual experiences. But probably the more meaningful autobiographical references are those which concern the author's feelings about race at that point in his life.

Michel Rey's reluctance to join the humdrum mediocrity of bureaucratic existence has given rise to speculation that there was a similar reluctance on Jacques Roumain's part. The circumstances of his life seem to justify this view. We may profitably quote what Roger Gaillard has written on the subject:

> On sait qu'un des héroes de "La Proie," Michel Rey finit par se laisser aller à la solution facile, en acceptant un poste dans l'Administration Publique.
> On sait aussi que J. R. a été aussi fonctionnaire. De façon d'ailleurs éphémère. Voici ce que m'écrit à ce propos un familier de notre romancier:
> "Jacques était Chef de division au Département de l'Intérieur quand il publia La Proie et l'ombre; mais il avait écrit les nouvelles de ce recueil avant son entrée au ministère.
> "Préface à la Vie d'un Bureaucrate," un des récits de "La Proie," aurait été, de quelque manière, l'expression d'une prémonition *sans être pour autant auto-biographique.* Prémonition de la capitulation des intellectuels d'une génération devant les "impératifs de la vie." Au reste, Jacques *savait* qu'il n'échapperait pas lui-même à la tentation." (Lettre reçue le 16 Mai 1965) (Gaillard, *L'Univers romanesque de Jacques Roumain,* p. 5, n. 1)

One can accept as coincidence the fact that both the author and the character were functionaries in the Départment de l'Intérieur; one can even accept the author's premonition as another testimony to Roumain's sensitivities and perceptions. However, we do find in subsequent fiction that certain incidents in the lives of protagonists strongly parallel those in the life of the author. The part of autobiography with respect to *events* as distinct from perceptions and poetic vision remains somewhat of a problem.

LES FANTOCHES

If, in *La Proie et l'ombre,* we find the indirect appeal to the sensitivities of the reader typical of poetry, we also find in it the direct appeal to the reader's powers of analysis typical of prose. While the indirect appeal constitutes an invitation to view the hero from within, to react as one with him, the direct appeal leaves us outside, scrutinizing, not only actions and the motivations for them, but also the milieu in which those actions unfold. In Roumain's first prose publication, the storyteller implicit in the novelist vies still with the impression-maker implicit in the poet. In *Les Fantoches,* published in 1931, the storyteller comes more clearly into his own, creating more fully developed characters, who move in a better delineated environment and who exteriorize their feelings to a much greater extent through conversation. We find the same motifs of light and dark, of gloomy days and monotonous seas, of nocturnal walks and sudden crowds, of mirthless laughter and fruit and peasant women, as in *La Proie et l'ombre.* But it is more the characters and the opinions they enunciate which carry the theme in *Les Fantoches.*

Les Fantoches traces the lives of three young men: Marcel Basquet, *enfant gâté* of Port-au-Prince society; Santiague, the idealistic and dreamy poet; and Lefèvre, a sincere and dedicated politician. Around them circulate a host of secondary characters, the people who make up their milieu: Irène Estienne, Marcel's sweetheart; Michel Rey, whom we recognize from "Préface à la vie d'un bureaucrate," but now older, resigned, and with a somewhat mellowed cynicism; Jeannette Lange, cool and calculating, who collects lovers almost in her husband's presence; Cosquer, the mathematician, who composes riddles on the theme of life; Albert Lecocq, a Frenchman and Marcel's persistent rival for the attentions of Irène; and Mlle Fattu, Irène's old-maid aunt, ever on the lookout for a suitable match for her ward. The story unfolds through a series of tableaux set in the last years of the American Occupation, just before the national legislative elections of October 1930.

In the first chapter, "Le Bal au Club Sélect," we meet most of the characters. Marcel drifts over to a group of his friends, among whom is the poet Santiague. In response to Marcel's witty nihilism, Santiague tries to warn him that he may one day become a "faiseur de mots croisés" (p. 14) or another Michel Rey. Such is Marcel's attraction to Michel Rey that he no sooner hears the name than he must leave the younger men to go seek out Rey, seated at the bar.

> — Mais enfin, disait Michel Rey à Marcel, pourquoi êtes-vous venu à ce bal stupide?
> — Chercher l'ennui, l'ennui me distrait quand il me change de ma vie habituelle.
> Michel le regarda profondément.
> — Voici la réponse d'un homme jeune, fort, beau. N'ayez pas l'immodestie de protester. D'ailleurs, fit-il sur un ton singulièrement douloureux et méprisant, n'ai-je pas été comme vous? (pp. 14–15)

This is not the response Marcel had expected:

> —Est-il fou, ou ivre? se demandait Marcel avec inquiétude.
> Michel eut un rire sec:
> — Vos yeux me disent bien votre pensée. Un jour, peut-être serez-vous assis en face d'un homme jeune, fort, beau, comme devant le reflet de votre adolescence: Vous aurez pitié de lui, vous lui parlerez—et dans son regard vous lirez: "est-il fou?" (p. 16)

But Michel Rey's words have nevertheless reminded Marcel of something Santiague had one day said to him:

> Ce qui m'inquiète, Marcel, dans votre hésitation à agir, à entreprendre une oeuvre quelconque c'est que je doute qu'un jour vous sachiez échapper à ce remords fait de lâcheté et de faiblesse que dénonçait si durement Spinoza. Il me semble que tout courage vous manque pour accomplir de bonnes ou de mauvaises actions. (p. 18)

In the second chapter, "Le Meeting électoral," we find Marcel at a political rally where chance and his boredom have led him. There he runs into Santiague, and the two friends listen to the debate between Lefèvre and Marau, opposing candidates:

> Jean Lefèvre venait de monter sur la table. Une lampe à huile l'éclairait à mi-corps, mais quand il bougeait, on distinguait ses traits fiévreux, son front élevé sous les cheveux crépus, sa bouche tourmentée et la lumière de ses yeux.

> Sa voix était froide, un peu criarde, le thème de son discours se développait avec méthode. Marcel apprécia l'honnêteté qu'il mettait à ne pas faire de concessions au goût de la foule, pour les phrases belles et creuses.
> Il le dit à son compagnon.
> — Oui, c'est dommage, répondit Santiague. . . .
> Lefèvre a trop d'estime de soi pour être démagogue et il est trop bête pour ne pas saisir qu'un démocrate intelligent doit être un démagogue. . . . (pp. 30–31)

On the other hand, Lefèvre's opponent, Aristide Marau, is the ideal demagogue, and as Santiague has predicted, he captures the crowd with references to the glories of Toussaint and Christophe, heroes of Haitian independence and black men. Santiague and Marcel leave in disgust. Outside, they reflect on the nation's political future: anarchy? dictatorship? Santiague considers the possibility of the latter:

> Mon Dieu, pourquoi pas? Même à la liberté il faut un maître. C'est Schiller qui l'a dit, mais le Roi Christophe le pensait certainement.
> Nom de Dieu! en voila un qui n'aimait pas les merdaillons, les sacrés petits morpions démagogues du type Aristide Marau (Santiague devenait extrêmement brutal, dans l'enthousiasme).
> Marcel ouvrit la bouche: oui, mais . . .
> — Fermez ça, mon vieux. Je sais que vous aller me parler de la cruauté de Christophe. Mais la cruauté est un des attributs les plus remarquables de l'homme fort. . . . (pp. 35–36)

Santiague continues at length. His lengthy discourse repeats almost verbatim, and with the deletion of very few paragraphs and sentences, Roumain's article "Eloge à la cruauté de Christophe," published the preceding year in *Haïti-Journal*. Santiague and Marcel have apparently had this debate in the past. Marcel preferred Pétion and often said of him:

> "Pétion fut un homme supérieur; il n'est pas à la portée du commun des mortels d'être cocu, comme lui le fut, avec un si charmant et philosophique bonheur." (pp. 38–39)

Marcel's flippancy vexes Santiague, but the two part company still on good terms. Santiague goes home to write an article promised to *Le Soir*, while Marcel goes to find a girl he knows who is knowledgeable in the art of love.

"A l'ombre des bougainvilliers," the next chapter, takes up the relationship between Marcel and Irène. Marcel arrives at Irène's house just as Lecocq leaves. The encounter provokes Marcel's intense racial feelings, yet Irène leaves no doubt that it is Marcel she loves. Seated with Irène on the porch under the bougainvilleas, he rages:

> En vérité l'aristocrate haïtien tient par des fibres profondes à la France; il n'a pas oublié que quelque sombre couloir de case coloniale fut le berceau de sa naissance, le soir qu'un blanc échauffé par d'excessives libations renversa la négresse esclave son aïeule.
> — Vous devenez impertinent, murmura-t-elle, mais très bas et tristement comme si elle allait pleurer.
> La colère de Marcel était passée. Il supplia Irène de lui pardonner. Son repentir était sincère, mais ce regard touchant de chien battu qui implorait pitié; il l'avait longuement étudié et appris devant un mirroir.
> Toute émue, elle lui prit la main:
> — Qu'avez-vous donc à vous reprocher Marcel, pour ainsi en vouloir à votre bonheur? Pauvre amour que le mien: est-ce donc parce que vous m'aimez et que vous vous haïssez, que vous vous tourmentez par ma souffrance et dois-je trouver la preuve de votre tendresse dans les blessures que vous m'infligez?
> Marcel tout en gardant une mine contrite, se disait ironiquement qu'elle s'exprimait réellment bien. . . .
> Et pourtant il s'avouait qu'elle avait vu clair en lui; au fond il l'aimait, mais comme si une puissance étrangère et mauvaise se fut emparée de sa volonté, il prenait un plaisir amer à réduire en cendres, ses joies les plus pures. (pp. 46–47)

In the chapter "La Rédaction du Soir," Marcel, Michel Rey, Lefèvre, and Santiague are at the office of the newspaper *Le Soir*. Michel Rey has written an article describing an Aztec ceremony in which the sacrificial victim is first given the name of the deity to whom he will be sacrificed, is venerated and pampered as though he were that god, then sacrificed and eaten. Rey concludes:

> — Or, le cannibalisme religieux symbolique tel qu'on le trouve dans la communion chrétienne.

The editor, Lafond, is scandalized:

> . . . vous voulez donc ruiner mon journal? Vous confondez avec un effroyable blasphème le Christ et Huitzilopochtli. D'ailleurs, ajouta-t-il avec beaucoup de dignité, oubliez-vous que je suis catholique?
> — Je ne crois pas avoir attaqué vos convictions; je ne fais qu'exposer de vieilles croyances universelles auxquelles n'a pas échappé le christianisme. (p. 67)

Lafond looks over Marcel's article:

> — "Haïti, Mur des lamentations de la race noire." Vos titres sont épatants, mon vieux. . . . Je suppose que comme d'habitude, le titre vaut mieux que l'article. . . . Maintenant voyons ça: "Démoralisation . . . hérédité éducationnelle . . . conscience raciale." Très bien, très bien, personne ne lira ça . . . puisque justement il n'y a pas de conscience raciale dans notre bourgeoisie. (pp. 70–71)

The conversation turns to Marcel's abandoned essay on Gobineau. "A quoi bon?" says Marcel. His attitude toward politics is hardly any different:

> — Les nations sont assujetties implacablement au déterminisme. Qui m'assure que si aujord'hui, je lutte pour notre liberté, ce ne sera en vain: que notre histoire ne suivra un parcours cyclique et que le fait dont présentement nous pouvons nous débarasser—l'occupation américaine—dans quarante ans ne se renouvellera point? (p. 77)

Lefèvre, who is of a family of dedicated politicians, and who had been put in jail by the Occupation in its first years, cannot accept such a view. When he tries to protest, Marcel tells him:

> — Je vous estime Lefèvre, autant que je me méprise, mais je vous plains. Votre plus grand défaut, c'est avoir des idées. (p. 79)

In the following chapter, "La Surprise-Party chez Madame Lange," the cream of Port-au-Prince society is seen moving about in a world crumbling from within but still magnificent from without. Here we meet Jeannette Lange and watch her systematically seduce an indifferent Marcel.

While Marcel is thus occupied, Santiague, intrigued by the

house and by what it represents, has wandered away from the crowd:

> Dans la salle à manger déserte, il y avait de lourds meubles Renaissance, vermoulous et dépareillés, des tableaux à moitié effacés, une atmosphère de décrépitude et d'abandon. Son cerveau travaillait activement à associer ses impressions. Il avait souvent rêvé d'écrire l'histoire d'une famille de l'aristocratie politicienne, ruinée par l'arrivée des troupes américaines en 1915, et qui serait en même temps le miroir et l'éclairage du bouleversement social haitïen. (p. 88)

In an out-of-the-way corner of the house, Santiague comes upon a narrow flight of stairs leading up into darkness. He pushes a door open at the top and comes face to face with Mme Lange's senile old father, General Gesner St Martin, "boutonné jusqu'au cou dans une redingote de coupe militaire" (p. 90). With his toy soldiers on the floor before him and an old army march on the record player, the general speaks excitedly to Santiague of the military campaign he would wage to liberate Haiti:

> — Alors moi, je les attaque, ces Américains, je les attaque du Sud, du Nord, de L'Est; je les pousse vers la mer, ici, ici.
> Sa voix se brisa; le gramophone pleurardait sa musique dérisoire, le vieux général restait là, à quatre pattes devant ses soldats renversés. Une bave lente coulait dans sa barbe, et ses mains, dans la poussière, tremblaient.
> Santiague s'échappa sur la pointe des pieds. La gorge serrée, il tâtonnaient dans l'escalier branlant. . . . (p. 94)

The party draws to an end. As the guests leave, Mme Lange finally succeeds in seducing Marcel as he comes into a dressing room to get his hat and cane. Irène enters the room just in time to find them locked in an embrace.

"La Lettre," the last chapter, opens with Santiague bent over his desk at work in his studio. He hears the noise outside—rumbling automobiles and excited shouting: "A bas Mayard—Vive Mayard . . . —A bas Lefèvre— . . . Vive Lefèvre . . ." It is election night. The commotion outside contrasts sharply with the poet's mood:

> Adorable quiétude de la lampe, incomparable noblesse du silence. Le tumulte sautant par la fenêtre, comme une poignée de cailloux, à la fin, découragea Santiague.

Il rangea ses papiers, alluma une cigarette.

Les jambes confortablement allongées, il laissait aller sa pensée à la dérive. . . .

De l'autre côté de la cloison, une voix enfantine répétait avec l'inlassable patience d'une source:

Amalyllis, ô

Calalou Gombo

Bon Dieu mouri

Divi-divi

Diaguido-Digo

A travers la fumée, Santiague contemplait un paysage de mornes et de vallons, éclaboussé de verdure, de soleil, de cris d'oiseaux: une petite fille chante auprès d'un ruisseau en puisant une pleine callebasse, et sa voix se mêle au murmure de l'eau, glisse un peu sourde, comme l'onde cherchant chemin sous les galets, et puis s'épanouit en gouttelettes sur la pierre. . . . (pp. 114–115)

When Lefèvre arrives, weary from the campaign he has been waging, he and Santiague discuss his chances of winning and the political climate in general. The two friends were in agreement that Haiti needed a "vrai chef: énergique et pondéré, nationaliste intraitable tout en étant assez fin pour risquer le moins possible notre pays." (p. 127)

Meanwhile, Charmantine comes and goes. Lefèvre is intrigued by her songs. Santiague tells him the story of their meeting:

J'allais lentement, goûtant l'heure, dans une de ces rues désertes et mal éclairées de Port-au-Prince, où l'électricité souligne plutôt qu'elle ne combat l'obscurité.

Dans le ciel, les étoiles montaient comme des bulles à la surface de l'ombre.

— M'sieur?

Une fillette se tenait devant moi. (p. 136–37)

The girl had been put out of the house where she worked as servant and had been wandering the streets for days. Instead of giving her money, Santiague decided to take her home. He has fed her, clothed her, sheltered her ever since. He confesses he does not know why he took her in, but admits that he is proud of Charmantine's virginity, even though he has known many women:

C'est un désert terrible que la luxure. Charmantine est l'oasis fraternelle où j'aime à me reposer.

> Nous nous voyons peu. Mais je sais qu'elle est là à côté,
> dans la cuisine ou dans sa chambre. Je l'entends chanter.
> J'en ai le coeur réchauffé.
>   Parfois elle est triste, elle pense à son village, à ses jeux
> d'enfants dans la savane ou les bois.
>   Je l'appelle et lui apprend à lire dans un bulletin du Service
> Technique d'Agriculture, un vrai poème, je vous assure, tout
> débordant d'exquis noms créoles, de plantes et d'arbres du
> pays. Elle cueille ces noms comme des fruits, en fait des
> chansonnettes, berce sa nostalgie.
>   Je l'écoute et m'évade avec elle de cette ville étouffante,
> vers de paisibles paysages.
>   Je ne suis pas trop malheureux et je le dois peut-être à
> Charmantine. (pp. 144–45)

When she is older, Santiague intends to marry her off to
"quelque brave artisan," and their children will call him
"Tonton" (uncle). Santiague suddenly falls silent, afraid of
appearing ridiculous. His friend contemplates him:

> Son visage sur lequel portait la lumière de la lampe, respirait
> une force ironique. Le front élevé et jeune avait quelque
> chose de serein et de dominateur qui contrastait avec la
> bouche robuste, bien dessinée, sensuelle et triste.
>   Lefèvre lisait à livre ouvert sur cette face, où se reflétaient
> les combats intérieurs, les défaites et les victoires définitives.
> Il savait Santiague maître de lui-même et après les plus rudes
> épreuves de l'existence et de l'esprit. (p. 146)

The two friends take their meal in an atmosphere of quiet
companionship. Santiague wonders why Marcel has not come.
But Marcel has received a letter from Irène: "Adieu, mon ami,
je vous ai tant aimé." (p. 152) The story closes on the image
of Marcel wiping away his tears "rageusement."
   We can recognize in *Les Fantoches* essentially the same
theme as in *La Proie et l'ombre*. Lefèvre and Santiague state it
in the last pages of the final chapter in a conversation where
the word *fantoches* is used twice and which seems intended
as the key to the whole book. There is, however, an important
difference between this and the fiction published the previous
year: the "A quoi bon?" of *La Proi et l'ombre* is no longer an
answer but a question which a few courageous men muster
enough courage to try to answer. Marcel, who poses the
question, is not typical of all the men of his group, but only

of those who accept defeat without fighting. Lefèvre is committed to action, even though he recognizes it as futile. Santiague continues his work, even though he has seen the ultimate irony of his accomplishments: they have led him to a state of nonpotentiality, a dead end. He has confided as much to Lefèvre: "Il n'y a rien de plus affreux . . . que de ne pouvoir devenir" (p. 149). Both Santiague and Lefèvre, remain therefore lonely heroes trying to reach beyond themselves and despairing at their inability to do so.

And what of Marcel? The last chapter, in which the two doers Santiague and Lefèvre give the "key" to the whole, is entitled "La Lettre." Yet Marcel's letter takes up only the last two pages of it. The fact is that Marcel's world has been profoundly jolted. Having lost Irène, who has provided something vital to his existence by believing in him, he must now either grow or die. He too must become, or must inevitably join the ranks of the *fantoches*. The two scenes of the ending chapter therefore seem to point all three characters in a single direction. The book thus ends on a more optimistic note than any of the stories of *La Proie et l'ombre*. Marcel, Santiague, and Lefèvre, the principal characters, are the only ones whom we are privileged to glimpse from the inside. Each of the three has a "story" which is in some way resolved at the end: Lefèvre becomes a legislator, Marcel loses Irène, Santiague finds a kind of meaning to existence in befriending Charmantine. Both Marcel and Lefèvre are in conflict, Marcel with himself and Lefèvre with an irrational social system and the irrationality of man, which has spawned it. The poet Santiague has captured through disciplined mental work a kind of visionary equilibrium. He is at a psychological center between the two other men. He is neither happy nor fulfilled; but he is no longer in conflict. But it is Marcel's problem that draws the author's attention. Most of the action involves Marcel, and of the three it is he who must make the most meaningful journey. He is a typical Roumain hero.

Characterization in Roumain's work tends often to be symmetrical or antithetical. The tripartite division of the hero/ protagonist in *Les Fantoches* is a case in point. Marcel shares with Santiague a talent for verbal expression. But whereas

Santiague becomes absorbed in his writing, Marcel is undis-
ciplined about it and does not believe in what he writes. He
professes a disrespect for action in any form, telling Lefèvre:
"On n'écrit que par vanité: on devrait assez mépriser
l'humanité pour considérer une oeuvre réalisée dès que conçue" (p. 72). Yet Marcel's words bear a curious resemblance
to those uttered by Lefèvre in Santiague's studio: "C'est notre
tempérament qui nous lance dans la lutte, notre esprit s'y
rebelle. C'est tout le tragique de notre existence" (p. 125). The
words could serve as an apology for Marcel's ultra-intellectual
"A quoi bon?" And if Lefèvre continues to act in hopes of
accomplishing that which seems impossible, his behavior
exemplifies a remark Marcel had once made in a moment of
cynicism: "Le méritoire n'est pas de faire ce que l'on peut,
mais ce que normalement l'on ne peut point" (p. 13). Marcel
seems to be a negative reflection of the two other men.

Roumain's tendency to pair off opposing characters extends
throughout the novel. Lefèvre is at antipodes in every way
with his political opponent Marau. Lefèvre is an aristocrat;
Marau is a parvenu. Lefèvre appeals to his audience's reason;
Marau, to its emotions. Lefèvre's motivations are selfless;
Marau's are interested. Lefèvre is quiet and restrained; Marau
is loud and boisterous.

Of the two writers, Santiague and Michel Rey, one is
productive, the other is a failure. And Marcel wanders between
these positive and negative poles. He is attracted very strongly
to both. He goes from one to the other, and they both deliver
exactly the same message to him: to beware of the empty life
he is preparing for himself.

Marcel and Jeannette Lange complement each other in that
both are cynical, destructive, and false. They seem to need to
destroy in order to convince themselves that they exist. And
indeed, they exist only as façades. If Mme Lange is hiding
poverty and impotence behind the walls of her stately mansion,
Marcel is a *poseur,* as he is called more than once in the novel,
and more impressed by Pétion's genteel manners than with
Christophe's accomplishments for the new nation of Haiti.
Both are going on the pre-Occupation steam generated by
their aristocratic backgrounds; the message seems to be that
they are running on borrowed time.

Les Fantoches shows also certain affinities with the work of the French Decadents. Mme Lange in particular seems to represent the degenerate end of a noble line. Her seduction of Marcel (who is only one of many) betrays her sadistic character; seduction is her way of controlling and manipulating others. Unlike any of the heroes of *La Proie et l'ombre*, Marcel and Mme Lange purposely inflict pain and destruction. Marcel denies his love for Irène; the only way he can feel competent to cope with it is by turning on it. All of his acts are premeditated; blasé and cynical, he fits rather well a description of the decadent supplied in a Parisian journal of the 1880s: "Le Décadent . . . ne fait rien qui ne soit prémédité, posé, préparé en vue d'un but unique: l'enquête personnelle."[9] Of course, the parallel is again valid only on the surface: Marcel's decadent symptoms do not serve as a source of strength to him. Rather, they mask a profound inadequacy to cope with the world and with himself.

In the case of the young women, Roumain has set up an opposition in *Les Fantoches* which he does not pursue in the rest of his fiction. Jeannette Lange and Irène Estiènne, both upper-class, well educated, attractive, and intelligent, may have opposing souls, but this type of opposition does not recur in Roumain's female characterization. What does recur is the antithesis between the bourgeois and the peasant women.

These two classes are invariably cast as representatives of the two extremes of Haitian society: the artificial and the natural, the false and the true. Roumain's young intellectuals are thrown into a dilemma: their need for purity and national-racial identity on the one hand, for intellectual stimulation, fulfillment, and understanding on the other, causes them to fluctuate between one and the other pole. The women of the elite accept unquestioningly the life for which they are destined: a round of parties and evenings on the veranda sipping cool drinks, a world where grace, wit, charm and social standing are ultimate goals. Even Irène, for all her sympathy and intelligence, never gives any indication that she is at variance with these ideals. The women are bewildered and

---

[9] *Le Décadent*, November 15–30, 1888. Cited by Carter, p. 109.

perplexed by the men, who are dissatisfied with that existence but can neither articulate nor actualize anything beyond it. These women are not unsympathetic characters; they are simply products of their upbringing, unquestioning receptacles of the assumptions which rule the society in which they live.

The peasant women are receptacles also, but unlike their European-oriented, upper-class counterparts, they represent the indigenous Haitian. Roumain takes over a device which had existed in Haitian poetry since Oswald Durand, though lately given new life by the generation of 1927, and incorporates it into his fiction: He has his peasant women evoke the native fruits, the free and natural sensuousness and grace of living beings at peace with themselves and their identity. Thus, Charmantine's songs are a long litany of the fruits and streams of the Haitian countryside, and in the nurturing presence of the poet Santiague, they grow as freely and as naturally from her as fruit ripening and falling from a tree. Roumain has a tendency also to describe his peasant women—even the very old ones—in terms of fruits, as has already been remarked in connection with *La Proie et l'ombre*. Such descriptions are much rarer in the case of the young women of the bourgeoisie, who tend to be described more by their mannerisms, their background, their dress. But it is somehow these sophisticated women who emerge as the more credible, the more three-dimensional. The peasant women tend to remain passive, idealized symbols, whereas the bourgeois women act, speak, and *react* to those around them.

The highly developed characterizations in *Les Fantoches* have their beginning far back into the past. Certain characters form a continuity of types. Daniel, Michel Rey, Marcel Basquet are in the main really the same personality but with different names. The hopelessness and despair of each successive character is more elaborately and clearly depicted as those characters acquire more depth under the novelist's pen. We see Michel Rey in youth at his moment of truth, and again, years later, when he has made some sort of compromise with life. His existence clarifies the life ahead for Marcel. That Marcel is a younger edition of Michel is made quite clear in

Les Fantoches in the beginning chapter where we see the two engaged in conversation at the bar.

Dialogue in Roumain's prose has two functions. Roumain's characters develop certain ideas in such a way that they seem to transmit a covert message to the reader. Roumain makes liberal "borrowings" from his own writing, from theories and experiences that have particularly impressed him or which he is in the process of thinking through. We find, for example, the Aztec god Huitzilopochtli associated in "Corrida" with other images of sacrifice. We find the same god called upon by Michel to illustrate the notion that Christianity shares certain essential traits with pagan rites. Years later, the notion of universal religious practices reappears in more thoroughly thought out form, and as revealed through anthropological investigation, in Roumain's pamphlet: *A Propos de la campagne "anti-superstitieuse"*. And Jacques Roumain the dialectical materialist discussing history as spiral vs history as vertical motion in 1942 newspaper articles ("Répliques au Révérend Père Foisset") recalls curiously Marcel Basquet in the copy room of the newspaper *Le Soir,* discussing the implacable determinism of nations and the *"parcours cyclique"* of history. In that same scene, Marcel is made to "borrow" the term *conscience raciale* in one of his essays. *Conscience Raciale* was the title Roumain had given to an essay on which he was working at the time *Les Fantoches* was published. Whether Roumain intended or not, he has invited the reader of *Les Fantoches* to alternate his attention between fictional circumstances and historical author, and thus has given further validity to discussions concerning the extent to which his works are autobiographical.

All of Roumain's literary efforts seem to be an extension of his own desire to do, his desire to push beyond. We see his own attempts to work out ideas and problems through the "borrowings" of his characters. Roumain's need to estheticize his own experiences in order to give ultimate meaning to his aspirations and his ability to sense the continuity between himself and his society rescue his work most of the time from being mere propaganda. (One might perhaps except most of the writings in *Le Petit Impartial.*) Partly because of this felt continuity between himself and others, partly because of the synthesis Roumain seems to have effected between his various activities and his literary expression, he does not distinguish greatly between what his characters do, feel, or say and what he himself does, feels, or says, or wants to convince others of. This synthetic nature of Roumain's own character is responsible for the inevitable (and by no means unjustified) perplexity on the part of the reader as to whether or not he is reading autobiography, whether certain passages at least may not contain autobiographical allusions, whether certain characters "are" Jacques Roumain. Marcel's irony and sense of futility correspond to the Roumain we saw in the letters from Switzerland and in the *Petit Impartial* polemics. But in the poet Santiague, we certainly see goals, ideals, and struggles which we recognize as Roumain's.[10] Roumain's tendency to display his inner life through his characterizations is also responsible for the sermonizing quality of much of the dialogue; the long harangue on Christophe and the discussion near the end of *Les Fantoches* between Santiague and Lefevre do not escape it.

Despite the more direct and overt presentation of theme through character and dialogue in *Les Fantoches,* motif symbolism still operates in this novel. Motifs are most noticeable in the final chapter. The hero Santiague appears at the beginning of the chapter, alone in a room bent over a table with a lamp providing the only bright arc of light, with the environing dark, and its negative associations, outside. Later in the scene, Lefèvre will look on Santiague's face and see it illuminated in that light. Santiague's lonely nocturnal walks, his sudden immersion in a crowd of common folk just before he stumbled onto Charmantine, and his alienation and recaptured identity through the peasant woman associated with fruits are all present in this last, important chapter.

The obvious symbolism behind the title is presented in

---

[10] Jacques Antoine has remarked to me that Santiague is the Spanish form of Jacques (the literal translation would actually be St. Jacques). This adds evidence to the case for an autobiographical

several different ways in this last chapter. When Lefèvre comes in, he flops down into a chair, exhausted:

> Son attitude exprimait la plus grande lassitude. Ses bras pendaient des deux côtés du fauteuil comme ceux d'un pantin désarticulé. (p. 120)

Santiague, speaking of his loneliness, says he peoples it with the insignificant, wretched folk he meets in his noctambulations:

> Ainsi, je meuble ma vie de quelques personnages, qu'à certaines heures je fais jouer devant mon imagination désoeuvrée ou pour me distraire de préoccupations importunes.
> Je distribue les rôles à cette petite troupe, j'invente son destin qui s'accomplit au gré de ma fantaisie. Ces fantoches m'amusent comme un Guignol. (p. 135)

The reader will tend to identify Santiague, as a result of this speech, as a man whose mental discipline leads him to control rather than be controlled. The author has made us acutely conscious of puppets, and we are prepared for Lefèvre's statement, several pages later: "Vous êtes . . . le seul parmi nous . . . qui ne soit pas un fantoche" (p. 149).

Along with the greater preoccupation with characterization, satire increases. Roumain's gift for incisive commentary manifests itself in *La Proie et l'ombre* and in *Les Fantoches* in his portrayal of bourgeois existence: "allez un midi à la Grand'Rue," says Daniel, a black man,

> et vous voyez passer dans leurs voitures luxueuses ces mulâtres, ces "grands nègres," fondant à la chaleur de leur graisse, comme du chocolat au soleil; alors vous comprendrez mieux la fable du pot de terre et du pot de fer. (*La Proie et l'ombre* pp. 10–11)

But there is also biting satire for the black Haitian aspiring to break into the middle class. Santiague remarks of the black politician, Aristide Marau, who speaks Creole to his mesmer-

---

reading of the novel. In "Propos sans suite," Roumain had used the Spanish form Emilio to designate his friend Emile Roumer.

ized audience, that his father's name is Jean-Baptiste Philidor:[11]

> Il [Marau] habite maintenant le Chemin des Dalles et grimpe lentement vers les hauts quartiers dont il prétend exécrer les riches habitants. . . . c'est un grimaud qui enrage de ne pouvoir faire son petit mulâtre. (*Les Fantoches*, p. 34)

But the satire of Haitian modes of existence is most prevalent and most biting in Roumain's portrayal of middle-aged Haitian women of the upper classes. They are the repository of all that Roumain's young men resist—complacent mediocrity, ridiculous ignorance, unwarranted snobbery, fossilized modes of thought. Michel Rey's reaction before his mother-in-law is seen again in Marcel's identical response before the spectacle of his fiancée's aunt. In "Préface à la vie d'un bureaucrate," Mme Ballin is proud of having, as she says, "vaincu l'atavisme." (That is, her features show no trace of her African ancestry.) When she tells Michel: "Dire que j'ai donné ma pauvre fille à un être pareil!" he cannot contain himself:

> — Peut-être eussiez-vous mieux fait en la mariant à un de ces intéressants petits messieurs types standard bien sages, à l'abri des excès, soupapes de sûreté marque Tartuffe garanties, que j'ai eu le désespérant honneur d'apercevoir quelquefois si gentiment assis dans votre salon, s'intéressant généreusement aux oeuvres de bienfaisance et au progrès général de l'humanité . . . Madame Veuve Ballin, Madame Veuve Ballin, que n'avez-vous choisi pour Jeanne ce haut idéal des mères de famille haïtiennes! (*La Proie et l'ombre*, pp. 69–71)

In *Les Fantoches*, Mlle Fattu has come onto the veranda

---

[11] The name Jean-Baptiste Philidor would normally be associated with a peasant background. "Aristide Marau" can pass for aristocratic; Marau has changed his name to hide his origin. The Chemin des Dalles, built on a slight incline, is a street leading directly up to the Turgeau and Bois Verna sections, the "haut quartiers" where the old aristocratic families built their stately homes. The image is doubly à propos, as in the heat of the day, the walk up the Chemin des Dalles can be slow progress.

expecting to find Lecocq, Irène's French suitor. Instead, she finds Marcel, but unable to contain her admiration for Lecocq:

> — N'est-ce pas qu'il est bien, . . . ah, ces français [*sic*], comme ils sont aimables!
> Marcel se pencha vers elle et sur un ton confidentiel:
> — Savez-vous, chère mademoiselle, qu'il se murmure dans le public que M. Lecocq prétend à votre main charmante. Permettez-moi de vous féliciter: vous ferez un couple remarquable; vous vous ressemblez tellement—c'est à dire, au point de vue de l'identité des contraires. . . . Mon ami Cosquer le mathématicien . . . professe précisément que le sentiment de l'amour rappelle un édifice moléculaire dans lequel une place est vacante; or, la pression naturelle des forces environnantes fait que cet édifice en recherche un autre dont une des parties puisse occuper cette vacance sans troubler son équilibre initial. (pp. 49–50)

Mlle Fattu, sputtering and stammering, leaves the room. These women are faithful reflectors, incapable of independent thought or behavior. If the young women do not exactly show opposition to their set of values, they at least do not press with such determination; they, at least, attempt to understand their men. The dowagers make no such concessions, and Roumain renders them ridiculous.

Les Fantoches hangs together primarily because it maintains the same cast of characters and the same milieu from one chapter to another. But the book is not yet a fully developed novel, and this lack is primarily due to the sparseness of plot. *Les Fantoches* is really a series of scenes, the drama of which revolves around the life of Marcel, Santiague, and Lefèvre. As such, it is a story of love chanced and lost, of personal tranquility, and of public success and failure. But the weakness of the structure lies not so much in the lack of plot as in the fact that we are shifted from the private world of Marcel Basquet to that of the poet Santiague, then to that of Lefèvre. This occurs at the point where Santiague is deeply moved by his encounter with the old general hidden in the attic, and again at the end of the novel, when we enter the private world of Lefèvre for the first time as, moved by the story of Charmantine, he contemplates Santiague and we are allowed to see his thoughts.

There are no such structural defects in the case of *La Montagne ensorcelée*, which, on the contrary, handles admirably such shifts in point of view. Published the same year, and yet so different from *Les Fantoches*, *La Montagne ensorcelée* is a truly well-written and well-balanced story, with none of the stylistic excesses which, if they revealed a developing talent and an intelligent, well-read young author, had marred *La Proie et l'ombre* and *Les Fantoches*.

CHAPTER IV

From Port-au-Prince to the Haitian Hills

LA MONTAGNE ENSORCELÉE

It had been generally known that Jacques Roumain was working on a peasant novel. Antonio Vieux had mentioned it in his preface to *La Proie et l'ombre*, and the January 10, 1931, issue of "La Revue Caraïbe" carried a notice that *La Montagne ensorcelée* would soon be released. The novel appeared in August 1931, marking an important step in the indigenist movement: it was the first peasant novel to appear in Haiti.

La Montagne ensorcelée is the story of a rural peasant community, which, beset by one natural calamity after another, finds a scapegoat in the person of Placinette, an old woman suspected of sorcery who lives aloof from the village with her daughter, Grâce. The village suffers from drought, the crops are threatened, and the animals grow thin and weak. Then Dornéval's son is taken suddenly ill and dies; Dorilas' fine new bull dies suddenly and mysteriously after having wandered into a stagnant pool near Placinette's house. The rain, when it finally comes, does not let up, and the crops, waterlogged and muddy, are ruined for good. The men, huddled in groups, begin to grumble that there is something unnatural in all this. The words of Désilus begin to take on new meaning. It takes Désilus to show them that the road passing by Placinette's door and leading to a mapou tree winds and twists like a serpent and becomes Damballah by night.[1] Balletroy, the

---

[1] In the vodun religion, Damballah is the snake god. The mapou, an enormous tropical tree, is often associated with vodun rites.

chef de section (rural policeman), tries to calm them, reason with them, and finally threatens them with arrest. Aurel, the young peasant, also objects. Both he and Balletroy, each without knowing of the other's feelings, are in love with Grâce. But it is Aurel to whom Grâce gives her love, Aurel who has had the marriage letter drawn up, Aurel with whom Grâce spends her nights. When Chéri Lazare's young son is suddenly stricken, all are sure that Placinette is working evil magic. Balletroy, unable to contain them, goes to warn Placinette that the village is about to rise up against her. But he surprises Aurel near her hut and soon learns everything. Balletroy, now full of bitterness, tricks Placinette into going into the village, knowing that the villagers will not dare come to her hut. When they see her climbing up the side of the mountain, they run her down and stone her to death. Then they set out after Grâce, whom Dornéval beheads with his axe.

It is immediately apparent that this *récit*, as the author terms it, is an abrupt departure from anything Jacques Roumain had written before it. The setting, the mentality of the characters, and the vantage point and style of the narrator seem to project us into a different world. Yet the theme running through this story maintains somehow a certain affinity with that of the urban fiction. In the minds of the villagers of *La Montagne ensorcelée*, their fate is determined by a set of principles which they cannot change and which they can only imperfectly recognize. Consequently, the poor and uneducated peasants, like the sophisticated urbanites, face the misery and despair of seeing everything slowly slip away. Both groups react to that despair: While one group seeks to gain control of its world through art, political involvement or aloofness and destruction, the other seeks the same ends through sympathetic magic. The very real difference in the peasant novel is that it offers not secular but mythical solutions. *La Montagne ensorcelée* exposes us to a world at once natural and supernatural.

In other respects, *La Montagne ensorcelée* represents an accomplishment which the urban fiction attained only imperfectly. *La Montagne ensorcelée* is the realization of the well-made story, so much so as at times to resemble slick fiction in its use of all the time-honored techniques of the modern novel.

Such techniques are in evidence in the plot and timing, in the characterization, and in the interplay between these two components.

The plot is really two plots that merge into one for their mutual resolution. The personal love story of Aurel and Grâce is for a time paralleled by the story of the village in distress. The problem of the village is how to turn away the misfortune. As events pile up, the inhabitants begin to piece together a cause, and their passivity turns into reaction. They are not, however, capable of acting without some stimulus, and the dénouement is in reality triggered by the resolution of the love story: Balletroy takes the decisive step after he learns that he has lost Grâce to Aurel.

Timing is important as a transitional device and as a way to build suspense. But it also contributes to characterization. Balletroy, the *chef de section*, is both part of the village yet distinct from the other men of the village. He is their leader and enjoys their respect and a certain stature within the group. Never there among the crowd at the beginning of a scene, he makes a dramatic entrance, plunging *into* the crowd at dramatic moments: The village is assembled at Dornéval's, waiting out the child's last hours of agony with the family. The women are inside the hut, the men under the *tonnelle*.[2] Desilus is entertaining the children with stories and riddles:

> — Cric?
> Mais une plainte profonde dans la case arrête toute réponse.[3] Un bruit confus de paroles, de sanglots étranglés.
> C'est à ce moment-là, que Balletroy le chef de section pénétra sous la tonnelle.
> — Honneur.
> — Respect, répondirent tous en choeur. On lui fit place.[4]
> (pp. 21–22)

---

[2] In Haiti the term denotes an open structure extending out from the hut, consisting of a roof of thatch or leaves supported by poles.

[3] In Haiti when one person wants to tell a story or a riddle, he sounds out his listener(s) by the question: "*Cric?*". "*Crac!*" is their affirmative response. A similar situation obtains in American folkways in the "Knock, knock!—Who's there?" question and response pattern, indicating that a riddle is about to be told.

[4] In the Haitian countryside, one person, encountering another (or others), greets him with the word "*Honneur.*" The conventional reply is "*Respect.*"

Thus we are introduced to Balletroy. Days later, a group of men have assembled at the bedside of Chéri Lazare's boy. Dorneval, his own son now buried, leans over the boy:

> — Placinette, dit-il simplement.
> — Non, fit une voix forte.
> Et Balletroy pénétra dans la chambre. (p. 79)

Balletroy's entrances tend to shift attention to himself. Even the verbs show him as a force which cuts through. Such a character can become a device for shifting attention also from one scene to another. The villagers, gathered around Désilus, have witnessed one of the women being possessed by the god Damballah, of whom Désilus has just spoken.

> Ils la regardaient, dans un silence plein de terreur, n'osant lui porter secours, n'osant affronter le dieu qui la possédait.
> Pendant ce temps, Balletroy atteignait le mapou, et sautait à pieds joints dans le sentier . . . (p. 89)

The mapou is the landmark by which we know that he is just a few steps from Placinette's house.

Timing in the encounters or near-encounters builds suspense because these encounters are significant enough to divert the course of events. Balletroy meets Aurel on the way to Placinette's hut. In their camaraderie, Balletroy slaps Aurel on the shoulder. Aurel thinks he can confide in him. But when Balletroy learns of the impending marriage:

> La main de Balletroy s'alourdit ainsi qu'une massue sur l'épaule d'Aurel et il respire comme un soufflet de forge.
> — Hein que dis-tu! fait Aurel.
> — Moi, hé, héhé, rien. Grâce, je la connais. C'est une belle fille.
> Il tapote l'épaule d'Aurel et rit d'un rire étrange. (p. 91)

As if adding insult to injury, the unsuspecting Aurel asks Balletroy to be his *parrain de noces*. He tells him:

> J'en avais parlé à Grâce, elle était contente. Elle disait Tu fais bien: Balletroy est un homme âgé, un homme important, c'est un bon tonton. (p. 92)

In addition to the last-minute encounter, Roumain uses here various other devices that have become faithful standbys of the traditional novel: confidences made to an unknown rival, his equivocal reactions, and as a final humiliating blow, having him learn that the girl he loves looks upon him as an old man, an uncle. There would be more honor for him if he were hated.

Quite a bit of suspense is built up at the end of the story by the split-second timing which causes the lovers to miss each other. Aurel rides desperately to save Grâce from the mob:

> — Grâce, ho Grâce?
> Personne ne réspond.
> — Grâce? . . . Tonnerre, foutre tonnerre de Dieu. Mais si elle n'entend pas, c'est qu'elle est loin. Comment affronter, arrêter cette vague furieuse. . . . En dix minutes on peut faire la route du bourg, aller et retour. Il aura le temps. Et il tourna bride.
> Grâce n'était pas loin; elle avait été ramasser du bois. Un bruit confus lui était parvenu, mais elle n'y avait prêté attention. Elle s'en revenait au moment où Aurel gagnait la route du bourg. (p. 111)

The timing produces even more suspense in the ending scene. Grâce is racing toward a clearing in the woods where she has a horse tied:

> Plusieurs fois elle se retourna pour apercevoir à travers le feuillage leurs mufles en sueur, leurs gueules béantes.
> . . . elle entendait tout près, derrière elle le bruit des branches cassées et leur piétinement sourd.
> . . . une angoisse affreuse l'emportait avec les arbres tournoyant vers ce trou bleu grillagé de branchanges, vers la savane . . .
> Eux, tiennent leur proie. A un moment, à deux portées de bras d'elle ils la saisissaient déjà, quand Dorilas butant contre une souche, s'affala, les entrainant dans sa chute, barrant le chemin à leur élan.
> Grâce a disparu, ou plutôt non, la revoici, qui file dans la savane, tout droit au cheval et ils restent là, hébétés de rage impuissante. (pp. 112–13)

But inexplicably she turns, and they rush in upon her.

Characterization in *La Montagne ensorcelée* is resolutely from without. We do not explore the inner life or sensibilities of any of the main characters; we do not relive meaningful experiences with them as in the urban fiction. There is no past and no future shown of their individual lives, only their present. The author describes the people and what happens to them, but he does not invite us to take sides. Aurel and Grâce are two young lovers. Beyond that, there is nothing in their behavior to differentiate them from any other young couple. Nothing turns our sympathies toward them or away from them. Placinette, though she is portrayed in deathly terms, does nothing herself either to alienate or draw our sympathies.

We find in the characterization the same tendency toward antithesis as in the urban fiction: Placinette is an old woman near death, whereas Grâce is a young girl, in love and full of life. These two are the only women of any importance (the mothers of the two stricken children are episodic), and they are opposites. We never see them in a scene together, so we never see to what extent they may have any human affection for each other. They are in no observable way related, so that any inference that they may be related by a common supernatural power takes on added weight.

Both Placinette and Désilus are believed to have links with unseen forces. But Désilus' supernatural powers are harmless; he can see but not *do*. He likes to withdraw from human company at certain times of the day, but he invariably rejoins the group. Placinette, on the other hand, is never with the others.

Balletroy and Aurel are cast as opposites in the sense that both are rivals. But their rivalry cannot be viewed entirely as a hero-villain confrontation. Aurel is a likeable enough young man, but he is motivated only by his love for Grâce. It is not Aurel but Balletroy who has the superior qualities associated with the hero. *La Montagne ensorcelée* is different from the rest of Roumain's work in the important respect that it is the only case where the hero is not clearly delineated. Balletroy, by his stature, his entrances, his movements, his capacity as decision maker, and his compassion for the two grieving families, easily emerges as a leader of men. It is noteworthy too that Balletroy stands out from Placinette and the other villagers by his faith in the efficacy of reason. He is the only character who seeks rational explanations for the phenomena besetting the village.

Balletroy, like Roumain's later heroes, has both a public and a private life, each with its problem to be resolved. Yet Balletroy, if a hero, is a fallen one who limits his own potential through a weakness that leads him to misuse his power.

Balletroy and Désilus, though they appear to oppose each other—Balletroy is logical while Désilus is mythical, Balletroy is respected and feared while Désilus is the village fool—actually work together to give final impetus to the movement against Placinette. From the start it is obvious that Désilus is smarting under the sting of the ridicule he suffers at the hands of the younger men. As days pass, the rain and the winds bring Désilus his share of hardship, exposing him to the elements, aggravating his rheumatism. He can contain himself no longer, and the men for their part are all too willing to listen to anyone who can explain what has happened to their world.

The style of *La Montagne ensorcelée* sets it well apart from the urban fiction. Roumain has effected a distillation, a purification in his images and metaphors. As a result, the panorama he paints is more plastic, less intellectual, and contains far fewer contrived comparisons. The drawing-room wit, the display of learning (elements little suited in any case to a peasant novel) have been resolutely pared out, and the dialogue, except perhaps in certain of Balletroy's remarks, does not serve as a medium for the author's ideas, as it often seems to in the urban fiction.

Certain motifs persist, such as the *rire/sourire*, which here too serves as a mask hiding the misery, bitterness, or hypocrisy of the character. When Dornéval, bent over Chéri Lazare's sick child, sees the sickness clearly:

> Un étrange sourire, une déchirure des lèvres—tandis que le regard demeurait fixe, sans lumière—fit grimacer sa face. (p. 79)

Balletroy, on learning from Aurel of his romance with Grâce, "rit d'un rire étrange" (p. 91). However, the message-carrying force of the *rire/sourire* is diffused by its association also with the smile of the lover, a smile of openness and happiness. The peasant woman is here also described in terms of fruits. Aurel admires in Grâce "ses lèvres mauve-caïmitte, ses dents plus éclatantes que des grains de grenade" (p. 47), but his admiring glance takes in other elements as well: her kerchief, her dress, her jewelry, so that again the symbolism is diffused by the fact that the elements describing the peasant woman are chosen from a variety of classes of things, a variety not found in the descriptions of peasant women in *La Proie et l'ombre* and in *Les Fantoches*.

These lingering motifs are of secondary importance. Of major importance in this novel are the recurrent vistas of man in nature. The sudden shifts from the immensity of nature to the minuteness and frailty of man and human life give the impression of a supernatural bond between man and nature. This impression is strongest at the beginning of chapters. Most of the early chapters begin with a panoramic, plastic view of the community, cradled in the expanse of nature, then slowly narrow down to focus on the specific character whose personal tragedy mirrors the collective fate of the village. Often one of the characters serves as a transitional presence through whom the focus is shifted from cosmos to man. Such is, more often than not, the role of Désilus. The seer Désilus is like a sieve through which the significant events taking place are filtered and caught. The technique is immediately evident in the opening passages of the novel:

> La case trapue, bien assise à même le sol rougeâtre et ceinturée à sa base d'une balustrade, s'appuie sur un horizon de mornes sombres. Le sentier qui y mène, luisant comme une peau de couleuvre abandonnée, s'arrête brusquement au haut d'une pente d'herbe de Guinée et se jette en tremplin vers le ciel transparent.
>
> Le calme est grand et s'augmente des vastes cercles de silence que trace un malfini dans l'azur; d'une voix de femme qui chantonne à l'interieur de la maison et du bruit sourd, régulier, d'un pilon écrasant des grains.
>
> Le village domine cette solitude. Agrippé au flanc de la montagne les huttes rapprochent leurs têtes de chaume et guettent toute la vie d'en bas. Le village est pauvre. La terre crayeuse se craquèle comme l'écorce, entr'ouvre des lèvres avides: le village a soif. La sécheresse dure depuis des jours, brûle la récolte de petit-mil. Le bétail maigrit et pousse de longs meuglements douloureux.

Aujourd'hui, les hommes sont rentrés des champs pour le repas du soir. Dans chaque cabane, les femmes s'affairent autour des chaudrons. Seuls les enfants crient au-dehors en jouant dans la poussière. Les hommes sont muets. La fatigue écrase l'esprit autant que le corps. . . .

Désilus, lui, est assis sous les goyaviers. Il se repaît de leurs derniers fruits . . .

Les jeunes gens noirs ne sont plus respectueux: ils disent que Désilus a l'esprit dérangé, mais les anciens ne sont pas de cet avis.

Ainsi Tonton Jean qui est mort l'année dernière . . . répétait souvent que Désilus savait beaucoup de choses. Houng!

Quand le jour incline vers le crépuscule, Désilus aime à s'éloigner des hommes. Accroupi ou couché sous un arbre, il tient d'interminables soliloques en grattant de ses vieux doigts crochus une sorte de guitare à deux cordes . . .

Maringouins ping'ga zombis, ping'ga zombis[1]

Voici ce qui fait rire ces jeunes nègres:

Les sots, ils ont la tête remplie de vent! Ils se croient malins quand ils se moquent, et c'est le vent qui leur sort par la bouche.

Désilus expulse dédaigneusement à travers la broussaille grise de sa barbe une bouffée de sa bonne petite pipe.

Maringouins ping'ga zombis, zanzamzam, zim, zim, zimzim.

Savent-ils seulement, hé savent-ils seulement qui coasse la nuit dans la mare, sous la lune jaune? les crapauds? Bichi! Il se rappelle, lui Désilus, avoir vu qui. Il y a très longtemps . . . En passant près de la mare, il s'arrête pour puiser un peu d'eau, quand . . . Ay! il en tremble encore: cinq petits bakas[2] noirs comme l'enfer, avec des yeux de braise, étaient assis dans l'herbe. La tête levée vers la lune, ils imitaient les crapauds et gobaient des lucioles. En vérité, en vérité. Croyez-moi si vous voulez.

Maringouins ping'ga zombis.

La nuit était venue. Désilus se leva. La mare luisait au bas du morne comme un oeil maléfique. Il ne fait pas bon rester tard dehors, par certaines nuits.

— Surtout, avec celle-là, grommela-t-il, en se tournant vers la case trapue de Placinette où une fenêtre s'éclairait à vif, sur la nuit.

Les paysans se réunissaient ce soir-là chez Dornéval dont le fils se mourait. . . .

Sous la tonnelle, les hommes ont pris siège sur des bancs et des caisses renversées. . . . Plus loin sont les enfants . . . Désilus se glisse de leur côté. (pp. 15–21)

[1] Maringouins prenez garde aux revenants [Roumain's note].
[2] Gnomes très redoutables de la démonologie vaudou [Roumain's note].

We have the impression that we are descending into the landscape, narrowing down our field of vision as we approach the ordinary people. We see them as from an airplane, going about their daily tasks. The technique itself is not new in Roumain's work. (A Balzacian zeroing-in occurs at the beginning of the chapter "La Surprise-Party Chez Madame Lange" in *Les Fantoches*). But the technique, as it is used in *La Montagne ensorcelée*, reveals man against a backdrop of nature. A man-in-nature motif develops which holds constantly up to view the interrelatedness of nature and of the supernatural, since it shows man constantly in the company of phenomena he is powerless to control. Désilus helps us adjust our view from the panorama of nature to the specific and human. He can do this because he possesses the metaphysical consciousness, as is shown in his long soliloquy on his own visionary powers, and his occasional ominous and mysterious references to Placinette. Désilus looks Janus-like in both directions, sounding out the mysterious forces at work in the vastness of nature and correctly matching them with the microcosmic life of the people of the village. Thus the unseen forces dominating man's world are constantly paraded before us. As the situation accelerates and the villagers begin to react, as momentum builds up, the author's technique changes. From the point where the villagers have determined that Placinette is behind everything, the author abandons the indirect suggestiveness of the man-in-nature motif and begins the final chapters with dialogue, placing the reader abruptly within the group, in the midst of the drama.

La Montagne ensorcelée is esthetically satisfying in that it is a unit complete within itself. That completeness owes much to the author's success in fitting together elements of description and plot in sequences which do not immediately reveal their real relationships. Only gradually does the total picture fit together, like a mosaic, in the reader's consciousness. And the remarkable style here too governs the whole operation. It is not until Désilus remarks quite late in the story that the path before Placinette's hut winds like a snake that we understand the reference in the first paragraph to the "sentier . . . luisant comme une peau de couleuvre." It is only after his insinuations that the pond by Placinette's house is poisoned and attracting children and animals to it that the full significance of the off-handed metaphor at the beginning—"la mare luisait . . . comme un oeil maléfique"—is grasped. It is only after we have been sufficiently immersed in the milieu that we recognize the full importance of the opening paragraph and that nothing in the description is gratuitous. It is Placinette's hut we have glimpsed, deceptively peaceful with the "voix de femme qui chantonne à l'intérieur." That voice is in all likelihood that of Grâce, unsuspecting of the horror she will soon experience. The opening scene also establishes the physical and psychological relationship between Placinette and the villagers. Her squat hut sits alone at the foot of the hill, while the other huts huddle together above, as though observing fearfully. In the same way, there is nothing gratuitous about the fact that Désilus is the first character we meet, for he sets the myth-making tone of the whole story. Nor is it by chance that Dornéval, the first villager on whom misfortune falls, holds himself apart from the stoning of Placinette. He is saving himself for the ritual murder of Grâce. In his capacity as executioner of a sorcerer's progeny, he ends the chain of misfortune which began in his household.

The first pages of the story show another very important element of style. The author shifts almost imperceptibly from the objective, descriptive narrative to a fashion of expression which is that of his peasant characters. This level of style is intermediate between the narrative reportage of a disinterested observer and the dialogue spoken by the characters themselves. The beginning lines of the *récit* describe the village and the villagers from the outside and introduce us to the character of Désilus. But with the sentence "Les jeunes gens noirs ne sont plus respectueux," we cannot be sure whether it is the impersonal, objective narrator or Désilus who is speaking. The style continues to shift until, with the exclamation "Houng!", it becomes clear that it is Désilus who is speaking. The words "Quand le jour s'incline" project us back into external objective reality, outside of the character, and the words in Creole, a direct quote, differ from either of the two styles encountered in the paragraphs before it. Désilus' soliloquy picks up with the paragraph immediately following, only to be interrupted again by the author's description of him puffing on his pipe. The perspective shifts from external to internal, then back again. The soliloquy may begin in third person only to shift into first person perspective, as in the paragraph describing the *bakas*, where *il* in the end gives way to *moi*. Désilus' audible comment, in the form of dialogue ("— Surtout avec celle-là"), seems to flow naturally from the previous sentence (or perhaps the previous two sentences).

Roumain's skill in shifting the point of view is of no small consequence. The point of view is the mysterious agent which guides the reader to perceive the life of the village and its inhabitants on several levels of reality. It also affords us, from a critical approach, the first real glimpse at a technique which, years later, will become an integral part of the much-discussed and elusive style of *Gouverneurs de la rosée*. The shifts in point of view function in *La Montagne ensorcelée* both to reflect a folk mentality and speech (through Désilus) and also on occasion to impart a lyricism which compares favorably in beauty and depth to that of *Gouverneurs de la rosée*. We see in both novels a mother's lament for her lost son. At the wake of her son, Anna, Dornéval's wife, contemplates the small corpse, listens to the litany of the *prêtre savane*,[5] and loses herself in her own world:

> La douleur est un autre monde où elle se meut aveugle et sourde à tout ce qui n'est pas ce petit cadavre, cette chair de sa chair, détachée d'elle comme un fruit pourri de l'arbre.
>
> Est-il vraiment mort? Pas plus tard qu'avant-hier, il jouait dans la poussière avec les autres, avec ceux qui sont encore vivants.

---

[5] The *prêtre savane* is a kind of bush priest, not ordained but usually a former sacristan, called upon in the back country where priests are rare, to perform essential rites of the Church.

Un cri tendrement blessé monte de ses entrailles, un sanglot patient, qui ne veut pas finir, qui toujours recommence, mouillé de larmes, brûlé de larmes. Et pourquoi y a-t-il ces bougies autour de lui, ces fleurs ces feuilles? Oh, il y a de puissants sorciers qui guérissent les enfants malades, avec des feuilles, avec des feuilles cueillies dans la savane, dans les nuits mauvaises. Où est le hougan qui guérira son enfant?

— . . . *piis supplicationibus consequantur: Qui vivis et regnas Deus* . . .

Que dit cet homme noir? Que chante-t-il? Non, non, ce n'est pas ça. Voici ce qu'il faut chanter:

— Feuilles ho, feuilles, vini sauvé mouin dans misè mouin yé.

Pitite mouin malade, ma allé caille hougan.[1]

— Paix, Anna, paix!

[1] O feuilles, feuilles, venez me sauver de ma misère. Mon enfant est malade, j'ai été chez le sorcier. [Roumain's note] (pp. 42–43)

The shift in point of view operates here also, and the result is a lyric interlude. We have entered the world of Anna's thoughts and, like her, have cut out the outside to the point where her thoughts and her speech are as one. The admonishing voice (probably Dornéval's) brings us abruptly back to the outside, and we suddenly remember that the scene includes a room full of people.

Roumain's style reproduces a peasant mentality which, though it manifests itself through language, emanates from a much deeper source. The peasant mentality is already evident a few paragraphs into the book in Désilus' soliloquy. But the *âme haïtienne* of which the *Revue Indigène* writers spoke can also be represented closer to the surface. That is, the flavor of the Haitian countryside can be captured through French spoken with a Haitian accent and with Haitian divergencies of morphology or syntax, as in the speech of Helvé, the Protestant, reciting:

Mais lé bonheu' n'est pas pour lé méchant, et il ne prolongera point ses jours, pas plusse qué l'ombre, parce qu'il n'a pas dé la crainte dévant Dié. (p. 81)

Roumain's manipulation of the point of view also allows great flexibility in the narrative style. The narrator can suddenly drop his neutral (but literary) descriptions and assume the peasant way of recounting an incident, as during Choute's possession by Damballah:

> Ou plutôt non, elle n'avait point crié ce nom, mais sa bouche l'avait *dessiné*, si visiblement que tous l'entendirent, et frémirent et sentirent une peur glaciale ruisseler dans leur dos, car la bouche de Choute était devenue mince et pointue— encore une fois, je prends Dieu à témoin, la fausseté n'est pas dans mes paroles—oui, mince et pointue comme la gueule d'une couleuvre, et elle s'ouvrait et se refermait et aucun son n'en sortait, ainsi que cela se passa quand le Seigneur Bon Dieu maudit le Reptile au Paradis terrestre. (pp. 88–89, italics in text.)

Such a use of language goes beneath the surface to bring up and reveal a basic attitude toward life, and it is this attitude which is transcribed into French. Here indeed was something new in Haitian letters.

Creole as such does occasionally appear in *La Montagne ensorcelée*, but its appearance does not seem to be random. The characters revert to Creole at moments of high tension: Grâce cries out, as she is being pelted with stones—"*A mouè, Aurel, à mouè*" (literally, *A moi, Aurel, à moi*) (p. 114); Balletroy blurts out to Placinette that he is trying to protect her: "*Pour Grâce, mouin r'ainmain li*" (Pour Grâce, je l'aime) (p. 66). Creole occurs where the use of French would be artificial, as in proverbs and riddles. Balletroy tells Dorilas: "*trop pressé pas fait jou' l'ouvri*" (*d'être trop pressé n'amène pas le jour*) (p. 103). The use of Creole in Haitian fiction, thought not frequent, was not new. At the turn of the century, Justin Lhérisson and, more notably, Antoine Innocent, had used it; they, however, did not deem it necessary to translate their Creole into French in footnotes, as does Roumain. Perhaps Roumain, in so doing, was attempting to reach a larger audience. Similarly, Roumain explains references to vodun gods, folk heroes and Haitian customs in footnotes or even in a parenthetical remark in the body of the text. The explanatory material tends to fragment the imaginative level on which fiction must be experienced. The anthropological dimension which Roumain added to his novel through his notes points up one of the problems of the new form with which he was experimenting.

Jacques Roumain subtitles his novel *"récit paysan."* The term *récit* seems à propos when we consider that the action of the story is tidy and complete, that the narrator abstains from taking sides with one or another character and appears at pains not to engage the reader's credulity, leaving him to determine whether sorcery or superstition, metaphysical or psychological forces direct the course of events. In effect, the author offers natural and psychological reasons for all turns of events, yet in so doing does not exclude a possible higher order. Balletroy acts out of jealousy, Désilus from wounded pride. Before he reversed himself, Balletroy had explained in purely psychological terms to Placinette why she was being singled out by the villagers:

> Ils sont dans la misère, leur tête travaille, alors ils cherchent—ils cherchent un coupable. . . .
> Ils savent que tu connais les feuilles qui guérissent; ils pensent: celle qui peut faire le bien, peut faire le mal, ils pensent: les démons étaient autrefois de bons anges. (pp. 57–58)

Later, at the bedside of Chéri Lazare's dying boy, Balletroy appeals to reason:

> Ignorants! Vous n'avez jamais entendu parler de fièvre intestinale? Les enfants mangent n'importe quoi, des mangos pleins de vers, de la viande qui n'est plus bonne, voilà tout.
> Et puis, qui a le droit de se plaindre? Dornéval et Lazare. Vous, que foutez-vous icitte? (pp. 79–80)

There is nothing extrahuman, nothing metaphysical which the reader is constrained to accept. Ponds become stagnant, children and animals lack the wisdom to avoid them. Drought, torrential rains, crop failure and hunger are not rare in the countryside. All the events can be and are explained on natural and psychological grounds.

On closer scrutiny, however, the duplicity of the author becomes undeniable. If, for example, Balletroy's words to

Placinette quoted above are sensible, if Placinette's words are equally logical, her actions are described in a way which renders them suspect. She can say "le Bon Dieu et le Diable, c'est comme le bras et la main" and explain away the blasphemy by pointing out that Balletroy and the rest take Holy Communion at the Easter obligation, yet observe the vodun rite of *manger marrassa* despite the priest's warning that "lé bon Dieu du vaudou, c'est le diable" (p. 60). It is not the conversation as transcribed but the narrative, the author's contribution to the scene, which imparts an ominous tone to the interview:

> Le ricanement de Placinette tissait une angoisse insup- portable autour de Balletroy.
> — C'est pas la même chose, articula-t-il avec effort.
> Il avait envie de s'en aller, il étouffait entre les murs étroits et c'était intolérable, cette Placinette qui tournait dans la pièce comme une araignée.
> — Tu n'a pas répondu, compère. . . .
> . . . il y avait en lui un désarroi singulier comme si sa langue n'obéissait plus à sa pensée et ses gestes à sa volonté.
> Placinette inscrivait dans la pièce des cercles de pas menus et sautillants. A la fin elle s'arrêta devant lui et il fut étonné de voir ses yeux tristes et pleins de larmes.
> — Balletroy, il y a beaucoup de choses, on ne peut pas les comprendre. (pp. 60–61)

Placinette's strange line of questioning can be logically explained on the basis that she is leading up to the point made in the last sentence quoted, which is her way of introducing the story she now proceeds to tell Balletroy of her father's mysterious seizures and his ultimate execution for the practice of witchcraft. The author, however, has himself turned the tone of the narrative away from the logical and into the metaphysical mode by his choice of metaphors, which liken Placinette to a spider spinning a web around its victim. Words such as *tissait* are not Balletroy's but the author's. The author's insistence on the fact that Placinette is describing a circle around Balletroy leads us to feel, along with Balletroy, that some sort of sorcery is being prepared. Thus, the tone of supernatural mystery is already set well before Placinette enters upon the story of her ill-fated father.

When Balletroy goes to pay a second visit, this time to send Placinette to her death:

> Il la trouva raccommodant une vieille robe, comme elle fripée, avec de longues rides; ses déchirures, une chose morte entre ses doigts maigres aux ongles mauves de cadavre.
> Elle ressemblait de plus en plus à une araignée, tissant son piège minutieusement.
> — Tire toujours sur tes fils, pensait Balletroy, je ne suis pas la mouche que tu attraperas. (p. 97)

Images of death join this time those of the spider spinning a web, and the former have intensified and clarified the latter. And again, the viewpoint shifts gently from narrator to character; Balletroy picks up the author's rather literary metaphor as though it were a cue.

Similarly, the beginnings of the first several chapters of the story, in their natural-supernatural focus, are an important part of the author's duplicity. The style, while appearing resolutely objective, is responsible for the metaphysical aura in which the story is bathed.

In his preface to *La Montagne ensorcelée,* Jean Price-Mars stated:

> C'est la note émouvante de nouveauté que la jeune littérature apporte dans l'analyse de notre milieu que cette préoccupation de se servir des possibilités de ce milieu pour élaborer l'oeuvre d'art. Ainsi nos jeunes écrivains s'ingénient à créer une esthétique haïtienne. . . . Jacques Roumain est l'un des promoteurs de ce splendide mouvement. (pp. 12–13)

La Montagne ensorcelée stands thus at the beginning of a tradition, that of the *roman indigène.* Although Jacques Roumain provides us with the first specimen, his efforts in this respect join those of a number of men of letters who were working intently toward the Haitianization of Haitian life and art. These men all radiated around the imposing figure of Dr. Jean Price-Mars, many years their senior. In 1928, Price-Mars had published *Ainsi parla l'oncle,* a compendium of lecture notes from courses he had given in the preceding years. The final chapter of the work, the one which had the greatest influence, took up folklore and literature. In it, Price-Mars maintained that tales, legends, riddles, proverbs and folk-beliefs are more faithful indications of the spirit of a people than political documents, because they are

> des oeuvres ou des produits spontanés jaillis à un moment donné, d'une pensée géniale, adoptés par tous parce que fidèles interprètes d'un sentiment commun, devenus chers à chacun et mués, enfin, en créations originales par le processus obscur de la subconscience. (*Ainsi parla l'oncle*, p. 188)

It is these popular works above all which constitute "une extériorisation de notre moi collectif" (p. 189), and Price-Mars counsels:

> il faudrait que la matière de nos oeuvres fût tirée quelquefois de cette immense réserve qu'est notre folk-lore. (p. 192)

Haitianism, then, in the truest sense, must reflect and portray the life of the folk.

The literary revolution which had begun in the years 1925–27 had been above all Nationalist. The preservation of Haitian culture had meant as much the preservation of the French modes of life as it had meant the rejection of the Anglo-Saxon. But as the revolution looked more and more to the island's own culture, it discovered more and greater ties with Africa than with France. Folklore and ethnography became supremely important guides to the soul of the people and hence to "*l'âme haïtienne.*" The literary movement shifted from Nationalism to Africanism in the decade of the 1930s, and the works and teaching of Jean Price-Mars became preeminent. *Ainsi parla l'oncle* was read by all the youth of the period. One contemporary termed *La Montagne ensorcelée*, along with Jean-Baptiste Cinéas' *Le Drame de la terre* (published in 1933), "vivantes émanations d'Ainsi Parla l'oncle" and found in them "les productions essentiellement indigènes parues en ces quinze dernières années."[6] The fact that we find Price-Mars's remarks prefacing *La Montagne ensorcelée* marks it as a literary event. Only one novelist before Roumain had built his work

---

[6] Lorimer Denis, in Lorimer Denis, François Duvalier and Arthur Bonhomme, *Les Tendances d'une génération* (Port-au-Prince: Imprimerie Haïtienne [1934]), p. 52.

around the folk culture. Antoine Innocent had published *Mimola* in 1906. The Haitian literary tradition, then, offers only one possible precedent.[7]

The story of *Mimola* is simple. Mimola (nicknamed Lala) is the only surviving child of Mme Georges. Mme Georges' mother, Tante Rosalie, had been from Africa, and on her death had commanded her daughter to throw a chest with her belongings into the sea. But the chest contained her *loa* (Spirits), and Mimola, from the time of her first communion, has become subject to strange, inexplicable nervous disorders. Mme Georges is advised by Tante Marguerite, who had been her mother's good friend, to recover the chest and make certain sacrifices to the *loa* and also make a pilgrimage to a holy shrine associated with vodun miracles. There Mme Georges meets Mme Dagobert, whose son Léon suffers from the same attacks as Mimola. But Léon rejects the *loa* and goes mad. Mimola accepts the vodun faith and is saved. She becomes a vodun priestess.

In a general way, both *Mimola* and *La Montagne ensorcelée* are drenched in folk beliefs. Both are at pains to describe carefully and graphically the vodun possession. Innocent describes at great length a series of vodun rites and Mimola's possession by various gods and *loa*, of which the following passage is typical:

> Tout à coup des cris prolongés se font entendre; une chaise est renversée, des femmes accourent: c'était Lala qui venait de s'affaiser à terre avec des crispations de mains et de pieds. On essaya de la mettre debout. Impossible. Ses jambes flageolaient; elle tremblait de tous ses membres comme si elle eut froid. Ses traits s'étaient altérés et prenaient soudain l'expression d'une vielle physionomie ridée par les ans.

---

[7] One scholar has said in this connection: "l'indigénisme, qui se donnera pour un mouvement original devra feindre d'ignorer Innocent qui cependant, dès 1906, lui avait fourni sa matière, son orientation et sa substance." (Ghislain Gouraige, *Les Meilleurs poètes et romanciers haïtiens: pages choisies* [Port-au-Prince: Imprimerie de la Phalange, 1963] pp. 129–30). Another Haitian scholar expressed the opinion to me that if one were to look for precendents for Roumain's indigenist novels in the Haitian tradition, the only likely possibility would be *Mimola* (Group II interviews).

. . . Lala était sous l'influence d'un esprit. Quel était cet esprit dont elle était possédée? Frè Ti Dor était seul capable de le savoir. C'était l'esprit de sa grand'mère *Dan-Maoua*.
Madame Georges, en entendant ce nom, et voyant sa fille dans cet état, pleura dans on mouchoir.
Lala ou plutôt *Dan-Maoua* la prit dans ses bras, l'étreignit longuement sur son coeur en versant des larmes. Quelques femmes émues par cet petit drame, se mouchaient dans leurs robes, ou essuyaient du revers de la main leurs yeux humides.[8]

When we compare this passage to the one in *La Montagne ensorcelée* describing Choute's experience, we recognize that the difference is enormous. The elemental nature of religious ecstacy, the direct knowledge of creator by created has been somehow tampered with in the scene quoted above, and one discerns the sentimentality of the eighteenth-century European novel. Underneath the vodun exterior, the familiar scene of recognition and reunion of long-lost loved ones shines through, embellished by the ever-present audience of effusive well-wishers overcome to tears by the tenderness of the moment.

One can speak of similarities between Innocent and Roumain as social thinkers without comparing the form their thought takes. Innocent's apology for vodun on the basis that it represents archetypal religious beliefs and is a stage through which all religions pass reminds us of the few allusions to religious parallelism in *Les Fantoches* and the anthropological remarks of *A Propos de la campagne "anti-superstitieuse"* of a number of years later. Innocent's chastisement of Haitians for their "dédain . . . pour tout ce qui a trait à notre origine" (p. 164) reminds us of Price-Mars's similar chastisement of Haitian "bovaryisme" (a desire to be other than what one is). But Innocent and Roumain have created works as dissimilar in attitude as in style. Innocent has not escaped the Continental writers' attraction for exoticism and local color, as shown by his insistence on the mammylike appearance of Tante Rosalie and Tante Marguerite, on their mysterious African origins. His pages and pages of detailed description of vodun rites, of

---

[8] Antoine Innocent, *Mimola, ou l'histoire d'une cassette* (Port-au-Prince: E. Malval, 1906) p. 147.

Lala's possession by first one *loa* and then another, seem meant to milk the possibilities dry. The story of Mimola serves as a pretext for presenting the vodun religion from as many aspects as possible, and the characters are not really drawn as Haitian peasants. In *La Montagne ensorcelée*, on the other hand, the peasant, vodun mentality is the very texture of the story, and specific rites and their meaning are singularly absent.

It is not to the Haitian but to the French that we must look for direct influences on Roumain. Among Giono's novels, *Colline* has striking affinities with *La Montagne ensorcelée*. Roger Gaillard has established through textual comparisons some undeniable parallels. The supernatural perception of Jannet, the old man of *Colline*, and of Désilus is alluded to in both novels by other characters (Gaillard, *L'Univers romanesque de Jacques Roumain*, pp. 11–12). In both novels, a small peasant community, perched on the side of a hill, scratching out a meagre existence from the unwilling land, is caught helpless in the vagaries of nature. In *Colline*, it is the spring which stops flowing, leaving the village without water, as if by complicity. As Gaillard observes: "Le mysticisme, c'est enfin l'atmosphère irraisonnée de malheur" (Gaillard, *L'Univers romanesque de Jacques Roumain*, p. 12). The statement is equally true of *Colline* and of *La Montagne ensorcelée*. In addition to the similarities noted by Gaillard, there is visible in *Colline*, just as in *La Montagne ensorcelée*, a system of motifs, a plastic portrayal of man set against the backdrop of nature, which depict its vastness and his littleness.

Despite these similarities and the professed influence of Giono on Roumain (Group I interviews), *La Montagne ensorcelée* is basically quite different from *Colline*. There is a difference in the mythic consciousness of the characters themselves. Désilus is within the group, but Jannet is an opposing force. Jaume, the hero figure of *Colline*, tries to elicit useful information from Jannet which might save the village, but in vain, for the old man has already crossed over to the other side, and the village has no contact with an intermediary. If Jannet is in league with malevolent forces, the villagers have no extralogical forces with which to combat him. If, on the other hand, the peasants of *La Montagne ensorcelée* must combat Placinette,

Désilus is more than willing to provide the mythical vision by which her powers can be perceived and conquered. Vodun has retained its animistic contours; the religion of the French peasants has been logicalized and symbolized out of all relevance to their daily struggle with the unseen forces. Their mythical explanations fall back on all-but-forgotten elements of a now submerged earlier mythical system. The black cat which Jaume sees on the horizon each time there is to be a calamity can provide only a very diffused and vague connection with the total workings of the misfortune of the French villagers when compared to the embodiment of Damballah in the path leading to the mapou tree before Placinette's house.

The art of the novelist is also influenced, and quite deeply, by his own point of view. Giono makes an effort to *prove* mythic reality; Roumain simply demonstrates it. In *Colline* it turns out to be true that the old man was, after all, the evil intrusion upsetting the cosmic balance; Giono is at pains to provide an epilogue proving the rightness of the action the villagers would have taken. The spring starts on its own to flow again after Jannet's death. Roumain senses that with the performing of the ritual, the true point of culmination has been reached. In the mythic consciousness, if the act does not set things right, it is because more acts of appeasement are necessary, which in no way destroys the validity of the first act. Therefore, Roumain does not bother to reveal whether the villagers' misfortune ceases.

Giono is operating on a more distilled level. He is satisfied with symbolism. The villagers go through a ritual killing of the old man in their elaborate meeting, but his timely death conveniently absolves them of the obligation to do so in actuality. The behavior of Roumain's villagers is much more elemental. And they see a continuity in the evil forces: Placinette's father was ritually destroyed; her daughter is hunted down and killed after her. But the peasants of *Colline* treat Jannet's daughter as one of them, take her into their confidence, and require her permission to kill the old man. Logic has in their case replaced the mythic mentality, and Giono's setting does not completely succeed in reflecting the mythic consciousness which it purports to. Roumain's does.

La Montagne ensorcelée did not receive unanimously favorable reviews. One contemporary critic wrote:

> Nous avons enregistré également la venue de la Montagne ensorcelée qui nous a déçu infiniment, infiniment. Ce n'est pas ce que nous réservait Jacques Roumain. L'oeuvre qu'il vient de faire publier est au-dessous, très au-dessous de La Proie et l'ombre.[9]

On the other hand, Edner Brutus wrote in 1933:

> Rien de tout ce qu'a produit, jusqu'à présent, notre littérature paysanne ne voisine, de trop près, cette oeuvre où se meut toute une série de sentiments, de contes, de légendes.
> (Brutus, "Jacques Roumain," p. 15)

In 1933, *La Montagne ensorcelée* was still Roumain's most recent literary effort. Brutus closes his discussion of Roumain's work with words that are heavily influenced by that last production, words that are strangely prophetic as we read them in retrospect:

> Je soupçonne dans son oeuvre déjà publiée, l'ébauche d'une humanité sans frontières, en dehors du cercle haïtien et gardant quelque chose du rire désolé de la race noire et de ce caractère particulier sorti du mélange des civilisations afro-latine. . . . En tout cas, nous avons pour notre part, Dieu merci, La Montagne Ensorcelée. Et ne serait-ce que d'avoir écrit ce petit roman de nos frères en vareuse bleue, Mr. Jacques Roumain s'est constitué un rang justement jalousé dans notre monde lettré. (p. 16)

THE MIDDLE POETRY

Although the bulk of Jacques Roumain's writing during the period 1929–32 was prose fiction, four poems were published in the pages of *Haïti-Journal* during 1931. They are: "Quand bat le tam-tam" (July 4, 1931), "Poème" (July 6, 1931), "Langston Hughes" (October 20, 1931) and "Guinée" (December 30, 1931). "Quand bat le tam-tam" and "Guinée" are among

---

[9] François Duvalier, in *Les Tendances d'une génération*, pp. 105–6. The essay was originally published as "A Travers la Littérature" in *La Presse*, September 1, 1931.

Roumain's most famous poems. Both have been anthologized.[10] "Guinée" and "Langston Hughes" have appeared in English translation.[11] The poem published simply as "Poème de Jacques Roumain" in *Haïti-Journal* exists in manuscript form under the title "Créole."

The four poems show a racial preoccupation not unrelated to that of the 1929–31 prose. The rather frequent anthologizing of these poems, the many references to them by scholars studying the literature of black consciousness, may tend to foster the impression that they are representative of the poetry Jacques Roumain wrote during the indigenist period of Haitian literature (roughly 1925–45). Janheinz Jahn's statement—"In the Revue Jacques Roumain had still been choosing folklorist themes for his poetry: C'est le lent chemin de Guinée . . ."[12]— is baffling. None of the four poems appears in the issues of the *Revue Indigène* (the review to which Jahn must be referring, since he uses the word *"Revue"* elsewhere to mean *Revue Indigène* and never mentions another *Revue*, such as the *Revue Caraïbe*). Moreover, Jahn gives as reference—as do all other writers except Trouillot—the Dudley Fitts anthology, a secondary source which does not indicate the original date or place of publication.

These poems, however, purged of romanticism and of surrealistic influences, written in a straightforward style and

---

[10] In Dudley Fitts, ed., *Anthology of Contemporary Latin American Poetry* (Norfolk, Conn.: New Directions, 1942). The Fitts anthology reproduces "Guinée" under the title "Sur le Chemin de Guinée." They are reproduced as well in Garret, *The Renaissance of Haitian Poetry*. German translations (as "Guinea" and "Wenn der Tam Tam Schlagt") appear in Erich Arendt, *Die Indios Steigen von Mixco Nieder: Südamerikanische Freiheitsdichtungen* (Berlin: Verlag Volk und Welt, 1951).

[11] In Edna Worthley Underwood, *The Poets of Haiti: 1782–1934* (Portland, Me.: The Mosher Press, 1934), and in Langston Hughes and Arna Bontemps, eds., *The Poetry of the Negro: 1746–1949* (Garden City, N.Y.: Doubleday and Co., 1949). "When the Tom-Tom Beats," translated by L. C. Kaplan, appeared in *Poetry*, May 1943.

[12] Janheinz Jahn, *Neo-African Literature: A History of Black Writing* trans. Oliver Coburn and Ursula Lehrburger (New York: Grove Press, 1969), p. 217.

pared of any superfluous imagery and of patriotic fervor, constitute, by all available evidence, the sole expression of Negritude (uncontaminated with proletarianism) in the poetry of Jacques Roumain.

Roumain must have at this same period been undergoing a personal identity crisis. In the 1927 interview with Antonio Vieux, he had alluded more than once to his Breton ancestry. Yet less than three years later, he replied in one curt sentence to a formal invitation extended by the American High Commissioner: "Le nègre Jacques Roumain ne daigne pas fréquenter les blancs."[13] It is now as a black man that Roumain considered himself, and all of his future references to himself would evoke his African heritage. We have noted in the first poetry an absence of racial themes. In the nationalistic poetry and the poetic journalism of Le Petit Impartial, race themes are manipulated as corollaries to the dominant Nationalist ones. But racial themes and allusions creep into the early urban prose as a more sincerely felt preoccupation. Daniel, Emilio, Michel and Santiague, in their lonely walks, their immersion in crowds, their nostalgia for peasant women, all show an urgent need to identify racially as well as nationally. Racial identity becomes closely associated with the life patterns of the Haitian masses. Marcel, in his hatred for whites and in the race-consciousness of his articles, shows the same needs.

Roumain, in his personal development, in the orientation of his urban prose, the preparation of a roman paysan, and the writing of the four poems considered here, seems to parallel the development of Africanism, following the publication of Ainsi parla l'oncle, in Haitian letters. As Haiti moved into the decade of the thirties, Jacques Roumain seems to have moved at first along with it into a growing racialism. It would not be long before he would strike out in a different direction. But whatever he might thenceforth undertake, his writings would never lose their racial moorings, even as his commitment to the welfare of all peoples grew.

---

[13] As reported in La Presse, February 26, 1930. It has been asserted however by one of Roumain's associates that his actual response was "Le nègre Jacques Roumain ne dîne pas avec le raciste Russell" (Group I interviews).

Unlike the prose, the poems "Langston Hughes," "Guinée," and "Quand bat le tam-tam" are concerned with race
more in the manner of Negritude than of Indigenism. That is
to say, the poems reflect not the local but the universal black
experience. When the Haitian countryside is evoked, it no
longer reflects the tropicalism of poems such as "Midi,"
"Après-Midi," and "Miragôane." The Haitian countryside no
longer serves the ends of regional poetry but now becomes a
link with universal blackness. Image reversal and a different
system of motif symbolism than that found in the poems
published in the 1927–29 period are also evident in these
poems. It is not the individual hero who is featured here, but
the group. Fulfillment now comes not through individual effort
but through racial identity.

The poem "Quand bat le tam-tam" provides several striking
examples of image reversal and a motif symbolism geared to
the celebration of race:

Ton coeur tremble dans l'ombre, comme le reflet
   d'un visage dans l'onde troublée
L'ancien mirage se lève au creux de la nuit
Tu connais le doux sortilège du souvenir
Un fleuve t'emporte loin des berges,
Entends-tu ces voix: elles chantent l'amoureuse douleur
Et dans le morne, écoute ce tam-tam haleter telle la gorge
   d'une noire jeune fille.

Ton âme, c'est le reflet dans l'eau murmurante où
   tes pères ont penché leurs obscurs visages
Et le blanc qui te fit mulâtre, c'est ce peu
   d'écume rejeté, comme un crachat, sur le rivage.
                       (*Haïti-Journal*, July 4, 1931)

Here, white is a totally negative concept and is associated with
the white race. This is the kind of image reversal we meet over
and over in the Negritude poetry soon to follow of the late
1930s and of the 1940s. Black, as the opposite of white, assumes
a positive symbolism and is associated not only with race, but
more importantly with racial continuity and the animistic
vision of nature which is part of the black world view. Images
of black join images of night to provide a sombre matrix. But
the night has become reassuring because it is in this matrix

that the spirits of the ancestors reveal themselves. Night is no longer a blind void encircling the lonely hero cut off from his moorings and out of reach of his desires, as it was in much of the poetry published in 1927–29. The symbolism in the earlier poetry is traditionally European; blackness and night are traditionally negative in it. In "Quand bat le tam-tam," night is no longer cause for anxiety but for reassurance, and like blackness in general, it is a Negritude motif. Conversely, white no longer represents clarity and hope; it is not the one bright hopeful spot in a gloomy immensity as it was in the 1927–29 poetry, but is impurity and dirt: *écume* is likened to a *crachat*. The soul in the earlier poetry seeks out the clarity of light, but here, the soul is attracted to the reassuring darkness.

The imagery of this poem echoes occasional isolated images of the 1929–31 prose. In *Les Fantoches*, Santiague's reference to the beating of the African drums seems almost a direct comment on the title of the poem "Quand bat le tam-tam":

> Alors quand s'épanouit le plain-chant africain, que les ridicules instruments se sont tus et que seul résonne encore le tambour ancestral, j'entre dans la foule et me perds dans ma race. (p. 133)

Closely allied with the images of night are the images of flow, of streams, of rivers or bodies of water. It is important that the "blanc" is "rejeté sur le rivage"; that is, the white part of the poet's ancestry is not in the continuity, is therefore incidental, not essential. Water functions in the same way in "Guinée":

> C'est le lent chemin de Guinée;
> La mort t'y conduira.
> Voici les branchages, les arbres, la forêt:
> Ecoute le bruit du vent dans ses longs cheveux
> d'éternelle nuit.
> C'est le lent chemin de Guinée;
> Tes pères t'attendent sans impatience
> sur la route; ils palabrent.
> Ils t'attendent.
> Voici les branchages, les arbres, la forêt:
> comme des chapelets d'os.
> C'est le lent chemin de Guinée;
> il ne te sera pas fait de lumineux accueil

au noir pays des hommes noirs;
Sous un ciel fumeux, percé de cris d'oiseaux,
autour de l'oeil du mangot
les cils des arbres s'écartent sur la clarté purissante.
La t'attend au bord de l'eaux un paisible village et
la case de tes pères et la dure pierre familiale
où reposer ton front.

(*Haïti-Journal*, December 30, 1931)

Water, the river, represents the flow of life from past to present, linking one generation to another (l. 10–11)[14] and is the agent which will carry the individual into the ancestral past (l. 18–20), where time dissolves into mythic eternity. Again, night and black, through phrases such as "éternelle nuit," "noir pays des hommes noirs," "ciel fumeux," evoke, not the anxiety of that which is obscure, impenetrable and mysterious, but the reassurance of one's own oneness with mystery, and one's bonds with the past; and a phrase such as "clarté pourrissante" associates white not with purity but with impurity and dirt.

The poem "Langston Hughes" portrays the Diaspora of the black race and stresses the global vision of blackness typical of Negritude poetry. The poem depicts, through its images of prostituted women, the disintegration of culture and the dehumanization of the race:

Tu connus à Lagos ces filles mélancoliques
Elles portent aux chevilles des colliers d'argent et s'offrent
     nues
Comme la nuit encerclée de lune

Tu vis la France sans prononcer de paroles historiques
—Lafayette nous voici—
La Seine parut moins belle que le Congo

A Venise, tu cherchas l'ombre de Desdémone
Elle s'appelait Paola
Tu lui disais: Amorossissima
Et parfois
Babe, Baby
Alors elle pleurait et te réclamait vingt lires

---

[14] Florence White, " 'Poesía Negra' in Latin America," (Ph. D. dissertation, University of Wisconsin, 1951), state that the "chapelets d'os" are necklaces of bones worn by African priests, and that as they dance their ritual steps, the bones "grelottent" (p. 455).

Tu as promené ton coeur nomade, comme un Baedecker, de
Harlem à Dakar
La mer a prêté à tes chants un rythme doux et rauque, et
ses fleurs d'amertume écloses de l'écume.
Maintenant dans ce cabaret où à l'aube tu murmures:
Jouez ce blues pou' moa
O jouez ce blues pou' moa
Rêves-tu de palmes et de chants de pagayeurs au crépuscule?
                    (*Haïti-Journal*, October 20, 1931)

Again, the rivers and the sea represent the channels of racial
continuity, and the last line, joining images of black with a
submerged image of the flowing river (in the image of the
pagayeurs), seems to allude to an ultimate merging with the
ancestors. The agelessness of rivers implied in all three poems
is pointedly suggested in this one by Roumain's title: one of
Langston Hughes's most famous poems, "The Negro Speaks
of Rivers," also extends the black man's presence over the
continents and the epochs.

The poem "Créole" (published under the title "Poème de
Jacques Roumain" in *Haïti-Journal*) shares certain elements in
common with the three just studied. Yet, it is different in style
and treatment from all the rest of Roumain's poetry. Of these
four poems, "Créole" is perhaps more indigenist than Negritude, as it confines itself almost exclusively to Haitian images
and, like much of the indigenist poetry of Roumain's contemporaries, and like his own 1929–31 prose, celebrates the natural
beauty of the peasant woman. However, it too contains a
Negritude system of motifs:

Sous la tonnelle,
L'as-tu rencontrée, sous la tonnelle
La négresse vêtue de blanches mousselines
—Viergine, je m'appelle
A votre service, monssié—

Au bord de l'eau,
L'as-tu vue au bord de l'eau, sous les bougainvilliers
La négresse fraîche et nue comme l'ombre.

Viergine, Grâce
Vêtues de blanches mousselines ou d'ombre en fleur,
Mes rieuses négresses,
Combien vous sutes bénir ce coeur toujours inapaisé.
                    (*Haïti-Journal*, July 6, 1931)

The phrase "nue comme l'ombre" evokes interestingly enough the girls who are "nues comme la nuit" in "Langston Hughes." The association of obscurity with freshness is further developed in the final stanza of "Créole," and it becomes possible to speak here too of image reversal, of things that blossom out not in light but in darkness. The native woman in her typical dress, glimpsed in her daily tasks (drawing water from the spring), in her typical pleasures (she might be seen under the *tonnelle* at a party), brings the poet an almost religious pleasure. His appeasement reminds us of Santiague listening to his servant girl Charmantine and seeing in his reverie visions of freshness and of the Haitian countryside.

CHAPTER V

Mobilizing the Haitian Masses and a New Use for Literature

Jacques Roumain produced in the years 1927–1931 more works of a literary nature than he would ever again in his brief life. Within those five short years, he seems to have gone through several identifiable phases; yet the constant underlying theme of heroism and of the human quest for something more seems to indicate that the broad outlines of his character do not change.

Jacques Roumain now began to look with a more discerning eye at the Haitian political scene, or which he had now become a recognized part. The time was approaching when the hated American presence would be gone, but the political machinery which would function after was already in operation, and the Haitian masses would continue their lives essentially unchanged in the presence of Yankee and bourgeois Nationalist alike. Marxist philosophy had begun to make inroads in Haiti as elsewhere in the early 1930s. The Haitian intelligentsia of Roumain's generation read Marx and Engels, as they had read Nietzsche, but they had little inclination to use the philosophy as a basis for social action. Roumain had probably begun to read Marx and Engels as early as 1929 or 1930, and his interest also remained largely academic. It was not until 1931, after his disenchantment with Nationalism, when it became apparent that the newly instituted Nationalist government would in no significant way change the social and economic condition of the great masses of Haitians, that Jacques Roumain began to turn to Communism as an alternative. Communism began to represent for him a new hope for social equity, and it became for him a system upon which to rebuild his faith.

Roumain was in his personal life undergoing a profound evolution, sloughing off with difficulty and not always with complete success the charming dandy he had been, strolling and riding about Port-au-Prince, fashionably dressed and generously giving away his money.[1] His own remarks at the outset of his Communist career reveal the distance travelled. The French writer Tristan Rémy had asked Roumain for biographical information to be used in an article about him. (The two men had been discussing the possibility of Rémy doing a French edition of *La Montagne ensorcelée*.) Roumain's response, written toward the beginning of 1932, goes into considerable detail about the development of his political consciousness. Roumain declares that close contact with the proletariat has caused him to revise his political ideas. He goes on to state:

> Je suis communiste. Non militant pour l'instant, parce que les cadres d'une lutte politique n'existent pas encore in Haïti. Je m'applique à préparer. . . .
>
> Fils de grands propriétaires terriens, j'ai renié mes origines bourgeoises. J'ai beaucoup vécu avec les paysans. Je connais leur vie, leur mentalité, leur religion,—ce mélange étonnant de catholicisme et de vaudou.
>
> Je ne considère pas ce prolétariat paysan comme une valeur sentimentale. Le paysan haïtien est notre seul producteur et il ne produit que pour être exploité, de la manière la plus effroyable, par une minorité . . . politicienne qui s'intitule L'Elite. Toutes mes publications ont combattu cette prétendue élite. En ce qui concerne la littérature, j'ai écrit depuis mon plus jeune âge des poèmes et des contes. En 1930, j'ai publié une plaquette de nouvelles qui dépeint le malaise de notre génération— . . . ce thème a été repris dans un bref roman "Les Fantoches." Je travaille au renouvellement de notre littérature par l'étude de notre très riche folklore. Jusqu'à ce jour nos écrivains, à de très rares exceptions près, n'ont fait

---

[1] Roumain's greatest shortcoming was, according to one person interviewed, his generosity; he had a tendency to give all his money away (Group I interviews).

qu'imiter les poètes et conteurs français. J'estime que notre littérature doit être *nègre* et largement prolétarienne. Je travaille également au rapprochement des écrivains nègres de tous les pays. C'est pour cela que je prépare sous le titre "poèmes afro-américains," une plaquette de traduction de poèmes de nègres américains, Langston Hughes, etc . . .[2]

The letter also shows that literature remained very much on Roumain's mind and in his plans, and gives indications that Roumain's race consciousness was at that period vying with his proletarian consciousness for priority. Roumain's literary output, despite indications in the letter, was interrupted during the period 1932–34, a period given over, after the resignation from his post as *chef de division*, to the organizing of a Communist party in Haiti, and to the writing of "tracts" or "brochures" as they are variously called by newspapers hostile to him.[3]

In February of 1932 (perhaps immediately after the letter to Rémy, since, in Roumain's words, it dates "du début de l'année 1932"),[4] Jacques Roumain made visits to New York City and to Washington, D.C.[5] He had been corresponding

---

[2] The volume never appeared. In later years, Roumain also planned to publish a volume of Nicolás Guillén's poetry, translated into French, but died before realizing that project.

[3] "Un mouvement communiste en Haiti étouffé dans l'oeuf par le Gouvernement," *Haïti-Journal*, January 4, 1933, p. 1. The exact same article was reproduced in *L'Action Nationale*, January 5, 1933. The document had been found among Roumain's papers by the police during a search of his home in December 1932. Both newspapers labeled the document as a part of a communist conspiracy and did not reproduce it in its entirety, but began their quotation with four rows of ellipses, followed by the words: "en étroit contact avec le prolétariat." In a letter of protest to *Haïti-Journal* dated January 5, 1933, Roumain states: "La lettre que vous publiez triomphalement n'est que le brouillon de ma réponse [to Tristan Rémy] qui date du début de l'année 1932.

"Ayant lu la lettre de Rémy et les questions qui'il me posait, vous saviez à quoi vous en tenir sur la valeur révolutionnaire de ma réponse que vous avez la déloyauté de faire passer pour un document important."

[4] See note 3 above.

[5] Letter from Jacques Roumain to Alain Locke dated Dewey Square Hotel, New York, February 17, 1932. Alain Locke Collection, Moorland-Spingarn Research Center, Howard University, Washington, D.C.

with the Black American scholar Alain Locke since October
1931. Locke was aware of Roumain's work and had expressed
an interest in translating *La Montagne ensorcelée* into English.[6]
Roumain and Locke met in Washington, D.C., during Roumain's 1932 visit, and the meeting appears to have been a very
rewarding one for Roumain.[7] Thus, it appears that Roumain,
in keeping with the concerns stated in his letter to Tristan
Rémy, was interested in making personal contact with the
Black American intellectual community.

However, he seems also to have had other than literary
motivations for the trip. Traveling in the company of a Haitian
comrade, Christian Beaulieu, he was ostensibly on a business
trip. The real aim of the two men, however, was to confer with
officials of the Communist party of the United States in order
to be recognized and accepted as Communists, and to obtain
the cooperation of the American party in creating a Communist
party of Haiti.[8] Their reception by the American Communist
party was at first very reserved. The apparent coldness seems
to have been due to the fact that on a previous occasion,
Haitians had presented themselves, seeking official sanction
for the establishment of a Communist party in Haiti, but had
not followed through with their plans (Group I interviews). It
is also possible that the American Communists were suspicious
of Roumain and Beaulieu due to their social position as part
of Haiti's élite class (Group I interviews). In any case, the two
men were in the end told to return to Haiti and to establish
a basic organization, working underground. When they felt

---

[6] Letter from Jacques Roumain to Alain Locke, dated Port-au-
Prince, October 3, 1931. Alain Locke Collection, Moorland-Spingarn
Research Center, Howard University. There is no record of such a
translation among the Locke Papers at the Moorland/Spingarn Center.

[7] Roumain states in his letter to Dr. Locke of February 17, 1932:
"Grâce à vos généreuses attentions, mon séjour à Washington a été
extrêmement agréable."

[8] Group I interviews. One source could not remember whether the
trip by Roumain and Beaulieu had been made in 1931 or 1932 but
stated with conviction that there had been only one trip. Another
source remembers a lengthy conversation with Roumain in New
York in 1932.

that the organization was sufficiently strong, they were to declare themselves openly.

Back in Port-au-Prince, Roumain and his co-organizers began by holding meetings with members of the laboring classes, those who lived in the poorest sections on the outskirts of the city, in Bel-Aire and La Saline, and with students. Roumain's following was small, in no way comparable to the large following of his Nationalist period. Most of those who listened now did so because they remembered him from the days not long past when, as a Nationalist leader, he had come into their neighborhoods to talk to them. Jean Brierre has evoked those days of party organization in his tribute to Jacques Roumain, *Nous garderons le dieu:*

> Sa chambre souvent restait fermée . . .
> Vous[9] trouviez, troublée, Karl Marx et Lénine
> ouverts sur sa table.
> Il rentrait, fatigué,
> accueillant des inconnus mal habillés,
> des étudiants de province, dans son bureau tapissé
> de livres.
> Et vous écoutiez à travers la porte
> sa voix sobre leur parler de travail,
> d'organisation scientifique du monde,
> de prolétariat et d'oppression . . ..
> Ils sortaient avec des livres,
> des brochures,
> et laissaient après eux
> une sensation étrange de misère.[10]

In the beginning, Roumain limited his activities in this way to the indoctrination of small groups of men. After his trip to New York, his movements were closely watched by the government. There is indication too that Roumain and Beaulieu, while in New York, had been under surveillance by American authorities, and that a report from New York was later relayed to the Haitian government. His behavior must have certainly seemed unusual: he seemed not to want the favors the government was prepared to grant him. Sténio

---

[9] The poet is addressing Jacques Roumain's mother.
[10] Jean Brierre, *Nous garderons le dieu* (Port-au-Prince: Henri Deschamps, 1945) p. 19.

Vincent had offered him the post of secretary to the Haitian legation in Paris. Roumain's refusal, for no apparent reason, must have been among the factors which rendered him suspect.

In the early 1930s, Marxist Communism was looked upon in Haiti as synonymous with anarchy. Among intellectuals, there was a marked interest in Marxism, and Marx's ideas were read and discussed but not actively espoused. Haitians were just beginning in those years to see the triumph of their Nationalist efforts. Nationalism was still the vanguard movement. Not until the late 1930s, when Nationalism began to reveal its ineffectiveness in coping with the structure of society, would socialism acquire a sizeable number of adherents in Haiti.

During the early years of the decade, however, there were others in addition to Roumain who were actively engaged in seeking a solution to Haiti's political and economic woes. One such man was Max Hudicourt. Although a Nationalist, he felt that Haiti's economic problems could be solved if the government were to take out a loan from foreign capitalists in order to develop state cooperatives.[11] But Hudicourt, in addition to these ideas, apparently used his newspaper, Le Centre, as an organ of diffusion for Communist ideas (L'Action Nationale, December 29, 1932). Through its pages, he waged a constant attack against the dictatorial nature of the Vincent government. The government thus saw him as an anarchist and a communist. Both he and Roumain were called before the public prosecutor in December 1932. Roumain was, at the time, still chef de division at the Department of the Interior, but declared himself to be a Communist (L'Action Nationale, December 29, 1932). In January of the following year, Hudicourt stated in quite definite language that he was not a Communist.[12] Thus, although Roumain and Hudicourt were to espouse divergent solutions and to attract different sets of followers, when the

---

[11] Letter from Max Hudicourt to the Secretariat du Caribe, New York, dated September 6, 1931, confiscated by the government and published in L'Action Nationale, December 29, 1932.

[12] "Une Lettre de Max Hudicourt au Directeur du 'Temps'," Le Nouvelliste, January 9, 1933. (It should be added that the letter was written from the National Penitentiary.)

furor over a Communist conspiracy broke out, they were lumped together as Communist agitators and anarchists in the eyes of the government and of the government press.

The accounts in *Haïti-Journal* and *L'Action Nationale* during their January 1933 campaign against the reputed conspiracy told of clandestine activity and secret messages sent back and forth during the years 1931 and 1932, and of the government's quickened interest in such activities, an interest going back to the autumn of 1932. The Haitian minister in Paris, it was reported, sent word back to President Vincent that it was rumored among the Haitian students on the Left Bank that Communist activities were in full swing. There seems to have been a significant input by foreign agents; letters were addressed to nonexistent persons or to those whose involvement was less direct, in efforts to hide the identity of sender and recipient. Clubs were organized in the open, while cells were organized under cover. Although one must allow for the possibility of error and alarmism on the part of the progovernment press[13] in reporting them, it is clear that clandestine operations were kept under close scrutiny by the government.

There were, in effect, a vast number of clandestine operations. Toward the end of December 1932, Roumain wrote to the secretary of the American Communist Party, giving an account of the work accomplished in the months since his return from New York. (Group I interviews). Also in late December, the government stepped up its surveillance. On December 23, 1932, a certain Pequero, a national of the Dominican Republic, was arrested. Letters meant for him but addressed to several women were confiscated, as well as a document entitled "La Prochaine récolte en Haïti et les devoirs qui incombent aux Partisans de la C.S.L.A." The document contained detailed instructions calling for the mobilization of

---

[13] All the Haitian papers of the period were anti-Communist. However, *L'Action Nationale* was very close to the Vincent government, and *Haïti-Journal* had been founded by Vincent. These two papers give the greatest amount of coverage to the Communist and "anarchist" movement; both are manifestly anti-Roumain. *Le Nouvelliste*, on the other hand, felt that the Communist scare had been blown out of proportion and is decidedly more objective in its reporting.

workers in preparation for a strike against the Haitian American Sugar Company (HASCO), timed for the 1933 harvest:

> A cause de leur analphabétisme, les ouvriers ne parlant que créole, notre tâche immédiate est d'établir de solides contacts avec ceux qui sont les plus exploités, principalement ceux de la HASCO, car toute l'agitation devra se faire de bouche en bouche de la manière suivante:
>
> a) visiter leurs cases, en leur parlant des conditions misérables de leur vie présente, et laissant à ceux dont l'action peut être utile, l'impression qu'ils trouveront en nous un solide appui.
>
> b) organiser de petites réunions dans leurs propres cases où on les entretiendra des conditions du travail qui doivent régir la prochaine récolte et de la nécessité d'une amélioration.
>
> c) faire une sélection des éléments les plus militants pour les utiliser comme agitateurs afin de développer la préparation de la grève. (*L'Action Nationale*, Décembre 30, 1932)

L'Action Nationale termed the document a "manifeste." Roumain later stated publicly that it was simply an article from the newspaper *El obrero del Caribe*.[14]

Upon learning of Pequero's arrest, Roumain fled from his home to avoid arrest. He sent a telegram to New York the morning of December 24: "Pequero and other friends arrested don't send any mail till further instructions," and another on December 28: "Have written instructions about correspondence" (*Haïti-Journal*, January 4, 1933; *L'Action Nationale*, January 5, 1933). For a ten-day period, Roumain was a fugitive, depending on friends to provide for his food and housing. He seems to have formulated a plan during this time to leave the capital, travel to the south of Haiti where, according to information sent him, militants were at work organizing the rural proletariat and were inviting him to join in their work. Roumain had thought to live clandestinely among the peasants of the South. However, both entrances to Port-au-Prince were heavily guarded on the chance that he might try to leave the city, and there was no way of verifying the true situation in the South. Roumain abandoned the plan and decided instead to turn himself in, in order to avoid possible reprisals against

---

[14] In a letter dated January 5, 1933, to *Haïti-Journal*. See "Une Lettre de M. Jacques Roumain," *Haïti-Journal*, January 6, 1933, p. 1.

friends and family. (Group I interviews) On January 2 or 3, 1933, he surrendered and was imprisoned in the National Penitentiary.[15]

In the years 1928–30, Roumain had been in and out of jail on arrests stemming from his role in the Nationalist struggle. He now stood accused of Communist activities. The distinction is important. Nationalism had been the battle-cry around which Haitians had rallied. Communism as expressed through the Third International was suspect because controlled by outside forces. Its ideology, moreover, was manifestly counter to traditional Haitian political structures. The affair was given extensive coverage; progovernment and other establishment-oriented sectors were shocked. What they could not forgive was the invitation extended by native Haitians to foreign elements to infiltrate and undermine the existing system. Roumain and others came under fire for attempting to pull down the very class from which they sprang. One writer accused Roumain of wanting to "faire du marxisme dans un cadre de prince" (L'Action Nationale, January 10, 1933). The excitement was short-lived, however, subsiding by mid-January. Meanwhile, Roumain, Pequero, and Max Hudicourt (who had also been arrested) continued to be incarcerated under charges of "délit communiste." On February 9, Roumain and Hudicourt began a hunger strike to protest the slowness with which their trial was proceeding. They were released, along with Pequero, on Feburary 11, 1933 (Gaillard, Carl Brouard, p. 75).

For a time afterwards, the government and the press seemed to take the position that Communist agitation in Haiti was not to be taken seriously. However, Roumain and his comrades continued their extralegal activities. An inconspicuous article in the November 4, 1933, issue of L'Action Nationale reported testimony from a certain Fernande Juste:

Au commencement du mois de juin de cette année, Mar-

---

[15] L'Action Nationale of January 5, 1933, states that Roumain surrendered "avant-hier"; Haïti-Journal of January 3, 1933, states that he surrendered "hier matin"; Le Nouvelliste of January 3, 1933, states that Roumain surrendered "hier matin"; Group I interviews give the date as January 3, 1933.

cellus Sajous m'a demandé mon concours dans une campagne
communiste avec Jacques Roumain aux fins de soulever les
protestations des trieuses de café chez Berne, Wiener, et Cie
au sujet de leur salaire; . . . il m'a fourni des brochures, pour
étudier. Après les avoir bien lues, j'ai fini par comprendre
que pareille idée ne peut pas prendre corps en Haïti, et que
Jacques Roumain n'a qu'un seul but, celui de nuire au
Gouvernement, d'exploiter l'ignorance des simples pour
servir la cause communiste. Le samedi sept octobre courant
ayant soupçonné que la Police était au courant de ses menées
Marcellus Sajous était venu me dire que Jacques Roumain lui
a donné l'ordre de débarrasser la maison de tous les objets
suspects. . . . Le dimanche on me chargea du soin de les
mettre en lieu sûr. . . . je les pris et les ai déposés en plaine
pour les remettre au Gouvernement. Mardi de cette semaine,
M. Marcellus Sajous me demanda de lui remettre les objets
pour Jacques Roumain. Jacques Roumain et Marcellus Sajous
ont déclaré que la personne qui aurait dénoncé la campagne
communiste sera tuée.

Shortly thereafter, the Minister of the Interior, Elie Lescot,
questioned about Roumain's activity, had this to say:

Le Gouvernement est bien décidé à ne pas tenir compte
des activités de *soi-disant* communistes haïtiens qui ne sont,
en réalité, que de jeunes arrivistes ou des naïfs que d'autres
mènent. . . . (*L'Action Nationale*, November 9, 1933; italics in
text)

Roumain continued his activities, writing, now and again,
letters of denunciation to the Establishment press, "tracts" in
which he expressed his Marxist convictions. One has the
impression that Roumain wrote a great amount of pamphlet
literature during this period. Very little, however, has been
preserved. An isolated three-page "Introduction" in manuscript form (perhaps the first part of a projected book) can
probably be taken as a representative sample of his writing
during this period. It is obviously incomplete. In the first
section ("Nécessité de la Théorie"), Roumain combats at length
a tendency among men to discredit theory as an unnecessary
step:

Quel que soit son champ d'activité, il découvrira bientôt,
qu'à chaque tournant il se heurt [*sic*] à la théorie tant
méprisée. Il se trouvera soumis à la question: "Que faire

maintenant"? Et la réponse contient toujours cette autre question: "Quel but essayez-vous d'atteindre"? Afin de justifier l'action entreprise (une grève par exemple), il est forcé de faire appel à des raisons *générales* (dans ce cas: le but général envisagé et l'expérience *générale* de la tactique de la grève). Mais de tels faits généraux sont liées [*sic*] à ce que nous appelons: la *théorie* et si de plus ils présentent la caractéristique d'avoir été vérifier [*sic*] par l'expérience, nous les appelons *théorie scientifique*.

La théorie qui est à la base de toute activité socialiste consciente est le Socialisme Scientifique (Marxisme).

Roumain states that scientific socialism seeks a "vue d'ensemble du monde" based on scientific fact, whether physical, sociological, or the science of human thought. A world concept developed along these lines is inevitably at odds with the bourgeois world view, which is conservative, religious (in that it considers "l'ordre existant comme ayant reçue [*sic*] en quelque sorte la sanction divine"). The bourgeois world view is therefore doggedly opposed to "l'étude scientifique de la societé humaine avec toutes ses conséquences révolution-naires."

This then is an attempt to interpret Marxist theory to a Haitian audience, which must have been much like the one described by Brierre in his poem to Roumain's memory. Roumain's long apology for theory has the effect of discouraging action and agitation for the sake of action and agitation. The initial step must be study, which leads to a clear understanding of the historical processes involved. At the end, Roumain's audience would presumably realize that confrontation with the existing closed-circuit system was inevitable. The lapses in style and grammar probably bear witness to the hurried nature, the sense of urgency, of Roumain's work at this period.

In 1934, after two years or so of underground activity, Roumain and his associates decided to establish the Communist Party out in the open. *L'Analyse schématique*, published in June 1934 as an official publication of the Comité Central du Parti Communiste Haïtien, was the document which launched it. The pamphlet bears Jacques Roumain's signature and designates him as a member of the central committee. We know, however, that the work was a joint effort, various members being responsible for various parts of the tract. But Roumain, impatient to have the pamphlet published and circulating, assumed final responsibility for it in its entirety. It seems very likely that sections dealing with race, color, and class are the work of Jacques Roumain (Group I interviews).

L'Analyse schématique was in the main a critique written in response to a pamphlet published by the Réaction Démocratique (R.D.), led by Max Hudicourt. The Réaction Démocratique, continuing the platform Hudicourt had put forth earlier in his newspaper, *Le Centre*, had circulated a manifesto calling for the constitution of state farm cooperatives. *L'Analyse schématique* vigorously contested this move and sought to prove the inaccuracy—which it considered dangerous—of the Réaction Démocratique in both its philosophy and programs. The bulk of *L'Analyse schématique* (the seventeen pages of part C) refutes what Roumain and his coauthors appear to consider revisionist philosophy in the areas of economics, political organization, and the class struggle. This critique is preceded by a part A, which bears the title "Ecroulement du mythe nationaliste" (pp. i–iv) and a part B: "Préjugé de couleur et lutte de classe" (pp. i–vii). These first two parts are a more general statement of the ideology of the Haitian Communist Party. They are important for our purposes, since it is here that we can discern most clearly attitudes and preoccupations recognizeable as those of Jacques Roumain.

The pamphlet begins with a single-sentence paragraph:

Le fait le plus considérable, le plus riche en enseignements c'est, entre 1932–1934, l'écroulement du mythe nationaliste en Haïti. (p. i)

The author argues that the Nationalism provoked by the Occupation was not a movement uniting all classes in a common cause, but that the interests of the masses and of the bourgeoisie were, from the beginning, conflicting. It was the Haitian masses who resisted the Occupation, and their resistance was triggered by the reestablishment of the *corvée* by the Americans and the massacre of Haitian peasants. Bourgeois opposition, on the other hand, grew up not as a class struggle, but as a revolt by individual dissidents, who were able to bring the masses along with them through persuasive oratory and vain promises:

> . . . le nationalisme contenait des contradictions internes qui devaient se désagréger. Le mouvement nationaliste fut incapable de remplir ses promesses, parce que les promesses du nationalisme bourgeois se heurtaient dès la prise du pouvoir, à ses intérêts de classe, et se révélaient une duperie électorale. (p.iii)

The words reveal all the disillusionment of the crusader for social justice who turns away from the existing order at the moment when his place in it seems assured. It is easy to see how scientific socialism, with its confidence that the solution to the problem lay in the proper analysis of events, might appear in the hour of need as the only possible salvation to a character such as Roumain's.

If part A of L'Analyse schématique seems to mirror the stages through which Roumain's thought was passing during the period 1932–34, we cannot know for certain whether he drafted or had a hand in drafting it. We can be fairly certain, however, that he is the author of part B: "Préjugé de couleur et lutte de classe" (Group I interviews). A footnote explains that the title is taken from a work by Roumain soon to appear, which will examine the question in detail. Section B exhorts the same class consciousness as section A but attempts to show that color prejudice is "le masque sous lequel politiciens noirs et politiciens mulâtres voudraient escamoter la lutte de classes" (p. v.). The real phenomenon, according to Roumain, is the progressive pauperization of the middle classes. The petty bourgeois is oppressed by a small minority, while the upper middle class mulatto is "prolétarisée par la grosse industrie internationale." The author implies that it is no accident that the race issue is raised at a time when all classes are tending to gravitate downwards; the sentimental fallacy of race pride is invoked by those who govern in order to obfuscate economic reality. Against this emotional appeal, the author proffers scientific analysis:

> Il s'agit, on le voit, d'une oppression économique qui se traduit socialement et politiquement. Donc la base objective

du problème est bien la lutte des classes. Le P. [arti] C. [ommuniste] H. [aitïen] pose le problème scientifiquement sans nier aucunement le bien-fondé des réactions psychologiques des noirs blessés dans leur dignité. . . .
Mais le devoir du P.C.H. parti d'ailleurs 98 pour cent noir . . . où la question de couleur est vidée systématiquement de son contenu épidermique . . . est de mettre en garde le prolétariat, la petite bourgeoisie pauvre et les travailleurs intellectuels noirs contre les politiciens bourgeois noirs qui voudraient exploiter à leur profit leur colère justifié. (p. v–vi)

A section of part C ("La R.D. et la lutte de classe") seems to echo and elaborate the dialectical view hinted at in the last sentences of the unfinished "Introduction" dealing with the value of theory. The exploited class, according to this section of L'Analyse schématique, "par nature épouse toute tendance évolutioniste, puisqu'elle se résume à changer le statut quo" (p. 8).

Redundancies, stylistic lapses, and structural weaknesses suggest that the work was hurriedly put together and published in response to events of the moment. (It is possible that Jacques Roumain retouched certain passages in order to prepare the pamphlet for publication.) The fact that he allowed the entire pamphlet to go out over his signature justifies our assuming that he was in agreement with the ideas expressed throughout.

Toward the middle of 1934, the government apparently reversed its stance regarding Roumain's activities, and in the early part of August, he was arrested. He was tried not in civil court but before a military tribunal, on a charge of Communist conspiracy. The trial was held October 15–17, 1934.[16] The government's case rested largely on correspondence exchanged between Roumain and a certain St Juste Zamor, a Haitian residing in New York. One letter in particular, in which Roumain mentioned a *"commission"* and *"matériel,"* arrested the prosecutor's attention. Roumain protested the government's interpretation of *"commission,"* stating that he had been referring to a bottle of rum which a friend had requested, and of *"materiel,"* by which he meant simply newspapers and

---

[16] Unless otherwise noted, information is based on accounts in *Le Nouvelliste*, October 6, 12, 15, 1934, and *Haïti-Journal*, October 16 and 18, 1934.

pamphlets. The same words appeared, however, in a letter addressed to Roumain from New York. The prosecutor read parts of the letter into the record:

> ". . . le même ami qui vous a apporté des commissions et du matériel vous en apportera encore. Dites à Pierre d'aller à l'endroit habituel et d'amener avec lui un ami sûr. Deux hommes viendront, un Américain et un Espagnol. Pierre leur causera séparément. Dites-lui de ne pas marcher dans les rues avec ces messieurs de peur d'attirer des soupçons."
> (*Haïti-Journal* October 16, 1934)

Next, the prosecutor read a police report from New York indicating that the word *"matériel"* meant bombs or explosives, that the Haitian president's life might be in danger, and that all docking ships should be watched closely for accomplices. Again Roumain protested, stating that there was a distinction between terrorism and Communism, and declared that no Communist had ever attacked a chief of state or his ministers. The prosecutor, pursuing his initial line of argument, sought to establish through a series of witnesses that a network of subversive activity existed. For example, Mme Emilienne Millien, the mother of St Juste Zamor, had been visited by a certain non-French-speaking white foreigner who had her name and address written on a scrap of paper and had come to her house to deliver a package from her son for Jacques Roumain. She opened the package and found that it contained books. A day or so later, Roumain came for the package.

Mlle Léonina Millien, the daughter of Emillienne and sister of St Juste Zamor, was also questioned. She had previously been arrested by the police and held for questioning in connection with letters she had received from her brother intended for Roumain.[17] Roumain had written a letter of protest

---

[17] It is not clear when this arrest took place, but it must have preceded that of Roumain. At the time of the trial she was not in jail. Mlle Millien may have been arrested more than once; she is listed, along with Hudicourt, by the black worker's paper *Le Cri des Nègres* (Paris) in its June 1934 issue. The November 1934 issue of the same paper carries an article by St Juste Zamor in which he states that Vincent, unable to arrest him personally, had arrested his sister ("Le Gouvernement de Sténio Vincent sous les mots d'ordre de 'Liberté et Nationalisme").

to the Garde d'Haïti and had visited the jail to bring her food. The officer who had interrogated Mlle Millien at the time of her arrest had learned from her that Roumain often received mail and packages by boat. The officer began a surveillance of the docks, noting in particular activity around the ship *Pastores*. At the trial, he gave the following account:

> . . . le trente Septembre vers les huit heures et demie j'atteins la machine numéro 170 stationnée sur le quai. . . . A neuf heures quinze, le "Pastores" accosta. Du "Pastores" descendirent deux colis qui furent saisis par un Anglais qui les remit à un canotier. Immédiatement, je m'approchais du canotier et réclamais les deux colis. Il me dit qu'il venait de les recevoir d'un Anglais. Celui-ci, arrêté et intérrogé sur la provenance des colis, déclara qu'il les avait reçus d'un blanc du "Pastores" pour être transportés à terre. Un moment après le blanc fut arrêté et sur l'authorisation du capitaine du bateau, on fouilla sa cabine. On y trouva une collection du journal "Le Matin" et trois lettres à l'adresse de M. Camille Julien.
>
> Q.— Que contenaient les colis?
> R.— Des brochures et des journaux sur les activitiés communistes à l'étranger. (*Haïti-Journal*, October 16, 1934)

The same witness also revealed something of Roumain's work of indoctrination among the inhabitants of the city's slums:

> Q.— Savez-vous si M. Roumain avait eu des réunions secrètes? demande M. Lechaud. [Roumain's attorney]
> R.— Oui. A la Saline, à Carrefour, au Wharf aux Herbes.
> Q.— Savez-vous si au cours de ces réunions il s'agissait de troubler l'ordre des choses établies?
> R.— M. Roumain, dans ces réunions, disait toujours que l'on ne payait pas assez aux travailleurs, il les excitait à la grève. Il disait que s'il n'y avait pas de travail c'était la faute du Président de la République. (*Haïti-Journal*, October 16, 1934)

In addition to the letters, packages, and meetings, the prosecution produced what *Haïti-Journal* termed a "profession de foi de l'auteur dans une brochure portant la signature de Jacques Roumain" (October 16, 1934). Roumain's response was that the pamphlet was in no way secret, and that five copies had been deposited with the Department of the Interior, as prescribed by law. There is no direct reference by either the prosecution or the defense which would identify the document definitively, but there is reason to believe that the pamphlet in question was none other than the *Analyse schématique*.[18] The fact that Roumain was arrested shortly after its appearance would support this view.

In his final remarks, Roumain sought to justify his use of unusual methods for receiving mail and packages by exposing the difficulties he had had in ordering Marxist books through Port-au-Prince dealers, who had been afraid to accept his orders. Roumain's attorney sought to show that the government had not established a case for Communist conspiracy in its interpretation of the language in the letters offered in evidence, nor had it established a case for disrupting the public tranquility, as charged. The court retired to deliberate. On October 23, 1934, the verdict became public: Roumain had been sentenced to three years in prison (*Le Nouvelliste*, October 23, 1934, p. 1).

The incarceration raised protests among Roumain's friends and sympathizers, particularly in the United States. The March 27, 1935, issue of *New Republic* bears a notice from the Committee for the Release of Jacques Roumain, organized by Mrs. Francine Bradley (to whom Roumain was later to dedicate "Bois d'ébène"), which appealed for letters of protest from readers. According to Mrs. Bradley, a letter in French had been sent to Roumain from New York announcing the shipment of literature (*matériau*) which Roumain had ordered in connection with a defense drive in behalf of the Scottsboro boys. Langston Hughes, writing in *Dynamo*, appealed to readers to send telegrams to the Haitian government. According to Hughes,

---

[18] The term, *"profession de foi"* brings to mind the letter sent to Tristan Rémy by Roumain. Hénock Trouillot does not mention the letter to Remy but states: "Le principal chef d'accusation contre Roumain, devant la cour Prévotale, fut son ANALYSE SCHEMATIQUE 32–34. Il protesta que ce livre n'était pas publié dans la clandestinité. In en avait envoyé les cinq exemplaires règlementaires au Département de l'Intérieur" (*Dimension et Limites de Jacques Roumain* [Port-au-Prince: Editions Fardin, 1975], p. 102).

Roumain had been incarcerated for circulating the newspaper, *Le Cri des nègres*.[19]

The confusion and discrepancies in accounts published outside of Haiti as to the reasons for Roumain's trial and conviction were partly due to problems of communication. However, the confusion also stemmed from the tendency shown by the government and the government press to lump together as one conspiracy all opposition elements. Jacques Roumain had been arrested in August of 1934 in the same government drive which swept up Max Hudicourt, Leonina Millien, and signers of an anti-Vincent article published in the June 1934 issue of *Le Cri des nègres*. The October 1934 issue of this newspaper carries an unsigned article stating that neither Roumain nor Emile Roumer (who had also been arrested) had signed the June 1934 article, but that they had been arrested on suspicion of being Communists. The article in *Le Cri des nègres* had been smuggled into Haiti, reproduced in typed form, and circulated in several provincial capitals. It was primarily this action which triggered the government's pursuit of Max Hudicourt and the other signers. The trial of the co-signers of the article was being held at the same time as Roumain's trial, but the two cases were entirely separate.

LE CHAMP DU POTIER

Jacques Roumain did not serve out the three-year term, but was released on June 8, 1936.[20] Shortly after his release, Sténio

---

[19] "Free Jacques Roumain: A letter from Langston Hughes," *Dynamo: A Journal of Revolutionary Poetry*, May-June 1935. The same, or a similar, letter from Hughes was published in *Commune* (Paris) in January 1935, as is stated in a letter from Port-au-Prince dated February 17, 1935 and signed "Un Groupe d'amis de 'Commune.' " The February 17, 1935 letter is published in the April 1935 issue of *Commune* and corrects the inaccuracies in Hughes' letter.

[20] Letter from Jacques Roumain, August 16, 1936. There is no specific person (or persons) addressed, but the contents make clear that the letter is to members of the Committee to Free Jacques Roumain. I am endebted to Mrs. Francine Bradley for permission to use the letter.

Vincent decreed Communism outlawed. The years in prison had done serious damage to Roumain's health. He had contracted malaria,[21] and there are some who feel that the periods spent in prison were responsible for his early death (Group I interviews). The time spent in prison was not without its productive aspect, however. Friends brought him books to read, and because of his social position and the circumstances of his incarceration, he was not made to do forced labor (Group I interviews). Roumain thus had the leisure, during the 1934–35 incarceration, to begin his novel "Le Champ du potier."

Unpublished to date and little known outside of Haiti, the work had been conceived (probably in 1934) as part of a larger project which also included *Gouverneurs de la rosée*. Roumain, after completing *Les Fantoches* and *La Montagne ensorcelée* had thought to write another "cycle" of novels, as it were, one dealing again with urban middle-class society and the other taking up again the Haitian peasant and the countryside. The greater part of the urban novel, "Le Champ du potier," seems to have been written while Roumain was in prison. It remained incomplete at his death, lacking perhaps one or two chapters. The second peasant novel, *Gouverneurs de la rosée*, was begun in Belgium during the year following Roumain's release (Group I interviews), but it was not to be finished until some eight years after its conception. (See also Gaillard, *L'Univers romanesque de Jacques Roumain*, p. 3.) The novel which Roumain began in prison seems to utilize his own experiences during the years immediately preceding his incarceration.

"Le Champ du potier" is the story of three men and a movement. Pierre Martial is a young lawyer, devoted to his dying father and caught in a hopeless love for Pauline Deville. Doris Jean, black and born on a plantation owned by the Deville family, is now a Communist organizer among the Haitian masses; he is kept under surveillance by the police. Monier, a hunter attracted to the kill yet repulsed by death and

---

[21] Ibid. Roumain did not write specifically that he contracted malaria *in prison*, but the letter does create that impression. On the other hand, Langston Hughes makes a specific statement to that effect in his letter "Free Jacques Roumain," published in *Dynamo*.

dying, habitually intoxicated, is often in the marsh with his guide, Josaphat.

The narrative opens on Pierre driving up to the imposing Deville home. As he waits for Pauline, he chats with Mme Deville, her rather dull and contented mother. Mme Deville's marriage has brought her security, status, and the affection, if not the love and fidelity, of her husband. She hopes for the same for her daughter and looks on Pierre as a good possibility: "Il n'était pas riche, mais il était jeune et d'excellente famille. . . . Bruno lui trouverait une place dans un ministère." Pierre, meanwhile, reflects wryly on the irony of his situation:

> Ses phrases tombaient de ses lèvres, avec indifférence, dans le vide. Il était étrange qu'elles trouvassent un écho chez cette vieille petite dame qui tricotait infatigablement son ouvrage et une conversation où il était englué comme dans une toile d'araignée, par l'ennui. Il se mouvait avec écoeurement dans ce monde bourgeois, dans ce décor où se donnait en spectacle l'abjecte satisfaction de vivre. Tout ce qui faisait la réalité de l'homme s'y transposait sur un plan inférieur: l'espoir, une spéculation; l'amour, un marché; la souffrance des autres, une anécdote; la volonté de conquérir la vie, de la transformer, de créer de nouvelles valeurs humaines et morales: solidarité féroce de troupeau serré autour des appetits et des préjugés. Des milliers d'individus dans les caféières, les champs de canne, les cotonneries, les usines, n'avaient entre la naissance et la mort, d'autre raison d'être que de produire, dans le dénouement, l'ignorance et la servitude, l'existence de ce monde dérisoire.
>
> Ce monde n'avait que des prétextes, pas de raison de vivre. Si misérable que fussent ces prétextes, Martial ne pouvait plus ne leur opposer que le mépris. Le temps était passé où il se réfugiait dans la solitude. Ce qu'il préservait alors, c'était l'intégrité de sa pensée contre la dégradation. Il comprenait maintenant que la pensée n'est qu'action ou jeu stérile. L'ordre bourgeois ne lui semblait plus une caricature, mais un obstacle à la vie. Et il éprouvait comme une responsabilité personnelle impérative, l'obligation de participer à sa destruction.

When Bruno Deville makes his entrance (Mme Deville discreetly withdrawing), he speaks with the affected good humor of the man of authority, always in control of the conversation, making statements and allusions which carry more than superficial meaning. It is not lost on Pierre that Bruno Deville means to uphold the order of things, in which the elite governs the country like a smooth-running plantation. Deville considers Pierre's activities—his role as defense attorney for Communist agitators, his idealistic articles—just as chimeric as those of his brother, Julien, whose good-heartedness led him to neglect his class and his business interests. Julien died in poverty, he tells Pierre, with only the thanklessness of Doris to show for his efforts. When Bruno Deville broaches the subject of Pauline, Pierre rises: "Inutile d'en dire plus: j'ai compris." He leaves the house. Pauline, who has overheard some of the interview, intercepts him in tears outside. Pierre looks at her and remembers what she had once told him:

> "Tu es mon refuge, le plus doux," disait-elle. Peut-être n'étaient-ils l'un à l'autre que cela et c'était la faiblesse déchirante de leur amour. Une zone désertique le séparait de Pauline. [E]lle le rejoignait dans l'illusion de son bonheur et n'étreignait qu'un fantôme, mais lui ne pouvait se reconnaître en elle et se perdait amèrement.

Doris, alone in his apartment, is raving with malaria. His life flashes before him in disconnected scenes: his early childhood on the plantation, his service in the Deville household, school, the disdain of the mulatto boys who chased him from their play: "va-t-en domestique. Restez avec. . . . Ils le renfonçaient à coups de poing dans sa classe." Julien Deville "son seul lien avec un monde hostile." He had mourned Julien's death, then gone away to serve as stoker on a Dutch ship sailing West Indian ports. Then New York, menial jobs, despair: "Il était au centre d'une solitude d'où sa haine rayonnait sur le monde avec violence. Et un soir cet ouvrier blanc: camarade—Il leva la tête, regarda avec méfiance, le vieil ouvrier juif qui souriait." Abe was his name. Abe initiated him into a world of labor meetings, of strikes, of agitation, and of hope. Finally, Doris must flee New York to avoid deportation: Detroit, Chicago, Pittsburgh.

> Abe lui avait passé un colis de brochures. Il y trouva des bouquins aux titres étranges; des auteurs dont il n'avait jamais entendu parler: Marx, Engels, Lénine, Staline. Il les

lut pendant des mois, des nuits durant, peinant patiemment, puis dans un enthousiasme, un éblouissement, une clarté aveuglante.

More study, then Communist Party membership, and years of "dur apprentissage révolutionnaire" passed. Finally, he had returned home, and during a campaign to mobilize peasants in the countryside, had contracted malaria.

It is Sunday, an elegant crowd, turned out for the weekly concert, strolls about *Champ de Mars* square. Pierre and Doris, meeting in an obscure spot at the edge of the square, exchange news:

On vient d'arrêter quatre de nos camarades dominicains: Mario, Enrique, Antonio Lopez et sa femme.
— Mais quand? s'écria Martial. Cet après-midi même, j'étais en prison et je n'ai rien vu.

Doris gives his friend a few instructions: A telegram must be sent, collections must be made. The conversation turns to an article Pierre had given Doris to read:

— Tu vas l'envoyer à New Masses? Je l'ai lu. Pas mal. Mais tu es encore plus théologien que communiste. Tu as l'air de vouloir sauver ton âme, à l'aide du marxisme. C'est juste d'écrire comme tu le fais, que la vie est une mise en accusation, mais il faut donner à ces mots un sens humain, historique, et non pas métaphysique. — Pas fâché, j'espère?
. . .
Mais non il n'était pas fâché. Le communisme avait été pour lui avant tout une prise de conscience morale. Il se refusait avec dégoût à sa classe qui ne lui offrait que la plus basse tentation: la facilité de vivre, la satisfaction, un bonheur aveugle, indigne. Mais ce que Doris devrait savoir c'est que le communisme était devenu l'essence de sa pensée et de ses sentiments: sa raison de vivre. Si je cessais d'être communiste, ce serait un suicide intellectuel et morale; je ne serais plus qu'un cadavre vivant. . . .

Doris leaves. Pauline drives by and persuades a rather unwilling Pierre to meet her at his home. Once there, Pauline again opens her heart to him:

Ton amour a été pour moi comme une initiation à la beauté. Je croyais que vivre, c'était cette connaissance partagée, une

communion que rien ne pourrait détruire. Mais quelque chose maintenant t'arrache à moi; un monde inconnu qui me refuse. . . .
Il se taisait; maintes fois, il avait éssayé de lui expliquer. Elle ne manquait pas de générosité et son intelligence était réelle. Mais Martial s'effrayait de découvrir, combien pro-fondément, s'étaient enracinés en elle, les préjugés de sa caste.

But finally he has to give in:

Il ne se raidissait plus. Il était vaincu; sa tendresse longtemps refoulée jaillissait avec des mots dont il avait à peine con-science. . . . "Je n'ai que toi au monde. Tu es ma seule joie." Il sut cependant dans une atroce lucidité, qu'il ne faisait que différer une échéance, mais l'amour l'emportait au-delà du remords de se mentir.

Pauline, contented, goes home, while Pierre, alone in the house, "errait plein de détresse."

We are suddenly in the Haitian countryside with Monier and Josaphat, crouching amid the thorn acacia in the marshes, listening to the marsh hens and watching the wild ducks flying above:

Parfois avec un cri sinistre, des aigrettes à coups d'ailes puissants, s'enlevaient au-dessus des joncs. Elles montaient presque verticalement, d'un vol disgracieux, puis s'aban-donnant à quelque courant, flottaient comme de grands linges déchirés, une lessive immaculée. Elles se tenaient à distance du rivage, instruits du péril. Monier, pour le plaisir haineux de détruire, les abattait dès qu'elles approchaient.

Monier finally wearies of hunting. He hears drums in the distance, and Josaphat explains that there is a party at a village nearby. Monier, following his impulse, decides to go.

Ce qui l'attirait, c'était le mauvais tafia de canne, la chance d'une ouverture sexuelle, d'une brève et brutale étreinte, et à l'aube la fin pathétique de l'orgie dans le chant ronronné des coqs, quand se ralentit le rhythme du tambour comme un coeur cesse de battre, harassé; que la campagne assoupie s'était enveloppé de silence encore, et qu'avec le petit jour la vie reprend son goût de nausée.

An agreement is worked out that Monier will have the hostess.

But as he gets more and more drunk, he is side-tracked by a young peasant girl dancing gracefully with her partner. She repulses him. An old man tries to console him:

> — Ca c'est la vie. . . .
> Monier se retourna vers lui vivement:
> — Une définition? Un songe, je constate. Un peu verdi, dartreux et vermoulu comme de juste. Ces gens boivent, dansent, font l'amour. Par conséquent, c'est la vie? Peut-être, peut-être. Avoir notion de l'existence, c'est d'abord sentir. Pas sentir, surtout pas penser: dès que l'homme pense, il ment. Je pense, donc je ne *serai* pas. La douleur et le plaisir, voici les sources de la notion d'exister. Quel dommage qu'il n'y ait pas de linguistique fossile. On pourrait suivre le verbe être depuis le langage physiochimique de la masse protoplasmique de l'amibe; le bafouillage de l'Homo Pekinensis, traduisant qu'il vient de coucher avec sa femelle ou qu'il a reçu un éclat de quartz dans l'occiput, jusqu'à Descartes, jusqu'à Kierkegaarde . . . Le vieillard se tourna lentement vers Josaphat et demanda, les yeux ronds, avec un étonnement sans bornes:
> — Li fou?

Monier tries again, more aggressively, for the girl. The result is a commotion in which he makes a tipsy and arrogant spectacle of himself. The crowd of villagers, incensed, rushes in on him. He is finally rescued and rushed away by Josaphat. When Monier comes to, he discovers himself back in the marsh with his patient guide, whom he now attacks in his frustration and anger. Josaphat registers no emotion, but reaches for his knife:

> Des secondes intolérables s'écoulent, puis il entend la voix de Josaphat, plein de grave tristesse qui murmure:
> — Ah, Christian, ah desgraciado.[1] Tu as perdu ton bon ange. Sa main pend le long de son corps, viole.
> — Non, crie Monier, avec une rage désespérée, tu n'as pas le droit. Je ne veux pas! Je te frapperai encore.
> — Allez, Christian, à l'heu qu'il est, allez à la grâce de Dieu.

> [1] Malheureux [Roumain's note].

Josaphat withdraws, and Monier is left alone in the night.

Martial roams about the empty house filled with memories of his father, evidence of his life there—his piano, his books. He has just received news of his father's death. He remembers their walks alone together, his own sudden inexplicable sadnesses, his father's voice—"Ah, toi aussi." Once, Frédérick Martial had told him:

> — Vois-tu, ce qui importe, c'est la pureté—une volonté de pureté. Ne pas se soumettre, ne pas abdiquer. Jamais. Et quoi qu'il en coûte de ce que les hommes appellent le bonheur. . . . Pierre . . . étendu dans l'herbe, voyait les nuages se presser avant la nuit, comme un troupeau qui rentre du paturage. Il allait avoir quinze ans.

Frédérick Martial's attitude was the source of constant conflict with his wife; her voice had been

> une voix perçante, qui vrillait: "Existence stupide . . . l'argent . . . vos livres, votre musique, votre prétendue fièrté . . . de la vanité en réalité et de l'imbécilité. . .

Years later, she was now reproaching Pierre for his own lack of worldly success, holding up the example of André, his older brother.

André, in effect, enters in the midst of Pierre's reverie. His presence and his platitudes are like an intrusion. André, for his part, has used his position in the government to build a fortune. He is powerful, envied, and respected. Their interview becomes inevitably strained.

> — Je ne le déteste pas, pensait Pierre. Seulement tout nous sépare—le même sang et le même nom comme une étiquette pour deux matières, deux destinées si dissemblables qu'il était singulier que le mot: frère, maintînt encore entre eux une fiction sociale, des relations forcées.

As these thoughts are going through Pierre's mind, André is admonishing him, professing his affection as the older brother:

> . . . je suis soucieux de te voir prendre un chemin plus réaliste, plus conforme à ton avenir, au lieu de te livrer à de chimériques utopies qui ne te mèneront à rien; ou plutôt, si: à la pauvreté, au déclassement social et probablement à des ennuis sérieux avec le gouvernement.

But understanding is impossible between the two. After some

rather heated words, they turn to the business of settling their father's estate, which, though heavily mortgaged, André hopes to save. Pierre thinks to himself that he will return the land back to the peasants who have worked it all their lives.

Just as in the case of "Préface à la vie d'un bureaucrate," and more generally of all of the early prose, the question of autobiographical fiction imposes itself in a study of "Le Champ du potier," and it seems possible to draw the same conclusions here as earlier. The question of autobiography continues to present itself in several forms, the most obvious of which is whether personalities and relationships among characters mirror those of historical people. On this level, *La Proie et l'ombre* was able to generate a certain amount of discussion. But here, there seems to be no such room for speculation; Pierre's family configuration and his profession bear no resemblance to the author's. And Pauline, instead of being a historical figure, is simply a further projection of Roumain's need for the sustaining human contact of a truly understanding woman, a need seen in his early poetry as well as his prose, and certain metaphors (that of Pauline clinging to a *"fantôme,"* for instance) support this interpretation.

One can speak of autobiographical fiction, here as in the earlier prose, in those cases where the protagonist's thoughts and feelings reflect the author's inner life. This function, in "Le Champ du potier," falls to Pierre Martial. Some passages, when set side by side with others from Roumain's letter to Tristan Rémy, reproduced in *L'Action Nationale*, seem to be an esthetic reworking of them. This is the case particularly in the scenes where Pierre reflects upon his meaningless conversation with Mme Deville, and where Doris returns Pierre's article to him and comments upon it. Pierre's use of the word *suicide* moreover, seems to parallel almost exactly feelings Roumain is known to have voiced. He had once confided that if he ever came to doubt the validity of scientific socialism, the effect would be like suicide (Group I interviews). The considerable amount of repetition of the same ideas and attitudes in those passages where Pierre's thoughts are revealed to us would seem to be another indication of the author's own attempts to work through a problem, to crystallize a concept.

The author's inner life is also reflected, and more subtly so, in the way his characters develop. From one story to the next, the young men themselves undergo a change. The young Michel Rey and Marcel Basquet are *enfants gâtés*, taking out their despair on those who love them. They exhibit certain lingering adolescent traits. In *Les Fantoches*, these traits are in part counterbalanced by the appearance of Lefèvre and Santiague, who have managed to leave those struggles with the self behind. But Pierre Martial has matured to the point where he acts in full awareness of the consequences, not the least of which is alienation from a world for which all of his background has prepared him. The inner struggle has subsided, and we meet Martial at a point in his life when allusions to that struggle place it well in the past. Pierre's reflections on his moral development—disdainful withdrawal from a world of pretexts in order to preserve the integrity of his thinking, then the realization that "la pensée n'est qu'action ou jeu stérile"— go straight to the character of Marcel, whom Santiague accused of playing with his thoughts as with fire, who asserted to Lefèvre that a work was realized "dès que conçue." We cannot help but realize that Pierre is describing Marcel in describing his former self.

As the heroes have changed, so have the women. The dowager Mme Deville is empty and pretentious, but harmless in herself, and not ridiculous. She is perhaps even a bit pitiful. Pierre, though he finds himself in the same position of confrontation with her as Michel with Mme Ballin, as Marcel with Mlle Fattu, does not send her off in anger and confusion, but reflects instead on the inequities of the system which can have produced her. He has posed the question, as *L'Analyse schématique* exhorts, not on the level of personality but on the level of class. Even the frustrated Mme Martial, Pierre's mother, is described with a certain amount of detachment and in a style which recalls neither the *couperet* mouth and vanquished atavism of Mme Ballin, nor the fatuous Mlle Fattu (can her name also have been chosen for reasons of satire?). Pauline has acquired a certain warmth and compassion unknown to Jeanne Rey, and she lacks the trappings of emulationist thinking, the too obvious taste and wit associated with Irène, which

is to say that she too has matured. If she still cannot share
Pierre's world, he is neither bitter nor vicious toward her for
it; he is simply unhappy. It is not he but the force of
circumstances which causes Pauline to suffer.

It is significant that, just as the younger women are no
longer attacked by the protagonists (in their amorous relationships), the older women are no longer attacked *by the author*
(in his satirical descriptions). These characters have mellowed
and matured because the author has. Similarly, satire in other
contexts is less in evidence. Bruno Deville and André Martial
are too powerful to be ridiculed out of existence. Roumain's
characters continue to project his same basic preoccupations.
But their proportions have changed as Roumain's perceptions
have adjusted to the greater wisdom of his accumulating years.

If an autobiographical interpretation seems not at all trust
worthy as concerns allusions to the lives of those close to him,
it is undeniable that Roumain utilized certain elements from
his own life as plot elements in his prose. The borrowed events
are more obvious in "Le Champ du potier" than in the earlier
prose, because whereas many of the events in *La Proie et
l'ombre* and in *Les Fantoches* are typical of a class or of a
generation, those events in "Le Champ du potier" which
allude to Communist organizing are typical only of a small
group of persons in the Haiti of the 1930s, of which Jacques
Roumain was a key figure. Allusions to courts-martial of
persons accused of seditious activities (whom the protagonist,
Pierre Martial, defends), their hunger strikes, the search of
domiciles, the arrests of nationals of the Dominican Republic
and seizure of propaganda pamphlets, the telegrams sent to
comrades out of the country notifying them of arrests, all these
incidents remind one of newspaper accounts that implicate or
name Jacques Roumain as a principal participant in such
activities.

As *La Proie et l'ombre* and *Les Fantoches* show influences of
the French Decadents, as *La Montagne ensorcelée* was influenced
by Giono's *Colline,* so "Le Champ du potier" also seems to be
influenced by a literary movement, that of the proletarian
novel. In "Le Champ du potier," Doris asks Pierre if he is
sending his manuscript to *New Masses.* The pages of that

journal (published in the United States) are filled with studies of the proletarian novel as a new revolutionary genre responding to the ideals of the Marxist ethic and to the social needs of the time. In 1934, Granville Hicks wrote for *New Masses* a long series of articles on "Revolution and the Novel." Other articles appear with a certain amount of regularity through the end of 1935, when the wave begins to taper off. We know that Roumain had corresponded with editors of *New Masses* well before his stay in the United States in 1939 (Group I interviews), though it cannot be determined whether that correspondence was prior or subsequent to his imprisonment in 1934.

The fact remains that he was aware of the movement in full swing in the United States at the time he was writing "Le Champ du potier." The movement was not confined to the pages of *New Masses. Partisan Review*, another revolutionary Marxist literary journal published in the United States, also carried in the mid-thirties several critical articles on what it sometimes termed the proletarian, at other times, the revolutionary, novel. At an American writers conference held in 1935, revolutionary and proletarian literature was the topic discussed by most of the participants. There was thus in the mid-thirties a full-scale proletarian, revolutionary Communist-inspired literary movement in the United States. It seems likely that Roumain, in his links with the American Communist Party, his friendship with American socialists and liberals, and his characteristic openness to the movement of ideas in the world would have been aware of what was then regarded as a promising new literature.

In America, still in the midst of class struggle and disunity, the writer's role was to portray the dichotomized bourgeois/proletarian world as it existed. To this end, the proletarian novel was a vital concept.[22] A growing number of writers looked to proletarian literature not as propaganda but as the literary phalange of the creative, liberating humanitarian forces at work in the world. These forces were viewed within the framework of dialectical materialism. Literature, it was held,

---

[22] Edwin Seaver, "The Proletarian Novel" in *American Writers Conference*, ed. Henry Hart (New York: International Publishers, 1935), pp. 102–03.

had social (i.e., class) origins and functions. It followed that literature could be bourgeois or proletarian. But since bourgeois values had become reactionary forces, forces of the status quo, bourgeois literature represented decadent art, ingrown and unable to contribute to human progress as it had at its inception against the forces of feudalism. In the view of the Marxist critics, this decadence accounted for the dichotomy between art and life, art and politics, art and human needs.

The proletarian or revolutionary writer felt that the class struggle, which would give rise to a new social order, provided the widest basis of human experience on which to build a work of art. The far-reaching, all-inclusive experiences of the class struggle transcended in his view the personal experiences or emotion of the parasitic class, of the bourgeoisie. Therefore, against the personal orientation of bourgeois literature, proletarian literature presented the epic of the masses.[23] If the working class was the core around which the new order was to crystallize, then man's eternal search for the better life could best be portrayed through situations and characters that dealt with the working class, or more specifically, with the worker's struggle. Consequently, proletarian novels typically took place in a political context. Despite the claim that their mission was to portray the whole of modern experience, proletarian writers tended to deal with a fairly restricted set of characters and circumstances: the strike leader, the capitalist "boss," the intellectual seeking a new faith.[24] It is easy to see how these ideas lead to the rehabilitation of the concept of hero in the novel: they reintroduce epic character in the person of the

---

[23] See Joseph Freeman, "Introduction," *Proletarian Literature in the United States: An Anthology,* ed. Granville Hicks et al. (New York: International Publishers, 1935), p. 16: "It does not require much imagination to see why workers and intellectuals sympathetic to the working class—and themselves victims of the general social-economic crisis—should be more interested in unemployment, strikes, the fight against war and fascism, revolution and counter-revolution than in nightingales, the stream of the middle-class unconscious, or love in Greenwich village."

[24] Ralph Fox, *The Novel and the People* (New York: International Publishers, 1945), p. 91.

worker-organizer. In this respect such ideas fit well into the general corpus of Roumain's work.

To a large extent, the characteristics of the proletarian novel show through in "Le Champ du potier." The title itself is indicative of its theme.[25] It is a novel of the dispossessed. But the dispossessed are not only among the peasant masses who find themselves servants in Port-au-Prince households. Pierre, alienated from his own background, is also among the dispossessed. Monier, too, attempting to reintegrate himself into the African part of his heritage, is morally dispossessed. The specifically proletarian perspective of the novel shows through above all in the case of Doris Jean. Doris is a true proletarian hero. He is of the people and has come to political awareness through a combination of experience and study. Abe, who is white and Jewish, but a worker like himself, befriends him in his hour of need. The lesson is obvious: these are men who have suffered disenfranchisement each in his own way, but whose class consciousness transcends racial and religious antagonisms and frees them to work for the underlying community of interests of all workers. Doris is capable of love, but his love is generalized, and, concerned as he is with the broad sweep of history, he is impassioned by the epic nature of the events of his time: strikes, mobilization, revolution. His own individual love story, if he has one, is unimportant, and we do not see it. If we are allowed to glimpse his private, personal life, it is only insofar as it explains the man that he has become, and it is significant that the personal aspect is in the past. His slow upward climb becomes a sage of the struggle of Ordinary Man to free himself from the arbitrary restraints placed on him by the superstructure of class society.

The capitalist "boss," a standard character of proletarian fiction, is represented by men like Bruno Deville and André Martial, men who keep tight rein on the system, build an ideology to fit their privileged position, and so mean to go on

---

[25] The title alludes to the Bible, Matthew 27:6–10. The elders and rabbis buy a potter's field with the thirty pieces of silver paid to Judas and returned to them by him in remorse. There they bury strangers. The term designates generally a piece of ground adjoining a cemetery and used as a burial place for strangers and paupers.

forever in the status quo. Pierre too represents a type in proletarian literature. He is the intellectual who has found a new faith. But Pierre's story, unlike that of Doris, unfolds on two levels: he is a party organizer and has acquired a sense of man-in-society which will not let him stop short at the level of individual fulfillment. But he also has an intense personal life; his emotions and his conduct grow to a great degree out of his love involvement with Pauline and his grief at the loss of his father. Pierre is living two lives—a public and a private one—and both must be kept secret one from the other. Pierre is a proletarian hero, but in a much deeper sense, he is a continuation of a type of hero we meet over and over in Roumain's fiction. There can be no doubt that his neo-Marxist musings complement the lesson of Doris' lived experiences. But his proletarian accoutrements are as though superimposed on a sensitive, searching, and sincere nature which we already recognize in Santiague, in Lefèvre, and even in Michel Rey and Daniel. Pierre himself is a Marcel Basquet who has been saved. Monier also seems to fit into the scheme of heroes already established in Roumain's early fiction. His frantic attempts to annihilate himself by destroying everything around him suggest the final disintegration of a Marcel Basquet, but of a Marcel who, unlike Pierre, has been unable to find himself.

But if "Le Champ du potier," for all its proletarian orientation, cannot be considered as purely or completely within the genre of the proletarian novel, Roumain's Marxism is clearly revealed through it. This novel sheds light on the author's own dialectical progression and allows us to better understand the underlying proletarianism in *Gouverneurs de la rosée*.

If we look at the formal structure of "Le Champ du Potier," it is immediately apparent that the work is unfinished. As the novel stands, it is difficult to see how Christian Monier's story is connected with that of Pierre Martial or of Doris Jean. His name is never mentioned by Pierre or Doris or by any of the characters which radiate around them. One has the impression, however, that the lives of all three were to run together in some way at the end, each life lending more profound meaning to the saga of the whole. In this regard, we can only speculate . . . .

Characterization is by far the most important aspect of "Le Champ du potier," as it was in *Les Fantoches*. It is curious to note here, as in the earlier urban novel, a similar division of the hero into three characters. Pierre Martial is the major figure. His story and his sensitivities are treated at length. However, there are three men whose stories we follow, and follow from the perspective of their inner lives. Doris Jean is a man who has come to a true understanding of himself and his mission. In this he recalls the poet Santiague of *Les Fantoches*. Although both devote themselves tirelessly to their work, their self-awareness puts them in a philosophical state of motionlessness. They are no longer becoming but have completely become. Pierre acts out of idealism in much the same way as the politician Lefèvre, while Monier's destructiveness, his rage at confronting an inner emptiness, are strongly reminiscent of Marcel. Yet the characters have personalities and are surrounded by circumstances which are not at all those of *Les Fantoches*. Doris and Pierre move in a more serious and purposeful world; they do not think of themselves as puppets moved by inscrutable forces. And even Monier, bent on self-destruction, comes closer to actually succeeding, and by acts of will of which Marcel is incapable.

The political framework of "Le Champ du potier" is also, like the characters, more definite, more sure of itself. Moreover, "Le Champ du potier" is less exclusively urban than *Les Fantoches*. City and countryside, bourgeoisie, peasantry, and proletariat are more closely intertwined in the later novel, yielding far greater variety in setting and style than is found in *Les Fantoches*.

The technique of antithesis and symmetry in characterization is in plentiful evidence in "Le Champ du potier," perhaps because that technique lends itself so easily to an essential aim behind proletarian fiction: to portray the confrontation of neatly opposing interest groups. On the one hand, Pierre continues his father, while Doris is Lucien Deville's spiritual successor, and in a sense, his adoptive son. André, Pierre's brother, continues in his generation the attitude and social standing represented not by Frédérick Martial, but by Bruno Deville. Pierre is obliged to confront first Bruno then André, and both offer him the same arguments and advice.

There appears to be an antithesis—but with less mathematical precision—in the stories of Pierre and of Monier. Monier's relationship with Josaphat seems to be a negative rendering of Pierre's genuine affection for Doris. Pierre accepts Doris' guidance, while Josaphat must guide Monier through the mire while the latter resists all the way. It is also possible to see in Monier's gratuitous witticisms on man's perception of his own existence a travesty of the same philosophical quest for meaning in existence which we see in Pierre's reflections.

The style of "Le Champ du potier" is more varied than that of any of the fiction that precedes it. The same striking plasticity is in evidence in descriptions of nature as in *La Montagne ensorcelée*, and Roumain often begins chapters or scenes with the same panoramic sweep and gradual narrowing of perspective which was so effective in the peasant novel. His ability to draw characters through close attention to telltale physical particularities is here more apparent than ever. Each of the supporting characters is carefully described, physically and morally, at the time we are first introduced to him. Characters are thus thoroughly encamped and particularized. It is perhaps an important point that the same is not true for Pierre, Doris, and Christian. A few words here and there give us a hint of their physical appearance, but it is almost exclusively their inner being that we are exposed to.

Thus we experience the universe of "Le Champ du potier" through the eyes of the major characters; all that is external to them we see from without, but we never see *them* as façades. (The same may be said, in fact, for all of Roumain's heroes.) Roumain uses a straightforeward narrative prose in telling Pierre's story, a reflective style, suitable to the character. He introduces a clipped, telegraphic style in recounting Doris' life. The style (which we have seen briefly before in such poems as "Cent mètres") reflects the urgency of Doris' life, his dedication to the tasks at hand. But it also reflects the effects of his illness, as it hampers the smooth, connected flow of his thought. The author employs still another style in describing the marsh, where the slow accumulation of details eventually builds up a murky, gloomy spiritual aura. A passage describing a strange dream Monier has as he comes to himself after the party reproduces the shifting forms of dream imagery.

Motif symbolism is minimal in "Le Champ du potier," the major themes being transmitted almost entirely through characterization. Roumain does, however, return briefly to the image of light surrounded by darkness, as when at the end of their meeting, Pierre's eyes follow Doris, disappearing down the street: "Il traversa la chaussée et Pierre le vit sur le trottoir passer dans le rayon d'un réverbère: une ombre noire qui se hâtait." It is worth noting that Doris has taken leave of Pierre with the words: "Je ne peux pas mourir. C'est impossible. Tout simplement. Au revoir, Martial, il se fait tard et j'ai encore à travailler." The motif of the hero as the bright spot of light surrounded by darkness seems thus to reappear.

Jacques Roumain did not finish "Le Champ du potier" after his release from prison. Although it had probably been his intention to do so, it was not long before new avenues of exploration, probably long on his mind, absorbed his attention.

CHAPTER VI

Exile

THE SECOND EUROPEAN PERIOD: IN THE SERVICE OF MAN AGAINST THE FORCES OF GLOBAL OPPRESSION

Roumain was released from prison in June 1936 and left Haiti on August 15 of the same year with his wife and son on a cargo ship bound for Europe.[1] Aboard ship, he sent a letter of thanks to friends in New York who had worked on the Committee for the Release of Jacques Roumain. In the letter, he reveals his reasons for leaving Haiti:

> A ma libération j'ai été placé sous la plus stricte surveillance de la police. Cette vigilance paralysante dans un milieu aussi limité que le nôtre et où je ne suis que trop connu signifie: être réduit à l'impuissance. Dans l'impossibilité de me déplacer en échappant aux persécutions policières et même de visiter mes camarades—car cela les compromettait—j'ai senti que décidément la terre me brûlait sous les pas et que j'étais sous la constante menace d'une nouvelle machination du gouvernement. D'autre part, ma santé sérieusement atteinte par la malaria réclame au dire du médecin un changement de climat et des soins appropriés. C'est ainsi que je me suis vu forcé de prendre, avec l'assentiment du C.C. [Comité Central?] la decision de m'exiler momentanément d'Haïti.

He goes on to relate the increasingly dictatorial powers which the Vincent government had assumed and speaks of government-created conspiracies designed to draw attention to and discredit Communism.

With his family, Roumain went first to Belgium, where he

---

[1] Letter from Jacques Roumain dated August 16, 1936 referred to in note 20, chapter 5, above.

spent perhaps a year. He spent many hours in museums and libraries during that year and did a good deal of reading. He met archeologists, among them specialists in pre-Columbian archeology, and he began to do some serious readings in the field. Ethnography had long interested him. Jean Price-Mars had been an early influence on him, and the choice of subject in *La Montagne ensorcelée* (and its treatment) attest to such an interest, as do references to Aztec culture in some of his other writings. In September of 1937, Roumain left Brussels and took up residence in Paris.[2] The decision seems to some extent to have grown out of his desire to pursue formal training in ethnology. He did, in fact, study at the Sorbonne, the Institut de Paléontologie Humaine, and the Institut d'Ethnologie, and was an assistant to Professor Paul Rivet at the Musée del L'Homme. His interests led him to join the Société des américanistes de Paris.[3]

But other considerations as well had led Roumain to leave Brussels for Paris. His political perceptions had evolved in Haiti from Nationalism to socialism. But he had come to the socialist position for the most part through his readings in Marx and Lenin. When, in Haiti, he had attempted to put the tenets of his socialist philosophy into action, the Haitian government had promptly and effectively checked his plans by putting him and his associates in prison. In Belgium, Roumain had sought ways of acquiring a more first-hand experience of the life of a militant Communist; he had sought contact with laboring classes and trade-union organizers. But Belgium afforded little opportunity for a militant foreigner. The Belgian political climate and Roumain's status as an alien unwelcome in his own land were such that open activity would

---

[2] According to Group I interviews, Roumain left Brussels for Paris in September of 1937 or 1938. Articles by Roumain begin to appear in Parisian journals in 1937, and we can infer his presence by November of that year from repercussions following the publication of one of his articles that month. Langston Hughes puts him in Paris in December of 1937 (see Hughes, "Happy New Year," *I Wonder as I Wander* [New York: Hill and Wang, 1964]).

[3] "Notice Biographique," *Gouverneurs de la rosée* (Port-au-Prince: Collection Indigène, 1944) pp. x–xi.

have been hazardous, and the Belgian Communist party counseled against it.[4] On visits to France while residing in Belgium, Roumain had had occasion to meet antifascist journalists and had been introduced to a circle of leftist intellectuals, proponents of the cause of the Spanish Loyalists, and it seemed to him, therefore, that Paris provided a much greater range of militant activity than Brussels.

Roumain's articles, short story and poetry reflect in varying degrees his other activities and the milieu in which they unfolded, but more important for our purposes, they illustrate a militancy based on ever-widening horizons. With the exception of some of the poetry of the 1927–29 period, all of Roumain's writing shows a commitment to social or human betterment and reflects an active striving after it. However, there is an urgency in the work of the period 1936–41 which stems from Roumain's perception of impending global disaster, and his speeches and essays are less studied and rhetorical, more direct and straightforward than his work in *Le Petit Impartial* and *Haïti-Journal*. The Spanish Civil War, Hitler and fascism especially have greatly affected Roumain's humanist thought. His work takes on an international, even global, quality. Survival is no longer merely that of a nation, but of mankind.[5]

Roumain had sought out the company of writers who, like himself, viewed the continuing advances of fascism and racism

---

[4] Gaillard, in *Carl Brouard*, records without comment the following information: On October 7, 1937, the Port-au-Prince newspaper *Le Matin* "fait état de l'existence à l'étranger d'un "Parti Révolutionnaire Haïtien", appelant à renverser le président Sténio Vincent. Ce Parti, d'après le journal, a pour leaders MM Lucien Hibbert et Jacques Roumain" (p. 81). Other sources indicate that the *Matin* article has no basis in fact, that Lucien Hibbert and Jacques Roumain were not even on speaking terms at that period; their simultaneous presence in Belgium was the result of coincidence (Group I interviews).

[5] Langston Hughes was in Paris in December 1937 and has recorded his encounters with Roumain and the milieu in which he moved: "The Parisian intellectuals declared Spain was only a training ground for Hitler and Mussolini. . . . The coming war, they predicted, would be everywhere. The charming but sad Jacques Roumain said, 'I expect the world will end.' " (*I Wonder as I Wander*, p. 401).

as a threat to human civilization. This concern had prompted the calling of conferences such as the two *Congrès des écrivains pour la défense de la culture*, the second of which was held in the beseiged city of Madrid and in Valencia July 4–8, 1937 and in Paris July 16 and 17, 1937. Although ill health prevented Roumain from attending that portion of the Congress held in Spain (Group I interviews), he was present at the Paris meetings where, not having prepared a written speech, he spoke *ex tempore*. He began with reflections on the historical willingness of the Haitian people to aid in the independence struggles of other peoples. He then went on to tie in past struggles with present ones:

> It is my pride also to belong to that same people of Negro slaves who were the first, now one hundred and thirty-three years ago, to seize arms for the overthrow of the domination of their masters.
>
> Perforce, I am a Communist, an anti-Fascist. Amongst a thousand other reasons, because I am a Negro; because Fascism condemns my race to every indignity.
>
> As a writer I take my stand for the defence of culture threatened by Fascist barbarism. This means that everything impels me to consider as mine both the sufferings and the will to victory of the Spanish people who are fighting for liberty against Fascism, who are fighting for the dignity of the human race.[6]

The same concerns were mirrored in journals such as the ones on which Roumain collaborated during his second stay in Europe: *Commune, Regards, Les Volontaires*. The poem "Madrid" amply illustrates Roumain's solidarity with the ideas and goals of Paris-based liberals and radicals. "Madrid" appeared in the April 1937 issue of *Commune, Revue Littéraire Française pour la Défense de la Culture*, an anti-Fascist, socialist journal published in Paris by such notables as André Gide, Romain Rolland, and Louis Aragon, among others. The journal devoted a considerable amount of space to the cause of the Spanish Loyalists and had, in the months preceding the appearance of Roumain's poem, published articles and poetry on the beseiged

---

[6] Nancy Cunard, "Three Negro Poets," *Left Review*, October 1937, pp. 529–30. I am indebted to Professor Edward Mullen for bringing this article to my attention.

city of Madrid and on the meaning of the death of the Loyalist poet Federico García Lorca, assassinated by rebel elements. With "Madrid," Roumain's poetry truly comes of age. The poem portrays in compact, sweeping images, against the backdrop of the devastated landscape, the helplessness of the victims of the war, the inhabitants of Madrid. Striking effects are achieved at times through an ironic use of language and of metaphors not too unlike the image-reversal of Roumain's Negritude poetry:

> et dans le petit square abandonné où règne maintenant la
> paisible épouvante il y a
> mais oui il y a sur le visage sanglant de cet enfant un
> sourire
> comme une grenade écrasée à coups de talon[7]

Shapes, outlines, profiles and silhouettes come alive, become flesh-and-blood animals, wreaking destruction, like monsters advancing over the desolation of the battlefield:

> Voici avec la neige la denture cariée des montagnes
> l'essaim des balles bourdonnant sur la charogne de la terre
> et la peur au fond des entonnoirs est comme le vers dans
> une pustule crevée

The accumulation of plastic animistic horror is an effective initial statement. These hallucinatory visions preface the essential message of the poem, stated in the final stanza in less plastic, more metaphoric terms:

> C'est ici l'espace menacé du destin
> la grève où accourue de l'Atlas et du Rhin
> la vague confondue de la fraternité et du crime déferle
> sur l'espoir traqué des hommes,
> mais c'est aussi malgré les sacré-coeurs brodés sur
> l'étendard de Mahomet
> les scapulaires les reliques
> les grigris du lucre
> les fétiches du meurtre
> les totems de l'ignorance

---

[7] The poem is reprinted in Léopold Sédar Senghor, ed., *Anthologie de le nouvelle poésie nègre et malgache de langue française* (Paris: Presses Universitaires de France, 1948, second edition, 1969) pp. 112–13. Quotations are from this source.

tous les vêtements du mensonge les signes démentiels du
passé
ici que l'aube s'arrache des lambeaux de la nuit
que dans l'atroce parturition et l'humble sang anonyme
du paysan et de l'ouvrier
naît le monde où sera effacé du front des hommes la
flétrissure amère de la seule égalité du désespoir.

"Madrid" transposes the meaning of the Spanish Civil War
and the implications of the Loyalist cause into poetic terms.
War and religion merge: the series of objects from various
religious systems placed after images of war becomes like a
litany recited over the wreckage of the battlefield, in the wake
of the onslaught. The poet thus symbolizes the bankruptcy of
religion in man's struggle to reconstitute his world. Yet despite
the horror and the desolation and the bankruptcy, the poem
ends on an optimistic note: Man, in the person of the peasant
and the worker, will, through his own sacrifice, bring his own
salvation in his own world. The final lines point up the
universal importance of the seemingly local struggle and
prefigure the proletarian emphasis of the poems which follow
in the next year or two.

In the November 18, 1937, issue of *Regards*, Roumain
published an article entitled "La Tragédie haïtienne" (pp. 4–6),
which dealt with the massacre of Haitians living in the
Dominican Republic. The publication of the article put Roumain once again in the center of controversy. In October of
1937, thousands of Haitian workers residing in the Dominican
Republic had been massacred with no apparent provocation.
The Dominican government appeared implicated.[8] When news
filtered out via the American and Latin American press, the
Haitian people were horrified. The Dominican government's
behavior at first only added to the confusion. In Paris, Roumain
wrote his article based on newspaper and other accounts sent

---

[8] According to the historian Dantès Bellegarde, "La simultanéité
des scènes d'horreur, qui s'étaient produites dans plusieurs endroits
différents de la Partie de l'Est [i.e., of the island of Hispaniola, or the
Dominican Republic], montrait que les auteurs de ces crimes avaient
obéi à un mot d'ordre et ne laissait aucun doute sur la participation
qu'avaient prises certaines autorités dominicaines, civiles et mili-
taires" (Bellegarde, *Histoire du peuple haïtien*, p. 303).

to him by friends in Haiti and Mexico. But Roumain does not limit his article to the Dominican massacre. His concern with the inequities of life in Haiti under the existing social order, his anguish at the misery of the peasant masses, have not diminished in exile. He strikes out not only against Trujillo but against the duplicity of Haitian politicians who perpetuate a system in which the ordinary Haitian is forced to migrate to the Dominican Repúblic in order to sustain himself and his family.

Roumain precedes the text of his article with an excerpt from an article by Léon Laleau (minister plenipotentiary and commissary general of Haiti to the Paris Exposition, and one of Haiti's finest poets), which had appeared in the November 1937 issue of the journal *Continent*. Laleau had painted Haitian life as simple and graced with laughter. The beginning of Roumain's article is a commentary on such passages. After a sustained diatribe against those who misrepresent Haitian reality, Roumain sets the scene for the massacre: he paints the Haitian border village of Ouanaminthe in terms vaguely reminiscent of his description of the village in *La Montagne ensorcelée*, and his insistence on the barrenness of the landscape recalls the earlier article "Port-au-Prince—Cap Haïtien" and the descriptions of rural Haiti in the fiction to follow. But Roumain's objective here is to sketch the landscape and the peasants who inhabit it on either side of the border in such a way that the message he preached in Haiti during the years of Communist organizing once more surfaces: Beneath an identical poverty and barren life, the Haitian and Dominican masses are manipulated into conflict by the reigning powers on both sides of the border on the illusory basis of racial difference:

> . . . Ce qui le sépare [Ouanaminthe] du village dominicain de Dajabon, c'est un mince cours d'eau: la Rivière du Massacre, au nom atrocement prophétique. . . .
> Même paysage aride à Dajabon, même terre chauffée à blanc où l'extrême lumière vibre comme un essaim. Ce qui distingue les deux villages, c'est moins les cases, ici de torchis, et là palissadées avec les fûts du palmiste royal, que la population, nègre en Haïti et de langue française, métisse à Santo-Domingo et parlant espagnol. . . .

> . . . il est douteux . . . que la différence de race suffise à
> expliquer l'explosion de haine qui fit de la région de Dajabon-
> Montéchristi le théâtre d'une orgie sanglante. Je crois, de
> préférence, que ce peuple exacerbé par la détresse à laquelle
> l'a réduite la dictature de Trujillo, a obéi aux mêmes mobiles
> obscurs qui poussent, dans le sud des Etats-Unis, une meute
> de "poor withes" [sic] a lyncher un nègre, et en Hitlérie un
> petite [sic] bourgeois ruiné à maltraiter un Juif. Les classes
> dirigeantes et les dictatures s'entendent à entretenir, à prov-
> oquer ces sentiments qui détournent d'elles, à la manière de
> paratonnerres, la fureur des misérables. (p. 5)

Roumain stresses the sameness of the struggle against
tyranny of all oppressed peoples, whether of a remote corner
of the world—as Hispaniola must have been to most of his
audience—or of those who, like the Jews under Hitler, were
very much an immediate reality. Roumain makes some specific
charges against Trujillo: he has had all his enemies shot, has
appropriated public funds to his private bank account, has
given his family important political and governmental positions. (A seven-year-old son is an army general.) Roumain
suggests, by these accusations, an atmosphere of tension and
frustration in which the massacre of Haitians, described in
vivid terms, unfolded:

> . . . les machetes, achèvent sur les femmes, les
> enfants, les blessés, l'oeuvre des fusils
> et des armes automatiques. (p. 5)

Roumain accuses the Dominican government of responsibility,
but he goes still further and accuses Sténio Vincent, "président
d'Haïti et compère en dictature de Trujillo," of having tried to
keep word from getting out, and thus of complicity by silence,
a silence which, according to Roumain, is easily explained by
the fact that the two regimes support each other in their
tyranny. Roumain then shifts to the Haitian situation and
presents a lengthy exposé of the Vincent dictatorship and its
origins and of the political origin of the economic misery of
the peasantry.

Roumain's profile of Vincent the man is even more biting
than the barbs he has thrown at Trujillo:

> D'une paresse proverbiale, le bonhomme [Vincent], qui

possède une extraordinaire agilité verbale et souffre mani-
festement de ce qu'un conseiller financier américain a appelé,
avec une brutalité yankee, une diarrhée de paroles et une
constipation d'idées, excelle á exposer en d'éloquents dis-
cours, les vertus de l'économie dirigée. (p. 6)

Roumain accuses Vincent of selling out the Haitian peasant:
he is not allowed to migrate to Cuba and the Dominican
Republic except by special permission of the government,
whose favorites are thus able to set up a new and lucrative
slave trade; he is forced out of small industry and off his land
by large American concerns for which Vincent is an agent; he
has no recourse but to accept the twelve-hour day at low wages
working for the Americans, or to immigrate to Cuba or the
Dominican Republic, or to come down to the capital, where
he swells the ranks of the unemployed and where he is very
likely to be picked up for vagrancy and summarily put at
forced labor on public works projects, providing Vincent with
a corps of free laborers. Roumain concludes by linking the
Vincent and Trujillo governments together as a specific Caribbean variant of fascism.

Although much of what Roumain recounts is indeed a
faithful reporting of facts and events, the militant, sometimes
snide tone, and the disparaging remarks, make "La Tragédie
haïtienne" a bold article, especially so in light of Roumain's
status as an alien. Although the Haitian government came
under the greater attack, it was the Trujillo government which
reacted.

The day after the article appeared in Regards, a Dominican
diplomat demanded of the French authorities the arrest of both
Jacques Roumain and Pierre Saint-Dizier, the editor of Regards.
It was mid-April of 1938 before the French government acted,
although the reasons for the delay are not clear. Roumain and
Saint-Dizier were arrested for "outrages à un chef d'état
étranger," as provided for by the Laval Decree of October 30,
1935. Regards, which carried the report in its April 28, 1938,
issue, stated that this was to its knowledge the first time that
that law had been invoked against the French press.

In the weeks that followed, numerous workers' organizations and several liberal and socialist papers rallied to the

support of Roumain and of *Regards*.[9] The argument consistently put forth was that Roumain had only reported the truth, the same truth about the massacre which newspapers throughout the world were reporting at that time. A far greater issue, however, was that of freedom of the press, which, in the eyes of *Regards* and of many of its colleagues, was placed in serious jeopardy by the precedent-making invocation of the Laval Decree.

Roumain and Saint-Dizier were tried December 13, 1938, after several postponements.[10] The court opined that Roumain's remarks about Trujillo were "en termes violents et virulents" and quoted at length from Roumain's article, focusing upon passages which spoke directly of Trujillo and on the connection Roumain made between the motives of the poor whites in the United States against Negroes and the petty bourgeoisie in Germany against the Jews.[11] These passages, in the court's opinion, "constituent une attaque brutale, volontaire et directe contre le Président de la République Dominicaine" and therefore "une offence envers un chef d'Etat." The court did not base itself on the Laval Decree, but instead invoked an old law of July 29, 1881, against attacks on the honor and "délicatesse de la personne publique" of a person in public office. Roumain's words, the court opined, were designed to ridicule Trujillo and his acts. Roumain and Saint-Dizier based their defense on the right of the journalist to criticize public figures. But the court felt that Roumain's facts were amplified and denatured and found both men guilty of public offense against a chief of state. The 1881 law stipulated imprisonment of three

---

[9] "L'Ecrivain haïtien Jacques Roumain poursuivi . . . ," *Regards*, April 21, 1938, p. 4; "Regards sur le monde—Nous sommes poursuivis," *Regards*, April 28, 1938, p. 2; "Les Travailleurs aux côtés de 'Regards' poursuivi," *Regards*, May 19, 1938, p. 10; "Ce que nous pensons des poursuites intentés à Regards," *Regards*, June 16, 1938, p. 8. See also May 1938 issues of *Ce Soir, Messidor, Le Canard Enchaîné, L'Humanité*, and *La Lumière*.

[10] Postponements of July 11 and December 5, 1938. *Greffe Correctionnelle, XIIe Chambre*, Palais de Justice, Paris, France.

[11] The court must have been quoting from memory. The text of the records at the *Greffe Correctionnelle* does not exactly coincide with that of Roumain's article.

months to one year and a fine of from 100 to 3,000 francs. The court felt it could be lenient, as it was a first offense for both men, and suspended the prison sentence but ordered both men to pay a fine of 300 francs. Roumain and Saint-Dizier appealed the decision, and the case was sent to the Court of Appeals on January 18, 1939.[12]

In the midst of all the controversy about the trial and freedom of the press, *Regards* published a piece of writing by Roumain of a quite different nature. A short story appearing in August of 1938, though it did not provoke the reaction of his earlier article, is of far greater importance for the study of Roumain's fiction. The story, like the article, dealt with the Haitian peasant, and was entitled "Gouverneurs de la rosée."[13]

It has been said that the idea which was to blossom into the novel *Gouverneurs de la rosée* had begun to develop in Roumain's mind as early as his first year in exile, in Brussels (Group I interviews). The term "gouverneurs de la rosée" is already present in the November 1937 article "La Tragédie haïtienne," a work which must have been done toward the end of Roumain's stay in Belgium or during the first month or so in Paris:

> Mais la terre ne nourrit plus ces paysans noirs, travailleurs acharnés dont il suffirait de citer le titre magnifique qu'ils se décernent à eux-mêmes: *gouverneurs de la rosée*, pour définir leur dénouement et l'orgueil qu'ils éprouvent de leur destin. ("La Tragédie haïtienne," p. 6; italics in text)

We can, on this evidence, almost see beginning to crystallize in Roumain's mind the universe of the Haitian peasant and its profound human meaning, a meaning which Roumain was seeking to express creatively. The short story affords us a more

---

[12] Records at the *Greffe Correctionnelle, XIIe Chambre*, Palais de Justice, Paris, France. The *Greffe de la Cour d'Appel* had no record of the appeal and informed me that they destroy their records after thirty years.

[13] "Gouverneurs de la rosée," *Regards*, August 25, 1938, pp. 9–10. I have seen no references to this short story in any of the writing by or about Jacques Roumain which has come to my attention, nor has it been mentioned by any of the persons interviewed. Perhaps Roumain did not speak of it, in order not to take attention away from the novel of the same name.

striking and sharply defined picture of that universe than could the simple reference in the article. It is obvious that Roumain, in writing the story, was reaching for a philosophical statement which he later fully realized in the novel of the same name. However, the short story echoes certain concerns of the article published the preceding year, notably the dispossession of the Haitian peasant of his land by the large American business concerns. The same issue had been treated to some extent in "Le Champ du potier," written just prior to exile.

"Gouverneurs de la rosée," though much of the time possessing the poetry of the novel, has its own, entirely different, setting, plot and cast of characters. Jean-Gille Duplessy has for two years been a *caco* leader, engaged in struggle against the American Occupation. As the story opens, he is seated on an elevation, waiting for his men to assemble. It is daybreak. His friend Mirville joins him, and the two men wait in silence. Jean-Gille contemplates the countryside and allows his thoughts to flow. When all are assembled, Jean-Gille gives the order and they all march off, presumably to engage the U.S. Marines in still another skirmish. Although the words "Marines," *caco*, and "Occupation" are never mentioned, it is clearly that historical moment which Roumain uses as his setting and as catalyst for the scant action which take place. The *caco* in this fictional work is no longer the larger-than-life hero which Roumain had made of Charlemagne Péralte in the youthful Nationalist ardor of his articles in *Le Petit Impartial*. Roumain's portrayal of Jean-Gille Duplessy is much more complex. Jean-Gille is not a device for the evocation of Haitian national consciousness. He is much more valid, though fictional, than the real-life heroes of Roumain's early work.

The validity of the characters is still slightly flawed, however. Roumain appears at pains to describe the people and their customs, so much so that we suspect he is consciously speaking to an audience which knows little or nothing of the culture or the region about which they are reading.[14] Thus,

---

[14] Roumain's two contributions to *Regards* are quite different from the usual offerings in that journal. There are occasional references to Black American entertainers, and two short stories by Langston Hughes appear in French translation. However, the primary concern

the anthropological dimension and the problems it creates for imaginative literature appear here once again, as they did in *La Montagne ensorcelée*. Yet even though a passage may start out focusing on visible details, the emphasis ultimately shifts, fixing attention not so much on the outer description as on how that outer crust mirrors an inner, spiritual reality:

> Deux "habitants," Mirville et Jean-Gille, rien que des nègres-des-bois, comme les appellent avec dédain les gens de la ville. Ils portent de vastes chapeaux de paille, la vareuse de toile bleue, ils sont nu-pieds, et parlent un créole chantant où les mots sont comme le fruit qui fait ployer la branche, mais c'est surtout à leurs mains qu'on reconnaît le paysan, à cette peau crevassée et rêche où se noue un réseau de veines gonflées comme affleurent de sous le sol de gros paquets de racines; la couleur en est plus noire que la face parce que la terre s'est mêlée à la chair, et on dirait même, au sang. (p. 9)

This shift in point of view, from exterior to interior of the character, with its attendant alternation between objective description and the oral style of the story teller, already successfully developed in *La Montagne ensorcelée*, becomes even more poetic in "Gouverneurs de la rosée." Throughout, Roumain puts across his philosophical message by allowing us slowly to perceive the human condition of his people, their despair and struggle, their inner life. The story is skilfully constructed in such a way that we find ourselves placed immediately and abruptly in the middle of the scene, and then, slowly, from one sentence to the next, we absorb the atmosphere, become aware of the circumstances of the characters and the conflict in which they are locked. As in *La Montagne ensorcelée*, the shift in point of view from objective to subjective is often associated with the man-in-nature motif. Jean-Gille, with Mirville at his side, silently surveys the scene below:

> Maintenant, on distingue mieux le pays où la route qui s'enfonce dans une courbe boisée reparaît plus loin tendant

---

of *Regards* was the antifascist struggle and the Spanish Civil War. Those feature articles which occasionally appear about non-Europeans tend toward exoticism and a sense of cultural difference.

à bout de bras une poignée de palmiers, et le travail de la
rivière au fond de la barranque, son travail patient qui
entraîne dans les eaux sombres la terre rouge du morne, et
. . . mais Jean-Gille a dit: "Regarde la fumée," et c'est vrai,
la fumée monte d'une case et ça, c'est la paix: tu imagines
la femme accroupie devant le feu, faisant cuire la cassave, et
les enfants autour, et c'est le moment où l'homme prend sa
machete et dit: "Adieu, femme à moué," et il part à son
travail.

Jean-Gille et Mirville savent que plus loin, derrière la
montagne, il y a une autre fumée, mais ça, c'est la guerre et
la femme n'est pas à préparer le manger, elle est couchée, le
ventre ouvert comme un gros fruit pourri; quant aux enfants:
"Seigneur, paix à ma bouche," et l'homme, et bien! l'homme
est ici avec sa rage et son fusil. (p. 9; ellipses in text)

Roumain's style achieves here an intensity which reveals
at once the circumstances and the conflict of the story, and the
heroism and sense of destiny of the men living it. The style
allows us to perceive, moreover, that Jean-Gille's personal loss
is part of the common lot. His misery shares and understands,
responds to that of his fellows. There is a sympathy between
man and man which is borne on the man-in-nature motif. The
Haitian peasant is somehow in harmony with his surround-
ings, no matter how vast, and a cosmic understanding circulates from one being to the other, no matter how separated by
geographical distance. Jean-Gille becomes repository and con-
duit of the common misery, hope and destiny, as he continues
to contemplate the countryside below. Somewhere, women are
washing clothes beside a stream:

Là-bas, cette coulée crayeuse, c'est le lit à peu près desséché
d'un torrent—la "galette" nous disons nous-mêmes—les
lessiveuses battent le linge, . . . L'indigo et la mousse de
savon font les flaques à l'image du ciel. Les battoirs s'abattent,
claquent, et quand les femmes s'interrompent pour frotter,
la tête inclinée de biais sur l'épaule, elles chantent une
mélopée, comme ça, du fond d'elles-mêmes, sans paroles:
c'est inutile: tu comprends que ça veut dire la tristesse de
s'user à travailler sans profit du lever au coucher du jour, et
cette robe a été reprisée cent fois et je ne peux en acheter une
autre, et mon garçon à moi qui est malade et le docteur
demande cinquante piastres pour le traiter, . . . alors la
chanson, c'est pour oublier la grande peine des bras, ou si

tu veux pour essayer de l'endormir comme un enfant récal-
citrant.

Dans l'accalmie, le silence reprend son pouvoir, il coule
frais: un énorme soupir qui couvre le bavardage de l'eau
dans les pierres, le chant désolé, le jacassement des vieilles
femmes desséchées et flétries, alignées comme des feuilles
de tabac au soleil, et lorsque les battoirs retombent et
retentissent, le silence s'élève et plane comme un oiseau
effarouché. (p. 9)

The plasticity of the author's images describes the scene from
without, but gradually the language becomes the inner voice
of the woman herself, and it is as though Jean-Gille, observing
her gestures, hears her misery and understands and sympathizes with it, just as he understands and sympathizes with
nature. Things follow a predictable, understandable and essential order:

> Tout est si calme, si simple. Jean-Gille le connaît bien ce
> paysage où chaque chose est à sa place pour un rôle tracé par
> le travail et la misère, la vie et la mort. (p. 9)

Jean-Gille is the first truly heroic figure in Roumain's
fiction. The young bourgeois intellectuals of *La Proie et l'ombre*
accept defeat before they begin to fight. Those of *Les Fantoches*
have, at least in some cases, the moral courage to act, but their
actions are futile, like the gestures of puppets. Pierre, of "Le
Champ du potier," is commited and courageous enough to act
in accordance with his principles. He is an activist. But he is
also a dreamer, not a visionary, and too given to intellectual-
izing and too involved in his personal sorrows to be completely
effective. Doris Jean's commitment to the struggle for human
betterment is largely the result of conversion to a specific
dogma, and the portrayal of this conversion does not rise
above the prescribed formula for the Marxist novel. Moreover,
Doris' life is lacking an essential human dimension; he has no
intimate relationship, nor any need for fulfillment on a personal
level. On the other hand, Jean-Gille's wisdom, his commitment
to struggle arise not from intellectual musings nor from any
doctrine, but from the authenticity of his lived experience and

from an intuitive understanding of misery, struggle and destiny:

> Oui, on avait aussi sa part de chagrin et sa part de douleur et son compte de tracas et beaucoup de bouleversements, mais c'était la destinée, on ne se résignait pas; la vie, on la prenait à bras le corps et on se gourmait avec elle, en homme tout de bon, les dents serrées. (p. 9)

But Jean-Gille's heroism is marred because of the hate he feels welling up within him at the thought of the Americans. To continue the passage just quoted:

> Puis ils étaient arrivés ces blancs américains, soi-disant pour te civiliser et pour ça il leur faut prendre la terre, et toi, sale nègre, tu feras la corvee toute la sainte journée, payé à coups de pied et de nerf de boeuf.
>   Sa face se couvrit d'un orage de haine.
>   — Ah! ces blancs 'méricains, murmure-t-il du dedans de sa gorge; on eût dit qu'il étouffait. (p. 9)

The image of the hero is somewhat dissipated too by the sense of defeat which hangs over everything. Jean-Gille himself is described as "encore épais, . . . noueux et dru malgré l'âge, mais il y avait dans ses épaules quelque chose d'un ressort détendu" (p. 10). It is not just the Americans that one has to struggle against. Life was no idyll before their coming; it has always been hard. But it has been theirs to grapple with according to their own lights. Jean-Gille is caught up in the eternal dilemma of the hero: the tension between implacable destiny and human volition, between man in harmony with the natural cosmic order and in a conflict with it which he does not want and cannot bring to an end. His thoughts keep coming back to this essential cosmic conflict:

> . . . ce qu'il voulait expliquer, c'était que: tuer, être tué peut-être, c'était naturel, c'était la guerre, mais la guerre est une catastrophe, une tempête, ça vous arrachait à la terre comme un arbre par les racines: on laisse après soi une plaie béante: c'était un accident en dehors de la vie véritable qui était d'être planté au milieu de son champ, de son jardin de vivres, d'être reglé sur le soleil et la nuit, la pluie et la sécheresse. Forcément, quand cela vous est enlevé, c'est la rage, on se défend, pas vrai, on n'est pas bon marché, on a

son poids de courage, sa valeur d'homme et la mort pour
t'acheter doit y mettre le prix sans marchandage—mais tout
ça, c'est le désespoir, c'est pas la vie et alors, qu'est-ce que
tu veux, on regrette et on se ronge. (p. 10)

It is in their understanding that they must grapple with
life according to their own lights, in their talent for making
life come alive by an act of will, that the Haitian peasants of
Roumain's fiction become noble and heroic. The key to the
meaning of destiny and volition is contained in the story's
title, an expression, Roumain tells us, which the Haitian uses
to describe himself. The expression appears twice in the course
of the story and both times seems to be an articulation of man's
right to determine his own destiny in conformity with his
traditional, agrarian, way of life, a life ordered by traditional
values and by the familiar phenomena of cosmic nature. The
expression thus appears in conjunction with the man-in-nature
motif so noticeable in Roumain's work:

> . . . de bons habitants, travailleurs de la terre, nègres sérieux,
> gouverneurs de la rosée, des mille et des mille, saisis par la
> mort face à l'ennemi, ou bien arrêtés aux champs, tourmentés
> et torturés, fusillés, brûlés vifs, pendus. . . . (p. 10)

These men are sidetracked from their natural function of
governing the dew and must now reinterpret their destiny as
a struggle for the right of self-determination against American
imperialism. The struggle has ravaged their world and jarred
their lives out of harmony, has caused a detour in the natural
bent of their will:

> Une trentaine de paysans, par groupes, apparurent. Machetes
> croisées en bandoulière sur la poitrine, vareuses bleues en
> haillons, foulards rouges autour du cou; certains n'avaient
> pas de fusil. Nègres des bois, gouverneurs de la rosée,
> *dépossédés de leur destin,* tous pareillement dans la griffe du
> malheur et chacun a son histoire, différente et semblable, de
> sang, de violence et de mort. (p. 10; italics added)

The Haitian peasant is, above all, a cultivator. As such, he
knows the value of water in the cultivating of his fields, in the
bringing forth of life. Who is master of the dew is cultivator
of life, can coax life into being. Jean-Gille thinks back to those

days of peace and harmony, and we can feel, through the poetry of Roumain's words, how all of nature responds, a vast symphony:

> —Je songe, je songe quand je me réveillais à la nuit noire pour aller arroser. Je rencontrais mon voisin Aristide: "Voisin, je lui disais comme ça, tu as fini d'arroser?" (Je lui demandais parce que l'eau, c'est la bénédiction de tous), et il me disait: "Oui, voisin"; alors, je faisais: "Adieu oui, voisin," et il répondait de même, voisin Aristide. J'ouvrais le canal et l'eau se mettait à courir devant moi comme un bon chien, et moi je la suivais et elle m'emmenait dans ma terre et tu sentais que la terre était contente: son odeur montait comme un merci, comme une louange. (p. 10)

In the short story, except in this passage, the expression *gouverneurs de la rosée* does not emphasize the meaning of water in the life of the cultivator. The emphasis, rather, is on the first element of the term, on the word *gouverneurs*. Water will become the major element in the complex symbolism of the novel to follow. And what is here only a parenthetical remark—"l'eau, c'est la bénédiction de tous"—will become an essential lesson in the novel, the learning of which becomes crucial to the realization of harmony. The above-quoted passage, in which Jean-Gille recounts his dream, encapsulates the whole meaning of the title, and is the nuclear idea developed at length in the novel, for Jean-Gille's dream is one of man at harmony—with himself, with his neighbor and with nature.

But in the short story, Roumain explores primarily the tension between the natural role of the Haitian peasant, as master of the dew, and the unnatural one—which Jean-Gille recognizes as such—of *caco* guerrilla. The tension gives way in the end, the role of *caco* prevails over that of cultivator, and the defeat in the air overwhelms the heroic gesture of the *caco* band. The story ends on an equivocal note, for Jean-Gille and his men contribute to make the gesture:

> — Parés? leur crie Jean-Gille.
> — Oui.
> — Alôsse, en avant.
>   Jean-Gille, lui, ferme la marche. Il conduit comme un berger, par les défilés de la montagne, la petite troupe de paysans vaincus. (p. 10)

In addition to the time spent writing poetic fiction, committed poetry and militant journalism, Roumain also engaged to some extent in scholarly writing during his exile in Europe. In pre-World War II Paris, academic efforts were also under way to explore the problem of relationships among peoples in the modern world. A collection of articles entitled *L'Homme de couleur* appeared in Paris in 1939.[15] The dual question to which the essays addressed themselves is posed in a preface: "Comment s'éstablissent aujourd'hui les relations entre Blancs et Hommes de couleur? Dans quel sens doit-on souhaiter de les voir se développer?" The list of contributors, both white and black, was considerable. Among them was Jacques Roumain, whose article, "Griefs de l'homme noir," set out to demonstrate that

> des prétextes pseudo-scientifiques, historiques et . . . bibliques servent aux Etats-Unis, et plus spécialement dans le sud, de paravent et de disculpation à la mise en action du préjugé de couleur. . . . nous verrons encore que les slogans sur la protection de la femme blanche, l'irrémédiable infériorité de la race noire, la mission de l'homme blanc . . . dissimulent un égoïsme de classe rapace et sans scrupple; et enfin que le préjugé de race manié à la fois comme un instrument de division, de diversion et de dérivation, permet l'asservissement de larges couches de la population blanche des Etats-Unis. (pp. 98–99)

The study is unusual among Roumain's published work in its heavy use of statistical data, and in that Roumain cannot have experienced, first-hand or through field research, the material which he treats. He brings the whole notion of race under scrutiny, citing studies of prehistoric man to demonstrate that racial admixture was an accomplished fact as far back as the Stone Age. The notion of pure race is therefore unscientific, and the notion of a French race, of a German race, and so on is a metaphor. Of course, it is true that physical attributes vary from one race to another. Roumain makes liberal use of sarcasm to counter the argument often advanced on the basis of such differences that racial mixing leads to degenerate offspring:

---

[15] S. E. le Cardinal Verdier et al., *L'Homme de couleur* (Paris: Librairie Plon, 1939).

> Il est, ma foi, possible que l'observation—entre dix-sept caractères—d'un talon généralement proéminent chez l'embryon nègre, alors qu'il l'est avec une extrême rareté chez le foetus blanc, fasse du quarteron Pouchkine un être particulièrement bestial. . . . (p. 103)

Roumain cites figures charting the accumulation of wealth, the proliferation of institutions, the number of physicians and professors among blacks in America, pointing out the adverse conditions under which these acquisitions were made. The contention that the white woman must be protected against the rapist desires of the black man, an argument traditionally used to justify racist brutality on the model of the Ku Klux Klan, is, in Roumain's view, the most treacherous of all arguments:

> Pour notre part, nous nous refusons de faire l'injure à la femme américaine d'admettre qu'il faille à la sauvegarde de sa vertu, la contrainte légale et les fureurs du lynchage. Contre un être aussi abominable dans l'ordre biologique et moral, que le nègre, une répulsion toute naturelle devrait suffire à brandir devant les paradis interdits le glaive flamboyant de la pudeur. . . . Mais l'existence même de . . . millions de métis prouve suffisamment qu'il n'a jamais été question d'une . . . "protection de la femme noire." . . . (pp. 109–10)

That the Southern white man can have a black mammy and a black mistress (and black children by her), yet become irate at the prospect of eating in the same restaurant or riding in the same railroad car with blacks, must be due to reasons other than natural aversion. Roumain finds these reasons in the psychological strategems of the ruling class, who keep blacks in their place by fear, and poor whites too in their place by persuading them of their racial superiority. In this scheme of things,

> Le lynchage fait une utile diversion et joue le rôle de paratonnerre quand l'atmosphère est surnaturée de l'électricité des antagonismes sociaux. (p. 111)

The same situation holds true in the North, where white labor unions had until recently barred all black workers:

> Il est impossible de voir dans le préjugé de couleur autre chose qu'une expression idéologique de l'antagonisme des

classes, celui-ci reflétant à son tour les contradictions du système de production. (p. 112)

Thus Roumain's analysis results, not surprisingly, in the same Marxist interpretation as that found in *L'Analyse schématique*. The study ends with what may be termed a prose version of the theme of "Bois d'ébène," "Sales nègres," and "Nouveau sermon nègre," the famous revolutionary poems which Roumain wrote also during this period:

> . . . un jeune héros comme Angelo Herndon, symbolise le nègre nouveau, résolu, conscient de sa jeune force et qui a lié dans la fraternité du combat son destin à celui de l'ouvrier blanc. . . . personnellement je salue la noblesse et la grandeur de la tâche entreprise par des hommes de bonne volonté, hier frères ennemis, aujourd'hui réconciliés sur les ruines des préjugés, pour une nouvelle Abolition de l'Esclavage et la reconstruction du monde. (p. 113)

In these ending lines, as in the three revolutionary poems, the past sufferings of the black man provide the springboard for the revolution which will release all oppressed men everywhere from bondage. The black collectivity becomes the epic hero who will lead mankind beyond his present state, beyond himself as he now exists.

The poems "Bois d'ébène," "Sales nègres," and "Nouveau sermon nègre" were written sometime in 1938–39. ("Bois d'ébène" is dated Brussels, June 1939).[16] It has been stated that the poems "Bois d'ébène," "Sales nègres" and perhaps also "Nouveau sermon nègre" were published in European periodicals during the time that Roumain was in Brussels and Paris.[17] The three poems have been included in the posthumous collection *Bois d'ébène*. However, the first eighteen lines of the poem "Bois d'ébène"—the "Prélude"—were erroneously in-

---

[16] According to Group I interviews, Roumain did not return to Belgium to live once he had moved to Paris. He would, according to the same testimony, have been living in Paris in 1939. It is not clear under what circumstances he was in Belgium in June 1939, but it is quite possible he may have been on a visit.

[17] Group I interviews. I have not, however, been able to identify the journals in which these poems would have appeared.

serted in the poem at the time the collection was prepared for publication, as was the poem "L'Amour la mort." Both belong to a later period (Group I interviews.) "Prélude" and "L'Amour la mort" do, in effect, reflect a vastly different tone and spirit than the other poems in the collection. It is immediately apparent that the remaining three poems are uniformly militant and revolutionary. Peasants and workers, the oppressed masses, the vanguard of the revolution feature prominently in "Bois d'ébène," "Sales nègres" and "Nouveau sermon nègre." It is the peasants and workers who link these three poems to "Madrid," written somewhat earlier, although in "Madrid" they appear only briefly, at the end.

The alternation in this poetry between strongly racial themes and the common revolutionary cause of all oppressed peoples is viewed by some critics as contradictory, reflecting perhaps conflicting impulses on the part of the poet. For example, G. R. Coulthard states:

> All these writers [of Negritude] revel in being primitive, iconoclastic, in being black, anti-Christian, anti-white, although some are careful to point out that the are not racialist except in the context of a "white" civilization which rejects them. For example . . . Jacques Roumain in Bois d'ébène after a furious embittered rhapsody on the sufferings of the Negro, stops himself short with a "POURTANT" [in the poem "Bois d'ébène"] in capital letters. . . .
> The tone of impassioned vituperation against "white" civilization and its values is, however, prevalent.[18]

Coulthard says of "Sales nères" that it "sputters out a furious invective only capable of expression in argot crudities" (p. 82). Yet Coulthard sees in "Bois d'ébène" Roumain's belief that black revolt was "part of a great world-wide proletarian uprising," and that he had to remind himself that his attacks against the white world were actually against the white capitalist world (p. 84). Sartre's famous essay "L'Orphée noir" cites "Bois d'ébène" as evidence not of contradictory currents among

---

[18] George Robert Coulthard, *Race and Colour in Caribbean Literature* (London—New York—Toronto: Oxford University Press, 1962), pp. 65–66.

Negritude writers but of a dialectical progression, a widening of consciousness:

> . . . la notion subjective, existentielle, ethnique de *négritude* "passe," comme dit Hegel, dans celle—objective, positive, exacte—de *prolétariat*. . . . la Négritude apparaît comme le temps faible de'une progression dialectique: l'affirmation théorique et pratique de la suprématie du blanc est la thèse; la position de la Négritude comme valeur antithétique est le moment de la négativité. Mais ce moment négatif n'a pas de suffisance par lui-même et les noirs qui en usent le savent fort bien: ils savent qu'il vise à préparer la synthèse ou réalisation de l'humain dans une société sans races. . . . un poème de Jacques Roumain, [i.e., "Bois d'ébène"] communiste noir, . . . fournit sur cette nouvelle ambiguité le plus émouvant témoignage. . . .[19]

The militancy of these poems recalls the Nationalist poems, such as "Appel," and the frequent references to the black race recall the Negritude poetry: "Sur le chemin de Guinée," "Quand bat le tam-tam," and "Langston Hughes." But these Negritude poems are more a nostalgic identification with Africa and the African heritage of Haiti; they contain none of the calls for justice nor the show of confraternity with other races of the later poems, which go visibly beyond Nationalist and Negritude themes. Written in a cosmopolitan milieu, in an atmosphere of global struggle, they form part of a far-flung Euro-American movement. Revolutionary poetry had become a genre with rather well defined themes; those themes must of necessity be portrayed against a global background. Roumain's poetry occupies a special place in this scheme of things, for it is, in the European tradition, representative of the times, and, in the Haitian tradition, stands at the beginning of an era. While Roumain was in Europe writing revolutionary poetry, poets of Haiti were coming to a full and clear statement of Africanism. Haiti, on the other side of the Atlantic, was simply not living in the same daily crisis as was Europe. A short while later, in the 1940s, a type of poetry which could be called revolutionary would be written in Haiti. In the section

---

[19] J.-P. Sartre,, "L'Orphée noir," in Senghor, *Anthologie* . . ., pp. xl–xli.

of his work significantly entitled "Sous le Signe de la Solidarité Humaine," Professor Gouraige writes:

> Le *Langston Hughes* de René Piquion[20] élargissait en 1940 un horizon que les poèmes de Jacques Roumain avait fait entrevoir. "L'armée innombrable des opprimés, écrit Hughes, n'est pas seulement comprosée de Noirs, mais aussi d'hommes au visage blanc, jaune, brun; qu'en définitive ils ont tous les intérêts identiques; que leur libération résultera de leur union, de leur esprit de solidarité." Le poème *Sales Nègres* de Jacques Roumain n'a pas une autre signification. (Gouraige, *Histoire de la Littérature Haïtienne*, p. 384)

Another Haitian scholar, Roger Gaillard, has reflected:

> Je pense qu'il y a en Haïti une tradition de poésie patriotique et indépendentiste, mais il n'y a pas eu de poésie révolutionnaire . . . parce que la seule révolution que nous ayons eu, c'est 1804, et cette révolution a eu un caractère national . . . La poésie révolutionnaire est une poésie qui veut secouer l'ordre étabi . . . Dans le cas de Jacques Roumain, il faut bien voir que l'essor de la poésie révolutionnaire . . . a coïncidé avec la Deuxième Guerre Mondial, c'est-à-dire, entre la période de Franco, la Guerre d'Espagne et Stalingrad. (Group II interviews)

The experience of the black man vis à vis the white provides from a Neo-Marxist point of view an unusually rich example of the dialectial pull toward violent overthrow of the existing order. Although Roumain's three revolutionary poems are conceived against a backdrop of global revolution, it is significant that all three titles refer specifically to the black race, and more specifically still, to the exploitation of that race by the existing order. "Nouveau sermon nègre" points to the role of the church in brainwashing the black man into servility. "Sales nègres" examines a term which has been used as an epithet to reinforce the black man psychologically in his lowly station in the order of things. "Bois d'ébène" refers metaphorically to the mass transport of black men across the seas

---

[20] René Piquion, *Un Chant nouveau* (Port-au-Prince: Imprimerie de l'Etat, 1940). Piquion studies Hughes from the perspective of his commitment in the cause of black liberation.

like so many logs to be put to use in the construction of the New World. The titles alone make it clear that an epic role is assigned to the black race.

Image reversal, a technique of Negritude poetry, is clearly present in "Nouveau sermon nègre," where Christ's misery and Passion and the black experience merge:

Ils ont craché à Sa Face leur mépris glacé
Comme un drapeau noir flotte au vent battu par la neige
Pour faire de lui le pauvre nègre le dieu des puissants

. . . .

De son doux chant de misère
De sa plainte tremblante de banjo
Le tumulte orgueilleux de l'orgue
De ses bras qui halaient les lourds chalands
Sur le fleuve Jourdain
L'arme de ceux qui frappent par l'épée
De son corps épuisé comme le nôtre dans les plantations de
    coton

. . . .

Le bouclier d'or de leur fortune
Ils ont blanchi Sa Face noire sous le crachat de leur
mépris glacé

. . . .

Roumain attacked the church whenever he saw it prostituting its spiritual vocation; but he admired the humanitarianism and the spiritual strength of the historical Jesus. The poem reveals both his rage at the Christian institution and his admiration of the man Jesus. While images are iconoclastic, they also portray the basic sameness of Christ's sufferings and those of the black race; the image reversal in this poem thus rehabilitates the meaning of Christ, prostituted by the conspiracy of church and Western society. The true Christ is the Christ of the oppressed, not of the oppressor. More than a symbol of suffering, the black man becomes the sacrificial victim. His experience illuminates the meaning of Christ's mission. The metamorphosis of Christ into a hollow symbol, a tool of the capitalists, is expressed through images of his mutation from black to white, and the white is impure (Ils ont craché . . . Ils ont blanchi). It is that point that a new redeemer of men emerges, the proletarian vanguard, and the images surrounding him suggest that he is black:

Ils ont lynché John qui organisait le syndicat
Ils l'ont chassé comme un loup hagard avec des chiens
à travers bois
Ils l'ont pendu en riant au tronc du vieux sycomore
Non, frères, camarades
Nous ne prierons plus

. . . .
Nous ne chanterons plus les tristes spirituels désespérés

Un autre chant jaillit de nos gorges
nous déployons nos rouges drapeaux

. . . .
Debout les damnés de la terre
Debout les forçats de la faim

"Sales nègres," on the other hand, proclaims from its opening lines the revolt of the black man from his white slave masters:

eh bien voilà:
nous autres
les nègres
les niggers
les sales nègres
nous n'acceptons plus
c'est simple
fini
d'être en Afrique
en Amérique
vos nègres
vos niggers
vos sales nègres

The abuses hurled out at all that the white man has taught the black to hold sacred fit into the tradition of image reversal also. Such reversals are cathartic; they clear the air for the building of new, black values:

Surprise
jésusmariejoseph
suprise
quand nous attraperons
en riant effroyablement
le missionnaire par la barbe
pour lui apprendre à notre tour

à coups de pieds au cul
. . . .
que nous nous foutons
d'un Dieu qui
s'il est le Père
eh bien alors c'est que nous autres
. . . .
faut croire que nous ne sommes que ses bâtards

Toward the middle of the poem, the images of black revolt suddenly acquire a new dimension:

trop tard
car nous aurons surgi
des cavernes de voleurs des mines d'or du Congo
et du Sud-Afrique
trop tard il sera trop tard
pour empêcher dans les cotonneries de Louisiane
dans les Centrales sucrières des Antilles
la récolte de vengeance
des nègres
des niggers
des sales nègres
il sera trop tard je vous dis
car jusqu'aux tam-tams auront appris le langage
de l'Internationale
car nous aurons choisi notre jour
le jour des sales nègres
des sales indiens
des sales hindous
des sales indo-chinois
des sales arabes
des sales malais
des sales juifs
des sales prolétaires
et nous voici debout
Tous les damnés de la terre
. . . .
pour en finir
une
   fois
      pour
         toutes
avec ce monde
de nègres
de niggers
de sales nègres

It now becomes apparent for the first time in the poem that the *"sales nègres"* are not only black men but all oppressed peoples. The black experience has widened into a symbol; the epithet flung traditionally at the black man has been enlarged to include all exploited peoples, and the *sales nègres* of the last line clearly refer to all the races and classes enumerated in the lines preceding. The poem may have begun as an expression of Negritude, but has shifted to a statement of global revolution.

"Bois d'ébène" exhibits the same shift. The poet begins by painting images of the black man throughout history in every servile situation, from the slave labor which built the pyramids to the sweat shops and factories of the modern industrial world:

Nègre colporteur de révolte
tu connais tous les chemins du monde
depuis que tu fus vendu en Guinée
une lumière chavirée t'appelle
une pirogue livide
échouée dans la suie d'un ciel de faubourg

. . . .

Voici pour ta voix un écho de chair et de sang
noir messager d'espoir
car tu connais tous les chants du monde
depuis ceux des chantiers immémoriaux du Nil
Tu te souviens de chaque mot le poids des pierres d'Egypte
et l'élan de ta misère a dressé les colonnes des temples

. . . .

These images form part of a first movement, and their meaning is not fully revealed until the second movement (after the line *POURTANT*). The long-term oppression of the black man is symbolic of the oppression of man; his longing for Africa symbolizes the universal longing for freedom. The whole poem up to the line *POURTANT* builds up images of black suffering; all the lines after it exhort all the exploited of the earth to join forces:

Afrique j'ai gardé ta mémoire Afrique
tu es en moi

Comme l'écharde dans la blessure
comme un fétiche tutélaire au centre du village

fais de moi la pierre de ta fronde
de ma bouche les lèvres de ta plaie
de mes genoux les colonnes brisée de ton abaissement . . .

POURTANT

je ne veux être que de votre race
ouvriers paysans de tous les pays

. . . .
Est-ce tout cela climat étendue espace
qui crée le clan la tribu la nation
la peau la race et les dieux
notre dissemblance inexorable?

Et la mine
el l'usine
les moissons arrachées à notre faim
notre commune indignité
notre servage sous tous les cieux invariable?
Mineur des Asturies mineur nègre de Johannesburg métallo
de Krupp dur paysan de Castille vigneron de Sicile paria
des Indes
            (je franchis ton seuil — réprouvé
            je prends ta main dans ma main — intouchable)
garde rouge de la Chine soviétique ouvrier allemand de la
prison de Moabit indio des Amériques

. . . .
Ouvrier blanc de Détroit péon noir d'Alabama
peuple innombrable des galères capitalistes
le destin nous dresse épaule contre épaule
et reniant l'antique maléfice des tabous du sang
nous foulons les décombres de nos solitudes

. . . .
nous proclamons l'unité de la souffrance
et de la révolte
de tous les peuples sur toute la surface de la terre

The first movement of the poem is Negritude in outlook,
the second is revolutionary. Negritude has been pressed into
the service of the international revolution, becomes subsumed
under it. There is thus the same progression in all three poems:
the revolutionary message is prefaced by a Negritude movement. There is no fluctuation back and forth nor ambivalence
but, as Sartre observes, a progression.[21] The black man in
Roumain's revolutionary poetry symbolizes all oppressed,

---

[21] In "L'Orphée noir," pp. xl–xli. See note 19.

toiling masses. His example can provide a clear perception of the oppression of all. Because of the stress laid on the black man's suffering, it is his affectivity which is prominent in these poems. The black man's sensitivity is valued above his intellect as the truly human element in his experience. The effectiveness of the poetry in relaying this message stems, to a very great degree, from the presence of the poet himself. The reactions of the poet, who identifies himself as black, are an essential component of the poems. Here, as elsewhere in his work, Jacques Roumain's spiritual itinerary cannot be separated from the literary value of his work.

Running through the works written during the period of exile, works stressing Roumain's identity as a Haitian and as a black man in relationship to whites, is the more basic issue of man in his relations with his fellow man, regardless of race. The responsibility of the individual is a concern which weighed heavily on Roumain, and it appears consistently in his writing, but undergoes certain transformations. Roumain reached a turning point somewhere between *Les Fantoches* and "Le Champ du potier." From that point on, bitterness and hopelessness in his writings disappear. It is now clear to him that man must accept the responsibility for some form of action.

Roumain's close proximity to the war in Europe, his own growing conviction that the different forms of oppression in the world were all to be fought with the same steady determination, that they were all aspects of the same inhumanity, his associations while in exile with writers and intellectuals in the cosmopolitan setting of Paris, all these factors no doubt gave him a more specific material out of which to mould in his own mind an ethic of responsibility. Up to now, Roumain had been above all a writer. Henceforth, his essays were to concern themselves specifically with the responsibility of the writer. Shortly before he left Paris, his essay, "Sur la liberté de l'écrivain," appeared in the Parisian journal *Les Volontaires*.[22] Its message is that there can be no neutral ground, no ivory tower nor desert isle to which the writer can retreat. Such a

---

[22] Jacques Roumain, "Sur la liberté de l'écrivain," *Les Volontaires*, June 1939, pp. 556–57.

retreat, in view of the world situation, is an abdication. This position is stated in strictly uncompromising terms:

> Il n'y a plus de dignité dans le bonheur. . . . L'homme est désormais contraint de participer, et dans un monde partagé entre victimes et bourreaux, s'il veut rester libre, de se sentir enchainé à la nécessité de choisir. (p. 556)

Roumain's own growing conviction that the different forms of oppression in the world must all be fought equally on the basis of their common inhumanity is stated just as categorically:

> . . . de lointaines colonies sont intégrées dans le jeu mortel des diplomaties au même titre que des frontières d'Europe Centrale, et la même page de journal nous apprend que dans une petite ville d'Alabama neuf jeunes nègres innocents [the Scottsboro case] ont été condamnés à périr, brûlés vifs sur la chaise électrique et qu'un écrivain a payé derrière les barbelés d'un camp de concentration hitlérien, le crime d'être juif . . . poursuivant un nouveau et sanglant partage du monde, toute une géométrie belliqueuse d'axe et de triangle rend solidaire le destin d'un coolie chinois et d'un ouvrier tchèque, d'un mineur asturien—demain peut-être d'un paysan alsacien. (p. 557)

In the chaos toward which Roumain felt the world was marching, no writer could be allowed the presumptuousness of liberty and solitude. The urgency of the situation for Roumain is well illustrated by the image he chooses to close the article:

> Dès maintenant l'homme (et l'écrivain plus que tout autre), l'homme est traqué, *il faut* qu'il soit traqué, mis au pied du mur acculé à être interrogé—et à répondre. (p. 557; italics in text)

THE UNITED STATES AND CUBA

The urgent tone of "Sur la liberté de l'écrivain" reflects the urgency of European realities. With Hitler's war building up, Roumain found his position as an antifascist alien increasingly precarious. Perhaps, too, his conviction by the French court for publicly offending a chief of state made his presence in France less than welcome to the authorities (Group I interviews). Roumain left Paris for the United States in September 1939, the same month that France declared war on Germany.

When Roumain left Europe, he was not immediately allowed entry into the United States. He went first to Martinique, where he spent a portion of September while friends in the United States arranged for his entry. Finally able to come into the United States, he took up residence in New York, staying at least part of the time in the home of friends. Roumain's arrival in New York in the fall of 1939 did not pass completely unnoticed. A banquet-reception was given in his honor at the Harlem YWCA on November 15, 1939, and the occasion was duly noted in the local black press.[23] Well-known persons among the guests and sponsors included Alain Locke, Langston Hughes, Richard Wright, and Jessie Fauset. Although slated to speak at the banquet on the history and culture of Haiti, Roumain spoke instead of the events in Europe, the buildup of war and the threat of fascism, the need for human solidarity, and the defense of civilization—still fresh in his experience and uppermost in his mind. The speech, given in English, is in effect a refinement and an enlargement of the ideas already put forth just months earlier in "Sur la liberté de l'écrivain:

> At this very moment, the entire world, because of the war, is facing problems which affect our fate in a most fundamental manner: Politically the facts cannot remain localized and isolated any longer in time and space. They are immediately internationalized by the very substance of a war for a new redivision of the world. They have made as one the destiny of all mankind, no matter to what country or race they may belong.[24]

If Nazi Germany and fascist Italy were obvious examples of oppression, Roumain cautions that men of good will must not be fooled by other powers, who deal in words such as

---

[23] "Haitian Scribe to be Honored—Jacques Roumain Guest at Big Banquet . . . ," *New York Amsterdam News*, November 11, 1939, p. 7; "Dinner Reception to be Given Haitian by Writers and Artists," *New York Age*, November 4, 1939, p. 3.

[24] Jacques Roumain, typescript of untitled speech, vertical file, Schomberg Collection, New York Public Library.

"democracy" but continue in their imperalist domination of other peoples:

> Our sympathy is with the persecuted Jews: but it is also with the Negro people of South Africa, deprived of their land, pillaged, oppressed and reduced to the ranks of untouchables by English Imperialism. . . .
> We oppose a spurious crusade for liberty when this same liberty is refused to India. We oppose the bloody carnival of a holy war for democracy when the most modest enjoyment of this same democracy is refused to Africa and Indo-China. . . . We cannot be *for* freedom of Austria and Czekoslovakia and *against* the freedom of 550,000 colonial slaves, *against* the dictatorship of Herr Hitler and *for* the dictatorship of Monsieur Daladier.
> Under different masks, the drama is played by actors motivated by an identical will to power and in spite of clever orchestration, the old theme "to save democracy and civilization" rings terribly false. In reality this means such far from idealistic things as raw materials, oil, gold, mineral riches; world hegemony and colonial domination.

Particularly noteworthy in this speech is Roumain's continually developing conception of the role of the intellectual, of the writer, and, by implication, of literature. The following passage is strongly reminiscent of Pierre's moral awakening in "Le Champ du potier":

> The moral results of this interdependence [i.e., of the destiny of all peoples] is that we writers who like to believe ourselves to be the reflecting consciousness of the universe, have once and for all lost the right—if ever it was ours—to the artifice of solitude and to the mysticism of introspection. This more or less subtle phraseology is but a screen of smoke, hiding imperfectly a panic to desert. It is a renunciation of the primordial mission of a man of thought: *To Be A Man Of Action.*

The theory of literature implied in these remarks seems to be Roumain's first discursive formulation of an art-for-people's-sake (as opposed to an art-for-art's-sake) position, a position typical of the revolutionary writer. We have here a clear picture of the distance traveled since the days of the *Revue Indigène* interview and of the "Mon Carnet" article in *La Presse.* There is nothing incompatible in those early formulations with the

opinions voiced here, and Roumain's manifesto poetry of the
Petit Impartial days can even be viewed as a prefiguration of
them. But it is not until the letter directed to Tristan Rémy in
early 1932 that we begin to see anything approaching the
position taken here. And it is a position already illustrated in
the proletarian novel "Le Champ du potier" and in the
revolutionary poetry of *Bois d'ébène*. Romain's remarks now
lead him ultimately to a fully developed Marxist criticism:

> I believe that a rather good definition of "writer" should
> be that essentially he is not free, that thoughts are so deeply
> determined by history, that they have no real value if they
> do not reflect and express the dialectic pulsation of life.
> The humanist of today is not the anemic intellectual who
> retreats into his ivory tower, it is von Ossietsky in a concen-
> tration camp, expiating the crime of having been a pacifist.

Roumain made an even clearer statement of his philosophy
of literature shortly before leaving New York. On November
13, 1940, he participated in a symposium sponsored by the
League of American Writers at the Newspaper Guild Club in
New York. The symposium topic was "The Frustrated Poetry
Renaissance."[25] Roumain applies the dialectical materialist
view, of which there are glimmerings in the 1939 speech, to
the case of literature. The result is a prime example of the
Marxist criticism practiced in certain intellectual circles of the
era. Poetry, Roumain asserts, is contingent upon the society
which produces it:

> Poetry is not a pure idealistic distillation, a sort of magical
> incantation: it reflects that which in common language one
> calls an epoch; that is to say, the dialectical complexity of
> social relations, of contradictions and antagonisms of the
> political and economic structure of a society at a definite
> historical period. (p. 22)

These words diametrically oppose Roumain to all that a poet
such as Mallarmé stood for:

> Mallarmé is the product of an epoch when the progressive
> curve of capitalism has already reached its dead climax, when

---

[25] "Exiled Haitian poet at Guild Club Dec. 13," *New York Amsterdam
News*, December 7, 1940, p. 12. The speech was later printed in the
January 7, 1941, issue of *New Masses* (pp. 22–23) under the title "Is
Poetry Dead?" Page references are to *New Masses*.

bourgeois society has entered its declining stage, at which, to the destruction of the productive forces, it adds the negation of cultural values. (p. 22)

Mallarmé's failure to find a meaningful replacement for the obsolete social structure which he experienced led him into an escape from reality through a rare, obscure, and elitist poetry. Roumain, pursuing this line, views Mallarmé's idealist, metaphysical position within the process of class confrontation:

> . . . the world has reached an historical cross-roads; the forces of socialism and of capitalism are facing each other in decisive struggle. On the eve of a fundamental historical transformation, the crumbling old society finds in idealistic construction, in the submission to the metaphysical idols, in recourse to the dark forces of mysticism, the ideological weapons of counter-revolution. (p. 22)

Roumain's statement of the poet's role seems to echo the terms of his essentially political speech of a year or so earlier:

> Above all, one has to put an end to the myth of the liberty of the poet. Far from being an "Urmensch" as Valéry claims, the poet is, I submit, before all a man of his time: the reflecting conscience of his period. He is not free if he is not bound to the imperative necessity . . . of making a choice between García Lorca and Franco, between Nehru and Churchill, between Thaelmann and Hitler, between peace and war, between socialist democracy and imperialism. . . .
>
> The poet is at the same time a witness and an actor of the historical drama. He is engaged in it with full responsibility; specifically, at present, his art must be a first-line weapon at the service of the struggle of the masses. . . .
>
> Poetry today must be a weapon as effective as a leaflet, a pamphlet, a poster. If we succeed in fusing with the class content of the poem the beauty of form, if we know how to listen to the lessons of Mayakovsky, we will be able to create a great human revolutionary poetry worthy of the cultural values we have the will to defend. (pp. 22–23)

Public speaking and poetry seem to have occupied only a relatively small part of Roumain's time in New York. He also continued for a time his anthropological studies, enrolling immediately after arriving in the Graduate School of Arts and Sciences at Columbia University in September 1939. He withdrew however in February of the following year without having completed his course of studies.[26] From all evidence, Roumain must have had many social contacts in New York. His continued concern for literature led to collaboration with other writers, as was revealed by his speech at the symposium of the League of American Writers. He often discussed the concept of the social ends of art with friends from the *New Masses* group. He appeared much taken with Mayakovsky and Walt Whitman as socially committed poets. Haiti and her problems continued to preoccupy him, and he often discussed with American friends his hopes for the freedom of the Haitian masses and his long-range socialist objectives (Group I Interviews). Roumain was apparently a well-known figure in the black New York literary community. He was, on at least one occasion, guest of honor at a special celebration. On Saturday evening, May 25, 1940, a "Night in Haiti" program was held in Harlem as a tribute to Haitian culture, and "many prominent Haitian leaders" were expected to be present.[27]

But the time in New York also brought a new kind of loneliness. The bitterness of exile has been somewhat softened during the time in Belgium and France by the presence of family. Roumain's wife and son had accompanied him, and a daughter had been born in Europe. When the family left Europe, Nicole Roumain and the children returned to Haiti. Roumain's letters to her from New York and later from Cuba speak of the help and support she had provided him, speak of the children: "aimez-les pour moi," he tells her. The letters of this period show also a longing for home, a sense of isolation from his native, familiar land. Certain days make exile harder to bear: the snow turning to muddy slush as it settles in the New York streets, the biting wind. The thought of his long absence makes him reflect, "Quand je retournerai en Haïti, je serai entouré de visages étrangers. Une génération naît et une autre a grandi depuis mon dernier emprisonnement et ces jours d'exil."[28]

---

[26] Letter from office of the registrar, Columbia University, February 22, 1972.

[27] "To Honor Toymain[sic] at 'Night in Haiti' Program," *New York Age*, May 25, 1940, p. 4.

[28] Letters dated December 25, 1939, New York; October 14, 1940, New York; November 29, 1940, New York; March 21, 1941, Havana.

Sometime between November 30, 1940, and March 21, 1941, Roumain left New York. He had been invited to Cuba by Nicolás Guillén, a Cuban mulatto poet and journalist whose poems depicting the life and language of the black Cuban had been widely acclaimed. Guillén, like Roumain a member of the Communist party, had been in Spain and Paris in 1937 and had met Roumain there. The two men had become friends. During the months which he spent in Cuba, Roumain worked primarily as a journalist, in close association with Guillén, editor of the socialist newspaper *Noticias de Hoy*. He also contributed articles to literary reviews (Group I interviews). Guillén has since recalled those days:

> Jacques Roumain nos quiso mucho, y parte de su exilio lo compartió con un grupo de sus amigos, aquí en la Habana, casi en las vísperas de su muerte. Era en los tiempos heroicos de nuestro *Hoy,* cuando éste se hacía en una mala imprenta de la Habana vieja, donde como en la cárcel cervantina toda incomodidad tenía su asiento. Jacques iba en las tardes al periódico y allí tertuliabamos en la medida del trabajo de cada quien. Hasta que ya de noche, nos sentábamos todos en una pequeña fonda de chinos, frente a grandes platos de arroz con frijoles negros y carne asada.[29]

In this congenial atmosphere, Roumain appears to have been more politically active than had been possible in Europe or the United States. His political and public life would, however, soon find fuller expression once again in Haiti, after the change in the government which would make possible an end to exile at last.

---

[29] Nicolás Guillén, "Sobre Jacques Roumain," *Prosa de Prisa: Crónicas* (La Habana: Imprenta Nacional, 1962), pp. 324–25. The article originally appeared in *Hoy,* May 25, 1961.

CHAPTER VII

The Second Homecoming

In April 1941, Sténo Vincent's term of office drew to a close and Elie Lescot was elected president of Haiti. Lescot had promised during his campaign that if elected, he would not harbor ill feelings toward opponents of the previous government. Roumain was thus able to arrange for permission to return home. He returned that August, after nearly five years in Europe and America.

ETHNOLOGY AND DEBATE

Once home, Roumain went to work almost immediately. Putting to use the ethnological knowledge he had acquired during the course of his exile, he established in October the Bureau d'Ethnologie. The anthropologist Alfred Métraux seems to have suggested it to Roumain: he was in Haiti in August and publicly discussed the topic of the future of ethnographic studies in that island country.[1] But is it probable that the idea had already been maturing in Roumain's mind for some time (Group II interviews). President Lescot, persuaded that the Bureau would be of benefit to the nation, officially established it on October 31, 1941, naming Jacques Roumain as director.[2] Such an agency was altogether new in Haiti, although the climate for it had been well established over the past decade or so by such men as Jean Price-Mars, and by the ethnological

---

[1] *Le Nouvelliste,* August 20, 1941 announced a speech given by Métraux on that topic.

[2] *Bulletin du Bureau d'Ethnologie,* no. 1 (1942), p. 3.

orientation of the Africanist journal *Les Griots* and the men of that movement. There were, in effect, a considerable number of Haitians working in anthropology. The Bureau (and later the *Institut,* founded by Price-Mars) thus filled a recognized gap in the needs of the Haitian community.

The Bureau d'Ethnologie was charged with a number of tasks: it was to make inventory of, classify, and conserve previously collected archeological items; investigate and preserve archeological sites, and publish a quarterly bulletin bearing the results of research conducted by the Bureau and reporting on ethnological activities outside of Haiti.[3] During Roumain's directorship of the Bureau, several excavation expeditions on the Haitian islands of La Tortue and La Gonave were organized. Additional excavations were undertaken near Pétion-Ville and at Mariani and Gressier, on the Bay of Port-au-Prince. Roumain ultimately classified over two thousand items found by him and other ethnographers during these trips or contributed by private collectors, and prepared them for display. Such work led quite naturally to the creation of a museum, the functions of which Roumain considered both social and pedagogical. A museum, he wrote

> est essentiellement destiné à l'enseignement des couches les plus larges de la population. Il doit être semblable à un livre ouvert et expliqué. Sa mission n'est pas de séduire une curiosité désoeuvrée mais d'instruire et de stimuler l'étude.[4]

During the time of his directorship of the Bureau, Roumain wrote several ethnological studies: *Contribution à l'étude de l'ethnobotanique pré-colombienne des Grandes Antilles* (published as the first issue of the *Bulletin* in 1942); "L'Outillage lithique des Ciboney d'Haïti" (incomplete, comprising pages 22–27 of an unnumbered 1943 issue of the *Bulletin*); and *Le Sacrifice du tambour-assoto(r)* (published in 1943, after Roumain had left for Mexico, by the Imprimerie de l'Etat). These works are extremely technical, and seem to have been written with an audience of colleagues in mind.

---

[3] "Création d'un Bureau d'Ethnologie avec Jacques Roumain comme Directeur," *Le Nouvelliste,* October 16, 1941, p. 1.

[4] "Notice: Le Musée du Bureau d'Ethnologie," *Bulletin* (unnumbered) 1943, pp. 34–35.

The first work, *Contribution à l'étude de l'ethnobotanique* . . . , studies the uses to which plants and parts of plants were put by the pre-Columbian Indian (Taino) population of the island. Roumain listed and described plants under headings according to their functions and uses in society: myths, religious beliefs and material culture (i.e., medicinal uses). He drew heavily on the chronicles of the first European travellers, Bartolomeo de las Casas and Oviedo, for information as to how plants were prepared, their effectiveness and the plant families to which they belonged.

"L'Outillage lithique des Ciboney d'Haïti" was to have been a study of stone objects uncovered in the course of expeditions by Roumain and his colleagues. The study was to have appeared in the second issue of the *Bulletin*. The short report which was published implied that the importance of the study lay in the fact that the stone implements unearthed afforded for the first time ample evidence of a pre-Arawak (i.e., pre-Taino) Indian culture of nomadic gatherers and hunters (the Ciboney people) in Haiti and Cuba, which, by the time the Spaniards first appeared, had been submerged and almost eliminated by the invading Arawaks. Roumain proposed in a subsequent report to attempt a reconstruction of the cultural sequences of the Ciboney people through careful analysis of "La courbe de fréquence de chaque type d'objet par site; la présence ou l'absence de ces objets caractéristiques dans les divers sites étudiés (*Bulletin*, p. 25). No further parts of the study were published.

The third study to appear, *Le Sacrifice du tambour-assoto(r)*, is a step-by-step description of the manufacture, preparation and consecration of the large vodun drum, the *assotor*. Roumain spent several months assisting at ceremonies performed by his informant, the *houngan* Abraham. The ceremony is extremely complex and according to Roumain is the most important in the Arada cult.[5] Roumain incorporates numerous chants into the text, giving both the Creole and its French translation.

Aside from these scholarly writings and the directorship

---

[5] There are three vodun cults in Haiti, of which the Arada is the most important.

of the Bureau, Roumain also devoted time to teaching. About a month after the institution of the Bureau, Dr. Price-Mars founded the Institut d'Ethnologie. Unlike the Bureau, the Institut was devoted exclusively to teaching. It had a well-defined two-year curriculum and granted a diploma. It numbered among its faculty members those ethnologists and anthropologists associated with the Bureau; Roumain was professor of pre-Columbian archeology and of prehistoric anthropology.[6]

Although the bulk of Roumain's work during this 1941–42 period was technical, he did devote considerable efforts to the dissemination and popularization of the results of ethnological inquiry. Roumain gave a speech on vodun at the Cercle Militaire in Port-au-Prince, in which he sought to dispel the sensational and exotic picture created by novels and movies, which he called a "pittoresque facile." In the speech he stressed the historical development of vodun, pointing out that vodun is not a mosaic but is directly traceable to a single African tribal religion:

> Telle est la force da la tradition africaine qu'à travers quatre cent ans les vocables dahoméens se sont conservés intacts en Haiti et certaines chansons vaudouesques le sont si bien restées, que de nos jours encore, elles ont pu être comprises par les membres d'une société secrète du Dahomey.

The speech dwells at length on the sociological role of vodun, and Roumain does not pass up the opportunity to show that during the period preceding Haitian independence, vodun played the role of a "société secrète révolutionnaire."

Other popularizing work stemmed from the immediate problems within Haitian society. Three articles published in the newspaper Le Nouvelliste (March 11, 13, 18, 1942) under the title "Sur les superstitions" put ethnology in the service of the people.[7] The campagne anti-superstitieuse to which the

---

[6] The Bureau d'Ethnologie has continued to function and to publish its Bulletin and has maintained the museum with Roumain's exhibits intact. The Institut, now public, has been incorporated into the Université d'Haïti as the Faculté d'Ethnologie.

[7] The articles were published in pamphlet form with the title A Propos de la campagne "anti-superstitieuse": las supersticiones (Port-au-

articles refer had been a relentless crusade launched by the French clergy in October 1941 in the Haitian countryside, apparently with the sanction of the Lescot government. It was aimed at wiping out "superstition," that is, vodun. Vodun alters and sanctuaries were smashed, ceremonies routed. The campaign never had much lay suport, but it came to an end only after certain retaliatory measures were taken in late February 1942.

Le Nouvelliste became indignant when it learned that Monseigneur Silvani, the papal ambassador to Haiti, had boasted on a visit to the Dominican Republic in February 1942 that a crusade against the "parody" of the Christian rites by the Haitian peasants had resulted in the surprising results of twenty thousand "converts" per week. *Le Nouvelliste* could not pardon Silvani's representation of the Haitian people as, to use its words, "des primitifs encore fidèles aux pratiques du fétichisme africain . . . alors qu'il y a quatre-vingt-deux ans que nous avons signé un Concordat avec le Saint-Siège" (*Le Nouvelliste*, February 27, 1942). Roumain considered the crusade imperious and unenlightened. His articles attempted to show from an anthropological perspective that vodun represented a stage in religious development characteristic of all peoples:

> L'homme primitif ayant été incapable de comprendre le méchanisme des phénomènes naturels et la structure du monde extérieur, inventa autant d'esprits et de divinités, qu'il se posait de questions sur les rapports de sa pensée et de son être. . . .
> Au fur et à mesure que par une action réciproque les techniques et les exigences matérielles de l'homme non seulement changeaient le monde, mais *l'expliquaient*, transformaient la société, bouleversaient les rapports de classe, ces divinités multiples personnifiant les forces magiques du ciel, de la terre, des éléments, etc. par ce procès d'abstraction qu'Engels a remarquablement appelé un procès de distillation des dieux, cédaient la place au Dieu des religions monothéistes. . . .

Prince: Imprimerie de l'Etat, n.d.) in a bilingual (French and Spanish) edition. Whether publication in pamphlet form preceded or followed the *Nouvelliste* articles cannot be determined from available evidence.

> Tous les peuples ont conservé le résidu de cet héritage des
> âges obscurs dans leurs croyances religieuses populaires, les
> pratiques magiques et même leur philosophie. . . .
> L'Haïtien n'est pas plus—ni moins—superstitieux qu'un
> autre peuple.
> Les pratiques dites superstitieuses auxquelles il se livre
> ont un caractère universel. (pp. 3–4; italics in text)[8]

Roumain cites example after example in support of these
conclusions, showing the same or similar rites, practices or
beliefs among members of widely separated folk cultures. He
draws heavily from the peasant cultures of France to show, for
instance, that animal sacrifice in thanksgiving or propitiation
is practiced not only in vodun ceremonies but after the wheat
harvest in Guyenne, Picardy, Briançon, and Pouilly. As concerns the religious syncretism which so scandalized the ini-
tiators of the crusade, Roumain points to the syncretism in
Catholicism: Christmas is a replacement for the ancient festival
of the winter solstice; the Platonic theory of the immortality
of the soul was combined with elements of the dogma of the
Resurrection. The syncretism of Christianity and vodun is
likewise a purely historical event, and is now an accomplished
fact:

> L'amalgame est total; et puisqu'il y a syncrétisme, la
> persistance d'un des facteurs—le vaudou—dépend de
> l'existence de l'autre: le catholicisme.
> En somme, il faut être catholique, pour être vaudouiste.
> (p. 10)

Roumain criticizes the naïve assumptions of a crusade
conducted on the basis of fear (the peasants were threatened
with being refused the Sacraments) and repression (by chop-
ping down trees held to be sacred by vodun worshippers, the
clergy proceeded as though it were dealing not with fiction
but with a dreaded reality):

> Il faut naturellement débarrasser la masse haïtienne de ses
> entraves mystiques. Mais on ne triomphera pas de ses
> croyances par la violence ou en la menaçant de l'enfer. Ce
> n'est pas la hache du bourreau, la flamme du bûcher, les
> autodafés qui ont détruit la sorcellerie. C'est le progrès de

---

[8] Page references are to the articles as published in pamphlet form.

la science, le développement continu de la culture humaine, une connaissance chaque jour plus approfondie de la structure d l'Univers. (p. 11)

Thus, Roumain proposes to bring the Haitian peasant out of his "mentalité archaïque" through intellectual and material progress:

> Ce qu'il faut mener en Haïti, ce n'est pas une campagne anti-superstitieuse, mais une campagne anti-misère. Avec l'école, l'hygiène, un standard de vie plus élevé, le paysan aura accès à cette culture et à cette vie décente qu'on ne peut lui refuser, si on ne veut pas que ce pays tout entier périsse, et qui lui permettront de surmonter des survivances religieuses enracinées dans sa misère, son ignorance, son exploitation séculaires. (p. 12)

Roumain's articles provoked an immediate response in Haiti's Catholic newspaper, *La Phalange*. In issue after issue, Père Foisset attacked Roumain's ideology. On March 30, 1942, Roumain began his "Réplique au Révérend Père Foisset" in the columns of *Le Nouvelliste*. The "Réplique"—because of Foisset's persistence—continued through fourteen articles and did not end definitively until July 31, 1942.

What locked the two in their circular deadlock was their diametrically opposed world view, which Roumain described at the end of the debate:

> . . . ce qui nous oppose et d'une manière irréductible c'est l'essence de notre conception du monde. Elle est chez vous métaphysique, et vous savez que je lui oppose fondamentalement une philosophie scientifique qui s'appelle le matérialisme dialectique. (July 31, 1942)

The whole of the debate goes back to this difference. In the beginning, Père Foisset had labeled Roumain's comparative, historical approach "évolutionisme linéaire rigide." In his first "Réplique," Roumain had answered:

> . . . s'il fallait définir graphiquement la dialectique, ce n'est pas la rigidité linéaire qui l'exprimerait, mais l'infini mouvement de la spirale.

Heraclitus' notion of flux, "ce perpétuel mouvement des choses à travers leurs contradictions," lost to the empiricist philoso-

phers of the seventeenth and eighteenth centuries, was redis-
covered by Hegel:

> Mais pour l'illustre philosophe, la réalité n'est que la forme
> phenoménale de l'idée absolue. La triade hégélienne: thèse,
> antithèse, synthèse boucle un cercle, transforme la fleuve
> d'Héraclite et un lac: la logique hégélienne était en somme
> comme le remarquait Feuerbach la forme dernière de la
> théologie transportant l'essence de la nature hors de la nature,
> l'essence de l'homme hors de l'homme, avec cette différence
> capitale que chez Hegel l'idée remplace les créations méta-
> physiques imaginaires.
> C'est la philosophie scientifique, le matérialisme dialec-
> tique qui eut l'incomparable mérite de démontrer que la
> synthèse n'était pas statique, qu'elle contenait les éléments
> d'une nouvelle contradiction, demandant à être résolue à
> travers de nouveaux antagonismes sans cesse supprimés,
> constamment renouvellés, dans un procéssus de transfor-
> mation énergique qui est le mouvement même de vie: c'est
> au marxisme que revint l'honneur de démontrer que le
> mouvement de la pensée, n'est que le reflet du mouvement
> du réel transporté et transposé dans le cerveau de l'homme.
> Hegel enseignait: tout ce qui est réel est rationnel. Le Père
> Foisset, lui, semble croire que tout ce qui est irréel est
> rationnel et que le fait pour l'homme 'primitif' d'avoir créé
> des dieux à l'image de son ignorance, prouve l'existence de
> Dieu. (March 30, 1942)

The rest of the Répliques are almost entirely a refinement
or enlargement of this basic position, spiced by a considerable
amount of sarcasm. Foisset's grounding in Christian dogma
led him to assert that man went from the perfect to the
imperfect, having been created in God's image. This position,
of course, does not easily admit of biological evolution from
the less to the more complex forms of life. Roumain labeled
Foisset's position the "Homo Metaphysicus Edenensis" theory
and quipped:

> je supplie le Révérend Père Foisset de renoncer à sa théorie.
> . . . J'estime qu'il y a une suprême impertinence de supposer
> que l'on pourrait un jour découvrir un molaire, la calotte
> cranienne ou le cubitus de "l'image de Dieu." (March 31,
> 1942)

Père Foisset's system of belief, based as it was on revelation,
could not admit to a historical accumulation of knowledge.

Roumain saw the conflict as one between metaphysics and science:

> Pour les métaphysiciens, les vérités scientifiques ne sont que des empirio-symboles, une systématisation théorique sans racine dans la réalité objective, mais pour le philosophe, la question gnoséologique fondamentale est la correspondance de nos perceptions avec la nature objective des choses perçues. C'est la pratique expérimentale qui démontre cette identité. "Les substances chimiques produites dans les organismes végétaux et animaux restèrent des 'choses en soi' jusqu'à ce que la chimie organique se fut mise à les préparer l'une après l'autre." (Engels: Ludwig Feuerbach). Certaines proteines restèrent des "choses en soi" jusqu'en 1936, quand Bergman en découvrit la formule chimique. . . .
> . . . La science est une méthode d'investigation et de connaissance progressive du monde. Elle a un caractère transitoire, relatif approximatif; elle va de l'ignorance à la connaissance selon une courbe ascendante d'erreurs et de vérités relatives vers une appréciation de plus en plus exacte de la réalité objective. Mais ce relativisme ne nous conduit pas au scepticisme, à l'idéalisme philosophique; chaque parcelle de vérité scientifique, relative contient un élément de la vérité absolue qui est égale à la somme des vérités relatives en voie de développement. . . .
> C'est la distinction dialectique entre l'absolue et relative vérité qui donne à la science son caractère vivant et progressif.
> . . . Apparemment, la conscience de l'homme pas plus que sa physiologie, n'a réussi à surmonter parfois les survivances du passé: nous possédons encore des ongles et des canines qui ne nous servent plus à saisir et à déchirer une proie. . . .
> De même une conception religieuse peut survivre malgré les progrés de la science.
> La métaphysique n'est qu'une sorte d'appendicite idéologique. (April 21, 1942)

Roumain thus reiterates the major points of his three articles "Sur les superstitions." He ends the debates with a restatement of his beliefs regarding the need to concentrate more on the material well-being of the masses:

> Mais il y a des problèmes, tels que le chômage, la guerre, la lutte anti-fasciste, la liberté, la justice, la droit à une vie décente pour toute l'humanité qui sont des problèmes TERRESTRES que les hommes, aux religions et aux philosophies

les plus variées peuvent ensemble sincèrement essayer de résoudre. . . .

. . . Si telle est aussi votre opinion, je suis heureux de vous tendre une main loyale. (July 31, 1942)

During this year back from exile, Roumain seems to have engaged in relatively little literary activity. He did, however, write a preface to Edris Saint-Amand's critical study of *Dialogues de mes lampes*, a volume of poetry by the Haitian surrealist poet Clément Magloire Saint-Aude which had aroused considerable discussion.[9] In his preface, Roumain continues the same Marxist criticism he had professed during the period in New York. His preface even reproduces verbatim, in French translation, passages and phrases from his *New Masses* article, "Is Poetry Dead?" He applies the general concepts extracted from it to the Haitian situation and to the work of Saint-Aude, in which he sees a negative reflection of the era through which he is living. His judgment of Magloire Saint-Aude's work, within the context of historical necessity, is almost a direct parallel of what he had to say about Mallarmé:

Il [Saint-Amand] a saisi, avec une parfaite clairvoyance, l'importance de ce poète, de ce révolté anti-révolutionnaire . . . qui se refuse à changer le monde, fuit le réel, le nie, par l'artifice amer d'une réinvention du langage, qui lui permet, loin de la surdité bourgeoise à tout ce qui n'est pas musique vulgaire, de retrouver le chant terrible d'une irrémédiable solitude.

Aside from this brief preface, Roumain was at work on a book of translations of Nicolás Guillén's poetry.[10] Translations of two poems—"Je ne sais pas pourquoi tu penses" and "Ballade des deux ancêtres"—appeared in the August 14 and 17, 1942, issues respectively of *Le Nouvelliste*, almost certainly in anticipation of Guillén's visit to Haiti, which occurred in September 1942. Guillén was received in Haiti with considerable acclaim. The newspapers reported all of his movements,

---

[9] Edris Saint-Amand, *Essai d'explication de "Dialogues de mes lampes,"* Preface by Jacques Roumain (Port-au-Prince: Imprimerie de l'Etat, 1942).

[10] The work was never completed.

and Roumain was one of his constant companions. Guillén often found himself before an audience reciting his poetry upon request, and it has been stated that Jacques Roumain would often translate extemporaneously into French as Guillén recited (Group I interviews).

Although Roumain's literary activity was restricted, his public life continued to expand. His movements and activities were newsworthy items and faithfully reported in the papers. It seemed inevitable that the government should offer him some sort of official post.

DIPLOMACY AND DEATH

In October 1942, President Lescot named Jacques Roumain chargé d'affaires to Mexico. Roumain's acceptance of the post in a government which in effect exercised dictatorial powers has been widely criticized. Some have seen it as a contradiction of Roumain's ideas. It is to them a source of consternation, as Roumain had become for the youth of the country a champion of democratic principles.[11] Others have viewed the appointment as a kind of honorary banishment by the Lescot government of a man who, because of his stature, could not be overlooked.[12] According to one account, Lescot had become apprehensive of Roumain's ethnographic work because it brought him in contact with the people. The government, fearing that such contact might lead to the further polarization of Haitian society—that is, to Communist indoctrination of the proletarian and peasant sectors—felt it best to have Roumain out of the country (Group I interviews). Still others see no essential contradiction, reasoning that Roumain joined the government because it was resolutely anti-Nazi, and in a time when the international situation demanded solidarity against fascism, Roumain had understood that it was necessary to put

---

[11] See especially Jacques Stéphen Alexis, "Jacques Roumain vivant," in Jacques Roumain, *Oeuvres choisies* ([Moscow]: Editions du progrès, 1964).

[12] Langston Hughes and Mercer Cook, "Introduction," in Jacques Roumain, *Masters of the Dew* (New York: Reynal and Hitchcock, 1947) p. ix.

aside differences on the smaller scale of internal politics (Group I interviews).

Shortly after his appointment, Roumain, interviewed in Havana en route to his post in Mexico, spoke of President Lescot in terms which would seem to substantiate to some extent the latter view, even after allowing for the inevitable fact that a member of the government would not publicly criticize it:

> Le Chef de la nation haïtienne a une vision très précise de la nécessité impérieuse que constitue l'union de toutes les Républiques d'Amérique, et comme le Président est appelé par l'Unité nationale du peuple haïtien, sa politique d'alliance avec les Nations Unies qui luttent contre l'Axe exprime exactement les exigences des conditions de la victoire.
>
> Je tiens à rappeler que Monsieur Lescot fut le premier Président d'Amérique à contribuer matériellement par sa présence au succès d'une fête donnée au bénéfice de la Croix Rouge Soviétique. Cela est une expression de la conception que s'est formée le gouvernement haïtien de sa responsabilité.

During the course of this interview, Roumain also praised certain aspects of the government's internal policy:

> Le Gouvernement . . . a exprimé d'une manière réitérée sa volonté d'améliorer les conditions matérielles et intellectuelles du peuple haïtien. . . . Son action s'est concrétisée en décrets et en lois sociales fixant le salaire minimum, augmentant considérablement le prix de la tonne de canne . . . , préscrivant aux jeunes médecins d'exercer leur profession pendant deux années dans les campagnes, pour soigner et conseiller les paysans. . . .[13]

While Roumain was in Mexico the situation in Haiti did in fact change, and he began to have serious doubts as to his position in the Lescot government. Lescot had suddenly

---

[13] "Jacques Roumain interviewé à La Havane," *Le Nouvelliste,* November 20, 1942. It is worthy of note here that Roumain had written an article just a few months earlier in which he had deplored a social system which made the physician into another merchant selling his wares and sought to treat social illnesses by private methods. ("Le médicin rural ou la science au service du peuple," *Le Nouvelliste,* June 17, 1942).

decided to postpone legislative elections until after the signing of peace treaties by all parties at war. The democratic process was left dangling, since no one could say when all treaties would, if ever, be negotiated. In addition, Lescot proposed an immediate vote of confidence for himself in lieu of regular presidential elections at the end of the normal six-year term. Rumors circulated that Lescot was playing off fears on the liberal side (that a reactionary might come to power) against fears on the conservative side (that an extreme leftist might come to power). Rumor had it further that Jacques Roumain's name was being held up as the extreme leftist threat. When he learned of these stories, Roumain apparently intended to resign his post in Mexico and become independently active in politics, but death overtook him before he could analyze the situation sufficiently to make a formal decision.

In Mexico, meanwhile, Roumain continued to fulfill his diplomatic functions, filing his reports on Mexican-Haitian economic and political relations. He had occasion to speak publicly, once giving a speech on Toussaint Louverture (Group I interviews). In addition to his public functions Roumain seems to have enjoyed in Mexico also a rich and varied social contact. He came to know Nationalist painters whose work he had admired: José Orozco, David Siqueiros, Diego Rivera. The war in Europe had forced many liberal writers and thinkers into exile. Roumain met or renewed contact with many of them, now in political asylum in Mexico, including Ludwig Renn and Anna Seghers.

In 1943, while in Mexico, Roumain suffered a serious attack—of what type is not clear—and returned to Haiti to convalesce. He returned to his post after roughly two months, but the following year, on a visit home, he suffered another attack. He died on August 18, 1944, at the age of thirty-seven. The circumstances surrounding his death have remained somewhat unclear.[14]

---

[14] Some maintain that he was poisoned, a victim of political intrigue. A story circulates that a woman agent followed him from Mexico and appeared beside him at a reception the night before his attack, but some discredit this story as groundless. Others attribute

The brief time in Mexico had yielded a poem or so. "L'Amour la mort" was written there, and "Prélude" (included in error at the beginning of *Bois d'ébène* in the posthumous published version) dates from perhaps a week before Roumain's departure; it appears that he had intended to complete it in Mexico.[15] These two poems, apparently the last ones written by Roumain, are more reflective, more introspective than either the Negritude or the revolutionary poetry for which he is most famous.

"Prélude" translates the reflections of a man about to leave his cherished and familiar home:

> Si l'été est pluvieux et morne
> si le ciel voile l'étang d'une paupière de nuage
> si la palme se dénoue en haillons
> si les arbres sont d'orgueil et noirs dans le vent et la brume
>
> Si le vent rabat vers la savanne un lambeau de chant funèbre
> si l'ombre s'accroupit autour du foyer éteint
>
> Si une voilure d'ailes sauvages emporte l'île vers les naufrages
> si le crépuscule noie l'envol déchiré d'un dernier mouchoir
> et si le cri blesse l'oiseau
> tu partiras
> abandonnant ton village
>
> Sa lagune et ses raisiniers amers
> la trace de tes pas dans ses sables
> le reflet d'un songe au fond du puits
> et la vieille tour attachée au tournant du chemin
> comme un chien fidèle au bout de sa laisse
> et qui aboie dans le soir
> un appel fêlé dans les herbages. . . .

---

his death to sclerosis of the liver and indicate that Roumain had an alcoholic problem. This seems the most widely accepted view, but others refuse to accept that this can have been the cause of death. The death certificate apparently indicates the cause of death to have been an inflammation of the gall bladder (Group I interviews).

[15] Group I interviews. The person supplying this information was quite definite about the time periods. However, it is puzzling to find, with the rough draft of "Bois d'ébène," a rough draft of "Prélude," executed on the same type of paper and in the same pencil and handwriting as "Bois d'ébène."

Again, Roumain was to experience exile, but this time a voluntary one, and the sadness at leaving is quiet, almost prayerful. Such is the mood suggested by the series of lines which begin the poem, each one containing the image of a familiar aspect of the Haitian landscape. The parallel structure of the language (each clause beginning with *si*) and the parallels in the content (all the images have in common that they are scenes of home) create a kind of litany.

"L'Amour la mort" was written in Mexico after Roumain's first attack, in 1943:

> Pour son désespoir une idole vénéneuse
>
> Regard hagard d'escarbille d'hirondelle
> sourire poignardé
> flétrissure aiguisée du sang
> l'araignée tire le fil d'une ride:
> toute honte bue au soupirail de cette bouche
>
> Un battement de cil de l'aube
> et le pollen du soleil couvre ta joue
>
> Un nid d'ailes ta chevelure
> Si l'haleine du vent l'effeure
>
> Beauté ravie au mouvement du sang
> tes mains offrent un sacrifice de colombes
> Sur tes genoux invincibles.

The surrealistic images of the first stanza are reminiscent of the visions one might experience in delirium. The associations here remind one both of the deathlike images surrounding Placinette in *La Montagne ensorcelée* (the venom, the wild and bitter smile, the spider) and of certain images in "Madrid" (the half-burned aspect of the landscape, the blood and the dead smiling boy in the square). Some of the images of the second movement recall certain scenes of *Gouverneurs de la rosée*, which Roumain must have just been completing when this poem was written. The dawning day and the sun passing over the poet's cheek, the cooling breeze, are strangely evocative of the scene where Manuel lies dying and sees the sun rise on the last day of his life. The hair blowing in the breeze, alive as with birds' nests, recalls the metaphors in *Gouverneurs de la rosée* where the commotion of birds in the tree tops seems symbolic of life. The image of the last three lines is curiously reminiscent of "Corrida," where, just as Armillita l'Aztèque kills the bull, "Des colombes palpitent soudain dans toutes les mains." The images of the first part of "L'Amour la mort" seem deliberately chosen from among motifs which Roumain had developed elsewhere in his work and which are associated with death. Those of the second part seem just as deliberately chosen from among motifs which symbolize a contact with or a renewal of life. It may be that the poem thus represents a struggle with death through a hallucinatory night (first movement), and the peace and renewed life brought by the new day (second movement).

CHAPTER VIII

Gouverneurs de la Rosée: *Song of Human Solidarity*

The post in Mexico had given Roumain the leisure to finish the novel begun six years or so earlier in Belgium, *Gouverneurs de la rosée*. He finished work on it sometime in 1943. When he returned to Haiti in 1944, a month before his death, he carried with him the completed manuscript, ready for publication. The work, published posthumously, enjoyed an immediate success. The story, though simple and undeniably Haitian in its setting, is universal in its meaning. It is the portrayal of man's eternal struggle against the elements, and against his own destructive tendencies.

After fifteen years of laboring on the sugar plantations of Cuba, Manuel Jean Joseph comes home to the village of Fonds Rouge in the Haitian hills. On the dusty road he meets a girl, Annaïse, but when she learns his name, her amiability soon turns to coldness. Manuel learns later that a feud has split the village into two enemy camps; Annaïse belongs to the enemy side. But that is not the worst of it: the land which he remembered as green and ripe has become dry and barren. The villagers have cut down all the trees on the hill, exposing the land to the constant fiery sun. The springs have dried up, and no rain has come to alleviate the drought. The crops have died and the villagers are hungry and disheartened. Manuel's aging mother, Délira Délivrance, prays constantly to the *loa* and the Trinity, while Bienaimé, his father, loses his grief in endless dreams of days when the land was rich in crops and the men gathered for the *coumbite*, the communal harvesting, and came in afterward from the fields to feasts prepared by the women.

Manuel is determined to find water. Day after day, he sets out with his machete, roaming the hills in search of a spring to bring water, the precious source of life, back to Fonds Rouge. He speaks of his dream to Laurélien, his friend, and to Annaïse, who meets with him in secret on the hills outside the village, for Manuel's sincerity and gentleness soon win her to him. Annaïse will work with her faction of the village for a reconciliation when the water is found, for directing it into the plain and through the gardens of Fonds Rouge will be no easy task. The work will require the cooperative efforts of all. It is Manuel's vision to reunite the village in a *grand coumbite de l'eau*.

Manuel finds water on a hill lush with growth and water-loving fowl. He brings Annaïse to the spring, and there they consummate their love. There is rejoicing in Fonds Rouge when the news of water breaks. But in the enemy camp, the men gathered at Larivoire's house are despondent. Gervilen has seen Annaïse with Manuel, and in jealousy, he fans the flames of the feud separating the village. It is then that Manuel surprises everyone by walking boldly into their meeting. But his manner is conciliatory, and his words paint visions of harmony and plenty, if they will only work together. When Manuel leaves, the men at Larivoire are all but won over. But Gervilen has slunk away, grumbling viciously, and as Manuel walks home from the meeting, Gervilen falls upon him and wounds him mortally. He gathers all his will and manages to drag himself back to his hut and his mother's arms before morning breaks. He dies soon after. But he has extracted a promise from Délira not to alert Hilarion, the *chef de section*. His death will be the seal that binds the village in their new effort. Annaïse leads the villagers to the spring. A month later, she and Délira watch from a hilltop as the water, tapped and channeled by the long and patient efforts of the villagers, courses through the valley and into the village gardens. Délira asks: "O Manuel pourquoi es-tu mort?" But Annaïse tells her he is not dead, and presses the old woman's hand to her abdomen, where a new life grows.

Gouverneurs de la rosée, by its plot, falls readily into the category of the traditional novel. There is a well-defined story with beginning, middle, and end. The hero discovers a problem, confronts it and resolves it. Nothing is left dangling at the end; the destinies of all the principal characters are accounted for, and any further action would be superfluous. As in "Le Champ du potier," the plot bifurcates into the public and private stories of the hero. But here, the winning of the water and the winning of Annaïse are intimately intertwined, converging in the end in one single story, where themes, characters and problem merge into one synthetic message.

Manuel does not appear immediately. The problem of the village and the character of Manuel are introduced as a kind of prologue to his appearance; the structure of the novel thus enhances Manuel's stature as a hero. The old parents are awaiting at the same time the return of their son and a solution to the problem; the two events become fused in the lonely aching biding of Délira and Bienaimé. Chapter 1 ends with Délira intoning prayers to the Virgin Mary, Legba and all the saints to protect her boy and bring him home. As her prayer ends, Bienaimé comes and silently sits beside her. Together the two watch the coming dusk, waiting with their lives in abeyance for the night and the following dawn.

Chapter 2 begins, by contrast, with the decisive tone of a man giving an order: "Il dit au chauffeur du camion: Arrêtez" (p. 25). *Il* is, or course, Manuel, as he steps out of the vehicle leaving the highway and disappears into the "sentier à peine visible entre cet amas de roches," immersing himself once again in his native environment. Manuel's return becomes an advent. His destiny as a savior has been heralded by the sharp contrast in the hopeless tone of the first chapter and the decisive, expectant tone opening the second. As Manuel's nature is revealed, we recognize him as the man described by

Pierre in "Le Champ du potier", whom Roumain himself had described in his speech in New York: the man for whom action is the necessary corollary of thought. Manuel's presence is at first like an intrusion on the dying hopeless countryside; it becomes an infusion of freshness and of hope for new life as the story unfolds.

The structure of the beginning of the novel reveals the important role symbolism will play in it. In effect, symbolism is woven into the very fiber of the story, and is nowhere more evident than in characterization. Each of the major characters is associated with a gesture, a physical attribute, an object used over and over to describe moods or attitudes, so that it becomes a *leitmotiv*. Bienaimé puffs triumphantly on his pipe, throws it in a fit of anger, fills it thoughtfully. Laurélien poses his big, rough peasant hands on his knees, uses their strength to make a coffin for his dead friend, Manuel. Manuel himself has a "pli têtu au coin de la bouche" which appears whenever his determination to bring a dream to fruition needs under-scoring. Annaïse is always seen walking along the roads with her "long pas nonchalant et balancé." We are told: "Elle seule avait ce jet pur et souple des jambes, cet oscillement des hanches dans la douceur." The grace of her movements and the ampleness of her physique are brought before us in almost every scene where she appears. Délira's motions are always described in images of weariness; she is waiting for the relief of death.

On a deeper level, however, symbolism operates through a more elaborate system of motifs, each intimately associated with major characters. Opening the book, we read:

> — Nous mourrons tous . . . —et elle plonge sa main dans la poussière; la vieille Délira Délivrance dit: nous mourrons tous: les bêtes, les plantes, les chrétiens vivants, ô Jésus-Marie la Sainte Vierge; et la poussière coule entre ses doigts. La même poussière que le vent rabat d'une haleine sèche sur le champ dévasté de petit-mil, sur la haute barrière de cactus rongés de vert-de-gris, sur les arbres, ces bayahondes rouillés. (p. 1)

Délira is immediately characterized as old and weary, passively appealing to the saints for deliverance (perhaps her name is

meant to support the image). It is she who performs the acts
of piety, offering the feast for Legba at Manuel's return,
cleaning the tombs of her ancestors. Her religious fatalism,
her resignation and her enduring become associated with the
dust which settles over everything in a blanket of hopelessness
and dehydration. Her weariness is attached consistently to
such images:

> elle se sentait épuisée, . . . son vieux corps usé abandonné
> à la mort qui la confondrait, enfin, avec cette poussière, dans
> une nuit éternelle et sans mémoire. (p. 23)

Bienaimé, on the other hand, has given up all hope and
retreated into the past. (His inability to accept present misfortune will intensify to the point of complete withdrawal after
Manuel's death.) Each of his dreams of the past—the feasts
after the *coumbite*, the coziness of the hut with the rain beating
on the roof, his wife beside him and a pot of coffee on the
stove—is ended by an abrupt appearance of the dust. It is the
first thing he sees on coming back to reality. Dust becomes a
motif associated with the old couple, a constant reminder of
the problem.

The motif of water, symbol of life, responds to that of dust.
Délira has waited, enduring, for her son to come home. At
several points in the story, it is remarked that the dusty soil
is in a state of abeyance, wanting only water to become once
more capable of yielding life. Water, associated with life, is
also associated with Manuel. Manuel brings the water and he
brings life back to Fonds Rouge. His search for the water
associates him with it, on a rather abstract level, from the
onset. However, in the scene where Manuel discovers the
spring, the two entities, Manuel and water, visibly merge:

> Manuel s'étendit sur le sol. Il l'étreignait à plein corps:
> "Elle est là, la douce, la bonne, la coulante, la chantante,
> la fraîche, la bénédiction, la vie."
> Il baisait la terre des lèvres et riait. (p. 172)

Manuel coupling with Annaïse by the spring symbolizes the
fertility which will be unleashed by the flow of the water.
Manuel *passes on* life, as much as sharing the secret of the
water as by the physical act of procreation. Annaïse associates

her first experience of her own dormant fertility with the
sensation of water rumbling underground:

> Elle était étendue sur la terre et la rumeur profonde de l'eau
> charriait en elle une voix qui était le tumulte de son sang.
> (p. 190)

The scene is the actualization of the symbolic gesture of Manuel
embracing the earth at the moment he discovered the spring.
Annaïse brings the added dimension of fertility, unselfcons-
cious and natural, through which Manuel's life-giving will is
actualized. The constant attention drawn to her size, to her
slow and gracious stride and movements, symbolizes her
bounteousness, her fertility.

But the life that Manuel brings is not only in the physical
growth within the moistened earth and in the impregnated
body of the woman. He brings new life also in the unity which
is a necessary first step in starting the village to functioning
again as an organism, with each person participating for the
benefit of the whole. The image of water fuses with the concept
of life in the scene where Josaphat and his wife (who has just
told him she is pregnant with their first child) try to decide
whether their side should join Manuel's in bringing the water
down into Fonds Rouge. Josaphat says:

> — C'est lui qui commande, ce petit nègre. J'irai dire oui
> . . .
> — C'est la vie qui commande, dit Marianna, et l'eau, c'est
> la réponse de la vie. (p. 230)

Later, talking to the men at Larivoire's, Manuel uses the same
terms:

> Cette source que j'ai trouvée demande le concours de tous
> les habitants de Fonds Rouge. Ne dites pas non. C'est la vie
> qui commande, et quand la vie commande, faut répondre:
> présent. (p. 250)

If the motifs of dust and water join characterization on the
one hand to convey the meaning of Manuel's mission, certain
themes are overtly expressed through Manuel's conversations
with those close to him. The themes of the peasant/proletarian
revolt, of human solidarity, of man's casting off the yoke of
superstition and finding his reward through his own efforts,

are expressed through Manuel in their positive mode, through the other characters—whether friends or villains—in their negative mode. At the service which Délira gives in honor of Legba for the safe return of her son, Laurélien remarks: "Ah, c'est qu'il faut servir les vieux de Guinée," and one of his companions responds: "Notre vie est entre leurs mains" (p. 93). Manuel knows the error of such passive resignation. He participates in the ceremony because it is the custom and he respects the tradition. But he has said several days earlier to Délira:

> — C'est traître, la résignation; c'est du pareil au même que le découragement. Ça vous casse les bras: on attend les miracles et la Providence, chapelet en main, sans rien faire. On prie pour la pluie, on prie pour la récolte, on dit les oraisons des saints et des loa. Mais la Providence, laisse-moi te dire, c'est le propre vouloir du nègre de ne pas accepter le malheur, de dompter chaque jour la mauvaise volonté de la terre, de soumettre le caprice de l'eau à ses besoins; alors, la terre l'appelle: cher maître, et l'eau l'appelle: cher maître, et n'y a d'autre Providence que son travail d'habitant sérieux, d'autre miracle que le fruit de ses mains. (p. 65)

The *houngan* Dorméus is portrayed as a capitalist entrepreneur. He extracts his payment and renders the service afterwards. He is hardly distinguishable as an exploiter from Hilarion, the conniving *chef de section*, who plots, even as Manuel lies dying, to put him in jail and torture him until he tells where the water is located. Hilarion would then withhold the water from the villagers until in desperation they sold him their land. And the *prêtre savane* who performs the funeral service takes Délira's last money with impunity and then rushes through the ritual so that he can join Hilarion for a drink.[1]

Manuel, like Doris Jean of "Le Champ du potier", is an enlightened peasant. In Cuba, he has learned that laborers,

---

[1] See Claude Souffrant, "Le Fatalisme religieux du paysan haïtien," *L'Europe*, January 1971, pp. 27–41. Souffrant states that Roumain develops in *Gouverneurs de la rosée* the ideas current in Haiti on the causes of underdevelopment among the peasants: a resignation which becomes "attentisme surnaturaliste" and the flight from misery afforded by the intoxication of feasts and dances.

united in a common goal, can overcome exploitation and material misery. When Laurélien asks him: "Alors qu'est-ce que nous sommes, nous autres, les habitants, les nègres-pieds-à-terre, méprisés et maitraités?" he is able to answer:

> . . . eh bien, nous sommes ce pays et il n'est rien sans nous, rien du tout. Qui est-ce qui plante, qui est-ce qui arrose, qui est-ce qui récolte? Le café, le coton, le riz, le canne, le cacao, le maïs, les bananes, le vivres et tous les fruits, si ce n'est pas nous, qui les fera pousser? Et avec ça nous sommes pauvres, c'est vrai, nous sommes malheureux, c'est vrai, nous sommes misérables, c'est vrai. Mais sais-tu pourquoi, frère? A cause de notre ignorance: nous ne savons pas encore que nous sommes une force, une seule force: tous les habitants, tous les nègres des plaines et des mornes réunis. Un jour, quand nous aurons compris cette vérité, nous nous lèverons d'un point à l'autre du pays et nous ferons l'assemblée générale des gouverneurs de le rosée, le grand coumbite des travailleurs de la terre pour déchifrer la misère et planter la vie nouvelle. (p. 106)

Certain passages seem to resolve questions the young Roumain had posed metaphorically almost twenty years earlier. Manuel tells Annaïse that he has faith in life:

> . . . la foi que les hommes ne peuvent pas mourir. . . .
> — Oh sûr, qu'un jour tout homme s'en va en terre, mais la vie elle-même, c'est un fil qui ne se casse pas, qui ne se perd pas et tu sais pourquoi? Parce que, chaque nègre pendant son existence y fait un noeud: c'est le travail qu'il a accompli et c'est ça qui rend la vie vivante dans les siècles des siècles: l'utilité de l'homme sur cette terre. (p. 183)

This speech seems to take to its logical conclusion the theme of man's reward through his own efforts. But it is also the speech of a man who has reconciled himself to his inability to escape material contingencies, weakness, and mortality, but who has discovered a noncosmic way to extend his efforts beyond his historical presence on the earth. One is reminded of the images in the early poetry of the poet floating in space attempting to "se pencher hors de [lui-même]." Here, Manuel has discovered the means whereby man can after all reach beyond his apparent limitations. Roumain's hero has renounced the metaphysical solution and embraced an authentically humanistic doctrine.

These themes, of the revolt of the damned of the earth, of man's reward through his own efforts, of human solidarity and the liberation of the mind from superstition, are, in the final analysis, simply various aspects of the same essential theme of human betterment. They are broached many times during the course of the story as Manuel speaks with one or another of the characters, or as he reflects on his hopes for the future. It is this aspect of the novel which has caused some critics to speak of Roumain's tendency to editorialize and to inject his Marxist doctrines into the novel. Perhaps the clearest such examples are the next-to-last passage quoted above and the passage where Manuel, returning from town where he has had the marriage letter drawn up (to be presented later to Annaïse's mother), reflects on the benefits of learning:

> C'est nécessaire l'instruction, ça aide à comprendre la vie.
> . . . si l'habitant allait à l'école, certain qu'on ne pourrait plus si facilement le tromper, l'abuser et le traiter en bourrique. . . . (pp. 245–46)

These words recall, of course, points Roumain has already made in his articles "Sur les superstitions" and in his "Réplique au Révérend Père Foisset." The tendency on Roumain's part to repeat or tranpose passages from his previous works is pronounced, and we have met with it several times before. Manuel tells Annaïse that all men are brothers and "ont le même poids dans la balance de la misère et de l'injustice" (p. 137). The words echo those of "Madrid," of "Griefs de l'homme noir," of "Bois d'ébène." The vision of men united in misery converting themselves through their efforts into men united in well-being seems to haunt Roumain from the time of his discovery of Communism.

Although the editorializing in these passages may be somewhat distracting, the full effect of Manuel's words and thoughts lies in the fact that they are repeated after his death by those in whose company he spoke them. Délira, Laurélien, and Annaïse, in attempting to understand the tragedy of their personal loss, as they repeat his words in a new context of action, come to realize suddenly that his life and his sacrifice have meaning far beyond the personal reach of Manuel's individual existence. Thus, Laurélien at the funeral service hears a woman moan, asking God to grant strength and resignation, and the situation triggers an immediate response: "Manuel n'était pas partisan de la résignation," he thinks, and he realizes that though Manuel is dead, his words have a life of their own:

> . . . et si un jour sur le chemin de cette dure existence la fatigue nous tente avec des: à quoi bon? et des: c'est pas la peine, nous entendrons ta voix et nous reprendrons courage. (p. 301)

Délira, at Larivoire's, speaks before the assembled men of the enemy camp. She tells them of Manuel's wishes:

> Il m'a dit, voici ce que Manuel mon garçon m'a dit: vous avez offert des sacrifices aux loas, vous avez offert le sang des poules et des cabris pour faire tomber la pluie, tout ça a été innutile. Parce que ce qui compte, c'est le sacrifice de l'homme, le sang du nègre. (p. 307)

> On chante le deuil, c'est la coutume, avec les cantiques des morts, mais lui, Manuel a choisi un cantique pour les vivants: le chant du coumbite, le chant de la terre, de l'eau, des plantes, de l'amitié entre habitants, parce qu'il a voulu, je comprends maintenant, que sa mort soit pour vous le recommencement de la vie. (p. 308-9)

Annaïse comes to a similar realization when she hears Délira say: "Si seulement, Anna, on pouvait repriser la vie, reprendre le fil cassé. . . ." Annaïse remembers Manuel's words:

> . . . il me disait: la vie c'est un fil qui ne se casse pas. . . . Parce que chaque nègre pendant son existence y fait un noeud: c'est le travail qu'il a accompli. . . . (p. 316)

The age-old themes of the savior-hero and of the return of the prodigal son merge with the newer, secular proletarian ideal of the enlightened peasant passing on his awareness to others, uniting them in the struggle which Manuel himself calls a *rébellion*. Yet the archetypal theme of the savior-hero in its older, religious manifestation is very much present in *Gouverneurs de la rosée*, and as we have already noted, Manuel's advent has been prepared from the beginning of the book. Here again, a motif helps to carry the meaning. It arises, not surprisingly, in the constant images of the passage of time, the cycle of day and night. A majority of chapters open on the rising of the sun, close on its setting or orient themselves by its progress across the sky, the length of the shadows it leaves, the shades of orange it projects onto the barren countryside. The sun dictates the movements of the inhabitants as it does the condition of the earth. Many allusions to the cycle of night and day are associated directly with Manuel. The most striking are those associated with the day of his death. The progress from night to day and to night again is meticulously described, as Manuel waits for nightfall to slip away from his mother's hut to Larivoire's meeting; as he returns home along the path, after Gervilen's attack; as he regains consciousness and drags himself home along the road; as Délira brings him in and watches anxiously over him, praying, as he sleeps:

> . . . mais à quoi servent les prières et les oraisons quand cette dernière heure est arrivée dont parle le Livre: quand la lune s'éteint et les étoiles s'éteignent et la cire des nuages cache le soleil et le nègre courageux dit: je suis fatigué . . . (p. 262)

At dawn he awakens:

> Le jour passait sous le battement mal joint de la fenêtre. Les poules piaillaient comme à l'ordinaire.
> Manuel ouvrit les yeux. Il happait l'air. . . (p. 263)

He asks his mother to open the window:

> Il contempla cette clairière de lumière qui s'agrandissait dans le ciel. Il sourit faiblement:
> —Le jour se lève. Chaque jour, le jour se lève. La vie recommence. (p. 264)

Moments later, he is dead. His death has been like a passion. The day of his death, like a symbolic repetition of that passion, the funeral preparations, the wake, the funeral, the internment and the sitting up with the family are described against a backdrop of the day's progress and ending, followed by night and the dawn of a new day:

> . . . c'est le dernier cantique, le dernier, car voici le jour avec ses arbres noirs et frileux contre le ciel pâli et les habitants commencent à prendre congé. . . . les coqs s'égosillent de cour en cour, un jeune poulain hennit nerveusement dans la

savane. "Adieu, Délira," dit Laurélien. Il hésite: "adieu,
Annaïse" . . . et l'aurore entre par la fenêtre, mais Manuel
ne la verra plus, il dort pour toujours et à jamais. Amen.
(pp. 291–92)

The remarkable style of *Gouverneurs de la rosée* can be
glimpsed through the passages quoted above. The style does
in fact owe much to the plasticity of the images, those
portraying daybreak and sunset, as discussed above, and also
those which display the panoramic view of nature and the
silhouettes of man and nature against the horizon. Most such
views are seen, significantly, from Manuel's perspective. Frequently Manuel is on a hill surveying the barrenness of the
countryside, or he is contemplating the expanse of the environing countryside from the plain. Sometimes Annaïse is with
him, and her presence adds peace and serenity to the scene.
Perception from a sweeping elevated position is associated
thus with the savior-hero, and with his public and private
loves, his love for his people and for Annaïse. But the plasticity
of style does not stop with the broad expanses or restrict itself
only to Manuel's point of view. It is present in the minute
detail as well, as when the irrigation ditch is described as
"craquelé comme une vieille faïence" (p. 6) The degree of
animism in these descriptions is small. However, the way in
which trees are described and the constant presence of birds—
the only wildlife depicted—in or near them, suggests that they
participate in the symbolism of life reborn in the barren land.

This is particularly striking in the description of the tree
appearing as a kind of interlude between images of charcoal
manufacture, an activity which destroys life and moisture:

> Au-dessus des bayahondes flottent des haillons de fumée.
> Dans les clairières, les charbonniers déblaient les tertres sous
> lesquels le bois vert a brûlé à feu patient.
>   Un arbre, c'est fait pour vivre en paix dans la couleur du
> jour et l'amitié du soleil, du vent, de la pluie. Ses racines
> s'enfoncent dans la fermentation grasse de la terre, aspirant
> les sucs élémentaires, les jus fortifiants. Il semble toujours
> perdu dans un grand rêve tranquille. L'obscure montée de
> la sève le fait gémir dans les chauds après-midis. C'est un
> être vivant qui connaît la course des nuages et préssent les
> orages, parce qu'il est plein de nids d'oiseaux.

Estinval essuie du revers de la main ses yeux rougis. De l'arbre mutilé, il ne reste que le squelette calciné des branchages épars dans le cendre: une charge de charbon que sa femme ira vendre au bourg de la Croix-des-Bouquets. (p. 13)

The secret of life appears thus to be locked in the moist growth of the tree. And the moisure lies hidden far below in the earth. The tree provides the means of tapping it, and birds guide Manuel to it, attracting his attention by the noise they make. This appears to be the meaning of the giant fig tree at the source of the spring:

Il monta vers le figuier-maudit, il sentait ce souffle bienfaisant lui sécher la sueur, il marchait dans un grand silence, il entrait dans une pénombre verte et son dernier coup de machette lui révéla le morne refermé autour d'une large plate-forme et le figuier géant se dressait là d'un élan de torse puissant; ses branches chargées de mousse flottante couvraient l'espace d'une ombre vénérable et ses racines monstrueuses étendaient une main d'autorité sur la possession et le secret de˙ce coin de terre.

The symbolism is continued in the scene where Manuel brings Annaïse to the same spot:

Il écarta les lianes. Elle entra dans le mystère du figuier-maudit.
— C'est le guardien de l'eau, murmura-t-elle, avec une sorte de terreur sacrée.
— C'est le gardien de l'eau.
Elle contempla les branches chargées de mousse argentée et flottante.
— Il a grand âge.
— Il a grand âge.
— On ne voit pas sa tête.
— Sa tête est dans le ciel.
— Ses racines sont comme des pattes.
— Elles tiennent l'eau.
— Montre-moi l'eau, Manuel. (pp. 188–89)

Their dialogue has become a kind of litany, a ceremony of consecration which culminates in the act of love beside the spring and the confluence of the life forces in Annaïse.

Plasticity and symbolism are an important part of the style. But there is still another salient aspect, equally important, which contributes to the beauty of *Gouverneurs de la rosée*. A technique we have already encountered in *La Montagne ensorcelée* is developed in this later novel to a greater degree and is largely responsible for the beauty and poignancy of the story. Roger Gaillard described this property of Roumain's style in his discussion of *Gouverneurs de la rosée* and saw in it an expression of lyricism:

> Dès les premières lignes, on ne sait plus, en effet, qui parle, si c'est le personnage, si c'est l'auteur, si c'est même nous autres qui lisons. Et c'est ainsi que le lyrisme prend son essor. . . .
> Le chant est parfois double.
> Il est alors celui de l'auteur et celui du personnage. Une sorte de style parlé, sans guillemets, vient s'entrelacer au style narratif proprement dit. (Gaillard, *L'Univers romanesque de Jacques Roumain*, pp. 17–18.)

Most of the time, when lyricism becomes a *"chant double,"* involving the point of view of one of the characters, it is Délira whom the author chooses as his accomplice. Délira's character, her religious fervor, and her selfless and enduring love as a mother combine with stylistic technique to create a true lyricism, as in the passage cited by Gaillard, in the first chapter of the story:

> Elle l'avait embrassé. Elle avait tendu dans ses bras ce grand gaillard qui avait été à elle dans le profond de sa chair . . . et qui était devenu cet homme à qui elle murmurait à travers ses larmes: Allez mon petit, la Vièrge Altagrâce vous protège; et il avait tourné au coude de la route, et il avait disparu, ô fils de mon ventre, joie de ma vie, chagrin de ma vie, mon garçon, mon seul garçon. (p. 22)

However, the shift from *elle* to *mon*, as seen above, is not necessarily present in passages where lyricism is expressed through Délira's character. What is important is that such passages express the mother's sensitivity to the fact of having brought forth life and her intimate connection with that life. Délira, standing before Manuel, thinks back to the day of his birth:

> . . . elle sarclait dans le jardin et les douleurs l'avaient surprise. Elle s'était traînée jusqu'à la case, elle avait mordu

ses cris dans la chair de son bras et il était né dans un immense déchirement de son être. Elle avait elle-même coupé le cordon, lavé et couché l'enfant dans du linge propre avant de se laisser couler au fond de ce puits noir d'où étaient venus la tirer plus tard la voix de Bienaimé et le bavardage des commères. Et aujourd'hui, il était devant elle, cet homme si grand, si fort, avec cette lumière sur son front, et qui connaissait le mystère du sommeil de l'eau dans les veines des mornes. (p. 197)

It is not by chance that Délira is chosen by the author to carry lyric intensity. The same lyric intensity has already been associated with Anna, in *La Montagne ensorcelée*, at the wake of her son, dead as the result (she believes) of supernatural powers. A similar lyric intensity arises in the short story "Gouverneurs de la rosée" from the grief of the mother whom Jean-Gille contemplates as she washes clothes by the stream, despairing for her sick child. Roumain's tendency to associate the grief-stricken peasant mother with symbols of mythic consciousness appears even as early as the 1930 article "Port-au-Prince—Cap-Haïtien," in which the mother of Charlemagne Péralte is described in an attitude of prayer and by words such as "mater dolorosa," "calvaire," "station de . . . chemin de croix." And the portrait of the mother's grief before her sacrificed son at the end of *Gouverneurs de la rosée* (where the same shift in point of view appears in the style) amplifies the portrait of Manuel as Christ figure. The two ways in which Manuel is associated with birth merge in the last passage quoted above: Manuel's birth as Advent; Manuel's intuitive knowledge of how to ressurect life underneath surface layers of apparent death. In this way, the symbolism of motherhood throughout Roumain's work merges with the symbolism of the savior-hero in this last novel.

Lyricism is, however, but one manifestation of the style of the novel, with its shifting point of view. Humor or peasant simplicity are just as easily revealed through it, as in passages such as the following:

Pendant des années, la haine avait été pour eux une habitude. Elle avait donné un objet et une cible à leur colère impuissante contre les éléments. Mais Manuel avait traduit en bon créole le langage exigeant de la plaine assoiffée, la plainte des plantes, les promesses et tous les mirages de l'eau. Il les avait promenés d'avance à travers leurs récoltes: leurs yeux brillaient, rien qu'à l'entendre. Seulement, il y avait une condition: c'était la réconciliation. Et qu'est-ce que ça leur coûtait? Un geste à faire, quelques pas comme pour enjamber un pont et on laissait derrière soi les mauvais jours de misère, on entrait dans l'abondance. Hein, compère, que dis-tu? L'autre, pieds nus dans la poussière, les hardes déchirées, amaigri et affamé, écoutait en silence. C'est vrai qu'on était fatigué de cette vieille histoire. A quoi ça servait à la fin des fins? . . . Ce qui était sûr et certain, c'est qu'on ne pouvait pas se laisser périr. Alors? Alors, puisque c'est comme ça, on est d'accord. Mais qui ira parler aux autres? Moi, répondait Manuel. (pp. 215–16)

One finds in *Gouverneurs de la rosée*, as in *La Montagne ensorcelée*, a profusion of what might be called creolizing elements, that is, Creole modes of expression translated into French: "Ça me fait songer au temps longtemps" (p. 104), "je t'ai cherché tout partout" (p. 104), "le coeur et la raison c'est du pareil au même" (p. 138). Professor Mercer Cook has also enumerated creolizing elements in *Gouverneurs de la rosée*: words added for emphasis ("Je t'écoute, oui, Anna," p. 128; "Ce n'est pas si tellement le temps qui fait l'âge," p. 32); use of *icitte* (for *ici*); use of archaic French, retained in the patois ("Je n'ai pas besoin qu'on me baille la malédiction," p. 3).[2] Other syntactical variations, the many simple metaphors (comparisons using *comme*) are also typical of the peasant conceptualization of the world. All these various techniques—the shifting point of view, the panoramic, plastic descriptions of nature, the various motifs and their meaning, the freshness and simplicity of peasant conceptions of life as revealed through their speech—work together to create a style peculiar to *Gouverneurs de la rosée*. But the style also contributes to the characterization of the major figures, who display the whole spectrum of human love: the enduring devotion of a mother, the union of man and woman in spiritual and physical wholeness, friendship between two men based on respect and good will, the altruistic love of a man for all of his fellow men.

---

[2] Mercer Cook, "The Haitian Novel," *The French Review*, 19 (May 1946): 411–12.

La Montagne ensorcelée begins in Haiti the tradition of the *roman paysan*. It is a tradition which has yielded a wealth of novels, the one through which modern Haitian literature has received its widest exposure to the general reading public outside of Haiti. *Gouverneurs de la rosée* is generally considered to be the high point of that tradition, though by no means the end of it, as a good number of novels have been published since. Curiously enough, these two works and the one peasant short story constitute Roumain's only efforts in the genre. Obvious similarities and parallels set the two novels apart from the rest of Roumain's literary efforts. They are, first of all, the only instances in Roumain's work where the action comes to a neat end, with every single element completed after the resolution of a clearly stated problem. The funeral scene in both novels is similar in its description of the two men building the coffins; both are overcome with grief, Dornéval for his son and Laurélien for his friend. They take the nails distractedly one by one from the youngster at their side and release their frustration in the exercise of hammering. Gaillard, in *L'Univers romanesque de Jacques Roumain*, has pointed out similarities in the love scenes between Aurel and Grâce and between Manuel and Annaïse, in which Roumain uses almost the same terms to describe the women's reactions, but he does observe that these are superficial similarities. More importantly, the panoramic sweep over the countryside, the plasticity of description, although they occur to some extent in "Le Champ du potier" and even in *Les Fantoches,* are a striking aspect of the two peasant novels and the short story, where they are an integral part of the tone and meaning, imparting a poetic quality which most other novels in the tradition of the peasant novel do not cultivate.

Yet, for all their similarities, there is a world of difference between *La Montagne ensorcelée* and *Gouverneurs de la rosée.* To perceive the movement of forces within the later novel, we must look at *Gouverneurs de la rosée* not in the light of *La Montagne ensorcelée,* but in the light of *La Proie et l'ombre, Les Fantoches,* and "Le Champ du potier." And we must look with particular attention at the distance travelled between the short story, "Gouverneurs de la rosée," and the novel of the same name. These works, and not *La Montagne ensorcelée*, are the expression of Roumain's personality and his goal. We have noted a progressive mellowing of the characters in the urban fiction, which seemed to correspond to the ongoing maturation of the author. The process is taken further in *Gouverneurs de la rosée*, where the generational conflict, so central in the earlier prose, has become entirely peripheral. The antagonisms which flair up occasionally between Manuel and Bienaimé (who does not want Manuel to marry Annaïse or to end the feud separating the village) is treated as of no consequence: Manuel goes ahead and has the marriage letter drawn up on the assumption that Bienaimé will deliver it. Manuel is diametrically opposed to his mother's prayer and resignation, her acts of propitiation. Yet their ideological differences seem to have no effect on their personal relationship. The love between Manuel and Annaïse expresses for the first time in Roumain's work a relationship between man and woman untroubled by any gulf in their understanding of what each is searching for in life. Rather, their philosophical position is at the core of their love, for it is only when Manuel tells Annaïse that she can *help* in the cause that she lets herself fall in love with him.

The peasants in *La Montagne ensorcelée* are united in misery but are completely unaware of it. With the advent of the enlightened peasant, Manuel, unity in misery is transformed into human solidarity. But Manuel does not spring from Roumain's pen as a fully developed hero with no precedents. He and those close to him are separated from the characters of the first peasant novel by two factors: Roumain's espousal of Marxism, and his first real attempt to integrate the Haitian peasant's own self-concept into the ongoing portrait of the hero figure. The espousal of Marxism must have led Roumain to a kind of revelation just as intense as the religious crises which have been known in less secular eras to establish unshakable faith. Roumain wrote "Le Champ du potier" in the wake of his revelation, and the novel is steeped in Marxist theory.

Between the first and second peasant novels, Roumain wrote, as far as can be determined, only two pieces of fiction: "Le Champ du potier" and "Gouverneurs de la rosée." There is a link between these works as concerns the tendency in Roumain's fiction toward topicality, a tendency extremely pronounced in the first novel, *Les Fantoches,* and in the short stories of *La Proie et l'ombre.* It is interesting to note, however, that although "Gouverneurs de la rosée" is set during the Occupation, the only specific references to it are the mention of sites of *caco* skirmishes with the marines. Missing also is the element of party-line dogma so prevalent in "Le Champ du potier." The characterization in the short story also shows a progressive disentaglement from the contingencies of immediate reality. In "Le Champ du potier," Pierre, unlike his predecessors, has risen above personalities. He sees the people about him and their values in the light of class conditioning. His constant musings establish a tension in the human condition between individual desires and historical process. The struggle in "Gouverneurs de la rosée" appears to be on *both* the historical and the essential human levels. The hero's dilemma arises from the tension created between the two levels.

In Roumain's last novel, the question of struggle against an oppressive social system is raised, but as a side issue. Nor is the issue a necessary ingredient in the portrayal of Manuel's character. The rural police, who represent oppressive political authority, and the vodun and Christian priests, who represent oppression by mystification, can both be overcome. The struggle is in overcoming disharmony on a more essential, human and humanitarian level. It is human nature itself, not the social structure (which is simply a reflection of it), which must strive to throw out the evil within it and respond to good. No longer is there the implication that, if only the social order can be changed, man will live in peace and freedom. Manuel's doctrinaire statements are reminiscent of "Le Champ du potier," but he knows what Pierre and Doris did not realize: that dogmas and systems cure symptoms and not causes. Man's first struggle is against weaknesses and destructive tendencies within himself. Once a man has grown into full humanity, he will recognize and correct weaknesses in the system, such as the passivity fostered by the religious heritage of vodun and Christianity, but he will wisely emphasize traditional sources of strength, such as the *coumbite*. He will also have the strength to learn from his mistakes and from the example and teachings of others. He will, for example, allow himself to be taught that the cutting down of the trees on the hills disrupts the natural cycle of moisture and growth; he will understand the implications for his own situation in the Cuban workers' struggle in the cane fields.

In *Gouverneurs de la rosée*, the Marxist message has become internalized, integrated into Roumain's pre-existing concerns for human progress and meaning and for human solidarity, which were already discernible in the poetry of *La Revue Indigène* and in the exhortations of *Le Petit Impartial*. Socialism in *Gouverneurs de la rosée* becomes more generalized, "prodigalized," in the sense that it recognizes and utilizes native Haitian communal systems (the *coumbite*), recognizes and turns to good use (after the internationalism of the revolutionary poetry) man's sentimental attachment to his native land and its customs. The need for united effort is "essentialized" in the sense that the struggle is with the earth itself and the source of life locked within it, essentialized too in that the struggle depends for success on the awakening in man of the source of all true unity: his capacity for love. The message of Roumain's writing thus becomes universalized in *Gouverneurs de la rosée*.

Roumain has also effected a certain distillation—to use one of his terms—in the characterization of Manuel over that of Jean-Gille. Some of Jean-Gille's commitment, some of his determination, seems to stem from personal loss suffered at the hands of the oppressor. The picture of his house in flames with his family inside is burned forever on his memory. He thinks out in great detail how he will deal with any traitorous Haitian member of the Garde d'Haiti, a black man like himself, who should happen to fall into his hands. Although we cannot positively say that personal loss has triggered Jean-Gille's militancy, it certainly sustains it, and more importantly, it forces him to fight in a way which he feels is unnatural. Manuel, on the other hand, has suffered no such personal loss. His militancy is completely disinterested. And since he has no personal stake in the feud—he has been away the whole time—

his battle involves no side issue of self-interest. Manuel's movements are regulated solely by the rhythms of nature: life, growth, death, and rebirth.

Yet the last novel retains a trace of pessimism. Manuel has all but become the hero envisoned in the early poetry; he has found a way to reach beyond himself. But he too fails. He dies when everything in him wants to live. He is struck down by Gervilen as he dreams, outside the hut where Annaïse lies sleeping with her mother and brother, of the hut which he himself will build and furnish for her, and of the daily routine of his and Annaïse's existence together in it. In the public sphere, he has fuilfilled himself; his death is inevitable and even timely, as it thwarts the plans being plotted by the power structure (in the person of Hilarion) to use him as an agent for further oppression of the people. But in the personal sphere, Manuel has died too soon. His sacrifice, like that of the poets crucified against the sky in Roumain's early poetry, is an unwilling one.

Conclusion

Jacques Roumain's death was felt as a loss by many, Haitians and others alike. The day of his funeral in Port-au-Prince has been movingly described by one of his contemporaries:

> On the evening Jacques "left for Guinée," the weather was abominable. Pain and tears dampened the clothes of the crowds assembled on the edge of the road to bid him farewell. Hundreds of people, from all over the Republic witnessed a hopeshattering spectacle. A ray of light which had illuminated our path vanished in the darkness. As the casket disappeared under brick and mortar, Anthony Lespès shouted: "nous garderons le dieu!"[1]

The cry was taken up by Jean Brierre as the title for a series of commemorative poems completed less than a month after his friend's death, and in which Brierre's personal loss and the personal loss of Roumain's wife and mother are presented side by side with Roumain's character and personality, and his goals.[2] Nicolás Guillén, too, felt the loss deeply. He wrote to Roumain's widow:

> Desde la muerte de Jacques me propuse hacer algo sobre él. Algo que rebasara el simple artículo periodístico y que reflejara la amistad fraternal que . . . nos unió desde nuestro primer encuentro . . . ¿Qué haría? ¿Un ensayo? ¿Un poema? Este último fue lo que más profundamente cuajó en mi espíritu . . .[3]

---

[1] Antoine, "Literature—From Toussiant Louverture to Jacques Roumain," p. 120. Quoted also in Garret, *The Renaissance of Haitian Poetry*, p. 117.

[2] A passage of the poem is quoted in the Chapter V.

[3] Letter from Nicolás Guillén to Nicole Roumain dated Havana, July 10, 1948.

The letter was accompanied by the poem "Elegía a Jacques Roumain." The Black American writer Langston Hughes, whose friendship with Roumain went back to the time of his first visit to Haiti in 1931, was sufficiently moved to write, in a lyricism rare in his work, "A Poem for Jacques Roumain" not long after Roumain's death. Hughes's poem bears witness to the lasting impact of Roumain's life:

> Always
> You will be
> Man
> Finding out about
> The ever bigger world
>
> . . . .
> Always you will be
> . . . .
> Hand that links
> Erzulie to the Pope,
> Damballa to Lenin
> Haiti to the universe,
> . . . .[4]

These men, as poets, must have felt the need to perpetuate the meaning of Jacques Roumain's life because they perceived that that life had meaning beyond its private and historical contingencies. Like that of his heroes, Roumain's life unfolded on both the private and public levels. Like theirs, its dogged search for something more passed from private lonely quest to public endeavor. In perpetuating his life, the elegies of men such as Brierre, Guillén, and Hughes—and of Antoine also, in a sense—attempt in reality to perpetuate Roumain's work. In this, their writtings join those of Jacques Roumain himself. For it is Roumain's literary effort, his own esthetization of intensely felt needs, which survives him.

Roumain's own actions and the writings associated with

---

[4] Langston Hughes, "A Poem for Jacques Roumain," MS dated March 25, 1945. James Weldon Johnson Collection, Collection of American Literature, Beinecke Rare Book and Manuscript Library, Yale University. The above lines are from what appears to be the definitive version.

his name in the period 1932–34 attest to his belief that the accomplishments of Nationalism—and therefore his own activities in his first years of adulthood—were spurious and illusory. His career as politician and diplomat, a career upon which he entered, to all evidences, with considerable misgivings, was short-lived and disconnected. And if his socialist activism in Haiti may now, forty years later, be viewed generally with detached admiration, it is nonetheless true that such activism virtually disappeared with him. His investigations into the Ciboney and Arawak cultures brought scattered additions to the body of ethnographic knowledge but joined the efforts of other men working more patiently and single-mindedly toward the accumulation of that knowledge. Of all of Jacques Roumain's varied activites, only his literature has survived, with a life of its own.

It is here that we find the record of Roumain's life, for it is through his poetry and his novels that we discern a being who, as Edner Brutus remarked, lived intensely.[5] That life, an "excès de vie" as Roumain himself called it,[6] he transposed onto the esthetic level, through words, with a consistency and a continuity in no way matched by his other endeavors. Yet all these other endeavors, in the public and the private spheres, are there. This characteristic is what Roussan Camille must have had in mind when he spoke of the "harmonie complète"[7] between Roumain and his work. Although Jacques Roumain may be remembered for many endeavors, it is the field of literature which can most comfortably claim him at its own, for he was above all else, both as witness and as participant, a painter of emotions and of character, a poet and novelist, bent on discovering man's best ultimate relationship with nature and with himself, and urging his fellows toward it.

Jacques Roumain was finally able to realize before his unexpected death a true synthesis, in *Gouverneurs de la rosée*,

---

[5] Brutus, "Jacques Roumain," p. 10: "Mr. Roumain m'a toujours paru un élégant ennuyé qui, par l'une de ces contradictions bizarres, intensément, vit" (written in 1933).

[6] In Vieux, "Entre Nous: Jacques Roumain," p. 105.

[7] The passage is quoted in the Preface of this study.

between an emotional state carefully worked into a piece of art, and a life's endeavor in which considerations of personal glory, philosophical withdrawal and bravado had been relegated to the background. Thus most readers of *Gouverneurs de la rosée* have clearly seen that Manuel Jean Joseph does not merely speak for Jacques Roumain; he perpetuates his life.

*Appendix
Bibliography
Index*

Appendix

TRANSLATIONS OF FRENCH AND SPANISH PASSAGES IN TEXT

PREFACE

Page vii (*Le Nouvelliste.*)

Jacques Roumain realizes in his engaging personality a very rare thing: the complete harmony between life and ideas, between the man and the writer.

INTRODUCTION

Page 2 (Group I interview)

And Jacques had it announced to us that he would come— he knew that we were always together on such and such a day, at such and such a time—and to wait for him . . . that he'd come . . . to kick the fellow in the shins. . . . And he really did come; he gave me his hand—How are you?—How are you?— and he gave the other fellow a kick . . . Just to show you how adventurous he was. A child of his age would not have gone attacking another child two years older and rather strong.

Page 3 (Letter from Grünau written in 1922)

"I am nervous, always looking into space, take walks by myself, speak and eat little."

"Reading is the only thing I do with enthusiasm: Schopenhauer, Nietzsche, Darwin, and the poems of Heine and Lenau."

Page 3 (Letter from Grünau dated October 23, 1922)

. . . leave aside all talk of philosophy. Let everyone look for truth where he finds it. What good does it do to discuss? Everything passes, everything goes back into nothingness. . . .

Page 4 (Letter from Grünau dated April 10, 1923)

"Faded Violets"

I contemplate you and a muted sadness invades me
On seeing your poor wilted petals.
Like lips of the dead, lips forever closed
You bend your pensive heads where perhaps a dainty mouth
Planted a kiss, dreaming of the loved one.
Do you think, o little flowers, of the oblivious hand
Which was to destroy you, caressing you the while?
Do you dream of the hour when, adorned in your charms,
You [. . .] when, with a kiss, you were given alms?
    Or perhaps you remember the minute
    when an unhappy lover
Confided to your colloras a tear
Which like the dew sparkled there a moment?!

Page 5 (Vieux, p. 107)

Who then affirms . . . that there are two men in each of us? Beside the sportsman . . . exuberant with life, there is in me a melancholy side, the elegant ennui of Byron. I feel these two men collide in my acts. In Switzerland we were joyful students, loving pleasure and, certain days, not refraining from a joyous brawl.

Page 6 (Vieux, p. 105)

As regards zootechny, I was above all interested in the bullfights. I loved most of all the full sun of the fights. It corresponded to that excess of life which I have. It was also at that time that I met Montherlant. His *Bestiaries* struck me to a degree that you would not be able to imagine. I felt in him a poet with whom I had certain affinities.

Page 7 fn. 10.

"While the literary movement of the present generation of youth was being set in motion, painting was revealed to me by Jacques Roumain and Philippe Thoby-Marcelin. What an explosion of joy as I skimmed through the books they passed to me! I saw the heralding of a new dawn."

Page 7 (Letter from Zurich dated January 15, 1925)

Mr. Director:

You will excuse my audacity in writing you, for I am completely unknown to you personally. You will excuse me surely when I tell you that I pride myself on being Haitian . . . forced, because of my studies in engineering, to prolong my exile in Europe for some time still, inaction is each day more and more unbearable. I am eager to return to Haiti, to aid in raising the courage of the masses and in easing the people's burden.

I will perhaps seem extremely presumptuous to you if I tell you that I am only eighteen; but patriotism, just as valor, does not wait upon the accumulation of years, and you would overwhelm me if you consented to do me the honor of considering me among the number of your most faithful allies.

CHAPTER I

Page 14, fn. 2

All Haitians vividly resented this jolt, but its repercussions in literary works were varied. The group whose members were already mature at the arrival of the occupant reacted by a return to patriotic poetry: they lamented the country's lot (*Threnody for Haiti*, by Edmond Laforest [1876–1915]) or else they set about exalting the exploits of 1804 [i.e., the Haitian war of Independence] (Christian Werleigh [1895–1947] *The Palmetto in the Light* [1938]); others chose to evoke the Quisqueyan [Indian] legends and landscapes (*Quisqueyan Poems* [1926], by Frédéric Burr-Reynaud) when they were not launching into vengeful anathemas against the occupant and his collaborators [i.e., Burr-Reynaud's *Anathemas*, 1930].

Page 14 (Vieux and Thoby-Marcelin, p. 30)

For Haitian literature to exist it would have been necessary for the works to reflect more the aspirations, tendencies, the very soul of the country. . . . Our elders could have written works which would have been profoundly ours. It would be necessary . . . to analyze the Haitian soul, bare it and dissect it. By that means and that means alone can be produced that originality which obsessed them and which they went so far in search of, except where it could be found.

Page 15, fn. 5

"How should one confront the all-powerful invader if not by a moral resistance in order to safeguard the ancestral heritage and the cultural and intellectual patrimony of the nation."

Page 16 (*La Trouée*, p. 1)

Literature is not what one thinks in Haiti. It is not an occupation of pedants and of the leisured. We shall banish both. It is the cry of a people that wants to say what ferments in themselves. It is not that agreeable "local-color" imitation of some, nor is it that pale affectation of certain others. It is the expression of Ideas, of our ideas, the ideas of Haitians.

Page 16 (*La Trouée*, p. 1)

We will study the great problems, those which present themselves to the present Haitian generation and which that generation pretends not to know about, even though they are staring them in the face. . . . We will tackle them, and the bundle made by our good wills united into one will prevail.

Page 17, fn. 9

"Oswald Durand is a precursor. He is an indigenist."

Page 18 (Sylvain, p. 4)

The reader whom we choose, the one who is most dear to us, is the young man of twenty whom . . . generous enthusiasm transports, who still has a foolish and heroic heart, who dreams of the absolute. . . .

Page 18 (*La Trouée,* p. 2)

. . . we appeal to all those who aspire: Young or Old. . . . To the old, whom the experience of men and of things has matured and who have the word of wisdom; to the young, that the reader might discover, among talents in search of themselves, talent which affirms itself.

Page 19 (Sylvain, p. 3)

The ideas, true or false, which one has of a country are those which the poets, the novelists, the painters, the sculptors give of it, faithful image of a deceptive canvas. . . .

Literature is the infallible expression of the soul of a people.

Page 19 (Sylvain, p. 7–8)

What we will try to do in our journal.—A faithful and living picture of the various manifestations of contemporary Haitian life and thought.

Intellectual and artistic, economic and commercial life. The Haitian point of view of issues . . . and since the word *native* has been made into an insult, we claim it as a title, the point of view of the native. A return to sincerity and naturalness, based on the living model, on direct description, a more pronounced tone of Haitianism, that is what seems to characterize our young poetry.

Page 20 (Sylvain, p. 52)

I find the true poetry in the refrains our black nurses used to sing to us in the evenings, which lulled us to sleep as children: "Go to sleep, my little one, crab in the soup. . . ."

The songs of the women singers who led the country dances. . . .

Our folklore is rich in such songs. It is the sound of the tom toms . . . the call of the conche. . . . It is the rhythm, vibrating and sensuous, of a meringue with its lascivious melancholy which should pass into our poetry.

Page 22 (*La Trouée*, p. 22)

"Rain"

The rain, monotonous typist, drums
at the closed windows.
Lights flicker
rose-colored
in the dense obscurity.
Flashes, serpentine giants,
dance
Twisted to patches
of black sky.
The night
unfurls its sails of moire
over distant
gardens
where noiselessly mourning tears
fall
for roses which shed their petals.

"Noon"

Palm trees watch over the weary
landscape. Orange trees carry clusters of sun
gold-ripened in the vermilion noon.
A solitary latania sweeps
clouds in the azure
where insects
flash, sparks
suddenly
born in incandescent
rays. I listen to the rhythm of the silence
embalmed with the incense

of unreal flowers.
My soul is attracted toward the tangent
of heavy desires haunted by
the shadow of implacable phantoms,
divinely out of reach.

Page 24 ("Miragôane," *La Trouée*)

Over the road treacherously cracked
the car like a crutch
jolts . . .
. . . Very low,
squatting upon the knoll,
huts
look on with indifference.
Then suddenly: Red,
The eyes of the monster crouching in the shadow
The heat of a thousand intense lives
Rises brutally toward me.

Page 24 ("Echappée," *La Trouée*, p. 00)

To believe oneself solitary and joyous
in the savannah. . . .
.   .   .   .
To run in the cane fields
among
the bristling of silver swords
in the sun. . . .
.   .   .   .

Page 25 ("Orage," *La Revue Indigène*, p. 112)

The wind chased a herd of white bison in the
vast prairie of the sky. Silent and powerful, they
crushed the sun; the sun went out
The wind howled like a woman in childbirth:
the rain came running . . .
and drew over the world curtains of mist. . . .
. . . came the thunder
and applauded. Then everything got quiet to let the thunder
applaud. . . .
A herd of black bison emigrated from the east to
the west, and the
        night came like a woman in mourning.

Page 25 ("A Jouer aux billes," *La Revue Indigène*, p. 208)

The sky is too vast for a child to be able to grasp it in his little arms. But tell him: Sky, bowler hat; then he will stretch his little child hands toward the firmament hanging on the hatpeg of the palm tree, will pluck the moon and put it in his pocket. O child poet!

Page 26 ("Insomnie")

Indecisive clarity.
The night
enters the room, somber veil
embroidered with stars.
The moon is a big fruit
balancing on my insomnia.

Page 26 ("Pluie")

Lights flicker
rose-colored
in the dense obscurity.
Flashes, serpentine giants,
dance
Twisted to patches
of black sky.

Page 26 ("Calme")

The midnight sun
of my lamp. The fleeing time
does not disturb my peace.

. . . .
My table is a luminous island
in the black cotton-wool of the silent
night.

Page 27 ("Horizon . . . soleil," *La Presse*, p. 3)

Thread stretched along the length
Of the rocks, it does not break
Only the white flash of a wing
interrupts it an instant

Rest is the fall
Toward the night. . . .

. . . .
Sun adrift
Your arch above the shore
casts to the sky the fan
Of which night soon deprives us.

. . . .
The net of night
Shields us from the boredom
Of all lasting pleasures.

O peace, at the bottom of the well.

Page 27 ("Angoisse," *Anthologie* . . . "*indigène*," p. 36)

The soul
   is too heavy to rise
   to the mirror of the eyes

Page 28 ("Attente," *Anthologie* . . . "*indigène*," p. 37)

The lead of the night drips into the silence,

Page 28 "(Attente," *Anthologie* . . . "*indigène*," p. 37)

O the eyes sad to watch the golden stream
which the one-eyed street-lamp spills over the asphalt
and by which you will come miraculously pale
and soft and your eyes full of petals.
   Here is the rain
   that falls, falls, falls, falls.
   The gutter laughs and rolls
   imaginary nuggets, but you will not come any more.
   The rain
      falls, falls, falls, falls.

Page 28 ("Après-Midi")

   . . . Fine javelins
of the palm trees—motionless
fans fixed in Time.

. . . .
Each minute like a century of boredom
yawns.

Page 29 ("Horizon . . . soleil")

> Rest is the fall
> toward night, minutes.
> Silence, a finger held to the lips

Page 29 ("Attente")

> The lead of night drips into the silence,
> The agony of being limited and the childish temptation
> to advance the pendulum which nibbles away at time with
> derisive teeth.

Page 29 ("Insomnie," *Anthologie . . . "indigène,"* p. 39)

> I lean outside of myself
> to listen to a tenuous
> voice, and sad like a fragrance

Page 29 ("Mirage")

> O to lean over
>   to gather stars
>   and a bit of the sky.

Page 29 ("Noir," *La Revue Indigène,* p. 62)

> . . . I want to hear my sadness
> sob. Then place your hand, o
> very softly on my heart;

Page 30 ("Insomnie," *Anthologie . . . "indigène,"* p. 39)

> I reach my hands
> toward you and clasp
> the sky
> —and emptiness.

Page 30 ("Mirage")

> To close the door,
> to open it:

Happiness remains always without.
If you were there
your hands would prolong my life.

Page 30 ("Corrida," *La Revue Indigène*, pp. 115–16)

Death stands before you with pointed horns.
Your arms prolonged by banderillas, you advance; you are
a young Aztec god nourished by sun and the hearts of the
defeated.

Page 30, fn. 15

hands which bleed
from having heaved up to the heart
the bitter emptiness

.   .   .   .

to feel the caress of multiplied arms
to mingle in one's multiplied arms.

Page 31 ("Mirage," *Anthologie* . . . "*indigène*," p. 39)

I watch
  the Milky Way tremble.
O to lean over
  to gather stars
  and a bit of the sky.
Farewell
  farewell
my arms are a too-heavy cross.

Page 31 ("Le Chant de l'homme")

I wanted for my distress
narrow streets, the caress
on my shoulders of good hard walls.
But you, o men, have
enlarged them with your footsteps,
with your desires,
with stale smells of rum
of sex and of "draught-beer."
I wander through your multicolored
labyrinths and I am weary
of my plaint.

II

Thus:
toward you have I come
with my great heart naked
and red, and my arms heavy
with armfuls of love
And your arms toward
me were extended quite open
and your hard fists
struck my face hard.
Then I saw:
your lowly grimaces
and your eyes slimy
with abuse.
Then I heard
around me croaking, pustulous
toads—Thus:
solitary, somber,
strong now in my shadow
my only faithful companion,
I project the arch of my arm
over the sky.

Page 33 ("Corrida")

On the sand the blood splatters little Spanish
flags of purple and gold;

Page 33 ("Corrida")

but as for you, you go trampling the flags and you go up
an invisible stair above the crowd, a-
bove enthusiastic hands,
above fainted women, with an
ambiguous smile at the corner of your mouth.

Page 34 ("Corrida")

Then, Armillita the Azter, you present with the
sacerdotal gesture of the priest of Huitzilopochtli the ear
of the victim to the adoration of the Spanish crowd.

Page 34 ("Nungesser et Coli," *La Trouée*, p. 49)

Nungesser and Coli, I think of your death,
—splendor of flight toward infinity
sidereal pleasure of the strong being—
Nungesser and Coli, I think of your fists reaching out
of the glaucous water, your burnt fingers still gripped
at the cruel immensity
of the sky.

Page 34 ("Cent mètres," *La Revue Indigène*, pp. 14–15)

Arms, propellers suddenly
set in motion by the pistol
turning madly in a quarter circle. Twenty meters.
All abreast. Well-being;
pleasure of the wind
between the teeth.
Fifty meters: two fall back.
Chop the air. Woodcutters of
fatigue which seals the
muscles to the ground.
Despair.
Two others abreast.
Eighty meters. One thinks: "Will I pass? Oh will I pass?
Agony,
Agony of the little hammer
against the anvil of my temples
agony of the black hole
between the misery of my legs and the
finish line. I will.
I'm passing. No.
I will. I pass."
The other: "Ha! my body weary
Ha! my lungs
aching carburators
in my chest on fire."
Last effort of the body projected
against the string. Rictus of Prometheus
delivered. Thrombus.
Finally.
(Newspapers of the next day:
So-and-so, overcome by lung failure).
The grass is a green and fresh tomb.

Page 35 ("La Danse du poète-clown," *La Revue Indigène,* p. 62)

O Agni! thou who blazest in
the blood of
the desperate dancer!

Page 35 ("La Danse du poète-clown")

. . . Turn around, o pure one
enough to make hot again your despair
turn so as to see them no longer
turn, already they are no more
than mist. Do you mean
now to live the wound
of your heart; they were
they were! to the death, turn
dance, turn, o poet, o flame, o clown.

Page 36 ("Appel")

This and that have caused my sorrow
to burst,
and my sorrow grew

. . . .
and a great clamor of rage
came

. . . .
I will go to you

Page 36 ("Appel")

Then I shall howl
and you will come running
for, at death
I will have howled
and death
attracts
with its long arms

You will rush up
with your eyes wild
like wild beasts pursued
by brush fire

Page 37 ("Appel")

> listen to my clamor;
> I want
> like a flame
> for it to penetrate you
>
> . . . .
> I want it to kindle
> like red blood
> in the veins of old men.

Page 37 ("Appel")

> "Ha cowards, ha dogs
> Ha, men-with-lowered-eyes
> Does death have to
> howl
> does fire have to
> burn,
> does the mouth have to
> spit
> for you to rush up in a crowd?

Page 37 ("Appel")

> And your eyes are they *put out*
> and your hearts
> *dried up*
> and your fists *mutilated*
> for you not to know
> *in* you
> *around* you
> *among* you
> death come from beyond the walls
> which *howls* insults
> *burns* your fatherland
> and *spits*
> its white disdain
> on your black foreheads?

Page 38 (Vieux, p. 106)

For me, the poem contains a drama. And only this dramatic aspect can elicit an emotion. What is called artistic emotion, and which is nothing more than the satisfaction of something well said, does not suffice for me. I am more demanding. I want for the poem the vibrant force that shakes. The motor. In "One Hundred Meters" I didn't want to paint a canvas. I am not a painter. I wanted to make come alive what I had run. Fever. The impressions . . . of that banal thing, extract its soul. The drama of the track. The drama in the nerves and the muscles. From the time that they are bent over, the runners, ready for takeoff, up to the minute when the white thread will make for one of them a fine lined sash.

Page 39 (Vieux, p. 106)

The image comes alone. It even imposes itself. It would hurt not to put it in.

Page 39 ("L'Aube," *La Presse*, p. 3)

. . . Adieu, here is the dawn; the cold light of awakening
— Stay yet. The rings of a ray of sunlight
Play in your curls and your body is soft to my lips!
. . . Adieu, beloved, here is the dawn. To each time its fevers.

Page 40 ("Mon Carnet," *La Presse*)

. . . the poet in general is an instinctive being who seizes life forcefully by all its senses. His mind intervenes in the poetic conquest only for the delicate booty, for the most subtle enjoyments of prosodic arrangement. This sensuality is translated in the lines of poetry by sounds, images, assonances, which are to reality what onomatopoeia is to the sense of the word it would express. Baudelaire, more than anyone else, will prove my point by this immense line:
    Descend, descend, lamentable victims . . .
Notice the extraordinary progression from the *d* of "descend" to the *t* of "lamentable" and of "victims": one has the impression of visually perceiving the "Dammed Women" slowly descending the steps: one has the impression of hearing their steps!

This sensuality thus exteriorized is the mark of all eminent writers.

Page 41 (Vieux, p. 110)

— What I intend to do I do not know yet. I have no literary ambition, you know. Nor do I anticipate publishing in less than three years. My volume of poetry will be entitled: *The Blotter.*

I'm taking notes for a novel.

But whatever my work, it is to my land that I will dedicate it. . . .

CHAPTER II

Page 44 (*Le Petit Impartial*, February 15, 1928)

In these times, when it is said that a vile mercantilism comes to sully the best intentions, when it is repeated that all activities tend toward a regressive materialism, one cannot praise too much the noble effort of that fine pleiade of intellectuals of the *Revue Indigène*, who out of good will devote their youthful fervor to the praiseworthy enterprise of continuing our traditions of strong and pure French culture, all the while renewing the outlines, in spite of the surrounding contingencies.

Page 45 ("Le Peuple et l'Elite," *Le Petit Impartial*, February 22, 1928)

We are today facing the American as our ancestors faced the armies of the First Consul.

And was there, at the Crête-à-Pierrot, at the Ravine-à-Couleuvres, an "elite" and a "rabble"? No. There were men determined to die rather than live as slaves. Men who knew that blind death strikes down indifferently rich and poor, literate and illiterate. . . .

All of us are suffering. Misery has equalized us. Harshly. Above all petty quarrels. There is the injured fatherland to be saved.

Therefore see this peasant. Put your hand in his hand, rough calloused and fine from touching, from laboring each day in the Blessed Earth.

Let us be brothers united. Without that, a death more cruel than physical death awaits us.

Let us break the barriers. Let us close ranks!

Page 46 ("Péralte Crucifié")

Show yourselves then, ghosts of Péralte and of Battraville and you, unknown soldiers of the plains of the North, rise up from the abyss with your poor limbs convulsed and torn, your chests riddled by American machine guns and precede us in the paths where warriors march.

Page 46 ("La Terre et les Morts")

This land cannot die: this magnificent field devastated by sacrilegious hands.

Devastated, but only on the surface. Its depths are swelled and rich with the blood and corpses of men nobly fallen: our fathers.

These men passed away. But after them remained that living thing, that flame: their sacrifices. . . .

The ancestors are that deeply rooted tree of which Louverture spoke, and its powerful sap has risen even to us and has fortified us.

We have heard the voice of the dead Heroes. Their call has sounded upon our hearts like a bell sounding the alarm.

Page 47 ("Jeune Haïti")

That is hard to say.

It is hard to denounce that cause of our nourishment: the generation which precedes us.

Isn't it they, the vanquished ones, who flounder about in the governmental mire? . . .

Bogged down in the ditch, they did not see us above them, ready to stride over them in a single bound, our hearts saddened by the will to sacrifice, but our legs agile and our eyes turned toward the ancestors.

Page 47 (Petit and Roumain, "A la Jeunesse")

Youth, where are you? . . .

For twelve years, indifferent for the most part, we have witnessed the dismemberment of the nation, the treason of those called to defend us, the capitulations of first this one and then that, the putting up for auction of the Heritage of the Ancestors by a minority faction at once servile and cynical.

Like degenerates, we have, under the pretext of "Honor and Happiness"—and by allowing the glory of the ancestors to be tarnished—accepted living in the most abject servitude, corrupted by the American dollar and cowards to the point of being incapable of generating any wholesome reaction. . . .

Youth, you are scattered! That should not be. Group yourselves!

Page 49 ("Un homme Contre un Empire—Mahatma Gandhi")

I shall not call him superhuman.

That word has taken on an almost exclusively Nietzschian sense, a meaning too harsh for he who recommends *Ahîmsa,* nonviolence.

We can directly grasp the essence of the superman.

For that, we need only lift our eyes, intensifying ourselves, looking higher up.

Such is Gandhi, so far outside of common humanity that, in order to understand him, one must purify oneself; in order to grasp him, one must look outside of oneself.

I shall call him extrahuman. . . .

Page 49 ("La Non-Violence")

"Nonviolence"

On hearing these words, one could think a cowardly pacifism stemming from some oriental fatalism.

One would be wrong. Gandhi's nonviolence is an ACTIVE RESISTANCE without violence. He has excluded from it the idea of pusillanimity to such an extent that he calls it the SWORD of self-sacrifice. He demands brave nonviolent men at his side. . . .

And what a fine blade he has in his hands. Supple, flexible, I would say fluid. Not initiating, but wounding immediately whoever would seize it . . .

Against such an enemy, the English government ran out of wind.

Page 49 fn. 4

"Why bother? The good Lord will take care of everything."

Page 50 (Article about Gandhi, *Le Petit Impartial*)

Through the aspirations common to all Indians—the Bramans, who are in the majority; the Muslims, who are 80 millions; the Buddhists, very numerous; and finally the weak Parsi, Jewish, and Christian minorities—he works for a strong union.

He calls them his "dear friends," lays down to them their duties as INDIANS ABOVE ALL, and they listen piously to him and obey him.

Page 50 (Last article in Gandhi series, *Le Petit Impartial*)

In his somber prison, I see the Mahatma, the great-souled one, who has taken onto himself all the sufferings, all the miseries of his country. I see him, weak, little, homely, but his eyes overflowing with love and weaving for a regenerated India the Khaddar of liberty.

Page 51 (Petit and Roumain, *Le Petit Impartial*, June 13, 1928)

. . . we protest against the French secular clergy, which, especially since the Yankee occupation, meddles in our politics in the most unfortunate, the most anti-Haitian manner. . . .

Page 51 (Petit and Roumain, *Le Petit Impartial*, June 13, 1928)

What we demand is respect for the Concordat, whose terms require the elevation of Haitian priests to ecclesiastical dignities.

Page 52 (Petit and Roumain, *Le Petit Impartial*, July 24, 1928)

We well knew that with the civic and mental deformation effected in our environment by the French priests and monks, we would have to deal with a coalition of infamous and shady people who cannot live outside of intrigues and orgies which the ill-served sacristy obtains for shirkers in search of pleasures who pass themselves off as Christians, even as ministers of God, when one has only to raise their soiled skirts to uncover there the grimacing antichrist sneering upon the heads of the "dirty niggers" they say we are!

Page 52 ("Le 'Nouvelliste' Inconscient")

This passage [containing the accusation] is a sin of high treason, for its author has forgotten that above Catholics and Protestants there is the HAITIAN, and he arms them with a stupid and useless bitterness one against the other.

Page 53 ("Défense de Paul Morand")

It is our fault if we are ugly, and that is not as paradoxical as it at first seems: there is no standard of beauty, or rather, each race has its standard of beauty. Thus the esthetic sense can only be relative and limited to each ethnic group. Thus we have become used to considering the white race as a standard of beauty. Since we are its opposite, we have *made ourselves ugly.* (Italics in text)

Page 54 ("Défense de Paul Morand")

certain passages . . . have the aspect of a Call to Arms: "The black people will win," swore Occide to himself. "They will never see any worse day than the past, but they will not be content with a short vengeance.

Page 55 (*Le Petit Impartial,* February 5, 1929)

. . . Guérin's article had been "in favor of the defense of the rights of the Haitian people." . . . According to Roger Gaillard, the arrest was made "following a manifest signed by them [Guérin, Petit, and Roumain] against the 'illegal consecration of the white bishops Juliot and Lebinhin' instead of the 'honorable Haitian priests' Mondésir, Qualo and Codada."

Page 55 (Roumain's response in court, April 1, 1929)

If, to defend myself against the accusation brought against me, I were to go back to the events of 1922, it would be easy for me to prove how Louis Borno . . .

Page 55 (Roumain's continued response in court, April 1, 1929)

The public prosecutor Mr. Lanoue is voluntarily deceiving himself when he insinuates that only a minority of men, dissatisfied because they have no share of the power, hate the Louis Borno government. No. That is the sentiment of all Haitians, if one excepts the small percentage of functionaries nourishing themselves at the garbage pails of Cooperation.

Page 56 (Guérin's response in court, April 1, 1929)

You are not our judge. It is you who should be in our place. Condemn us, assassinate us, your treason will smash you. You feed on the white man's dirt. He will choke you, his dirt will kill you.

Page 56 (*Le Petit Impartial,* April 6, 1929)

. . . the accused allowed themselves to be escorted to the lower level, under the guard of a sergeant of the Gendarmerie. When they got there and as they were receiving the loud encouragements and bravos of a crowd of youths who had stationed themselves in the street, the public prosecutor Lanoue loudly insulted Mr. Jacques Roumain.

The latter, in two leaps, escaped from the sergeant, who was trying to seize him, hurled himself toward the stairs, and irrupted violently into the courtroom.

He was restrained from throwing himself on Prosecutor Lanoue, who made a suspicious gesture toward his briefcase, in which he had placed a gun.

The tumult reached its height, and the accused were led to prison to the acclamations of a crowd which accompanied them up to the gate of the penitentiary. ("The Judgment of Mssrs E. Guérin, Georges Petit, and Jacques Roumain")

Page 57 (Gaillard, *Carl Brouard,* p. 72)

At the end of the first hearing, at the moment of the usual formalities, Jacques Roumain, believing that his sister (who was moving toward him) was going to be molested by a guard, throws himself in her direction; he is beaten and wounded.

Page 58 ("Mon Carnet," September 21, 1929)

Today, I feel morose: what am I really? A kind of clown perched at the top of a newspaper column capering about from one subject to the other to divert his readers. An employee who delivers his thought and sometimes his heart, in detail, in a daily chronicle.

Page 59 ("Mon Carnet," September 23, 1929)

Here we are. This morning, upon opening my window, I saw that it was a nice day. . . .

No; today, decidedly, it is too nice a day for the gathering up of paradoxes. In all tranquility, I declare to you, readers, that at this moment you weary me considerably and that I have no intention of entertaining you with little commentaries on marriage, friendship, or boredom.

Page 60 (Evan's letter to Roumain)

In view of the preceding, I advise you that the formation of your League appears to be a breach of existing laws relative to meetings of twenty persons or more.

Page 63 ("Idées et Opinions—Agissons!")

It is to this proposition that the whole of the Nationalist campaign should presently address itself. By it alone will well-being come to us. The Commission of Inquiry, aside from its limited powers, will arrive in Haiti too late for its report to represent an obstacle to the election of a president by the Cabinet.

It must be the houses of the legislature—that is, the Haitian people—which chooses the patriotic and conscientious arbiter of its destinies, for, to quote the great Hindu nationalist Mahatma Gandhi: "A government is an instrument of service only to the extent that it is founded upon the will of the people. It is but an instrument of oppression when it obtains obedience at the point of a bayonet."

Page 64, fn. 18

"Let no one deceive himself. The United States is a country of opinion. The more the Haitian cause appeals to the soverign power of public opinion, the more chance it will have to be heard, understood, and treated with justice and equity."
("Ideas and Opinions—An Aspect of the Haitian Problem")

Page 64 ("Idées et Opinions—Mahatma Gandhi")

Gandhi grafts the political question onto religious feeling. The extraordinarily religious character of the Hindu is not unknown. . . . from sunrise to sunset, his acts are controlled by pious precepts.

Page 65 ("Idées et Opinions—Mahatma Gandhi")

For my part I believe that nonviolence is not realizable in

countries of Occidental civilization precisely because it cannot be based upon the same religious grounds.

Page 65 ("Notes pour servir à un manuel de parfait arriviste")

I I know a sincere man who thinks that all faults are possibilities of qualities; that they want only to be surmounted and that they are susceptible, as it were, to transmutation: truth can become pride; envy, a will to superiority; grossness, sensuality; refinement, etc., etc.

You, do not trouble yourself with these preoccupations. Simply call your cowardliness prudence; your greed, noble ambition; your baseness, modesty; your repugnance for truth, tolerance; your cynicism, frankness; and your lack of frankness, moderation.

Page 66 ("Notes pour servir à un manuel de parfait arriviste")

XI For your excuse, to squelch your scruples and appease your remorse, tell yourself that life is a combat to the death.

Page 66 ("Idées et Opinions—Eloge à la 'Cruauté' de Christophe")

Cruelty is one of the most remarkable attributes of the strong man. . . .

All great work demands a total disdain for scruples: it is perhaps regrettable for the sentimentality of certain good souls that the mortar of vast political edifices is a bit mixed with blood, but that does not prove that they are less solid.

And is it not remarkable that those historians who accept without flinching the great collective crimes that are wars shudder with horror before little capital executions, far less important in their consequences, and above all, far less stupid! Cruelty is a constructive quality. . . .

Page 67 ("Idées et Opinions—Eloge à la 'Cruauté' de Christophe")

And can one call cruelty that intelligent discipline to which he bent his kingdom? Christophe had understood with the greatest clarity that a people risen by violence from the most abject slavery would not know how to make use of its new independence without excesses.

The Haitian people after 1804 was an improvised people, and as such was given to all the turbulence of new nations intoxicated by liberty. Christophe devoted himself to the political education of the North by imposing on it the routine of peace and of work. It matters little that he restricted to the utmost limits, and severely, a liberty which would have been misunderstood. Not caring a regal whit for the Declaration of the Rights of Man and of the Citizen, he put an end to the intolerable ultra-republicanism still raging in the West and in the South and began his labor as clairvoyant head of state by constructing schools, academies, institutes of arts and crafts, and by granting to agriculture the intelligent protection which the prosperity of the country required.

His cruelty was a civilizing factor in the accomplishment of his strong and great work.

Page 68 ("Idées et Opinions—Eloge à la 'Cruauté' de Christophe")

Christophe was the forger of a nation. He knew that an idea is worth more than a life: that is the excellent psychology of the great man of politics. And he hammered severely, as though on an anvil, the subdued people, whom he fashioned in his greatness.

Page 68 ("Port-au-Prince—Cap-Haïtien")

The endlessly renewed heat and monotony of the thorn acacias and cacti overwhelm the spirit.

Yet, I gave myself over to the pathos of a little sleeping cemetery at the side of the shining road, in its immaterial calm. Crows traced a black flight like a funereal aureole around a tragic cross, covered with rags. . . .

. . . The savannah is dead; and the dusty trees have heads of white hair; those trees which no sap can set straight and which lean on their twisted trunks.

Page 69 ("Portrait d'une paysanne rencontrée")

I dreamed her in a Gauguin landscape, a paradise recreated by the enchantment of colors; in the midst of trees tortured by vines and with slimy lichens around their monstrous trunks and their branches, giving way to the irresistible gushing of life which shatters the bark and causes an amber blood to flow; in the midst of broad leaves and of fruits laden with perfume. In the midst of fruits, of leaves, of trees, in the glaucous hue of a jade light which resists the lustre of flowers in full bloom: she, lying nude and finally restored to primitive nature; her arms flung at random in the grass, her bosom high, fragrant, and rounded, heaving with the violent rhythm of voluptuosity. Her hips, soft, a moving basket, were subtly prolonged by the gush of her fine, strong thighs—in animal innocence, lying naked and sweetly offered like a beautiful fruit filled with secret delights.

Page 69 (Portrait of Péralte's mother)

Here she is, framed by the doorway, quite tiny in her austere black dress. . . .

Her long fragile hands are hands meant to be joined in prayer. In a moment she will tell us how they were bruised by the awful labor of the *corvées* and what suffering they know when she places them, trembling, on her broken heart, as though to protect it against a suffering too great to bear.

They are long and fragile hands; the hands of *Mater dolorosa*: the hands of the mother of Charlemagne Péralte. . . .

She tells us her long calvary across the country, following her son everywhere, from town to town, and each of the prisons where he was confined marked one of the stations of her cross.

And when, her eyes raised above us toward the vision of Péralte in his convict's jacket, she says:

"Ay, my little one!"

She makes the moving gesture, which brings hot tears to our eyes, of cradling a tiny little child.

We kiss those venerable hands and take leave of her, so as not to prolong her sorrow of mother martyr in the vivid wound of memory.

CHAPTER III

Page 73 ("Propos sans suite")

The square was small, sordidly lighted by a lone streetlamp. The crowd flowed from it through a narrow alley, and half-starved dogs, chased away, fled barking and snarling.

But behind the flattened mass of houses, somewhere in the night, the sinister and joyous voice of a drum could be heard, the voice of a thousand African gods, hilarious and obscene, which perforated the silence with little frantic blows.

"Why were you saying, Daniel, that this crowd is sad? . . ."

"Because it goes toward pleasure. Joy doesn't attract joy. You seem to think that I lend my own discouragement to everything. . . . No. We could go under that arbor where a poor happiness is being meted out: dance and whiskey. I would show you those men and those women, their faces, and then you would know that a gay crowd is made up of sad men. You would see the despair of pleasure."

Page 74 ("Propos sans suite," p. 4)

"You mean that my will is not equal to my strength and that this imbalance only leads me to futile attempts, to sterile convulsions. And moreover, that one must know how to resign oneself; to accomodate oneself to a petty life: to be content to some extent. That, never; I reject that pitiful stoicism."

Page 74 ("Propos sans suite," pp. 21–22)

"Poetry, poetry. . . . It isn't made from life; in any case, not ours. Yet the work is there, it matures, grows—withers away. . . . Ah, to create a book, a poem, so perfect that in giving them birth, one could at the same time unburden oneself of a life ended in greatness."

"Excuse me, Emilio," said Daniel in a choked voice. "I thought you were happy."

"Happy? You thought so because I seize my existence passionately as one clasps a woman. But after love, Daniel, how the eyes become lucid, what a sudden awful clarity! . . ."

Page 75 ("Fragment d'une confession," p. 47)

Mediocre: I pronounced already that word which is the doleful fall of a man oscillating on the taut cord between desire and will. As far back as I go toward my young years, I run up against that image of the acrobat with his arms stretched out toward the goal, but always losing his balance, and which was my inability to see anything through to the end.

And I wonder today if the very heat of my desire was not the insurmountable, withering obstacle, for the more it grew, the more it removed from my reach a satisfaction which became from that point on incomplete, and which I sought to attain by going beyond it.

Page 75 ("Fragment d'une confession," p. 47)

sleeping, his head in his arms, against the table, and the cool wind, wafted by the fans of the palm trees, bathed his forehead, but did not awaken him.

Page 76 ("Préface à la vie d'un bureaucrate," pp. 73–74)

Michel Rey thinks that from now on his life will unfold like the coming and going of the sea, bitter and monotonous: with no fine storms. . . .

To while away the waiting for that final resting, there is left for him the prospect of insulting his mother-in-law, making his wife unhappy and drinking multicolored cocktails.

"Well then, let's continue our interesting day," he sighed.

Page 76 ("Préface à la vie d'un bureaucrate," p. 91)

Here are blank sheets of paper piled up on the table, and then others covered with his handwriting, yellowed by time, and the ink already pale.
His whole wasted life is there.

Page 76 ("Préface à la vie d'un bureaucrate," pp. 94–95)

But he felt afraid.
He didn't close the drawer, but suddenly grabbed a blank sheet of paper; he began, heavily, slowly:
Mr. Secretary of State,
It is for me an honor . . .

Page 76 ("Mon Ami Alcibiades," p. 27)

. . . it is not known exactly where he lives, no occupation is known to him; it often happens that he will disappear for two weeks or so, then one fine day he is seen again, floating in a suit too large for him and invariably a green one, with a panama hat on his head which age has not whitened.
Only one thing about him can be stated with certainty: his regularity at getting drunk.

Page 78 ("La Veste," p. 168)

Saivre . . . looked out of the window. The rain was melting the light from the street lamp. Fine needles of gold were falling. Behind, the great vague night, the great black silence.

Page 78 ("Attente")

O the eyes sad to watch the golden stream
which the one-eyed street lamp spills over the asphalt.

Page 78 ("Fragment d'une confession," pp. 45–46)

Here I am, more alone for being in this dark room; the window does not let enter anything but night, scarcely put to flight by the timid lamp around which it stirs like a somber butterfly.

Here I am on my desert island; this flat, pale rock of the table, entirely surrounded by eddies of silence and of shadow.

Peaceful and mediocre the hour. All noises go off on tiptoe, and softly, the reverie of half-closed eyes approaches.

It is like tempting once again the deceptive experience of being bent over the past as over a river agitated by the cries and rustling of wings of those furtive gulls: memories.

Page 79 ("Fragment d'une confession")

My table is a luminous island
in the black cotton-wool of the silent night. . . .

Page 79 ("Fragment d'une confession," p. 52)

. . . Ah, that that door might open and a woman enter on hesitant steps; that she might, with that mysterious smile that I never knew, come up to my heavy brow and useless arms.
. . .

Page 79 ("Fragment d'une confession," p. 53)

Dear Lord, that that door might open and a very small child come to my knees and that I might hear his sweet, stumbling voice and that he might put his childish hands on my old face. Perhaps, dear Lord, he would love me?

Page 80 ("Préface à la vie d'un bureaucrate," pp. 91–92)

His whole wasted life is there.

His head between his hands, he recapitulates it:

"Am I limited by my weakness, or is it rather an inhuman desire which goes beyond the frontiers of a goal I do not want, which I cannot propose for myself, except in the distance!

"At bottom, it is possible that all this is just a case of 'sour grapes' that I persuade myself to scorn, while in reality, I'm not capable of the leap that would place them within my grasp.

"The issue is simple: I am a failure, my teeth set on edge by life, that bunch of acid fruit which I cannot bite.

"But what good does this pitiful analysis do me? Every interrogation which one subjects one's life to begs the question: Why? And every truth painfully arrived at contains, ridiculously, the simplicity of its explanation within itself.

"Or rather, everything can be summed up in the words: 'What's the use? And, in effect, 'What's the use?' is not a question, but a reply."

Page 82 ("Propos sans suite," pp. 23–25)

Day was arriving; night slipped away like a mask, and glimmers of light were already shooting forward like pale fingers and leaving dirty traces above the hills.

They felt filled with sadness and abandoned and useless, like those smashed-in boxes, that debris of pottery, scattered on the ground around them.

Jean started off first.

Daniel took his companion's arm. . . .

They walked as far as the wharf.

The sea had metallic highlights.

They remained there, saying nothing more, listening to the silk-like sounding of the waves against the pilings.

Finally they separated, for a fine, cold rain was beginning to fall in the colorless morning.

Page 82 ("Propos sans suite," pp. 14–15)

"Let's go over there," he says. "That must be a beautiful and buxom Negress."

They left the deserted square, entered into a maze of black alleys lined with half caved-in shanties, foul-smelling like heaps of filth, lost themselves a moment in a blind alley; but Daniel, who knew the section rather well, found the way again by crossing through several small sleeping courtyards, and they arrived at the Wharf-aux-Herbes.

The place presented its familiar visage eaten away by the night and by a leprosy of squalor. Here and there, above the displays of the vendors of fries and rice and beans vacillated the smoky light of candles.

Page 83 ("Préface à la vie d'un bureaucrate," pp. 56–60)

It was five years ago . . . he remembered the day of his return to Haiti. The noonday sun subdued a silent sea stirred by soft, foamless waves. A profound joy possessed him; in the anonymous crowd which rose on the bridge, pushing and shoving on the narrow ladder—visitors, dock hands, relatives—he recognized himself at last, felt the happy echo of this black world, listened to the melting away in himself of the ice (?) which had built up in Europe, felt disappear from his heart what he bitterly called "the great white silence," and which was the racial abyss which his friendships, his loves, his relations over there had not been able to fill in. Now he was among his brothers and his people. He wanted to kneel down, kiss this cherished earth. . . .

Leading him toward town, his parents overwhelmed him with questions. He tried to answer, but he would rather have gone his own way, to walk alone, in solemn ecstasy, and hug that woman who passed by selling mangos, carrying her fruit on her head as a queen carries her crown, her back bent, bursting the blue cloth of her coarse dress, yes, hug her tight and say to her: "Sister!"; take in his arms that bedraggled child holding out his hand to an American tourist, press him against his heart: "Brother, little brother! . . ."

Page 83 (Daniel, in "Propos sans suite")

. . . he burst out laughing. His voice was white; it trembled and broke with a kind of rage.

Page 84 (Emilio, in "Propos sans suite")

Emilio made a curious grimace: one would have said that his laughter had taken refuge in a sudden wrinkle which pulled at his lips bitterly . . .

Page 84 (Michel, in "Préface à la vie d'un bureaucrate")

He laughed that laughter which was peculiar to him: a kind of painful rictus that drew his lips to one side in two divergent wrinkles.

An inner sneer tears at him

Page 84 (*"Fragment d'une confession,"* p. 47)

And I wonder today if the very heat of my desire was not the insurmountable, withering obstacle, for the more it grew, the more it removed from my reach a satisfaction which became from that point on incomplete, and which I sought to attain by going beyond it.

In this struggle with a shadow all my life, I was outdistanced.

Page 85 (*"Propos sans suite,"* pp. 7–8)

I love prostitutes. Their kisses ache: it is from having bruised the flesh of their mouths on so many strange lips, on so many vile caresses. I am appeased before them. I am like them. . . . Like them in suffering and in daily loathing. Prostituted also: to myself, to my weakness, my cowardliness before life.

Page 86 (Baudelaire, "Femmes Damnées," CXVI, *Fleurs du Mal*)
You whom in your hell my soul has pursued,
Poor sisters, I love you as much as I pity you,
For your gloomy sufferings, your unquenched thirsts,
And the urns of love of which your great hearts are full.

Page 86 (Marquis de Sade, *Justine*)

Evil alone moves me; I breathe only in committing it; my organism finds delight in it alone. . . . I like to see creatures perish in my experiments. . . . I am bestial and murderous.

Page 86 (*La Proie et l'ombre*, pp. i–iv)

I will not go so far as to say of this work, the first that Mr. J. Roumain gives us, that it is a confession. It is rather a testimony—and I prefer it so. The confession is limited to a single man, to a single soul. . . . The testimony is broader. . . . The testimony is useful for the history of the collective soul. . .

Profound and merciless analysis of ourselves, I believe. . . . This book? A testimony, I tell you.

Page 87 (Brouard, *Le Petit Impartial*, September 8–9, 1930)

It is not good for man to be too much with himself. The external world does not exist enough for ROUMAIN. That external world which expands the heart and renders it optimistic. . . . He should not apply *his own* reflexes, his own sensations to the peasants he develops in the forthcoming novel.

Page 87 (Georges J. Petit? *Le Petit Impartial*, September 10–11, 1930)

"The success of *The Prey and the Shadow* is no longer to be predicted. It is already a fact."

Page 88 (Brutus, *La Relève*, pp. 12–13)

Many see it as pure autobiography and hardly discern in it the result of an inquiry conducted through the meanders of the soul of the disoriented of our generation. This book is at once a testimony and a confession. The author has collected his observations just as much in himself as in us.

Page 88 (Brutus, *La Relève, pp. 9–11*)

His poetry translates a state of weariness of the heart and the sensation of repose given by the acceptance of that despondency. It gives forth that interior silence of a man drawn in upon himself, the better to catch his impressions. . . .

Mr. Roumain has always appeared to me a bored man of fashion who, by one of those bizarre contradictions, lives intensely. . . .

His malady, on certain occasions, gives him instants of calm alternating with periods of bitter depression. . . . In studying himself, he takes pleasure in posing his finger on the crack in his heart.

Page 90 (Gaillard, *L'Oeuvre romanesque de Jacques Roumain*, p. 5, n. 1)

It is known that one of the heroes of *The Prey*, Michel Rey, ends by allowing himself to go with the easy solution, by accepting a position in the administration.

It is also known that Jacques Roumain was also a functionary. Very briefly, however. This is what one close to our novelist writes me on the subject:

"Jacques was under-secretary at the Department of the Interior when he published *The Prey and the Shadow*; but he had written the stories of this collection before entering the Department. 'Preface to the Life of a Bureaucrat,' one of the stories of *The Prey*, was probably in a way the expression of a premonition *without, for that, being autobiographical.* Premonition of the capitulation of the intellectuals of a generation before the 'imperatives of life.' Moreover, Jacques *knew* that he himself would not escape the temptation." (Letter received May 16, 1965)

Page 92 (*Les Fantoches*, pp. 14–15)

"But tell me," said Michel Rey to Marcel, "why did you come to this stupid ball?"

"In my search of boredom. Boredom amuses me when it changes my habitual life."

Michel looked at him closely.

"There is the answer of a young, strong and handsome man. Don't be so immodest as to protest. Besides," he said in a singularly painful and scornful tone, "wasn't I like you?"

Page 92 (*Les Fantoches*, p. 16)

"Is he crazy, or drunk?" wondered Marcel uncomfortably.
Michel laughed dryly:
"Your eyes tell me your thoughts quite clearly. One day
you will perhaps find yourself sitting face to face with a young,
strong, handsome man, as though before the reflection of your
own adolescence. You will take pity on him, you will speak
to him, and in his look, you'll read: 'Is he crazy?' "

Page 92 (*Les Fantoches*, p. 18)

What makes me uneasy, Marcel, about your hesitation to
act, to undertake any work at all, is that I doubt that you'll
know one day how to escape that remorse stemming from
cowardliness and weakness which Spinoza denounced so
severely. It seems to me you are lacking the courage to
accomplish good or bad acts.

Page 92 (*Les Fantoches*, pp. 30–31)

Jean Lefèvre had just gone up to the table. An oil lamp lit
his body to the waist, but when he moved, his feverish
features, his high forehead under his frizzy hair, his troubled
mouth and the light in his eyes were visible.
His voice was cold, a bit shrill, the theme of his speech
developed methodically. Marcel noted with appreciation the
honesty with which he made no concessions to the tastes of
the crowd for fine-sounding, hollow sentences.
He said so to his companion.
"Yes, it's a shame," replied Santiague. . . .
"Lefèvre has too much self-respect to be a demagogue, and
he is too dense to realize that an intelligent democrat must be
a demagogue. . . .

Page 93 (*Les Fantoches*, pp. 35–36)

"My God, why not? Even liberty needs a master. It was Schiller
who said so, but King Christophe certainly thought so.
"Christ! there was one who didn't like damned little crab-

lice demagogues like Aristide Marau." (Santiague became extremely brutal in his enthusiasm).

Marcel opened his mouth: "Yes, but . . ."

"Can it, old boy. I know you're going to tell me about Christophe's cruelty. But cruelty is one of the most remarkable attributes of the strong man. . . .

Page 93 (*Les Fantoches*, pp. 38–39)

Pétion was a superior man. It is not in the reach of common mortals to be a cuckold, as he was, with such a charming and philosophical happiness.

Page 94 (*Les Fantoches*, pp. 46–47)

"In truth, the Haitian aristocrat prizes France, hangs onto it by fibers that go deep; he hasn't forgotten that some dark passageway in a colonial cabin was the cradle of his birth, the evening when a white man, heated by excessive libations, laid the negro slave woman, his ancestor."

"You're becoming impertinent" she murmured, but very softly and sadly, as if she were going to cry.

Marcel's anger was passed. He begged Irene to forgive him. His repentance was sincere, but that touching look, like a whipped dog imploring pity, was something he had studied at length and learned in front of a mirror.

Deeply moved, she took his hand:

"What are you reproaching yourself for, Marcel, to have such a grudge against your happiness? What a poor love is mine! Is it because you love me and hate yourself that you torment yourself by making me suffer? And must I find the proof of your tenderness in the wounds that you inflict on me?

Marcel kept his contrite look, but thought ironically to himself that she really expressed herself well. . .

And yet he admitted to himself that she had seen through him. Basically, he loved her, but, as if some strange evil power had taken hold of his will, he took a bitter pleasure in reducing to ashes his purest joys.

Page 94 (*Les Fantoches*, p. 67)

"Thus, symbolic religious cannibalism, such as it is found in the Christian rite of Communion."

Page 95 (*Les Fantoches*, p. 67)

". . . so you want to ruin my paper? You are confusing in a horrible blasphemy Christ and Huitzilopochtli. Besides," he added with much dignity, "are you forgetting that I'm a Catholic?"

"I do not believe I've attacked your convictions; I'm only exposing old, universal beliefs which Christianity has not escaped."

Page 95 (*Les Fantoches*, pp. 70–71)

" 'Haiti, Wailing Wall of the Black Race.' Your titles are splendid, old man. . . . I suppose that, as usual, the title is worth more than the article. . . . Let's see now: "Demoralization . . . educational heredity . . . racial conscience." Very good, very good, no one will read that . . . since, in effect, there is no racial conscience in our bourgeoisie.

Page 95 (*Les Fantoches*, p. 77)

"Nations are implacably subjected to determinism. Who can assure me that if today I fight for our liberty, it will not be in vain, that our history will not follow a cyclical course, and that the situation we can rid ourselves of at present—the American occupation—won't come back again in forty years?

Page 95 (*Les Fantoches*, p. 79)

"I admire you as much as I despise myself, Lefèvre, but I pity you. Your greatest fault is having ideas."

Page 96 (*Les Fantoches*, p. 88)

In the deserted dining room were heavy Renaissance

furniture, worm-eaten and unmatched, half-obliterated paintings, an atmosphere of decrepitude and desertion. His brain was working actively to associate his impressions. He had often dreamed of writing the story of a family of the political aristocracy, ruined by the arrival of the American troops in 1915, and which was, at the same time, the mirror and illumination of the social upheaval of Haiti.

Page 96 (*Les Fantoches*, p. 94)

"Then, as for me, I attack them, these Americans. I attack them from the South, from the North, from the East; I push them toward the sea, here, here. . . ."

His voice broke. The gramophone whined its absurd music. The old general remained there, on all fours before his overturned soldiers. A slow dribble trickled down his beard, and his hands, in the dust, trembled.

Santiague stole out on tiptoe. With a lump in his throat, he felt his way down the rickety staircase. . .

Page 96 (*Les Fantoches*, pp. 114–15)

Adorable quietude of the lamp, incomparable nobility of silence. The tumult flying in through the window like a fistful of pebbles in the end discouraged Santiague.

He put his papers away, lit a cigarette.

His legs comfortably stretched out, he let his thoughts wander. . . .

From the other side of the partition a childish voice repeated with the untiring patience of a stream:

Amalyllis, o

Gumbo soup

The Good Lord died

Divi-divi

Diaguido-Digo

Through the smoke, Santiague contemplated a landscape of hills and valleys, splashed with verdure, with sunlight, with the cries of birds. A small girl sings by a stream while drawing water into a gourd, and her voice mingles with the murmur of the water, becomes a bit muted, like the flow of water seeking out a path under the pebbles, then spreads out in droplets on the stone. . . .

Page 97 (*Les Fantoches*, pp. 136–37)

I was going slowly, enjoying the hour, through one of those deserted and badly lit streets of Port-au-Prince, where the electricity underscores the obscurity more than it combats it.

In the sky, the stars were rising like bubbles to the surface of shadow.

"Mister?"

A little girl was standing before me.

Page 97 (*Les Fantoches*, pp. 144–45)

"Carnal pleasure is a terrible desert. Charmantine is the fraternal oasis where I like to go to rest.

"We don't see each other very much. But I know that she is there, nearby, in the kitchen or in her room. I hear her singing. My heart is warmed.

"Sometimes she is sad, she thinks about her village, about her child's games in the savannah or in the woods.

"I call her and teach her to read from a bulletin of the Department of Agriculture, a real poem, I assure you, over-flowing with the exquisite Creole name of the plants and trees of the land. She gathers these names like fruits, makes little songs from them, cradles her nostalgia.

"I listen to her and I escape with her from this suffocating town toward peaceful scenes.

I am not too unhappy, and perhaps I owe it to Charmantine."

Page 98 (*Les Fantoches*, p. 146)

The light from the lamp was directed toward his face, upon which there breathed an ironic force. His young, high brow had a serene and domineering air which contrasted with his robust mouth, well formed, sensuous and sad.

Lefèvre read like an open book that face where were
reflected the internal struggles, the defeats and the definitive
victories. He knew Santiague to be master of himself and after
the rudest of trials of existence and of the spirit.

Page 105 (*Les Fantoches*, p. 120)

His attitude expressed the greatest lassitude. His arms
hung down both sides of the armchair like those of a disjointed
puppet.

Page 105 (*Les Fantoches*, p. 135)

"Thus I people my life with a few characters, which, at
certain hours, I parade out in front of my idle imagination or
to distract me from harassing preoccupations.

"I distribute roles to this little troupe. I invent its destiny,
which is accomplished according to the likings of my fantasy.
These puppets amuse me like a Punch and Judy show.

Page 105 (*La Proie et l'ombre*, pp. 10–11)

"and you see these mulattos passing by in their luxury
cars, these 'big Negroes,' melting in the heat of their blubber
like chocolate in the sun; then you'll understand better the
fable of the earthen pot and the iron pot."

Page 106 (*Les Fantoches*, p. 34)

He [Marau] now lives on the Chemin des Dalles and climbs
slowly toward the high sections of town, whose rich inhabitants he claims to loathe. . . . he's an ignoramus enraged at
not being able to make his little mulatto baby.

Page 106 (*La Proie et l'ombre*, pp. 69–71)

"Perhaps you would have done better marrying her off to
one of these interesting little gentlemen, standard type and
very correct, sheltered from excesses, safety valves of the brand

Tartuffe, guaranteed sanctimonious hypocrites whom I have had the heart-breaking honor of perceiving sometimes sitting so prettily in your living room, generously interesting themselves in works of charity and the general progress of humanity. . . . Madame Widow Ballin, Madame Widow Ballin, why didn't you choose for Jeanne that high ideal of the mothers of good Haitian families!"

Page 107 (*Les Fantoches*, pp. 49–50)

"Isn't he nice? . . . ah, these Frenchmen, how pleasant they are!"

Marcel leaned toward her and in a confidential tone:

"Do you know, dear mademoiselle, that it is rumored in society that Monsieur Lecocq is a pretender for your charming hand. Permit me to congratulate you: you will make a remarkable couple; you are so much alike—that is, from the point of view of the identity of opposites. . . . My friend Cosquer the mathematician . . . claims, in fact that the sentiment of love reminds him of a molecular structure in which one place is vacant; now then, the natural pressure of the surrounding forces works in such a way that that structure seeks out another of which one of the parts can occupy that vacant space without disturbing its initial equilibrium."

CHAPTER IV

Page 111 (*La Montagne ensorcelée*, pp. 21–22)

"Cric?"

But a profound moaning inside the hut stops all answers. A confused noise of words, choked sobbing.

At that moment, Balletroy, the local policeman, entered the *tonnelle*.

"Honor"

"Respect" answered all in chorus. A place was made for him.

Page 112 (*La Montagne ensorcelée*, p. 79)

"Placinette" he said simply.
"No" said a strong voice.
And Balletroy entered the room.

Page 112 (*La Montagne ensorcelée*, p. 89)

They looked at her, in a silence filled with terror, not daring to come to her aid, not daring to confront the god who possessed her.

During this time, Balletroy arrived at the *mapou* tree and made a standing jump into the path. . . .

Page 112 (*La Montagne ensorcelée*, p. 91)

Balletroy's hand becomes as heavy as a club on Aurel's shoulder and he breathes like a blacksmith's bellows.

"Hey, what do you say!" says Aurel.

"Me, he, hehe, nothing. I know Grace. She's a pretty girl." He taps Aurel's shoulder and laughs a strange laugh.

Page 112 (*La Montagne ensorcelée*, p. 92)

"I had talked to Grace about it. She was satisfied. She said:

'You're doing right; Balletroy is a mature man, an important man, he's a good uncle.' "

Page 113 (*La Montagne ensorcelée*, p. 111)

"Grace, ho Grace?"
No one answers.
"Grace? . . . Christ, Christ Almighty."
But if she doesn't hear, it's because she's too far off. How to confront, how to stop that furious wave. . . . In ten minutes, you can go to town and back. He'll have the time. And he turned his horse.

Grace wasn't far off; she had been out collecting wood. A confused noise had reached her, but she had paid no attention to it. She was on her way back just as Aurel turned into the road for town.

Page 113 (*La Montagne ensorcelée,* pp. 112–13)

Several times she turned around to see their sweating muffles through the foliage, their gaping snouts.

. . . she heard quite close behind her the noise of broken branches and their muffled trampling.

. . . an awful anguish carried her with the turning trees toward that blue hole lattice-work of branches, toward the plain. . .

For their part, they have their prey. In a moment, two arm-lengths away, they were already seizing her when Dorilas, stumbling against a stump, fell down, carrying them with him in his fall, barring the way to their impetus.

Grace has disappeared, or rather no, there she is again, running through the savannah, straight for the horse, and they remain there, dazed with rage and powerlessness.

Page 115 (*La Montagne ensorcelée,* p. 79)

A strange smile, a tear in the lips—while his look remained fixed, without light—made his face grimace.

Page 116 (*La Montagne ensorcelée,* pp. 15–21)

The squat hut, planted firmly on the reddish ground and girdled at its base by a balustrade, leans against a horizon of somber hills. The path leading there, glistening like an abandoned snake skin, stops abruptly at the top of a crabgrass-covered slope and flings itself as on a spring-board into the transparent sky. . . .

There is a great calm, augmented by vast circles of silence traced by a huge bird of prey in the azure; augmented by the voice of a woman singing inside the house and by the muffled measured sound of a pestle crushing grain.

The village dominates this solitude. Gripping the side of the mountain, the huts bring their thatched heads together and keep an eye on all the life below. The village is poor. The chalky earth crackles like bark, parts its avid lips; the village is hungry. The drought has lasted for several days, burns the millet crop. The livestock grows thin and utters long, painful lowings.

Today, the men are back from the fields for the evening meal. In each cabin, the women busy themselves about the cauldrons. Only the children are outside, shouting as they play in the dust. The men are silent. Fatigue crushes the spirit as much as the body. . . .

Désilus, for his part, is seated under the guava trees. He eats his fill of their last fruits. . . .

These young Negroes are not respectful any more: they are saying that Désilus is out of his mind, but the old folks are not of that opinion.

Thus it was that Uncle Jean who died last year . . . used to repeat often that Désilus knew a lot of things. Houng!

When the day declines toward twilight, Désilus likes to withdraw from the company of men. Squatting or lying under a tree, he holds interminable soliloquies while scratching with his old hooked fingers a kind of two-string guitar. . . .

Mosquitoes watch out for the zombis, watch out for the zombis.

This is what makes these young Negroes laugh:

The idiots, their heads are full of wind! They think they're smart when they make fun, and it's the wind coming out of their mouths.

Désilus scornfully blows a puff of his good little pipe through the gray scrub of his beard.

Mosquitoes watch out for the zombis, zanzamzam, zim, zim, zimzim.

Did they even know, eh, did they even know who croaks at night in the pond under the yellow moon? toads? Huh! He remembers, himself, Désilus, having seen who. A long time ago . . . Passing near the pond, he stops to draw a little water, when . . . Ay! he still trembles at the thought: five little gnomes black as hell, with glowing eyes, were sitting in the grass. Their heads raised toward the moon, they were imitating the toads and gulping down fireflies. Truthfully, truthfully, believe me if you want.

Mosquitoes watch out for the zombis.

. . . .

Night had come. Désilus rose. The pond was gleaming at the bottom of the hill like an evil eye. It is not well to stay outside, certain nights.

"Most of all with that one" he muttered, turning toward Placinette's squat hut where a window shown brightly lit against the night.

The peasants were gathering that night at Dornéval's house; his son was dying. . . .

Under the *tonnelle*, the men have found seats on benches and boxes. . . . Further off are the children. . .

Désilus slips off in their direction.

Page 120 (*La Montagne ensorcelée*, pp. 42–43)

Pain is another world where she moves about blind and deaf to everything that is not this little body, this flesh of her flesh, fallen away from her like a rotten fruit from the tree.

Is he really dead? Only day before yesterday, he was playing in the dust with the others, with those who are still living.

A tenderly wounded cry rises from her innermost being, a patient sobbing which will not end, which starts up always again, wet with tears, burned with tears. And why are there these candles around him, these flowers, these leaves? Oh, there are powerful sorcerers who cure sick children, with leaves, with leaves gathered in the savannah, on bad nights. Where is the vodun priest who will cure her child?

". . . piis supplicationibus consequantur: Qui vivis et regnas Deus . . ." What is that black man saying? What is he chanting? No, no, that's not it. Here is what should be sung:

Leaves, ho, leaves, come save me from my misery. My child is sick. I went to see the vodun priest.

"Peace, Anna, peace!"

Page 121 (*La Montagne ensorcelée*, p. 81)

But happiness is not for the wicked, and he will not prolong his days, no more than the shadow, for he has not the fear of God.

Page 122 (*La Montagne ensorcelée*, pp. 88–89)

Or rather, no, she had not cried out the name, but her

mouth had *formed* it, so visibly that everyone heard it, and shuddered and felt an icy fear running down their backs, for Choute's mouth had become small and pointed—again, as God is my witness, untruth is not in my words—yes, narrow and pointed like the mouth of a snake, and it opened and closed and no sound came out, just as it came to pass when the Good Lord cursed the Reptile in Paradise.

Page 123 (*La Montagne ensorcelée*, pp. 57–58)

"They are in misery, their heads work, then they look for, they look for a guilty party. . . .

"They know that you have the knowledge of leaves that heal; they think: who can do good can do evil. They think: demons used to be angels."

Page 123 (*La Montagne ensorcelée*, pp. 79–80)

"Fools! Have you never heard of intestinal fever? Children eat anything, mangoes full of worms, spoiled meat, that's all.

"And anyway, who has the right to lament? Dornéval and Lazare. You others, what the hell are you doing here?"

Page 124 (*La Montagne ensorcelée*, pp. 60–61)

Placinette's derisive laughter wove an insupportable anguish around Balletroy.

"It's not the same thing," he uttered with an effort.

He wanted to go away, he was suffocating between the narrow walls and it was intolerable, this Placinette who was turning around the room like a spider.

"You haven't answered, my friend."

. . . there was in him a singular disorder, as if his tongue no longer obeyed his thought and his gestures no longer obeyed his will.

Placinette inscribed little hopping circles around the room. Finally she stopped in front of him, and he was astonished to see her eyes sad and filled with tears.

"Balletroy, there are a lot of things we can't understand."

Page 125 (*La Montagne ensorcelée,* p. 97)

He found her mending an old dress, like herself, crumpled, with long wrinkles; its tears, a dead thing between her thin fingers, with their nails mauve like those of a corpse.

She looked more and more like a spider, carefully spinning her trap.

"Go on drawing your threads," thought Balletroy, "I'm not the fly you'll catch."

Page 125 (*La Montagne ensorcelée,* pp. 12–13)

This preoccupation to make use of the possibilities of our milieu to elaborate the work of art is the exciting note of novelty which the young literature brings to the analysis of that milieu. Thus our young writers create with ingenuity a Haitian esthetic. . . . Jacques Roumain is one of the promoters of this splendid movement.

Page 126 (*Ainsi parla l'oncle,* p. 188)

. . . works or spontaneous products at a given moment sprung from an inspired thought, adopted by all because faithful interpreters of a common sentiment, which have become dear to everyone and finally transformed into original creations by the obscure process of the subconscience.

Page 126 (*Ainsi parla l'oncle,* p. 192)

the material for our works should be sometimes drawn from that immense reserve which is our folklore.

Page 127 fn. 7

One scholar has said in this connection: "Indigenism, which puts itself forward as an original movement, will have to feign ignorance of Innocent who, nevertheless, as early as 1906, had supplied its material, its orientation and its substance."

Page 127 (Innocent, *Mimola* . . . , p. 147)

Suddenly prolonged cries are heard; a chair is overturned, women come running: it was Lala, who had just fallen to the floor with a nervous twitching of the hands and feet. They tried to help her up. Impossible. Her legs gave way; her arms and legs trembled as if she were cold. Her features had altered and suddenly took on the expression of an old face wrinkled by the years. . . . Lala was under the influence of a spirit. Which was the spirit possessing her? Brother Ti Dor was the only one capable of knowing. It was the spirit of her grandmother, Dan-Maoua.

Madame Georges, hearing that name, and seeing her daughter in that state, cried into her handkerchief.

Lala, or rather, Dan-Maoua, took her in her arms, pressed her a long time to her heart, shedding tears. Some of the women, moved by this little drama, wiped their noses on their dresses, or wiped their humid eyes with the back of their hands.

Page 131 (Duvalier, *Les Tendances d'une génération*, pp. 105–6)

We have also noted the appearance of *The Bewitched Mountain*, which has disappointed us immensely, immensely. It is not what Jacques Roumain had in store for us. The work he has just published is beneath, very much beneath *The Prey and the Shadow*.

Page 131 (Brutus, "Jacques Roumain," p. 15)

Out of all that our peasant literature has produced to this point, nothing comes at all close to this work where a whole series of sentiments, stories and legends stirs.

Page 131 (Brutus, "Jacques Roumain," p. 16)

I suspect in his already-published work the rough draft of a humanity without frontiers, outside of the Haitian circle and preserving something of the desolate laugh of the black race and of that particular character issuing from the mixture of African and Latin civilizations. . . .

In any case, we have for our part, thank God, *The Bewitched Mountain*. And if for no other reason than having written this little novel about our brothers in blue jackets, Mr. Jacques Roumain has made for himself a justly envied place in our world of letters.

Page 133

"The Negro Jacques Roumain does not deign to frequent whites."

Page 133 fn. 13

"The Negro Jacques Roumain will not dine with the racist Russell."

Page 134 ("Quand bat le tam-tam")

Your heart trembles in the shade, like the reflection of a face
    in the troubled water
The old mirage rises up in the hollow of the night
You know the sweet sorcery of memory
A river carries you far off from the shores
Do you hear those voices? they are singing in loving sadness
And on the hill, listen to the tom-tom panting like the throat
    of a young black girl.

Your soul is the reflection in the murmuring waters where
    your fathers bent their dark faces
And the white man who made you a mulatto is this bit of
    spume cast up, like spit, on the shore.

Page 135 (*Les Fantoches*, p. 133)

Then when the African plain-chant opens out, when the ridiculous instruments have become silent and only the ancestral drum still sounds, I enter the crowd and lose myself in my race.

Page 135 ("Guinée")

It's the long road to Guinea:
Death takes you down

Here are the boughs, the trees, the forest:
Listen to the sound of the wind in its long hair of eternal
night.
It's the long road to Guinea:
Where your fathers await you without impatience
Along the way, they talk.
They wait.
This is the hour when the streams rattle like beads of bone
It's the long road to Guinea:
No bright welcome will be made for you
In the dark land of dark men:
Under a smoky sky pierced by the cry of birds
Around the eye of the river the eyelashes of the trees
                            open on decaying light.
There, there awaits you beside the water a quiet village,
And the hut of your fathers, and the hard ancestral stone
    Where your head will rest at last.

                                        (L.H.)

Page 136 ("Langston Hughes")

At Lagos you knew sad-faced girls.
    Silver circled their ankles.
They offered themselves to you naked as the night
Gold circled by the moon.
You saw France without uttering a worn, shop-made phrase;
    Here we are, Lafayette!
The Seine seemed less lovely than the Congo
Venice. You sought the shade of Desdemona
Her name was Paola.
You said: Sweet, sweet Love!
And sometimes
Babe! Baby!
Then she wept and asked for twenty lire.

Like a Baedeker your nomad heart wandered
From Harlem to Dakar.
The Sea sounded on in your songs—sweet, rhythmic,
                            wild . . .
Of white foam blossom-born.

Now here in this cabaret as the dawn draws near you
                            murmur . . .
The blues again play for me!
O! for me again play the blues!

Are you dreaming tonight, perhaps, of the palm trees, of
Black Men down there, who paddled you down the
dusks?

                                                    (E.W.U.)

Page 137 ("Créole")

Under the *tonnelle*,
Have you met her, under the *tonnelle*
The negress dressed in white muslin
"My name is Viergine,
   At your service, Mister"

Beside the water,
Have you seen her beside the water, under the Bougainvilleas
The negress fresh and nude as the shade.

Viergine, Grâce
Dressed in white muslin or in flowering shade,
My laughing negresses,
How much you knew how to bless this heart forever
                                              unappeased.

CHAPTER V

Page 140 (Roumain, "Un mouvement communiste . . .")

I am a Communist. Not a militant one for the moment,
because the cadres of a political struggle do not yet exist in
Haiti. I am applying myself to their preparation. . . .

The son of owners of extensive land holdings, I have
renounced my bourgeois origins. I have lived a lot among the
peasants. I know their life, their mentality, their religion—that
astonishing mixture of Catholicism and vodun.

I do not regard this peasant proletariat as a sentimental
value. The Haitian peasant is our only producer, and he
produces only to be exploited in the most hideous manner, by
a minority, . . . politicians known as the elite. All of my
publications have combated this would-be elite. As concerns
literature, I have written poems and stories from my earliest

youth. In 1930, I published a slim volume of stories which depict the malaise of our generation . . . this theme was taken up again in a short novel *The Puppets*. I am working for the renewal of our literature through the study of our very rich folklore. Up to the present time, our writers, with very rare exceptions, have done nothing but imitate the French poets and storytellers. I am of the opinion that our literature should be *Negro* and largely proletarian. I am working equally for the coming together of Negro writers of all countries. It is to this end that I am preparing, under the title *Afro-American Poems*, a small volume of translations of poems by American Negroes, Langston Hughes, etc. . . .

Will this information be sufficient, my dear comrade? I hope so . . .

Page 141, fn. 3

"The letter you triumphantly publish is nothing more than the rough copy of my answer, which dates from the first part of 1932.

"Having read Rémy's letter and the questions he asked me, you knew what revolutionary value to attribute to my answer, which you have the disloyalty to pass off as an important document."

Page 142, fn. 7

"Thanks to your generous attentions, my stay in Washington was extremely agreeable."

Page 143 (Brierre, *Nous garderons le dieu*, p. 19)

His room was often closed . . .
Troubled, you would often find Karl Marx and Lenin
open upon his table.
He would come home, tired,
receiving badly dressed strangers,
students from the provinces, in his office covered
with books.
And through the door you would listen to

his sober voice speak to them of work,
of the scientific organisation of the world,
of proletariat and of oppression . . .
They would come out with books,
with pamphlets,
and would leave behind them
a strange sensation of misery.

Page 146 (*L'Action Nationale*, December 30, 1932)

Because of their illiteracy and the fact that the workers speak only Creole, our immediate task is to establish solid contacts with those who are the most exploited, principally those of HASCO, for all the agitation should be by word of mouth in the following manner:

a) Visit their huts, speaking to them of the miserable conditions of their present life, and leaving the impression with those whose action may be useful that they will find a solid support in us.

b) Organize small meetings in their own huts, where they will be engaged in conversation about the conditions of work that must govern the next harvest and the need for an improvement.

c) Make a selection of the most militant elements in order to utilize them as agitators in developing preparations for the strike.

Page 147 (*L'Action Nationale*, November 4, 1933)

At the beginning of the month of June of this year, Marcellus Sajous asked my help in a Communist campaign with Jacques Roumain with the end in view of stirring up protests among the coffee-sorters at Berne, Wiener and Co. regarding their salaries; . . . he supplied me with pamphlets to study. After having read them closely, I realized that such an idea could not take hold in Haiti, and that Jaques Roumain had only one aim—that of harming the government and of exploiting the ignorance of the simple-minded in order to serve the Communist cause. On Saturday October seven of the present year, having suspected that the police knew about his schemings,

Marcellus Sajous came to tell me that Jaques Roumain had
given him the order of clearing the house of all objects which
would render them suspect . . . On Sunday I was assigned the
task of putting them in a safe place. . . . I took them and
deposited them where I could later turn them over to the
government. Tuesday of this week, Mr. Marcellus Sajous asked
me to give him back the objects for Jacques Roumain. Jacques
Roumain and Marcellus Sajous have declared that any person
who informed against the Communist campaign would be
killed.

Page 148 (*L'Action Nationale,* November 9, 1933)

The government is firmly decided not to pay any attention
to the activities of so-called Haitian Communists who are, in
reality, only young parvenus or naive souls led by others.
. . .

Page 148 ("Nécessité de la Théorie")

Whatever his field of activity, man will discover that at each
turn he runs smack into that much-despised theory. He will
find himself reduced to asking: "What now?" And the answer
always contains this other question: "What goal are you trying
to attain?" In order to justify the action undertaken (a strike,
for example), he is forced to appeal to *general* reasons (in this
case, the general aim envisaged and the *general* experience of
the tactics of the strike). But such general facts are tied to what
we call *theory* and if, moreover, they offer the characteristic of
having been verified by experience, we call them *scientific
theory.*
  The theory which is at the basis of all conscious socialist
activity is scientific socialism (Marxism).

Page 149 ("Nécessité de la Théorie")

A world concept developed along these lines is inevitably at
odds with the bourgeois world view, which is conservative,
religious (in that it considers "the existing order as having

received in some way divine sanction"). The bourgeois world view is therefore doggedly opposed to "the scientific study of human society with all of its revolutionary consequences."

Page 150 (*L'Analyse schématique*, p. i)

The most considerable fact, the richest for what it teaches, is the collapse, between 1932–34 of the Nationalist myth in Haiti.

Page 151 (*L'Analyse schématique*, p. iii)

. . . nationalism contained internal contradictions which were to fall apart. The Nationalist movement was incapable of keeping its promises because the promises of bourgeois Nationalism came into direct conflict with its class interests once it came to power and revealed itself to be an electoral deception.

Page 151 (*L'Analyse schématique*, pp. v–vi)

It is easy to see that the question here is one of economic oppression which translates into social and political terms. Thus, the objective basis of the problem is certainly the class struggle. The H. [aitian] C. [ommunist] P. [arty] poses the problem scientifically, without in any way denying the valid basis for the psychological reaction of the blacks, wounded in their dignity. . . .

But the duty of the H.P.C., after all 98 percent black . . . where the color question is systematically relieved of its epidermic content . . . is to put the proletariat, the poor petty bourgeoisie and the black intellectual workers on guard against the black bourgeois politicians, who would like to exploit to their profit their justifiable anger.

Page 153 (*Haïti-Journal*, October 16, 1934)

". . . the same friend who has brought you messages and materiel will bring you more. Tell Pierre to go to the usual place and to bring a friend who can be trusted with him. Two men will come, an American and a Spaniard. Pierre will talk to them separately. Tell him not to walk in the streets with these men for fear of attracting suspicion."

Page 154 (*Haïti-Journal,* October 16, 1934)

. . . the thirtieth of September at about eight-thirty I arrived at car number 170 parked at the wharf. . . . At nine-fifteen, the "Pastores" came alongside. Two parcels were sent down from the "Pastores" and were immediately taken by an Englishman, who gave them to a boatman. I immediately approached the boatman and demanded the two parcels. He told me that he had just received them from an Englishman. The Englishman, arrested and interrogated as to the origin of the parcels, declared that he had received them from a white man on the "Pastores," to be transported on shore. A moment later, the white man was arrested and, upon authorization of the ship's captain, his cabin was searched. A collection of the newspaper *Le Matin* and three letters addressed to M. Camille Julien were found there.

Q. What did the parcels contain?

A. Pamphlets and newspapers about Communist activities abroad.

Page 154 (*Haïti-Journal,* October 16, 1934)

Q. Do you know if Mr. Roumain held secret meetings? asked Mr. Lechaud. [Roumain's attorney]

A. Yes. In the Saline, at Carrefour, at the Wharf-aux-Herbes.

Q. Do you know if, during the course of these meetings, the issue of disturbing the established order of things ever came up?

A. Mr. Roumain, at these meetings, would always say that the workers were not paid enough; he prompted them to strike. He said that there was not enough work and that it was the fault of the President of the Republic.

Page 158 ("Le Champ du potier")

His sentences fell indifferently from his lips into empty space.

It was strange that they should find an echo in this little old lady working tirelessly on her knitting and a conversation in which he was glued down, in boredom, as if in a spider web. He moved about disgustedly in this bourgeois world, in this decor in which the abject satisfaction of living made a spectacle of itself. Everything which comprised man's reality was transposed here onto an inferior level: hope, a speculation; love, a bargain; the suffering of others, an anecdote; the will to conquer life, to transform it, to create new human and moral values: a ferocious solidarity of the herd crowded close around appetites and prejudices. Thousands of individuals in the coffee groves, in the cane fields, the cotton fields, the factories, from birth to death, had no other reason to exist except to produce, in ignorance and servitude, the existence of this absurd world.

This world had only pretexts, not a reason for living. However miserable those pretexts might be, Martial could no longer confront them only with disdain. The time was passed when he sought refuge only in solitude. What he was preserving then was the integrity of his thought against degradation. He understood now that thought was nothing but sterile action or games. The bourgeois order no longer seemed a caricature to him, but an obstacle to life. And he felt a personal and imperative responsibility to participate in its destruction.

Page 159 ("Le Champ du potier")

"You are my sweetest refuge," she said. Perhaps they were only just that for each other and it was the heartrending weakness of their love. A desert-like zone separated him from Pauline. She attached herself to him in the illusion of her happiness and embraced only an illusion, but he could not recognize himself in her and was bitterly losing himself.

Page 159 ("Le Champ du potier")

Abe had passed him a packet of booklets. He found among them books with strange titles, authors whom he had never heard of: Marx, Engels, Lenin, Stalin. He read them for months, during entire nights, struggling patiently, and then with enthusiasm, a dazzling, blinding clarity.

Page 160 ("Le Champ du potier")

They have just arrested four of our Dominican comrades: Mario, Enrique, Antonio Lopez, and his wife.

"But when?" cried Martial. "This very afternoon, I was at the prison, and I didn't see anything."

Page 160 ("Le Champ du potier")

"Are you going to send it to *New Masses*? I've read it. Not bad. But you're still more a theologian than a Communist. You seem to want to save your soul, with the help of Marxism. It's well to write, as you do, that life is an indictment, but you must give those words a human, historical sense, not a metaphysical one. I hope you're not angry? . . ."

He was not angry, of course. Communism had been for him above all a moral awakening. He held himself disgustedly aloof from his class, which offered him only the basest temptation: an easy life, gratification, a blind, unworthy happiness. But what Doris should know was that Communism had become the essence of his thoughts and his sentiments, his reason for living. "If I should cease to be a Communist, it would be an intellectual and moral suicide; I would no longer be anything more than a living corpse. . . ."

Page 160 ("Le Champ du potier")

"Your love has been for me like an initiation into beauty. I thought that living was shared knowledge, a communion that nothing could destroy. But something is tearing you away from me, an unknown world which refuses me. . . ."

He kept silent. Many times he had tried to explain to her. She was not lacking in generosity, and her intelligence was real. But Martial was shocked to discover how profoundly the prejudices of her caste were rooted in her.

Page 161 ("Le Champ du potier")

He no longer held himself back. He was won over. His tenderness, so long repressed, spilled forth in words of which he was hardly conscious. . . . "I don't have anyone in the world but you. You are my only joy." He realized, however, in an awful moment of lucidity, that he was only putting off the time of reckoning, but love carried him beyond the remorse of lying to himself.

Page 161 ("Le Champ du potier")

Sometimes egrets beating their powerful wings took off above the rushes with a sinister cry. They rose almost vertically, in an ungraceful flight, then, abandoning themselves to some air current, they floated like great torn sheets, an immaculate washing. They kept at a distance from the shore, conscious of the peril. Monier, in the hate-filled pleasure of destroying, felled them as soon as they approached.

Page 161 ("Le Champ du potier")

What attracted him was the bad cane whiskey, the possibility of a sexual encounter, a brief and brutal embrace, and at dawn, the pathetic end of the orgy in the sustained and throaty chant of the cocks, when the rhythm of the drum slows down like a heart, harassed, ceasing to beat, when the dozing countryside was still enveloped in silence, and when at daybreak life takes on again its taste of nausea.

Page 162 ("Le Champ du potier")

"That's life . . ."

Monier turned toward him sharply: "A definition? A dream, I put it to you. A bit greenish, scabby and wormeaten, of course. These folk drink, dance, make love. Consequently, is that life? Perhaps, perhaps. To have a notion of existence is first of all to feel. Not to feel, above all, not to think. From the time man begins to think, he lies. I think, therefore I shall not *be*. Sadness and pleasure, these are the sources of the notion of existing. What a shame that there isn't a fossil linguistics. One could follow the verb 'to be' from the physiochemical language of the protoplasmic mass of the amoeba, the stammerings of Homo Pekinensis, translating the fact that he has just slept with his female or that he has got a chip of quartz in the back of his head, down to Descartes, down to Kierkegaard. . . ."

The old man turned toward Josaphat and, his eyes rounded in limitless astonishment, asked: "He crazy?"

Page 162 ("Le Champ du potier")

Seconds flowed by, intolerably. Then he hears Josaphat's voice, full of grave sadness, murmuring: "Ah, Christian, ah desgraciado[1]. You've lost your guardian angel. His hand hangs along his body. "No!" cries Monier, with desperate rage, "you don't have the right. I won't have it! I'll strike you again."

"Go, Christian, go now with the grace of God."

[1] Unfortunate fellow [Roumain's note; his translation: *malheureux*]

Page 163 ("Le Champ du potier")

"You see, what's important is purity, a will to purity. Not to submit. Not to abdicate. Never. No matter what the cost in what men call happiness. . . . Pierre . . . , stretched out on the grass, was looking at the clouds fleeing before the night, like a herd coming back from pasture. He was about to become fifteen.

Page 163 ("Le Champ du potier")

a piercing, boring voice: "Stupid existence . . . money . . . your books, your music, your so-called pride . . . really just vanity and imbecility. . . ."

Page 163 ("Le Champ du potier")

"I don't hate him," thought Pierre. "Only, everything separates us. The same blood and the same name like a label for two materials, two destinies so dissimilar that it was singular that the word 'brother' still maintained between them a social fiction, a forced relationship.

Page 163 ("Le Champ du potier")

". . . I am anxious to see you follow a more realistic path, one more in conformity with your future, instead of giving yourself over to chimeric utopias that will lead you nowhere, or rather, to poverty, to your coming down in the world and probably to serious trouble with the government.

CHAPTER VI

Page 175 (Letter from Roumain, August 16, 1936)

At my liberation, I was placed under the strictest surveillance by the police. This paralyzing vigilance in a milieu as limited as ours and where I am only too well known means being reduced to powerlessness. Due to the impossibility of moving and escaping police persecution and even of visiting my comrades—for that would compromise them—I felt that decidedly the earth scorched me at every step and that I was under the constant threat of new machinations by the government. On the other hand, my health, seriously damaged by malaria, requires a change of climate and appropriate care, according to the doctor. Thus I found myself forced to make the decision, with the consent of the C.C. [Central Committee?] to go into temporary exile from Haiti.

Page 177 fn. 4

On October 7, 1937, the Port-au-Prince newspaper *Le Matin* "reports the existence outside of Haiti of a revolutionary Haitian party calling for the overthrow of President Sténio Vincent. The party, according to the newspaper, has as leaders Messers Lucien Hibbert and Jacques Roumain."

Page 179 ("Madrid")

and in the little square where peaceful terror now reigns
there is
why yes there is upon the bloody face of that child a smile
like a pomegranate smashed by heel blows

Page 179 ("Madrid")

Here with the snow the decayed dentures of mountains
the swarm of the bullets buzzing over the decaying carcass
of the earth
and the fear at the bottom of the craters is like the worm in
a burst pustule

Page 179 ("Madrid")

Here is the threatened space of destiny
the shore where, rushing up from the Atlas and the Rhine
the confused wave of fraternity and crime breaks
upon the quarried hope of men,
but it is also despite the sacred hearts embroidered upon
Muhammad's standard
the scapularies the relics
the charms of lucre
the fetiches of murder
the totems of ignorance
all the clothing of lies the demented signs of the past
it is here that the dawn tears itself from the shreds of night
that in the atrocious parturition and the humble anonymous
blood
of the peasant and of the worker
is born the world where from the brows of men will be
effaced the bitter stigma of the sole equality of despair.

Page 180, fn. 8

"The simultaneity of the scenes of horror, which had occurred
in several different places of the Eastern Part [i.e., of the island
of Hispaniola, or the Dominican Republic], showed that the
authors of these crimes had obeyed an order and left no doubt
as to the participation of certain Dominican authorities, civil
and military."

Page 181 ("La Tragédie haïtienne," p. 5)

. . . What . . . separates Ouanaminthe from the Dominican village of Dajabon is a thin flow of water: the Massacre River, a name atrociously prophetic. . .

The same arid landscape in Dajabon, the same white-scorched earth where the intense light vibrates like a swarm. What distinguishes the two villages is less the huts, here of cob, and there, palisaded with palmetto boles, than the population, black and French-speaking in Haiti, mixed blood and Spanish-speaking in Santo Domingo. . . .

. . . it is doubtful that the racial difference can suffice to explain the explosion of hate which made of the Dajabon-Montechristi region the theater of a bloody orgy. I am inclined to believe that this people, exacerbated by the distress to which the Trujillo dictatorship has reduced them, obeyed the same obscure motivations which, in the South of the United States, pushes a mob of poor whites to lynch a Negro, and in Hitler country, a financially ruined petty bourgeois to mistreat a Jew. The governing classes and dictatorships have an understanding; they foster and provoke these sentiments, which turn away from themselves, in the manner of a lightning rod, the furor of those who are miserable.

Page 182 ("La Tragédie haïtienne," p. 6)

. . . the machetes fall upon the women, the children, the wounded, and finish the work of the rifles and the automatic weapons.

Page 182 ("La Tragédie haïtienne," p. 6)

With proverbial laziness this simple "good man" [Vincent], who possesses an extraordinary verbal agility and suffers manifestly from what an American financial counselor, with Yankee brutality, has called a diarrhea of words and a constipation of ideas, excells at exposing, in eloquent discourses, the virtues of directed economy.

Page 185 ("La Tragédie haïtienne," p. 6)

But the earth no longer nourishes these black peasants, eager workers for whom it would suffice to cite the magnificent title they bestow upon themselves—masters of the dew—to define their aim and the pride they feel about their destiny.

Page 187 ("Gouverneurs de la rosée," p. 9)

Two "inhabitants," Mirville and Jean-Gille, nothing but Negroes-from-the-sticks, as the townsfolk disdainfully call them. They wear huge straw hats, blue cloth work-jackets, they are barefoot and speak a chanting Creole in which the words are like fruit which makes the branch bend. But it is most of all by his hands that the peasant can be recognized, by that rough, cracked skin where a network of puffy veins knot, just as, under the ground, big bundles of roots crop out. The color of their hands is darker than that of their face, because the earth has become intermingled with their flesh, one would say even with their blood.

Page 187 ("Gouverneurs de la rosée," p. 9)

Now can be better distinguished the country where the road which plunges into a wooded curve reappears further on with a handful of palms stretching out at arm's length, and the work of the stream at the bottom of the ravine, its patient work which carries the red earth of the hill into its somber waters, and . . . but Jean-Gille has said: "Look at the smoke." And it's true, smoke is rising from a hut, and that, that's peace. You imagine the woman squatting before the fire, cooking the cassava, and the children around and it's the moment when the man takes up his machete and says: "Good-by, my wife," and he goes out to work.

Jean-Gille and Mirville know that behind the mountain there is another smoke, but that, that's war, and the woman is not about to prepare the meal. She is lying, her belly open like a great rotten fruit. As for the children—"Lord, peace to my lips"—and the man, well! the man is here, with his fury and his rifle.

Page 188 ("Gouverneurs de la rosée," p. 9)

Over there, that chalky flow, that's the bed of an almost dried-out torrent—"La Galette, The Cake," we call it. The women beat their wash, . . . the indigo and soapsuds make patches that look like the sky. The beetles of the washer-women crash down, clap, and when the women stop to rub, their heads inclined to one side over the shoulder, they kind of chant from their innermost beings, without words: it's useless. You understand that that means the dreariness of wearing yourself out working to no avail from sunup to sunset, and this dress has been mended a hundred times and I can't buy another one, my boy who's sick, and the doctor's asking fifty piasters to treat him . . . then, the song, that's to forget the great pain in the arms, or, if you like, to try to make it go to sleep, like a recalcitrant child.

In the lull, silence reigns again, it freshly flows, an enormous sigh that covers the chatter of the water in the rocks, the desolate chant, the jabber of the old women, dried out and faded, lined up like tobacco leaves in the sun. And when the beetles begin again to fall and resound, the silence rises and hovers like a startled bird.

Page 189 ("Gouverneurs de la rosée," p. 9)

Everything is so calm, so simple. Jean-Gille knows this country well, where everything is in its place for a role traced out by work and misery, life and death.

Page 190 ("Gouverneurs de la rosée," p. 9)

Yes, you also had your share of chagrin and your share of sadness and your measure of worry and a lot of setbacks, but that was destiny; you did not resign yourself. You took life by the waist, grappled with her without letting up, like a man, your teeth clenched.

Page 190 ("Gouvernerus de la rosée," p. 9)

Then they had come, these white Americans, supposedly to

civilize you and for that they had to take the land, and you, dirty nigger, you'll have to work the *corvée* the whole blessed day, paid with a kick and a bull whip.

A storm of rage covered his face. "Ah! these white 'Mericans," he murmured inside his throat. One would have said that he was choking.

Page 190 ("Gouverneurs de la rosée," p. 10)

. . . what he wanted to explain was that to kill, perhaps to be killed, was natural, that was war. But war is a catastrophe, a storm. It tore you from the earth like a tree by the roots; you left behind you a gaping wound. It was an accident, outside of real life. Life was being planted in the middle of your field, of your garden of foodstuffs, being regulated by the sun and the night, the rain and the drought. Certainly, when that is taken from you, it's rage. You defend yourself, don't you? You don't come cheap, you've got your weight of courage, your value as a man and death, if he's going to buy you, has to put up his price without bargaining. But all that is despair, it's not life. And then, what do you want? You regret it and it eats at you.

Page 191 ("Gouverneurs de la rosée," p. 10)

. . . good inhabitants, tillers of the soil, serious Negroes, masters of the dew, thousands and thousands, seized by death facing the enemy, or else taken in the fields, tormented and tortured, shot, burned alive, hung. . .

Page 191 ("Gouverneurs de la rosée," p. 10)

Thirty or so peasants, in groups, appeared. Their machetes strapped across their chests, blue work-jackets in tatters, red neckerchiefs around their necks, some had no gun. Negroes from the sticks, masters of the dew, *dispossessed of their destiny,* all similarly in the grip of misfortune, and each one with his story, different and the same, of blood, of violence and of death.

Page 192 ("Gouverneurs de la rosée," p. 10)

"I'm thinking, I'm thinking about when I used to wake up in the middle of the night to go and water. I would meet my neighbor Aristide. 'Neighbor, I'd say, like so, have you finished watering?' (I asked him because water is the benediction of all), and he would tell me 'Yes, neighbor'; then I'd say 'Good-by then, neighbor,' and he'd answer the same, neighbor Aristide. I'd open the canal, and the water would begin to run before me like a good dog, and me, I'd follow it and it would lead me in my land, and you felt that the land was happy. Its odor rose like a thanks, like praise.

Page 192 ("Gouverneurs de la rosée," p. 10)

"Ready?" cried Jean-Gille to them.
"Yes."
"Then, forward"
Jean-Gille brings up the rear. Like a shepherd, through the mountain passes, he leads his little band of defeated peasants.

Page 193 ("Griefs de l'homme noir," pp. 98–99)

pseudo-scientific, historical, and . . . biblical pretexts serve in the United States, and especially in the South, as a screen and as an exoneration for the activation of color prejudice. . . . we will yet see that slogans about the protection of the white woman, the irremediable inferiority of the black race, the white man's mission . . . hide an unscrupulous and rapacious class egoism; and, finally, that race prejudice manipulated like an instrument of division, diversion and derivation, permits the enslavement of large segments of the white population of the United States.

Page 194 ("Griefs de l'homme noir," p. 103)

It is, of course, possible that the observation—among seventeen characteristics—of a generally prominent heel in the Negro embryo, while it is so with extreme rarity in the white foetus, makes the quadroon Pushkin a particularly bestial being. . . .

Page 194 ("Griefs de l'homme noir," pp. 109–10)

For our part, we refuse to insult the American woman by admitting that her virtue needs to be safeguarded by legal constraints and the furors of lynching. Against such an abominable being as the Negro, in the biological and moral order, a quite natural repulsion should suffice to brandish the flaming sword of modesty before forbidden fruits. . . . But the very existence of millions of mixed bloods proves sufficiently that it has never been a question of the "protection of the black woman. . ."

Page 194 ("Griefs de l'homme noir," p. 111)

Lynching is a useful diversion and plays the role of lightning rod when the atmosphere is overcharged with the electricity of social antagonisms.

Page 194 ("Griefs de l'homme noir," p. 112)

It is impossible to see in color prejudice anything other than an ideological expression of class antagonism, the latter reflecting, in turn, the contradictions of the system of production.

Page 195 ("Griefs de l'homme noir," p. 113)

. . . a young hero such as Angelo Herndon symbolizes the new Negro, resolute, conscious of his youthful force and who has allied his destiny in the fraternity of combat to that of the white worker. . . . personally, I salute the nobility and the grandeur of the task undertaken by men of good will, yesterday bitter enemies, today reconciled upon the ruins of prejudices, for a new abolition of slavery and the reconstruction of the world.

Page 197 (Sartre, "L'Orphée noir")

. . . the subjective, existential, ethnic notion of *Negritude* "passes", as Hegel says, into the notion of *proletariat*—objective, positive, exact. . . . Negritude appears as the weak moment in a dialectical progression: the theoretical and practical affirmation of white supremacy is the thesis; the position of Negritude as an antithetical value is the moment of negativity. But this negative moment has no sufficiency in itself, and the Blacks who use it know that quite well; they know that it aims at preparing the synthesis or realization of that which is human in a society without races. . . . a poem by Jacques Roumain, [i.e., "Bois d'ébène"], a Black communist, provides the most moving witness to this new ambiguity. . .

Page 198 (Gouraige, *Historie de la Littérature Haïtienne*, p. 384)

René Piquion's *Langston Hughes* enlarged a horizon in 1940 which the poems of Jacques Roumain had allowed a glimpse of. "The innumerable army of the oppressed," writes Hughes, "is not made up only of blacks, but also of men with white, yellow, and brown faces; in fact, they all have identical interests, and their liberation will result from their union, from their spirit of solidarity." The poem "Dirty Niggers" by Jacques Roumain has no other meaning.

Page 198 (Gaillard, Group II interviews)

I think that there is in Haiti a tradition of patriotic and independentist poetry, but there has been no revolutionary poetry . . . because the only revolution that we've had was the one of 1804, and that revolution had a national character. . . . Revolutionary poetry is a poetry that wants to overturn the established order. . . . In the case of Jacques Roumain, one must see, certainly, that the rise of revolutionary poetry . . . coincided with the Second World War, that is, between the period of Franco, the Spanish War, and Stalingrad.

Page 199 ("Nouveau sermon nègre")

They have spit in His Face their icy disdain
As a black flag floats in the wind beaten by the snow
To make of him, poor negro, god of the powers that be
. . . .
Of his soft song of misery
Of his trembling banjo lament
The prideful tumult of the organ
Of his arms which hauled the heavy barges
On the river Jordan
The arm of those who strike with the sword
Of his body, spent like ours on the cotton plantations
. . . .
The golden buckle of their fortune
They have whitened His black Face under the spit of their
    icy disdain
. . . .

Page 200 ("Nouveau sermon nègre")

They have lynched John who was organizing the union
They chased him like a wild desperate wolf with their dogs
    across the woods
They hung him laughing to the trunk of an old sycamore
No, brothers, comrades
We will pray no more
. . . .
We will sing no more the sad desperate spirituals

Another song gushes from our throats
we unfurl our red flags
. . . .
        Arise damned of the earth
        Arise convicts of hunger

Page 200 ("Sales nègres")

okay, there you are:
we
the negroes
the niggers
the dirty niggers
we won't take any more
it's simple
through

being in Africa
in America
your negroes
your niggers
your dirty niggers

Page 200 ("Sales nègres")

Surprise
jesusmaryandjoseph
surprise
when we catch
laughing hideously
the missionary by the beard
to teach him in our turn
with kicks on the behind

. . . .

that we don't give a damn
about a God who
if he's the Father
well then, then it must be we

. . . .

must be we're only his bastards

Page 201 ("Sales nègres")

too late
for we will have risen up
from the caverns of thieves from the gold mines of the Congo
and of South Africa
too late it'll be too late
to prevent in the cotton fields of Louisiana
in the sugar plantations of the Antilles
the harvest of vengeance
of the negroes
of the niggers
of the dirty niggers
of the dirty hindus
of the dirty indo-chinese
of the dirty arabs
of the dirty malays
of the dirty jews
of the dirty proletarians
and here we are standing up

All the damned of the earth

. . . .

to finish
once
  and
    for
      all
with this world
of negroes
of niggers
of dirty niggers

Page 202 ("Bois d'ébène")

Negro bearer of revolt
you have known all the roads of the world
since you were sold in Guinea
a capsized light calls you
a livid canoe
run aground in the soot of a suburban sky

. . . .

Here is for your voice an echo of flesh and blood
black messenger of hope
for you have known all the chants of the world
starting with those of the immemorial building-sites of the
                                       Nile
You remember each word the weight of the stones of Egypt
and the impetus of your misery has set up the columns of
                                   temples

. . . .

Page 202 ("Bois d'ébène")

Africa I have kept your memory Africa
you are in me

Like the splinter in the wound
like a tutelary fetish in the center of the village
make of me the stone of your slingshot
make of my mouth the lips of your wound
of my knees the broken columns of your downfall . . .
    YET

I want only to be of your race
peasants workers of all countries

. . . .

Does all that climate expanse space
create the clan the tribe the nation
skin race and gods
our inexorable dissimilarity?
And the mine
and the factory
the harvests wrung from our hunger
our common indignity
our servitude under all skies invariable?
Miner of Asturia black miner or Johannesburg metallo
of Krupp hard peasant of Castille vineyard worker of Sicily
                                                                    pariah
of India
                                (I pass through your door sill, outcast
                            I take your hand in my hand, untouchable)
red guard of soviet China German worker in the
prison of Moabit Indian of the Americas

. . . .

White worker of Detroit black peon of Alabama
innumerable people of the capitalist galley
destiny sets us shoulder to shoulder
repudiating the ancient evil spell of the taboos of blood
we trample under foot the debris of our solitudes

. . . .

we proclaim the unity of suffering
and of revolt
of all peoples on all the surface of the earth

Page 205 ("Sur la liberté de l'écrivain," *Les Volontaires*, p. 556)

There is no longer dignity in happiness. . . . Man is
henceforth constrained to participate and, in a world divided
into victims and executioners, if he wishes to remain free, to
feel chained to the necessity of choosing.

Page 205 ("Sur la liberté de l'écrivain," *Les Volontaires*, p. 557)

faraway colonies are drawn into the fatal game of diplomacy
to the same extent as the frontiers of Central Europe, and the
same page of the newspaper teaches us that in a small town
in Alabama nine innocent Negroes [the Scottsboro case] have
been condemned to perish, burned alive in the electric chair,
and that a writer has paid behind the barbed wires of one of

Hitler's concentration camps for the crime of being a Jew
. . . pursuing a new and bloody division of the world, a whole
warlike geometry of axis and triangle renders one the destiny
of a Chinese coolie and a Czech worker, of an Austrian miner—
perhaps tomorrow of an Alsatian peasant.

Page 205 ("Sur la liberté de l'écrivain," *Les Volontaires,* p. 557)

From this moment man (and the writer more than any
other) is being hunted down. He *must* be hunted down, put
at the foot of the wall, brought to bay, and interrogated. And
he must answer.

Page 210 (Letter to Nicole Roumain dated March 21, 1941)

When I return to Haiti, I will be surrounded by unfamiliar
faces. A generation is born and another one has grown up
since my last imprisonment and these days of exile.

Page 211 (Guillén, "Sobre Jacques Roumain," *Prosa de Prisa,*
pp. 324–25)

Jacques Roumain loved us much, and he shared part of his
exile with a group of his friends, here in Havana, almost on
the eve of his death. Those were the heroic times of our *Hoy,*
when the paper was produced in a poor printing press in old
Havana, where, as in Cervantes' cell, every inconvenience had
its place. Jacques would go in the evenings to the paper and
there, in the midst of working, we'd laugh and talk. Until,
already night, we would all sit down in a little Chinese eating
place, in front of huge plates of rice and black beans and roast
meat.

CHAPTER VII

Page 214 ("Création d'un Bureau d'Ethnologie . . .," *Le Nouvelliste,* p. 1)

is essentially designed for the instruction of the largest segments of the population. It should be similar to a book opened and explained. Its mission is not to whet idle curiosity but to instruct and to stimulate study.

Page 216 (Roumain, speech on vodun at the Cercle Militaire)

Such is the force of the African tradition that throughout four hundred years Dahomeian words have been preserved intact in Haiti, and certain vodun songs have remained authentic to such an extent that even today the members of a secret society of Dahomey have been able to understand them.

Page 217 (*Le Nouvelliste*, February 27, 1942)

primitives still faithful to the practices of African fetishism . . . even though it has been eighty-two years since we signed a Concordat with the Holy See.

Page 217 (*Le Nouvelliste*, March 1942, pp. 3–4)

Primitive man, having been incapable of understanding the mechanism of natural phenomena and the structure of the external world, invented as many spirits and divinities as he had questions about the relationships between his thought and his being. . . .

Insofar as, by a reciprocal action, man's techniques and material needs not only changed the world but *explained* it, transformed society, overturned class relationships, these multiple divinities personifying the magical forces of the sky, of the earth, of the elements, etc., by that process of abstraction which Engels has remarkably called a process of distillation of the gods, gave way to the God of monotheistic religions. . . .

All peoples have conserved the residue of this heritage of obscure ages in their popular religious beliefs, their magical practices, and even in their philosophy. . . .

The Haitian is neither more—nor less—superstitious than any other people.

The so-called superstitious practices in which he indulges have a universal character.

Page 218 (*Le Nouvelliste*, March 1942, p. 10)

The amalgam is total; and since it is syncretism, the persistence of one of the factors—vodun—depends upon the existence of the other: Catholicism.

In short, one must be Catholic to practice vodun.

Page 218 (*Le Nouvelliste*, March 1942, p. 11)

Naturally, we must relieve the Haitian masses of their mystical impediments. But we will not win over these beliefs by violence or by the threat of Hell. It was not the executioner's axe, the flames of the stake, the auto-da-fés which destroyed sorcery. It was the progress of science, the continued development of human culture, an understanding of the structure of the universe, growing more and more profound each day.

Page 219 (*Le Nouvelliste*, March 1942, p. 12)

What needs to be staged in Haiti is not an antisuperstition campaign but an antimisery campaign. With schooling, hygiene, a higher standard of living, the peasant will have access to that culture and that decent life which one cannot refuse him if one does not want this whole country to perish, and which will permit him to surmount religious survivals rooted in his misery, ignorance, and secular exploitation.

Page 219 ("Réplique au Révérend Père Foisset," *Le Nouvelliste*, July 31, 1942)

. . . what puts us in opposition to each other, and uncompromisingly so, is the essence of our conception of the world. It is, in your case, metaphysical, and you know that I set against it in a fundamental way a scientific philosophy called dialectical materialism.

Page 219 ("Réplique au Révérend Père Foisset," *Le Nouvelliste*, March 30, 1942)

. . . if it were necessary to define dialectics graphically, it is not linear rigidity which would explain it, but the infinite movement of the spiral.

Page 219 (Heraclitus' notion of flux)

that perpetual movement of things through their contradictions

Page 220 ("Réplique au Révérend Père Foisset," *Le Nouvelliste*, March 30, 1942)

But for the illustrious philosopher, reality is only the phenomenal form of the absolute idea. The Hegelian triad—thesis, antithesis, synthesis—closes the circle, transforms Heraclitus' river into a lake: Hegelian logic was in short, as Feuerbach remarked, the last form of the theology which transported the essence of nature outside of nature, the essence of man outside of man, with this major difference that in Hegel the idea replaces imaginary metaphysical creations.

Scientific philosophy, dialectical materialism, had the incomparable merit of demonstrating that synthesis was not static, that it contained the elements of a new contradiction, demanding to be resolved through new antagonisms endlessly suppressed, constantly renewed, in a process of transformation of energy which is the very movement of life: to Marxism is due the honor of having demonstrated that the movement of thought is none other than the reflection of the movement of the real transported and transposed into man's brain.

Hegel taught: everything which is real is rational. Father Foisset, for his part, seems to believe that everything which is unreal is rational and that the fact for primitive man of having created gods in the image of his ignorance proves the existence of God.

Page 220 ("Réplique au Révérend Père Foisset," *Le Nouvelliste*, March 31, 1942)

. . . I pray the Reverend Father Foisset to abandon his theory.
. . . I deem that there is a supreme impertinence in supposing that one could one day discover a molar tooth, the cranium, or the ulna of "the image of God."

Page 221 ("Réplique au Révérend Père Foisset," *Le Nouvelliste*, April 21, 1942)

For the metaphysicians, scientific truths are only empirio-symbols, a theoretical systemization without basis in objective reality. But for the philosopher, the fundamental gnoseological question is the correspondence of our perceptions with the objective nature of things perceived. It is the experimental method which demonstrates this identity. "The chemical substances produced in vegetable and animal organisms remained 'things-in-themselves' until organic chemistry began to prepare them one after the other." (Engels: Ludwig Feuerbach). Certain proteins remained "things-in-themselves" until 1936, when Bergman discovered their chemical formula. . . .
Science is a method of investigation and of progressive knowledge of the world. It has a transitory, relative, approximative character; it goes from ignorance to knowledge according to an ascendant curve of errors and of relative truths toward a more and more exact appreciation of objective reality. But this relativism does not lead us to skepticism, to philosophical idealism: each parcel of relative scientific truth contains an element of absolute truth equal to the sum of the relative truths in process of development. . . .

It is the dialectical distinction between absolute and relative truth which gives to science its living and progressive character.
. . . Apparently, man's conscience has no more succeeded in surmounting the survivals of the past than has his physiology: we still possess nails and canine teeth which no longer serve the purpose of seizing and tearing apart a prey.

In the same way a religious conception can survive despite the progress of science.

Metaphysics is only a kind of ideological appendix.

Page 221 ("Réplique au Révérend Père Foisset," *Le Nouvelliste*, July 31, 1942)

But there are problems, such as unemployment, war, the antifascist struggle, liberty, justice, the right of the whole of humanity to a decent life, which are WORLDLY problems that men of the most varied religions and philosophies can try together sincerely to resolve. . . .

. . . If such is also your opinion, I am happy to offer you a loyal hand.

Page 222 (Roumain, Preface to *Essai d'explication de "Dialogues de mes lampes"*)

He [Saint-Amand] has grasped, with perfect clairvoyance, the importance of this poet, of this antirevolutionary rebel . . . who refuses to change the world, flees from reality, denies it through the bitter artifice of a reinvention of language, which permits him, far from the bourgeois deafness of all that which is not vulgar music, to recapture the terrible song of an irreparable solitude.

Page 224 ("Jacques Roumain interviewé à La Havane," *Le Nouvelliste*, November 20, 1942)

The Head of the Haitian nation has a very precise vision of the imperious necessity which the union of all the Republics of America constitutes, and as the President is called by the national unity of the Haitian people, his policy of alliance with the United Nations, which in fighting against the Axis, expresses exactly the exigencies of the conditions of victory.

Let me emphasize that Mr. Lescot was the first President of the Americas to contribute materially by his presence to the success of a benefit for the Soviet Red Cross. That is an expression of the conception which the Haitian government has formed of its responsibility.

Page 224 ("Jacques Roumain interviewé à La Havane," *Le Nouvelliste*, November 20, 1942)

The government . . . has expressed repeatedly its resolve to better the material and intellectual conditions of the Haitian people. . . . Its action has been implemented by decrees and social legislation fixing the minimum salary, considerably increasing the price per ton of sugar cane, . . . requiring young doctors to spend a two-year tour of duty in the countryside to care for and advise the peasants.

Page 226 ("Prelude")

If the summer is rainy and gloomy
if the sky veils the pool with an eyelid of clouds
if the palm comes undone in shreds
If the trees are proud and black in the wind and the fog

If the wind blows a wisp of funeral song toward the plain
If the shadow crouches around the dying hearth

If the sails of wild wings carry the island off toward the ship-
                                                          wrecks
if the dusk drowns the torn flight of a last handkerchief
and if the cry wounds the bird
you will depart
abandoning your village

Its lagoon and its bitter grape vines
the trace of your footsteps in its sands
the reflection of a dream at the bottom of the well
and the old tower at the road's turn
like a faithful dog at the end of his leash
and who barks in the evenings
a cracked call in the pastures. . . .

Page 227 ("L'Amour la mort")

For his despair a venomous idol
Wild look of swallow's half-burned cinder
stabbed smile
sharp withering of the blood
the spider draws the thread of a wrinkle
every shame drunk at the vent of this mouth
                        *
            *   *

A beating of the eyelash of the dawn
and the pollen of the sun covers your cheek

A nest of wings your hair
If the breath of the wind brushes over it

Beauty ravished at the movement of blood
your hands offer a sacrifice of doves
On your invincible knees.

CHAPTER VIII

Page 232 (*Gouverneurs de la rosée*, p. 1)

"We're all going to die," said the old woman. Plunging her hands into the dust, Délira Délivrance said, "We're all going to die. Animals, plants, every living soul! oh, Jesus! Mary, Mother of God!"

The dust slipped through her fingers, the same dust that the dry wind scattered over the high hedge of cactus eaten by verdigris, over the blighted thorn acacias and the devastated fields of millet.

Page 233 (*Gouverneurs de la rosée*, p. 23)

she felt exhausted. . . . her worn-out body given over to death that would in the end bring her to this dust.

Page 233 (*Gouverneurs de la rosée*, p. 172)

Manuel lay down on the ground. With his whole body he embraced the earth.

"There she is! The good, sweet, flowing, singing, cooling, blessed life!"

He kissed the earth with his lips and laughed.

Page 234 (*Gouverneurs de la rosée*, p. 190)

She was stretched out on the ground and the low rumble of the water echoed within her in a sound that was the tumult of her own blood.

Page 234 (*Gouverneurs de la rosée*, p. 230)

"He's the one who's giving the orders, that little black baby! I'm going to say yes."

"It's life that's giving the orders," Marianna said, "and water that's life's answer!"

Page 234 (*Gouverneurs de la rosée*, p. 260)

"This spring that I've found needs the help of all the peasants of Fonds Rouge. Don't say no. It's life that gives orders. When life commands, we've got to answer, 'Present!' "

Page 235 (*Gouverneurs de la rosée*, p. 65)

"Resignation won't get us anywhere." Manuel shook his head impatiently. "Resignation is treacherous. It's just the same as discouragement. It breaks your arms. You keep on expecting miracles and providence, with your rosary in your hand, without doing a thing. You pray for rain, you pray for a harvest, you recite the prayers of the saints and the *loas.* But providence—take my word for it—is a man's determination not to accept misfortune, to overcome the earth's bad will every day, to bend the whims of the water to your needs. Then the earth will call you, 'Dear Master.' The water will call you, 'Dear Master.' And there's no providence but hard work, no miracles but the fruit of your hands."

Page 236 (*Gouverneurs de la rosée*, p. 106)

"What are we? Since that's your question, I'm going to answer you. We're *this country,* and it wouldn't be a thing without us, nothing at all. Who does the planting? Who does the watering? Who does the harvesting? Coffee, cotton, rice, sugar cane, cacao, corn, bananas, vegetables, and all the fruits, who's going to grow them if we don't? Yet with all that, we're poor, that's true. We're out of luck, that's true. We're miserable, that's true. But do you know why, brother? Because of our ignorance. We don't know yet what a force we are, what a single force—all the peasants, all the Negroes of plain and hill, all united. Some day, when we get wise to that, we'll rise up from one end of the country to the other. Then we'll call a General Assembly of the Masters of the Dew, a great big *coumbite* of farmers, and we'll clear out poverty and plant a new life."

Page 236 (*Gouverneurs de la rosée*, p. 183)

"Faith in life, Anna. Faith that men can't die." . . .

"Naturally the day comes when each man must enter the earth. But life itself is a thread that doesn't break, that can't be lost. Do you know why? Because every man ties a knot in it during his lifetime with the work that he does—that's what keeps life going through the centuries—man's work on this earth."

Page 237 (*Gouverneurs de la rosée*, pp. 245–46)

Instruction was a necessary thing; it helped you understand life. . . . And if a peasant went to school, surely it wouldn't be so easy any more to cheat him, abuse him, and treat him like a beast of burden.

Page 238 (*Gouverneurs de la rosée*, p. 301)

And, if, one day on the hard road of this life, weariness should tempt us with, "What's the use?" and "It's not worth the trouble," we'll hear your voice and we'll be of good courage.

Page 238 (*Gouverneurs de la rosée*, p. 307)

"He told me, here's what Manuel, my boy, told me. 'You've offered sacrifices to the *loas*, you've offered the blood of chickens and young goats to make the rain fall. All that has been useless. Because what counts is the sacrifice of a man, the blood of a man.' . . .

It's customary to sing mourning with hymns for the dead, but he, Manuel had chosen a hymn for the living—the chant of the *coumbite*, the chant of the soil, of the water, the plants, of friendship between peasants, because he wanted his death to be the beginning of life for you."

Page 238 (*Gouverneurs de la rosée*, p. 316)

". . . he said to me, 'Life is a thread that doesn't break, that is never lost, and do you know why? Because every man ties a knot in it during his lifetime with the work he has done.' "

Page 239 (*Gouverneurs de la rosée,* p. 262)

But what good are prayers and supplications when that last hour has come of which the Book speaks? When the moon goes out and the stars go out and the wax of the clouds hides the sun, and the strong Negro says, "I'm tired."

Page 239 (*Gouverneurs de la rosée,* p. 262)

The daylight slipped through the badly hung flap of the window. Some hens started cackling as usual. Manuel opened his eyes. He reached for the air with little panting gasps.

Page 239 (*Gouverneurs de la rosée,* p. 264)

He looked at the patch of light that spread in the sky. He smiled feebly. "Day is breaking. Every day, day breaks. Life starts over again."

Page 239 (*Gouverneurs de la rosée,* pp. 291–92)

It was the last hymn, the very last, for day came with black chilly trees against a pale sky, and the peasants began to take leave. . . . Roosters strained their throats from yard to yard, and a young colt neighed nervously on the savanna.

"*Adieu,* Delira," Laurelien said. He hesitated. "*Adieu* Annaise." . . .

Dawn came in through the window, but Manuel would never see it again. He had gone to sleep for always and forever.

Amen!

Page 240 (*Gouverneurs de la rosée,* p. 13)

Above the thorn acacias floated wisps of smoke. In the clearings, the charcoal workers were clearing away the mounds under which the green wood had slowly burned.

A tree is made to live in peace in the color of the day and the friendship of the sun, the wind, the rain. Its roots sink deep into the rich fermentation of the earth, draw in the elementary juices, the fortifying juices. It seems always lost in a great tranquil dream. The sap, rising unseen, makes it moan in the hot afternoons. It is a living being that knows the passing of the clouds and senses the coming of storms because it is full of birds nests.

Estinval wipes his reddened eyes with the back of his hand. Of the mutilated tree, nothing remains but the burned skeleton of scattered branches in the ashes, a load of charcoal which his wife will sell in the town of Croix-des-Bouquets.

Page 241 (*Gouverneurs de la rosée*, p. 171)

He went up toward the giant fig tree. He felt the blessed breeze dry his sweat. He was walking through a great silence.

Then, he entered a deep green shade, and his last machete stroke revealed the mountain circling a wide level space where the giant fig tree proudly lifted its powerful trunk. Its branches, laden with floating moss, covered the spot with venerable shade, and its monstrous roots extended an authoritative hand over the ownership and secret of his corner of the earth.

Page 241 (*Gouverneurs de la rosée*, pp. 188–89)

He pushed the vines aside. She walked in the mysterious shade of the giant fig tree.

"That's the keeper of the water," she whispered in a sort of sacred terror.

"He's the keeper of the water."

She looked at the branches laden with silvery, floating moss.

"He's terribly old."

"He's terribly old."

"You can't see his head."

"His head's in the sky."

"His roots are like feet."

"They hold the water."

"Show me the water, Manuel."

Page 242 (Gaillard, *L'Univers romanesque de Jacques Roumain*, pp. 17–18)

From the first lines, we no longer know, in effect, who is speaking, if it is the character, the author, or even we ourselves who are reading. And it is thus that the lyricism takes wing.
. . .

The song is at times double.

It is in those cases, that of the author and that of the character. A kind of spoken style, without quotation marks, becomes intertwined with the narrative style, properly speaking.

Page 242 (*Gouverneurs de la rosée*, p. 22)

She had kissed him. She had taken in her arms this big fellow who had come from the depths of her flesh and blood, and had become this man to whom she whispered through her tears. "Go, my little one, may the Holy Virgin protect you!" And he had turned at the elbow of the road and disappeared. "Oh, son of my womb, sorrow of my womb, joy of my life, pain of my life! My boy, my only boy!"

Page 242 (*Gouverneurs de la rosée*, p. 197)

She had been weeding the fields when the pains struck. She had dragged herself to her hut, bitten her cries in the flesh of her forearm, and he was born from an immense laceration of her being. She herself had cut the cord, washed and laid the infant down in clean clothes before sinking into black unconsciousness, until Bienaimé's voice and the womenfolk's chatter had aroused her. Today, he was here before her, this man so tall, so strong, with that light on his forehead, this man who knew the mystery of water sleeping in the veins of the mountains!

Page 243 (*Gouverneurs de la rosée*, pp. 215–16)

For years, hate had become with them a habit. It had given an object and a target to their impotent anger against the elements. But Manuel had translated into good Creole the exacting language of the thirsty plain, the plaint of growing things, the promises and all the mirages of the water. He had led them in advance through their harvest. Their eyes gleamed just from listening to him. Only there was one condition: that was reconciliation. And what did it cost them? A mere gesture, a few steps like walking over a bridge, and they would leave behind the bad days of poverty, they would enter the land of abundance.

"Well, brother, what do you say?"

The other, his feet bare in the dust, ragged, skinny, and famished, listened in silence. It was true that they were tired of that old story. What good was it, after all? Suppose they had a mass sung at the same time for both Dorisca and Sauveur, for the repose of their souls? That would reconcile them in the grave, then they'd leave the living in peace. Restless dead folks are troublesome, they're even dangerous. What was sure and certain was that we mustn't let ourselves perish. Well?

"Well, since it's like that, we agree. But who'll go and talk with the others?"

"I will," Manuel replied.

CONCLUSION

Page 251 (Letter from Nicolás Guillén to Nicole Roumain, Havana, July 10, 1948)

Ever since Jacques' death, I had planned to do something on him. Something which would go beyond the simple newspaper article and which would reflect the brotherly friendship uniting us from our first meeting. . . . What would I do? An essay? A poem? This last was what took shape most firmly in my mind. . . .

Page 253, fn. 5

Mr. Roumain has always appeared to me a bored man of fashion who, by one of those bizarre contradictions, lives intensely.

Bibliography

PUBLISHED WORKS BY JACQUES ROUMAIN

"Absence." *Anthologie da la poésie haitienne "indigène."* Port-au-Prince: Imprimerie Modèle, 1928, p. 38.

"Agissons!" *Haïti-Journal,* January 25, 1930, p. 1.

Analyse schématique: 32–34. Publication du Comité Central du Parti Communiste Haïtien. Port-au-Prince: V. Valcin, June 1934, (with anonymous co-authors).

"Angoisse." *Anthologie . . . "indigène."* Port-au-Prince: Imprimerie Modèle, 1928, p. 36.

"Appel." Port-au-Prince: Imprimerie V. Pierre-Noel, 1928.

"Après-Midi." *La Trouée,* September 1927.

"Un Article tendencieux du 'Matin'." *Le Petit Impartial,* June 13, 1928.

"Attente." *Anthologie . . . "indigène."* Port-au-Prince: Imprimerie Modèle, 1928, p. 37.

"L'Aube." *La Presse,* September 14, 1929, p. 3.

Bois d'ébène. Port-au-Prince: Imprimerie Henri Deschamps, 1945. English translation: *Ebony Wood,* trans. by Sidney Shapiro. New York: Interworld Press, 1972.

"Calme." *La Revue Indigène,* September 1927, p. 114.

"Cent mètres." *La Revue Indigène,* July 1927, pp. 14–15. Reprinted in *Anthologie . . . "indigène,"* pp. 33–34.

"Le Chant de l'homme." *La Revue Indigène,* September 1927, p. 113.

Contribution à l'étude de l'ethnobotanique pré-colombienne des Grandes Antilles. Port-au-Prince: Imprimerie de l'Etat, 1942.

"Corrida." *La Revue Indigène,* September 1927, pp. 115–16.

"Une Critique importante." *Bulletin du Bureau d'Ethnologie,* no. 2?, (1943), pp. 33–34.

"La Danse du poète-clown." *La Revue Indigène,* August 1927, p. 64.

"Défense de Paul Morand." *Le Petit Impartial,* May 19, 1928, p. 3.

"Echappée." *La Trouée,* March 1928.

"Eloge à la cruauté de Christophe." *Haïti-Journal,* May 7, 1930, p. 1.

"Les Fantoches-Fragment." *Haïti-Journal,* June 27, 1931, p. 2.

Les Fantoches. Port-au-Prince: Imprimerie de l'Etat, 1931.
> Reviews: Luc Grimard, "Deux Romans de Jacques Roumain." *Haïti-Journal,* February 24, 1932, pp. 1–2. "Les Fantoches et la Montagne ensorcelée," *Le Nouvelliste,* December 21, 1931, p. 1. Fr(ançois) Duvalier, "Les Fantoches de Jacques Roumain," *Le Nouvelliste,* December 28, 1931, p. 1.

"Gouverneurs de la rosée." *Regards,* August 25, 1938, pp. 9–10.

Gouverneurs de la rosee. Port-au-Prince: Imprimerie de l'Etat, 1944; second edition, Paris: Bibliothèque Française, 1947; third edition, Paris: Editeurs Français Réunis, 1950, repr. 1971; fourth edition, Club Français du Livre, 1964.
> Reviews: Edner Brutus, "Gouverneurs de la rosée, "*Haïti-Journal,* January 11, 1945; Claudie Planet, "L'Edition française de 'Gouverneurs de la rosée' de Jacques Roumain." *Conjonction.* 7 (February 1947): 29–32.

English translation: *Masters of the Dew,* trans. by Langston Hughes and Mercer Cook. New York: Reynal and Hitchcock, 1947; second edition, New York: Collier Books (Macmillan Co.), 1971.

"Griefs de l'homme noir." *L'Homme de couleur.* Edited by S. E. le Cardinal Verdier. Paris: Librarie Plon, 1939. Spanish trans.: "Quejas del hombre negro." *Casa de las Américas,* May-August, 1966, pp. 147–54.

"Guinée." *Haïti-Journal,* December 30, 1931. This is the same poem which in the Dudley Fitts anthology bears the title "Sur le Chemin de guinée." [See "Anthologies Which Include Poems by Jacques Roumain."]

"Un homme contre un empire—Mahatma Gandhi." *Le Petit Impartial,* March 2, 1928, p. 1; March 7, 1928, p. 2; March 10, 1928, p. 1; March 14, 1928, p. 3; March 17, 1928, p. 3; March 21, 1928, p. 1; March 28, 1928, p. 1.

"Horizon . . . soleil." *La Presse,* September 7, 1929, p. 3.

"Insomnie." *La Revue Indigène,* September 1927, p. 111.

"Is Poetry Dead?" *New Masses,* January 7, 1941, pp. 22–23. Published version of speech given at Writers Guild, New York, December 13, 1940. Spanish trans. "La Poesía como arma." *Gaceta del Caribe,* January 1944. French trans. from Spanish version in *Cahiers d'Haïti* II, 4 (November 1944). Reprinted in Lakansièl II (1975): 26–27.

"Je rêve que je rêve." *La Presse,* September 14, 1929, p. 3.

"Jeune Haïti." *Le Petit Impartial,* March 3, 1928, p. 3.

"A la jeunesse." *Le Petit Impartial,* March 7, 1928, p. 1 (with Georges J. Petit).

"A Jouer aux billes." *La Revue Indigène,* January 1928, p. 208.

"Langston Hughes." *Haïti-Journal,* October 20, 1931, p. 1.

"Une Lettre de M. Jacques Roumain." *Haïti-Journal,* January 5, 1933, p. 1.

"Madrid." *Commune,* April 1937.

"Mahatma Gandhi." *Haïti-Journal,* May 14, 1930, p. 1.

"Manifeste à la jeunesse." *Le Petit Impartial,* April 4, 1928, p. 1 (with Georges J. Petit).

"Manifeste à la jeunesse des écoles." *Le Petit Impartial,* October 7, 1928, p. 3 (with Georges J. Petit).

"Le Médecin rural ou la science au service du peuple." *Le Nouvelliste,* June 17, 1942, p. 1.

"Midi." *La Trouée,* July 1927, p. 22. Reprinted in *Anthologie . . . "indigène,"* p. 32.

"Mirage." *Anthologie . . . "indigène."* Port-au-Prince: Imprimerie Modèle, 1928, p. 39.

"Miragôane." *La Trouée,* September 1927.

"Mon ami Alcibiades." *La Trouée,* July 1927, pp. 26–28.

"Mon Carnet." *La Presse,* August 21, 22, 24; September 21, 23, 1929 (signed Ibrahim).

"La Montagne ensorcelée." *Haïti-Journal,* (Feuilletons 1–15) January 20–24, 26–31; February 2–5, 1931.

La Montagne ensorcelée. Preface by Jean Price-Mars. Port-au-Prince: Imprimerie E. Chassaing, 1931.
> Reviews: Carl Brouard, *Haïti-Journal,* January 25, 1932, p. 1; Luc Grimard "Deux Romans de Jacques Roumain," *Haïti-Journal,* February 24, 1932, pp. 1–2. "Les Fantoches et la Montagne ensorcelée," *Le Nouvelliste,* December 21, 1931, p. 1.

La Montagne ensorcelée (précédé de *La Proie et l'ombre,* suivi de *Griefs de l'homme noir* et de poèmes). Preface by Jacques Stéphen Alexis. Paris: Editeurs Français Réunis, 1972.

"Le Musée du Bureau d'Ethnologie." *Bulletin du Bureau d'Ethnologie,* no. 2?, (1943), pp. 34–35.

"Noir." *La Revue Indigène,* August 1927, p. 62.

"Notes pour servir à un manuel de parfait arriviste." *Haïti-Journal,* January 25, 1930, p. 1.

"Nous sommes grossiers!" *Le Petit Impartial,* September 8, 1928, p. 1 (with Georges J. Petit).

"Le 'Nouvelliste' inconscient." *Le Petit Impartial,* June 16, 1928, p. 1.

"Nungesser et Coli." *La Trouée,* August 1927, p. 49.

Oeuvres choisies. Preface by Jacques Stéphen Alexis, study by Eugénie Galpérina. [Moscow]: Editions du progrès, 1964.

"Orage." *La Revue Indigène,* September 1927, p. 112. Reprinted in *Haïti-Journal,* January 20, 1932, p. 1.

"L'Outillage lithique des Ciboney d'Haïti." *Bulletin du Bureau d'Ethnologie,* 1943, pp. 22–27.

"Péralte crucifié." *Le Petit Impartial,* November 1, 1928, p. 1.

"Petite chronique." *Le Petit Impartial,* October 24, 1928, p. 3.

"Le Peuple et l'élite." *Le Petit Impartial,* February 22, 1928, pp. 1, 3.

"Pluie." *La Trouée,* July 1927, p. 22. Reprinted in *Anthologie . . . "indigène,"* p. 31.

"Poème de Jacques Roumain." *Haïti-Journal,* July 6, 1931, p. 2. This is the same poem which in MS bears the title, "Créole." [See "Manuscripts and Correspondence of Jacques Roumain."]

"Port-au-Prince—Cap Haïtien." *Haïti-Journal,* April 3, 1930, p. 1.

"Préface" to Edris Saint-Amand's *Essai d'explication de "Dialogue de mes lampes."* Port-au-Prince: Imprimerie de l'Etat, 1942.

"Préface à la vie d'un bureaucrate." *Haïti-Journal*, February 19–22, 24–25, 1930. Reprinted in *La Proie et l'ombre*.

"Présentation de Langston Hughes." *Haïti-Journal*, August 8, 1931, p. 2.

"Un Prêtre a le droit d'être un soldat quand sa patrie est en danger." *Le Petit Impartial*, June 20, 1928, p. 1.

La Proie et l'ombre. Preface by Antonio Vieux. Port-au-Prince: Editions "La Presse," 1931.
　　Reviews: Jean-Baptiste Cinéas, *Haïti-Journal*, October 4, 7, 11, 1930; L. G., *Haïti-Journal*, September 24, 1930; G. J. P. [Georges J. Petit?], *Le Petit Impartial*, September 11, 1930; Carl Brouard, *Le Petit Impartial*, September 8–9, 1930.

A Propos de la campagne "anti-superstitieuse": las supersticiones. Port-au-Prince: Imprimerie de l'Etat, n.d. The same study was published as "Sur les superstitions" in *Le Nouvelliste*, March 11, 13, 18, 1942.

"Quand Bat le Tam-Tam." *Haïti-Journal*, July 4, 1931, p. 2.

"Réplique au Révérend Père Foisset." *Le Nouvelliste*, March 30–July 31, 1942.

Le Sacrifice du tambour-assoto(r). Port-au-Prince: Imprimerie de l'Etat, 1943.

"Au Secrétaire Universelle." *Le Petit Impartial*, July 11, 1928, p. 1.

"Surgi d'une natte de paille peinte." *Anthologie . . . "indigène."* Port-au-Prince: Imprimerie Modèle, 1928, p. 40.

"Sur la liberté de l'écrivain." *Les Volontaires*, June 1939, pp. 556–57.

"La Terre et les morts." *Le Petit Impartial*, February 25, 1928, p. 2.

"La Tragédie Haïtienne." *Regards*, November 18, 1937, pp. 4–6.

"La Veste." *La Revue Indigène*, October 1927, pp. 167–71. Reprinted in *La Proie et l'ombre*. Spanish trans. "La Chaqueta," *Casa de las Américas*, May–June 1974, pp. 115–18.

"Voix de la jeune Haiti." *Le Petit Impartial*, March 10, 1928, p. 3 [Signed J. R.].

MANUSCRIPTS AND CORRESPONDENCE OF JACQUES ROUMAIN

"Bois de'ébène." Handwritten manuscript, n.d.

"Le Champ du potier." Handwritten manuscript, n.d.

"Créole." Poem. Handwritten manuscript, n.d.

"Introduction." Typed manuscript, n.d., appears to be first section of a Marxist speech, pamphlet, or study.

"Sur le vodou haïtien." Typed manuscript of speech, n.d. [1942?].

Untitled manuscript of speech given at Harlem YMCA, November 15, 1939. Vertical file, Schomberg Collection, New York Public Library.

"Violettes fanées." Handwritten poem inserted in letter dated April 10, 1923, from Grünau.

Correspondence:
Letter dated October 23, 1922, Grünau.
Letter [1922], Grünau.
Letter to Joseph Jolibois, Zurich, January 15, 1925. Published in Sylvain, Georges. *Dix années de lutte pour la liberté: 1915–1925.* Vol. 2. Port-au-Prince: H. Deschamps, n.d.
Letter dated October 3, 1931, Port-au-Prince. Alain Locke Collection. Moorland-Spingarn Research Center, Howard University.
Letter dated February 17, 1932, New York. Alain Locke Collection, Moorland-Spingarn Research Center, Howard University.
Letter dated August 16, 1936, en route for Europe.
Letter dated December 25, 1939, New York.
Letter dated October 14, 1940, New York.
Letter dated November 29, 1940, New York.
Letter dated March 21, 1941, Havana.

ANTHOLOGIES WHICH INCLUDE POEMS BY JACQUES ROUMAIN

Anthologie de la poésie haïtienne "indigène." Port-au-Prince: Imprimerie Modèle, 1928. Contains "Pluie," "Midi," "Cent mètres," "Orage," "Angoisse," "Attente," "Absence," "Mirage," "Surgi d'une natte de paille peinte."

Arendt, Erich, ed. and trans. *Die Indios steigen von Mixco Nieder: Südamerikanische Freiheitsdichtungen.*

endt. Berlin: Verlag Volk und Welt, 1951. Contains "Guinea" and "Wenn der Tam Tam schlägt."

Collins, Marie. *Black Poets in French*. New York: Charles Scribner's Sons, 1972. Contains "Bois d'ébène" (bilingual edition).

Fitts, Dudley. *An Anthology of Contemporary Latin-American Poetry*. Norfolk, Conn.: New Directions, 1942. Contains "Sur le chemin de Guinée" and "Quand bat le tam-tam."

Hughes, Langston and Arna Bontemps, eds. *The Poetry of the Negro: 1746–1949*. Garden City, New York: Doubleday, 1949. Contains "Langston Hughes," "Guinea," and "When the Tom-Tom Beats." (These poems are not reproduced in the 1971 edition of the anthology.)

Kesteloot, Lilyan. *Anthologie Negro-africaine*. Verviers, Belgium: Editions Gerard (Collection Marabout Université), 1967. Contains "Bois d'ébène."

Lubin, Maurice A. *Poésies Haïtiennes*. Rio de Janeiro: Livraria-Editora da Casa do estudante do Brasil, 1956. Contains "Insomnie," "Orage," "Angoisse," and "Le Chant de l'homme."

Saint-Louis, Carlos and Maurice Lubin. *Panorama de la poésie haïtienne*. Port-au-Prince: Henri Deschamps, 1950. Contains "Miragôane," "Après-Midi," "Insomnie," "Orage," "Pluie," "Calme," "Attente," "Midi," "Mirage," "La Danse du poète-clown," "Le Chant de l'homme."

Senghor, Léopold Sédar, ed. *Anthologie de la nouvelle poésie nègre et malgache de langue française*. Paris: Presses Universitaires de France, 1948. Contains "Madrid," "Bois d'ébène," "L'Amour, la mort," "Nouveau sermon nègre."

WORKS ABOUT JACQUES ROUMAIN

Achiriga, Jingiri J., "Jacques Roumain, Gouverneurs de la rosée: l'exemple haïtien" in his *Révolte des romanciers noirs*. Sherbrooke: Naaman, 1973, pp. 119–141.

Alexis, Jacques Stéphen. "Jacques Roumain vivant." *Jacques Roumain. Oeuvres choisies*. [Moscow]: Editions du progrès, 1964.

Antoine, Jacques. "Literature—From Toussaint Louverture to Jacques Roumain." *An Introduction to Haiti*. ed. by Mercer Cook Washington, D.C.: Pan American Union, 1951, pp. 93–120.

Balmir, Guy-Claude. "Gouverneurs de la rosée." *Négritude africaine, négritude caraïbe.* Université Paris-Nord (Paris XIII): Centre d'études francophones, 1974, pp. 135–39.

Berrou, Frère Raphael. " 'Gouverneurs de la rosée' ou la tragédie de l'eau." *Le Nouveau Monde,* August 24, 1970, pp. 1 and 6.

Bradley, Francine. "Political Prisoners in Haiti." *New Republic,* March 27, 1935.

Brierre, Jean. *Nous garderons le dieu.* Port-au-Prince: Henri Deschamps, 1945.

Brutus, Edner. "Jacques Roumain." *La Relève* 2, iv (October 1933): 4–16.

Camille, Roussan. "Jacques Roumain." *Le Nouvelliste,* October 27, 1942.

Cobb, Martha. "Concepts of Blackness in the Poetry of Nicolás Guillén, Jacques Roumain and Langston Hughes." *College Language Association Journal* 18, no. 2 (December 1974): 262–72.

Cunard, Nancy. "Three Negro Poets." *Left Review,* October 1937, pp. 529–36.

Dalmas, A. "Ecrire pour vivre." *Mercure de France,* no. 338 (1960): 706–8.

Dash, Michael. "The Marxist Counterpoint—Jacques Roumain: 1930's to 1940's." *Black Images* II, Spring 1973, pp. 25–29.

Dixon, Melvin. "Toward a World Black Literature and Community." *Massachusetts Review* 18: 750–69.

Dominique, Jean. " 'Délire ou Délivrance,' à propos d'une critique de Jean-Claude Fignolé sur *Gouverneurs de la rosée.*" *Conjonction,* no. 125 (May 1975): 85–100.

Fignolé, Jean-Claude. *"Gouverneurs de la rosée" (Hypothèse de travail dans une perspective spiraliste).* Port-au-Prince: Editions Fardin, 1974.

Fowler, Carolyn. "Motif Symbolism in Jacques Roumain's *Gouverneurs de la rosée.*" *College Language Association Journal* 18, no. 1 (September 1974): 44–51.

Gaillard, Roger. "Il y a vingt ans mourait Jacques Roumain . . ." *Le Matin,* August 18, 1964.

_____. "Le Théâtre: Eternelle jeunesse de 'Gouverneurs de la rosée'." *Le Nouvelliste*, July 29–30, 1967, p. 1.

_____. "Notes." Program notes for stage version of *Gouverneurs de la rosée*, July 23, 1967.

_____. *L'Univers romanesque de Jacques Roumain*. Port-au-Prince: Henri Deschamps, n.d. [1965?].

Galpérina, Eugénie. "Jacques Roumain: Sa vie, son oeuvre." *Jacques Roumain, Oeuvres choisies*. [Moscow]: Editions du progrès, [1964].

Gazarien-Gautier, Marie-Lise. "Le Symbolisme religieux dans 'Gouverneurs de la rosée' de Jacques Roumain." *Présence Francophone* 7 (Autumn 1974): 19–23.

Guillén, Nicolás. *Elegia a Jacques Roumain en el cielo de Haiti*. La Habana: Imprenta Ayon, 1948. French trans. "Elégie à Jacques Roumain." *Optique* 18 (1955): 9–13 and *Présence Africaine* 3, lxxxv (1956).

_____. "Prólogo" to *Gobernadores del rocío* (Spanish trans. of *Gouverneurs de la rosée*). La Habana: Imprenta National, [1961]. Reprinted with biographical information added as "Sobre Jacques Roumain." *Prosa de Prisa: Crónicas*. La Habana: Imprenta National (Universidad Central de las Villas, Dirección de Publicaciones), 1962.

Hoffman, Léon-François. "Complexité linguistique et rhetorique dans 'Gouverneurs de la rosée' de Jacques Roumain." *Présence Africaine* 98 (1976): 145–61.

Hughes, Langston. "Free Jacques Roumain: A Letter from Langston Hughes." *Dynamo*, May–June, 1935, p. 1.

"Interview de M. Jacques Roumain." *Le Nouvelliste*, March 18, 1930.

Jones, Graham C. "The Narrative Point of View in Jacques Roumain's *Gouverneurs de la rosée*." *Esprit Créateur* 17:155–22.

L., G. G. "Les Nouvelles Allures de la jeunesse—à batons rompus." *Le Nouvelliste*, November 6, 1930, p. 1.

Lamarre, Joseph M. "Le Militaire dans trois romans haïtiens." *Présence Francophone* 12 (Spring 1976): 131–40. Treats Lherisson's *Zoune chez sa ninaine*, Roumain's *Gouverneurs de la rosée* and J.-S. Alexis' *Les Arbres Musiciens*.

Laraque, Maurice. "En marge des 'Gouverneurs de la rosée'." *Optique* 18 (August 1955): 19–28.

Lespès, Anthony. "Ce qui compte, M. Laraque, c'est l'esprit de sacrifice—*Gouverneurs de la rosée*." *Haïti-Miroir* 1, nos. 12–13 (September 19–25, September 26–October 1, 1955).

———. "Pour defendre Jacques Roumain—Sur la sincerité." *Haïti-Miroir* 1, no. 17 (November 27–December 3, 1955). Reprinted in *La Voie* translated by Jacques Roumain. New York: En Avant!, 1977.

Locke, Alain. "Jacques Roumain." *Opportunity* 12 (May 1935): 134–35.

———. "Jacques Roumain." *New Masses*, May 22, 1945. Different article from preceding.

Magloire, Hébert. *Actualité de Jacques Roumain: Le Christ noir.* St. Léonard, Canada: Textes Francophones, 1975.

Makouta-Mboukou, J. P. "Jacques Roumain, essai sur la signification spirituelle et religieuse de son oeuvre." Thesis, Doctorat d'Etat ès Lettres et Sciences Humaines, Sorbonne, 1975.

———. "La Vision de Dieu chez Jacques Roumain dans *Gouverneurs de la rosée*." Thesis, Licence en Théologie, Faculté de Théologie Protestante, Paris, 1974.

Montas, Lucien. "Anniversaire de la mort de Jacques Roumain." *Optique* 18 (August 1955): 8.

Moraille, Yvon. "Hommage à Jacques Roumain." *Haïti-Journal*, April 12, 1932, p. 1.

Ormerod, Beverly. "Myth, Rite and Symbol in *Gouverneurs de la rosée*." *Esprit Créateur* 17: 123–32.

Paul, Cauvin L. *Manuel . . . ! Un Dieu tombé* (*Essai sur Gouverneurs de la rosée*). Astoria, New York: By the Author, March 3, 1975.

"La Pièce dont on parle—*Gouverneurs de la rosée*." *Le Nouvelliste*, July 20, 1967.

Serrès, Michel. "Christ noir." *Critique* 29 (January 1973): 13–25.

"Le Sort de Jacques Roumain." *Commune*, April 1935, p. 903.

Souffrant, Claude. "Le Fatalisme religieux du paysan haïtien." *L'Europe* 49 (January 1971): 27–42.

———. *Une Négritude Socialist: Religion et développement chez J. Roumain*, J.-S. Alexis, L. Hughes. Paris: Harmattan, 1978.

Trouillot, Hénock. *Dimension et limites de Jacques Roumain*. Port-au-Prince: Editions Fardin, 1975.

Vieux, Antonio. "Entre nous: Jacques Roumain." *La Revue Indigène*, September, 1927, pp. 103–10.

Williams, Eric. "Four Poets of the Greater Antilles." *Caribbean Quarterly* 2, no. 4:8–15. Reprinted in 8, no. 1:4–12.

Unpublished Materials About Jacques Roumain

Cobb, Martha. "The Black Experience: Poetry of Nicolás Guillén, Jacques Roumain, and Langston Hughes." Ph.D. dissertation, Catholic University of America, Washington, D.C., 1974.

Guillén, Nicolás. Letter to Nicole Roumain from Havana, July 10, 1948.

Hughes, Langston. "A Poem for Jacques Roumain." Langston Hughes Papers, James Weldon Johnson Collection, Collection of American Literature, Beinecke Rare Book and Manuscript Library, Yale University.

Office of the Registrar, Columbia University. Letter, February 22, 1972.

White, Florence. " 'Poesía Negra' in Latin America." Ph.D. dissertation, University of Wisconsin, 1951.

Literature, Critical Studies and Histories

Antoine, Jacques. "Les Moins de trente." *La Relève*, 2 (August 1933): 14–21.

Auguste, Y. L. "L'amour dans la littérature haïtienne." *Présence Africaine* 60(1966): 159–71.

Baguidy, Joseph D. *Aperçus sur la pensée haïtienne. Essai*. Port-au-Prince: Imprimerie de l'Etat, 1941.

Bélance, René. "Introduction à la poésie haïtienne." *Conjonction*, 4 (June 1946): 4–7.

Bellegarde, Dantès, ed. *Ecrivains haïtiens; notices biographiques et pages choisies*. Port-au-Prince: Société d'éditions et de librairie, 1947.

Bostick, H. F. "Toward Literary Freedom: A Study of Contemporary Haitian Literature." *Phylon* 17 (1956): 250–56.

Carter, A. *The Idea of Decadence in French literature, 1830–1900*. Toronto: U. of Toronto Press, 1958.

Cook, Mercer. "The Haitian Novel." *The French Review* 19 (May 1946): 406–12.

———. 'La littérature française et les Noirs." *Conjunction* 8 (1950): 74–80.

———. "Trends in Recent Haitian Literature." *The Journal of Negro History*, April 1947, pp. 220–31.

Coulthard, George Robert. *Race and colour in Caribbean literature*. London: Oxford University Press, 1962.

Damas, L. G. "Price Mars, le père du haïtianisme." *Présence Africaine* 32/33 (1960): 166.

Décius, Philippe. "Contes et réalités haïtiennes." *Europe* 501 (January 1971): 49–63.

———. "Pour situer Haïti." *Europe* (*spécial sur Jacques Stéphen Alexis et la littérature d'Haïti*) 501 (January 1971): 3–20.

Denis, Lorimer, François Duvalier and Arthur Bonhomme. *Les Tendances d'une génération*. Port-au-Prince: Imprimerie Haïtienne, n.d. [1934].

Dépestre, René. "Jean Price-Mars et le mythe de l'orphée noir ou les aventures de la négritude." *L'Homme et la Société* 7 (January–March [1969?]): 171–81.

Fardin, Dieudonné. *Cours d'Histoire de la Littérature Haïtienne*, vol. 4 (1915–1946), *Panorama de l'école Indigéniste*, 2nd edition. Port-au-Prince: Collection Régénération du Nord-Ouest d'Haïti, 1967.

Fleischmann, Rose-Marie. "Die haitianische Literatur, Ein Uberblick." *Die Neueren Sprachen* (Frankfurt/Main) 12 (1963): 117–29.

Foisset, J., ed. *Petit recueil de poésies*. Port-au-Prince: Imprimerie Telhomme, 1943.

Fouché, Franck. *Guide pour l'étude de la littérature haïtienne*. Port-au-Prince: Editions Panorama, 1964.

Fox, Ralph. *The Novel and the People*. New York: International Publishers, 1945 (first edition, 1937).

Freeman, Joseph. "Introduction" to *Proletarian Literature in the United States: An Anthology*, ed. by Granville Hicks et al. New York: International Publishers, 1935, pp. 9–28.

Gaillard, Roger. *La destinée de Carl Brouard*. Port-au-Prince: Henri Deschamps, 1966.

―――. "Notre Ami Langston Hughes." *Le Nouvelliste*, July-August 1967.

Garret, Naomi. *The Renaissance of Haitian Poetry*. Paris: Présence Africaine, n.d. [1963].

Gouraige, Ghislain. *La Diaspora d'Haïti et l'Afrique*. Ottawa: Editions Naaman, 1974.

―――. *Histoire de la littérature haïtienne de l'indépendance à nos jours*. Port-au-Prince: N.A. Théodore, 1960.

―――. *Les Meilleurs poètes et romanciers haïtiens: pages choisies*. Port-au-Prince: Imprimerie de la Phalange, 1963.

Hicks, Granville. "The Dialectics of the Development of Marxist Criticism" in *American Writers Conference*, ed. by Henry Hart. New York: International Publishers, 1935, pp. 94–98.

Hoffmann, L.-F. "L'image de la femme dans la poésie haïtienne." *Présence Africaine* 34/35 (1960–61): 183.

Hughes, Langston. "To Negro Writers" in *American Writers Conference*, ed. by Henry Hart. New York: International Publishers, 1935, pp. 139–41.

Jahn, Janheinz. *Neo-African Literature: A History of Black Writing*. Trans. by Oliver Coburn and Ursula Lehrburger. New York: Grove Press, 1969.

Kesteloot, Lilyan. *Les Ecrivains noirs de langue française: Naissance d'une littérature*. Bruxelles: Institut de Sociologie, 1963.

La Selve, Edgar. *Histoire de la littérature haïtienne depuis ses origines jusqu'à nos jours*. Versailles: Imprimerie de Cerf, 1875.

Lhérisson, Lélia Justin. *Manuel de littérature haïtienne et textes expliqués: Littérature des Amériques*. Port-au-Prince: Imprimerie du Collège Vertières, 1945.

Lubin, M. "Contribution d'Haïti à la poésie nègre du monde." *Présence Africaine* 14–15 (June–September 1957): 256–80.

Mariñas, Luis. "Evolución del pensamiento haitiano." *Cuadernos Hispanoamericanos* (Madrid) 182 (February 1965): 325–47.

Morisseau-Leroy. "La littérature haïtienne d'expression créole: son avenir." *Présence Africaine* 17 (December 1956–January 1957): 46–59.

Morpeau, Louis. *Anthologie d'un siècle de poésie haïtienne: 1817–1925, avec une étude sur la muse haïtienne d'expression française et une étude sur la muse haïtienne d'expression créole* . . . Préface de Fortunat Strowski. Paris: Ed. Bossard, 1925.

Paul, Emmanuel Casséus. *Culture, langue, littérature.* Port-au-Prince: Imprimerie de l'Etat, 1954.

Pierre-Louis, Ulysse. *Esquisses littéraires et critiques.* Port-au-Prince: Imprimerie de l'Etat, 1959.

————. "Le roman français contemporain dans une impasse. Perspectives communes du roman d'Haïti des peuples noirs et de l'Amérique latine." *Présence Africaine* 27/28 (August–November 1959): 51–68.

Pompilus, Pradel. "150 ans de littérature haïtienne." *Formes et Couleurs* (no. 1, 12th series) *La Revue International des arts, du gôut et des idées,* [Lausanne?] Tricinquantenaire de l'Indépendance d'Haïti.

————. and les Frères de l'Instruction Chrétienne. *Manuel historique de la littérature haïtienne.* Port-au-Prince: H. Deschamps, 1961.

————. ed. *Pages de la littérature haïtienne.* Port-au-Prince: Imprimerie de l'Etat, 1951.

Price-Mars, Jean. "L'Etat social et la production littéraire en Haïti." *Conjonction* 35 (August 1951): 49–55.

————. "A propos de la Renaissance nègre aux Etats-Unis." *La Relève,* no. 1 (July 1932): 15–19; no. 2 (August 1932): 9–15; no. 3 (September 1932): 8–14.

————. *De Saint-Domingue à Haïti; essai sur la culture, les arts et la littérature.* Paris: Présence Africaine, 1959.

Rose, Max. "La Jeune littérature française d'Amérique: Haïti." *La Relève* 4, no. 8 (February 1936): 3–9.

———. *La littérature haïtienne*. Bruxelles: Ed. Conférences et Théatres, 1938.

Sartre, Jean Paul. Preface to "Orphée Noir." In *Anthologie de la nouvelle poésie nègre et malgache de langue française*, ed. by Léopold Sédar Senghor. Paris: Presses Universitaires de France, 1948 (second edition, 1969).

Seaver, Edwin. "The Proletarian Novel." In *American Writers Conference*, ed. by Henry Hart. New York: International Publishers, 1935, pp. 98–103.

Trouillot, Hénock. *Les Origines sociales de la littérature haïtienne*. Port-au-Prince: N. A. Théodore, 1962.

Vaval, Duraciné. *Histoire de la littérature Haïtienne ou l'Ame Noire*. Port-au-Prince: Imprimerie Héraux, 1933.

Viatte, Auguste. *La Francophonie*. Paris: Larousse, 1969.

———. *Histoire littéraire de l'Amérique française*. Quebec: Presses Université Laval; Paris: Presses Universitaires, n.d. (1956).

SOCIAL SCIENCES, HISTORY, THE ARTS

Aubourg, Michel. *Haïti préhistorique—Mémoire sur les cultures pré-colombiennes Ciboney et Taino*. Bureau d'Ethnologie d'Haïti, 2nd series, no. 8. Port-au-Prince: Imprimerie de l'Etat, 1951. On page 24 of his study, the author reports on Jacques Roumain's field work and projected study of Ciboney material culture.

Bellegarde, Dantès. *Histoire du peuple haïtien: 1492–1952*. Port-au-Prince: Collection du tricinquantenaire de l'indépendance d'Haïti, 1953.

———. *La Nation haïtienne*. Paris: J. de Gigord, 1938.

Davis, Harold P. *Black Democracy: The Story of Haiti*. New York: Lincoln MacVeagh-The Dial Press, 1928.

Desanti, Dominique. *L'Internationale Communiste*. Paris: Payot, 1970.

Gaillard, Roger. *Les Cent-Jours de Rosaluo Bobo ou une mise à mort politique*. Port-au-Prince: Presses Nationales, 1973.

———. "Destin de la presence française en Haïti." *Culture Française* 16, no. 4 (1967): 22–29.

Hall, Robert Anderson. *Haitian Creole: Grammar, Texts, Vocabulary* . . . Philadelphia: American Folklore Society, 1953.

Herskovitz, Melville. *Life in a Haitian Valley.* New York: Octagon Books, 1937, 1964.

Leyburn, James Graham. *The Haitian People.* Rev. ed. New Haven: Yale University Press, 1966.

McCrocklin, James. *La Garde d'Haïti: Twenty years of organization and training by the United States Marine Corps.* Annapolis, Md: U.S. Naval Institute, 1956.

Métraux, Alfred. *Haïti: Black Peasants and Voodoo.* Trans. by Pierre Longyel. New York: Universe Books, 1960.

Millspaugh, Arthur Chester. *Haiti under American Control: 1915–1930.* Boston: World Peace Foundation, 1931.

Price-Mars, Jean. *Ainsi parla l'oncle . . . Essais d'ethnographie.* Port-au-Prince: Imprimerie de Compiègne, 1928. Second edition, Ottawa: Léméac, 1973.

————. "La Position d'Haïti et la culture française en Amérique." *Culture Française* 5, no. 4 (October 1956): 52–64.

Savain, Pétion. "De l'avenir et de l'intégratien de la Peinture Haïtienne dans la Peinture Moderne." *La Voix de la Génération de l'Occupation.* Port-au-Prince: Editions de l'Assaut, no. 2 (March 1936), pp. 45–47.

NEWSPAPERS AND PERIODICALS CONSULTED[1]

L'Action. Journal de la masse, organe de la Ligue de la Jeunesse Patriote Haïtienne, (Port-au-Prince)
  N. BC at SLG: Oct. 1, 3, 8, 13, 17, 22, 26, 1929; Jan. 7, 14, 16, 23, 1930; Feb. 6, 11, 18, 25, 1930; Mar. 1, 4, 6, 22, 1930
  R: Oct. 17, 22, 26, 1929; Mar. 22, 1930

---

[1] Abbreviations used in this section as follows: N—Newspaper; P—Other Periodical; SLG—Bibliotheque de l'Institution Saint Louis de Gonzague (Port-au-Prince); BN—Bibliotheque Nationale (Paris); NYPL—New York Public Library; BC—Broken Collection; R—by or about Roumain.

L'Action Nationale. Organe d'information quotidienne. (Port-au-Prince)
  N. BC at NYPL: Oct. 30, 1931; Nov. 20, 1931; Dec. 15, 28–31,
      1931; Jan. 4, 7, 8, 11, 13, 14, 16–18, 20, 22, 25, 27, 29, 1932;
      Dec. 29–31, 1932; Jan. 5, 6, 10, 12, 16–28, 31, 1933; Feb. 2–24,
      1933; Mar. 3–18, 20–23, 25–31, 1933; Apr. 2, 4–13, 17–29, 1933;
      May 2–13, 16, 17, 19–24, 1933; May 26–June 14, June 16–Aug.
      10, Aug. 29–Sept. 28, Sept. 30–Oct. 31, 1933; Nov. 3–15, 17,
      Dec. 1, Dec. 5–9, 12–14, 16, 19, 20, 23, 26–30, 1934; Jan. 4–10,
      1934; Jan. 12–Feb. 10, 1934; Feb. 14, 15, 17, 19, 21–27, 1934;
      Mar. 1, 3, 5–9, 12–20, 22–28, Mar. 31–Apr. 6, Apr. 9–13,
      16–May 9, 1934; May 11, 12, 19, 30, 1934; June 1–15, 18, 1934
  R.: Dec. 29, 1932; Jan. 5, 6, 1933; Nov. 4, 9, 1933; Mar. 19, 1934

Commune. Revue Littéraire Française pour la Défense de la Culture.
  (Paris)
  P.   April 1935 no. 20; April 1937 no. 44
  R: April 1935

*Communist International: Organ of the Executive Committee of the
Communist International.* (New York, N.Y.)
  P.   vol XI, Jan. 1934–vol. XVII, Dec. 1940

Conjonction. Bulletin de l'Institut Français d'Haïti. (Port-au-Prince.)
  P.   1946–62; 1974–75
  R: May 1975

Le Cri des Nègres (Paris)
  N. BC at BN: Oct. 1931; July–Aug., Sept., Nov.–Dec. 1933; Jan.,
      Apr.–May, July, Aug., Oct., Nov. 1934.
  R: Oct. 1934

*Culture Française. Association International pour la Culture Française à
l'Etranger.* (Paris)
  P.   Vol. I, 1952–vol. XVI, 1967

Daily Worker. (New York, N.Y.)
  N. June 18, 1934–Aug. 27, 1934

Dynamo: A Journal of Revolutionary Poetry. (New York, N.Y.)
  P.   1934–1935
  R: May–June 1935

Haïti-Journal. (Port-au-Prince)
  N. Jan. 27, 1930–Dec. 31, 1930; Jan. 5, 1931–Dec. 3, 1931; Jan. 20,
      1932; Jan. 25, 1932; Feb. 24, 1932; Apr. 12, 1932; Jan. 3,
      1933–Dec. 31, 1934

R: Jan. 25, 30, 1930; Feb. 19–25, 1930; Apr. 3, 4, 1930; May 7, 14, 1930; Sept. 24, 1930; Oct. 4, 7, 9, 11, 1930; Dec. 31, 1930; Jan. 20–24, 1931; Jan. 26–31, 1931; Feb. 2–5, 1931; June 27, 1931; July 4, 1931; July 11, 1931; July 18, 1931; Aug. 8, 1931; Oct. 20, 1931; Jan. 20, 1932; Jan. 25, 1932; Feb. 24, 1932; Apr. 12, 1932; Jan. 3, 1933; Nov. 30, 1933; Sept. 18, 1934; Oct. 16, 17, 1934

Hoy. (Mexico, D.F.)
N.   Nov. 1–Dec. 31, 1942; Aug. 1–31, 1944

New Masses. (New York, N.Y.)
P.   Jan. 1931–Dec. 1941
R: Jan. 7, 1941; May 22, 1945; Sept. 10, 1946

New York Age. (New York, N.Y.)
N.   Dec. 5, 1931–Apr. 5, 1932; Nov. 4, 1939–May 25, 1940
R: Nov. 4, 1939; May 25, 1940

New York Amsterdam News. (New York, N.Y.)
N.   Oct. 7, 1939–Feb. 10, 1940; Dec. 7, 1940–Feb. 1, 1941
R: Nov. 11, 1939; Dec. 7, 1940

Noticias de Hoy. (Havana)
N.   BC at NYPL: May 16–June 8, 1938; Dec. 16, 1941–Feb. 8, 1942

Nouvelle Optique. Recherches haitiennes et caraibéennes (Montreal)
P.   vol. 1, Jan. 1971

Le Nouveau Monde. (Port-au-Prince)
N.   Aug. 24, 1970

Le Nouvelliste. (Port-au-Prince)
N.   Apr. 23, 1929; Mar. 18, 1930; Nov. 6, 1930; Dec. 21, 1931; Dec. 28, 1931; Jan. 3–31, 1933; Nov. 3–30, 1933; Sept. 10–15, 1933; Oct. 1–16, 18–31, 1934; Nov. 3–10, 1934.
R: Mar. 18, 1930; Nov. 6, 1930; Dec. 21, 1931; Dec. 28, 1931; Jan. 3, 6, 1933; Nov. 30, 1933; Oct. 6, 12, 15, 16, 23, 1934

Optique. (Port-au-Prince)
P.   Vol. 18, Aug. 1955
R: Vol. 18, Aug. 1955

Partisan Review. (New York, N.Y.)
P.   Feb. 1934–July 1934; Sept. 1934–Dec. 1934; Jan. 1935–Feb.

1935; Apr. 1935–May 1935; July 1935–Aug. 1935; Oct. 1935–Nov. 1935

Party Organizer. (New York, N.Y.)
P.   BC: vols. V–VI, 1932–3; VIII–X, 1935–37

Le Petit Impartial. Journal de la masse, organe de la Ligue de la Jeunesse Patriote Haïtienne. (Port-au-Prince)
N.   Dec. 5, 1927–Oct. 10, 1931
R: Feb. 22, 25, 1928; Mar. 3, 7, 10, 14, 17, 21, 28, 1928; Apr. 4, 1928; May 16, 19, 1928; June 13, 16, 20, 1928; July 7, 24, 1928; Aug. 18, 1928; Oct. 17, 24, 1928; Nov. 1, 1928; Feb. 5, 14, 1929; Apr. 4, 6 1929; Sept. 8/9, 11, 1930; Feb. 12, 1931; Oct. 10, 1931

Le Peuple. (Paris)
N.   Jan 1, 1939–Jan. 31, 1939

Présence Africaine. (Paris)
P.   1947/48–1970
R: 1947/8, no. 1, (first series); 1955/56 no. 3, (new series)

La Presse. Organe d'information générale. (Port-au-Prince).
N.   (BC at both NYPL and SLG)
Aug. 21, 31, 1929; Sept. 7, 14, 21, 23, 25, 27, 29, 1929; Oct. 15, 16, 18, 19, 21, 22, 24, 30, 31, 1929; Nov. 4–8, 11, 1929; Nov 19–Dec. 4, 1929; Dec. 17–24, 26–31, 1929; Jan. 3–Feb. 7, 1930; Feb. 10, 11, 13, 14, 17–26, 1930; Feb. 28–Mar. 4, 1930; Mar. 6–19, 1930; Mar. 21–Apr. 5, 1930; Apr. 7–16, 19, 22–30, 1930; May 2–14, 16–23, 26–28, 1930; May 30–June 7, 1930; June 10–16, 20–24, 1930; June 26–Aug 14, 1930; Aug. 19–Oct. 13, 1930; Oct. 15–29, 31, 1930; Nov. 3–11, 13–17, 19–26, 1930; Nov. 28–Dec. 5, 1930; Dec. 8, 9, 11, 12, 20, 26, 29, 31, 1930; Jan. 5–14, 16–24, 1931; Jan. 27–Feb. 16, 1931; Feb. 18–Mar. 30, 1931; Apr. 4–13, 15–30, 1931; May 4–13, 1931; May 15–June 3, 1931; June 5–Aug. 14, 1931; Aug. 17–19, 1931; Aug. 22–Sept. 30, 1931; Oct. 2–16, 19–31, 1931; Nov. 3–13, 16–24, 1931
R: Aug. 21, 24, 31, 1929; Sept. 7, 14, 21, 1929; Oct. 21, 22, 1929; Dec. 30, 1929; Feb. 14, 26, 1930; Mar. 13, 21, 1930; May 3, 1930; Jan. 10, 1931

Regards. (Paris)
P.   April 21, 28, 1938; May 19, 1938; June 16, 1938; Aug. 25, 1938
R: April 21, 28, 1938; May 19, 1938; June 16, 1938; Aug. 25, 1938

La Revue Indigène. Les arts et la vie. (Port-au-Prince)
P.   July, Aug., Sept., Oct. 1927. Jan./Feb. 1928; *Anthologie* . . .
     "Indigène", 1928 [No other issues published]
R: in all issues

Le Temps. (Paris)
N.   July 1, 1938–Nov. 11, 1939

La Trouée. Rev. d'Intérêt Générale. (Port-au-Prince)
P.   July (no. 1), Aug. (no. 2), Sept. (no. 3), Oct. (no. 4), Nov.
     (no. 5), Dec. (no. 6), 1927; Mar. 1928 (no. 7)
R: July–Oct. 1927; Mar. 1928

Les Volontaires. (Paris)
P.   Dec. 1938 (no. 1)–June 1939 (no. 7)
R: June 1939

BIBLIOGRAPHIES

Bissainthe, Max. *Dictionnaire de bibliographie haïtienne.* Washington,
D.C.: The Scarecrow Press, 1951.

Duvivier, Ulrich. *Bibliographie générale et méthodique d'Haïti.* 2 vols.
Port-au-Prince: Imprimerie de l'Etat, 1941.

Lucien Jean, Frère. *Catalogue de la Bibliothèque haïtienne des Frères de
l'Instruction Chrétienne.* Port-au-Prince: Institution Saint Louis de
Gonzague, 1958.

Paricsy, Paul. *A New Bibliography of African Literature. Part 1: An
Additional Bibliography to J. Jahn's A Bibliography of Neo-African
Literature from Africa, America and the Caribbean. Part 2: A
Preliminary Bibliography of African Writing (from 1965 to the
Present).* (Studies on Developing Countries 24) Budapest: Center
for Afro-Asian Research, Hungarian Academy of Sciences, [nd].

Index

Abe (In "Le Champ du potier"), 159, 169, 313
Abolition of slavery, 195
Abrahan, the houngan, 215
"Absence" (Roumain), 21n
Action, Journal de la Masse, Organe de la Ligue de la Jeunesse Haïtienne, L', 59, 59n, 60, 60n, 61, 61n
Action Nationale, L', 141n, 144, 144n, 145, 145n, 146, 147, 148, 164, 309, 310
Administration Public, L', 90
Advent, 243
Africa, 126–127, 135, 197, 202, 207, 327–328
African beliefs, 46
African heritage, 128, 133, 169, 197
Africanism, 52, 106, 126, 133, 197, 214
Afro-American Poems (Roumain), 308
"Agissons!" *See* "Idées et Opinions— Agissons!"
Agni, 35
Agricultural School at Damiens, 61
Agronomy, 6
Ahimsa, 49. *See also* Nonviolence
Ainsi parla l'oncle (Price-Mars), 19, 125–126, 133
  excerpts, 126
  translations, 303
Alabama, 205, 329
Alcibiades (In "Mon Ami Alcibiades"), 76–77
Alcohol problem, 226n
Alexandrine meter, 39
Alexis, Jacques Stéphen, 223
Alienation, 82, 165
Altruism, 48
Amarou, 35
Amberger de Osa, Roni, 58
Ame haïtienne. *See* Haitian soul

American chargé d'affaires, 9
American authorities, surveillance by, 143
American business concerns, 183, 186
American Communist Party, 142, 145, 167
  secretary of, 145
American culture, 43
American High Commissioner, 10–12, 133
American intervention, 8
American Occupation, xi, 6–14, 14n, 15–16, 43, 49, 51–52, 54, 60–61, 63, 73, 91, 95, 139, 150, 186, 190, 247, 294
American public, 63
American Writers Conference (Hart), 167
"Amour la mort, L' " (Roumain), 195–196, 226–228
  text, 227
  translation, 336
Analyse schematique, L', (Comité Central du Parti Communiste Haïtien), 149–152, 155, 155n, 165, 195
  excerpts, 150–152
  translation, 311
Anarchy, 93, 144, 145n
Anathèmes (Burr-Reynaud), 14n, 258
Ancestors
  souls of, 46, 134
Anglo-Saxon America, x
Anglo-Saxon culture, 126
"Angoisse" (Roumain), 21n, 27
  excerpt, 27
  translation, 263
Anguish, 21
Animistic images, 24, 130, 134, 179
Anna (In "Gouverneurs de la rosée"), 138, 243–244, 339

365

Anna (In *La Montagne ensorcelée*), 120–121, 130

Annaïse, (In *Gouverneurs de la rosée*), 229–234, 236–238, 240–241, 245–246, 249, 340

Anthologie de le nouvelle poésie nègre et malgache de langue française, (Senghor), 179n, 197n

Anthologie de la poésie haïtienne "indigène", 21–22, 26–29, 58, 263–265

Anthology of Contemporary Latin American Poetry (Fitts), 132n

Anthropology, 187, 209, 213–214, 216–217

Anti-Americanism, 13

Anti-Christ, 52

Anticlerical tirades, 53

Antifascism, 177–178, 187n, 205, 223

Anti-intellectualism, 4

Antilles, 327

Antilles décolonisées, Les (Guérin, Daniel), 56n

Antoine, Jacques C., xii, 42, 42n, 104n, 251n, 252

"Appel" (Roumain), 21n, 32, 35–36, 38, 44, 53, 80, 197
  excerpts, 35–38, 53
  translations, 268–269

"Appel à la Jeunesse" (Sam), 61

Apollinaire, Guillaume, 40, 40n

"Apres-Midi" (Roumain), 21n, 24, 24n, 28–29, 134
  excerpts, 24, 28–29
  translation, 263

Arada cult, 215, 215n

Aragon, Louis, 178

Arawak culture, 215, 253

Archeology, 176
  pre-Columbian, 3, 176, 216

Arendt, Erich, 132n

Aristide (In "Gouverneurs de la rosée"), 192, 323

Aristocracy, 1, 42, 94, 100

Armillita l'Azteque, 33, 33n, 34, 228, 266

Armillita, the Aztec. *See* Armillita l'Azteque

Arms, motif of, 30–31, 36, 79, 125

Art, 110, 125, 168, 254
  decadent, 168

"Aspect du problème haïtien, Un". *See* "Idées et Opinions—Un aspect du probleme haïtien"

Assemblée des Délégués des Arrondissements de la République, 62

Assotor, 215

Atlantic Ocean, 34

Atlas, 179

"Attente" (Roumain), 21n, 28–29, 78–79
  excerpts, 28–29, 78–79
  translation, 263–264, 284

Aube (Medieval lyric genre), 39

"Aube, L' " (Roumain), 21n, 39, 58
  excerpt, 39
  translation, 270

Auguste, Tancrède, 1, 56

Aurel (In *La Montagne ensorcelée*), 110–114, 122, 245, 298

Austria, 207

Autobiographical elements in Roumain's writings, 86–90, 103–104, 164–166, 290

"Avenir et de l'intégration de la Peinture Haïtienne dans la Peinture Moderne, De l' " (Savain), 7n
  excerpt, 7n
  translation, 257

Axis, the, 224

Aztec culture, 3, 94, 103, 176

Bakas, 120

"Bal au Club Sélect, Le," (Chapter in *Les Fantoches* (Roimain)), 91

"Ballade des deux ancêtres," 222

Balletroy (In *La Montagne ensorcelée*), 109–112, 114–115, 122–125, 302–303

Ballin, Mme (In "Préface à la vie d'un bureaucrate"), 75–76, 89, 106, 165, 297

Basquet, Marcel (In *Les Fantoches*), 91–96, 98–104, 106–107, 133, 170–171, 290–292 , 297

Battraville, Benoît, 46

Baudelaire, Charles, 22, 38, 41, 85–86, 270, 288

Bay of Port-au-Prince, 214

Beaulieu, Christian, 142, 142n, 143

Bel-Aire, 143

Belgian Communist Party, 176

Belgium, 157, 175–177, 185, 195n, 210, 229. *See also* Brussels

Bellegarde, Dantès, 8n, 180n

Bergman, 221, 334

Berne (Switzerland), 3

Berne, Wiener, et Cie, 148, 309

Bestiares, Les (Montherlant), 6, 6n, 256

Bewitched Mountain, The (Roumain),
    304. *See also La Montagne ensorcelée*
Bhagavad-Gîtâ, 65
Bible, the, 169n
Bienaimé (In *Gouverneurs de la rosée*),
    230–233, 246, 342
Black American entertainers, 186
Black and white, motif of, 38, 53
Black consciousness, 132–134, 136–137,
    140. *See also* Race consciousness;
    Negritude
Black Democracy: The Story of Haiti
    (Davis), 8n
Black intellectuals, 152
Black Republic, 17
Black writers, 141–142
Blasphemy, 125
Blood, symbolism of, 37
Bobo, Rosalvo, 8, 8n, 9–10
"Bois d'ébène" (Roumain), 31, 155,
    195–198, 202, 208, 225, 226n, 237
    excerpts, 202–203
    translation, 328–329
"Bois d'ébène" (Roumain), 31, 195, 226
Bois Verna, 1–2, 8, 106n
Bombs, 153
Bonhomme, Arthur, 126n
Bontemps, Arna, 132n
Borno, Louis, 11–12, 51, 55, 55n, 63, 276
Borno government, 42–43, 51, 55, 61
Bourgeoisie, 42, 141, 293
Bourgeois literature, 168
Bourgeois nonauthenticity, 73–108
Bourgeois world view, 149, 158, 168
Bovaryisme, 128
Boycotts, 43
Blot, Probus, 9
Bradley, Francine, 155, 156n
Bramins, 50
Braun, Franck, 21
Breton ancestry of Roumain, 133
Brierre, Jean, 61n, 143, 143n, 149,
    251–252, 308
Britain, 64
British. *See* English government
Brother Ti Dor. *See* Frè Ti Dor
Brouard, Carl, 18, 42, 47, 55n, 57, 57n,
    59, 87, 87n, 89, 147, 177, 277, 289
Brussels, 176, 176n, 177, 185, 195
Brutus, Edner, 88, 88n, 131, 253, 253n,
    289, 304
Buddhists, 50, 274
Bull, image of, 33
"Bulletin de la Ligue de la Jeunesse," 61
Bulletin du Bureau d'Ethnologie, 213n,
    214, 214n, 215, 216n

Bullfights, 6, 33
Bureau d'Ethnologie, 213–214, 214n, 216
Burr-Reynaud, Frederic, 14n, 258
Buvard, Le (Roumain), 21, 21n, 41
Byron, Lord, 5, 256

Cacos, 8–10, 15, 43, 186, 192, 247
"Calme" (Roumain), 21, 21n, 26, 40,
    78–79, 81
    excerpts, 26, 79
    translation, 262
Camille, Roussan, ix–x, 253
Campagne anti-superstitieuse, 216
Canard Enchainé, Le, 184n
Cannibalism, 94
Caperton, Admiral, 9–10
Cap-Haitien, 8–9, 68, 181
Capitale de la Douleur (Eluard), 40n
Capitalism, 144, 168–169, 199, 235
Carl Brouard. See Destinée de Carl
    Brouard, La
Carrefour, 154, 312
Carrère, Benoît (In "Fragment d'une
    confession"), 75, 79, 81, 84
Carter, A.E., 85n, 101n
Casas, Bartolomeo de las. *See* Las Casas,
    Bratolomeo de
Caste, 45
Catalogue de la Bibliothèque haitïenne des
    frères de l'instruction chrétienne
    (Lucien), 59
Catholic Church, 51–52, 120n, 199, 275
Catholicism, 52, 140, 218, 307, 332
Cauvin, Victor, 60–61, 61n
Celestial imagery, 31
Cent-Jours de Rosalvo Bobo, Les
    (Gaillard), 8n
"Cent mètres" (Roumain), 21n, 34–36,
    38, 40, 66, 80, 172
    text, 34–35
    translation, 267
Centre, Le, 144, 150
Cercle Militaire, 216
Ce Soir, 184n
Champ de Mars square, 160
"Champ du potier, Le" (Roumain), 66,
    156–173, 186, 189, 204, 207, 231,
    232, 235, 245–246
    excerpts, 158–163
    translation, 312–313
"Chant de l'homme, Le" (Roumain), 21,
    21n, 32, 36, 86
    excerpt, 86
    text, 31–32, 86
    translation, 265–266

Chant Nouveau, Un (Piquion), 198n
Characterization, 99–100, 111, 113, 172
Charlier, Etienne, 14
Charmantine (In *Les Fantoches*), 97–99, 102, 104, 107, 138, 295
Chatelain, Yves, 60
Chef de division. See Roumain, Jacques: as *chef de division*
Chemin des Dalles, 106, 106n, 296
Chicago, 159
Children, 44, 98, 119, 123
Chirico, Giorgio di, 40n
Choute (In *La Montagne ensorcelée*) 122, 128, 302
Christ, 35, 95, 199, 292
Christianity, 103, 217–218, 247, 293
Christian priests, 247
Christians, 50, 52
Christmas, 218
Christophe, Henri, 66, 66n, 67–68, 93, 100, 104, 279–280, 291–292
"Chronique-Programme" (Sylvain), 17n, 18n
   excerpts, 18–19
   translation, 259–260
Churchill, Winston, 209
Ciboney culture, 215, 253
Cinéas, Jean-Baptiste, 126
Clandestine activity, 145
Class, 45, 89, 150, 160, 167–168
Class consciousness, 151, 169
Class struggle, 150–152, 167–169, 209, 248
Clothes, 42
Codada (Haitian priest), 55, 276
Coffins, 245
Coicou, Massillon, 44
Collaborationists, 54–55
Colline (Giono), 129–130, 166
Colonialism, 207
Color, 150, 193
Columbia University, 209–210, 210n
Comité Central du Parti Communiste Haïtien, 149, 317
Comité de Grève, 61
Comité Fédératif des Associations Partriotiques, 61
Comité Revolutionnaire, 9
Commission d'Enquète, La, 63
Committee for the Release of Jacques Roumain, 155, 175
Committee to Free Jacques Roumain, 156n
Communal elections, 61
Commune (Paris), 156n, 178

Communism in Haiti, 140–141, 141n, 142–145, 145n, 147–157, 159–160, 166, 175–176, 181, 237, 310–316. *See also* Dialectical materialism
Communist party of Haiti. *See* Parti Communiste Haïtien
Communist party of the United States. *See* American Communist Party
Concordat (with the Holy See), 51, 217, 275, 331
Congo, 136, 201, 306, 237
Congrès des écrivains pour la défense de la culture, 178
Conscience Raciale (Roumain), 103
Conseil d'Etat, 11, 63
Constitution (Haitian), 11
Continent, 181
Contribution a l'étude de l'ethnobotanique pré-columbienne des Grandes Antilles (Roumain), 214–215
Cook, Mercer, 42n, 84, 84n, 85n, 223n, 244n
"Correspondance" (Evans), 60
   excerpt, 60
"Corrida" (Roumain), 6, 21n, 22, 30, 33–34, 36, 103, 228
   excerpts, 30, 33–34
   translation, 265, 266
Corvée, 10, 150, 281
Cosmic despair, 28
Cosmic detachment, 32
Cosmic hero, 77
Cosmic imagery, 28, 116, 190
Cosmic nature, 26
Cosmic quest, 29
Cosmic setting, 26, 29, 31
Cosquer (In *Les Fantoches*), 91, 107, 297
Coulthard, George Robert, 196, 196n
Coumbite, 230, 233, 248, 339
Counter-revolution, 168n, 209
Countryside, 68, 102, 111, 123, 134, 138, 157, 161, 171, 181
Courage, 37, 64, 75, 98
Cour d'Appel, La. *See* Court of Appeals
Courrier Haïtien, 7
Court of Appeals, 185, 185n
"Création d'un Bureau d'Ethnologie avec Jacques Roumain comme Directeur," 214n
   excerpt, 214
   translation, 330–331
Creole (language), 20, 47, 82, 97, 105, 117, 120, 122, 187, 215, 244
"Créole" (Roumain), 132, 137–138
   excerpt, 137
   translation, 307

Crête-à-Pierrot, 45, 271
Cri des nègres, Le (Paris), 153n, 156
Croix-des-Bouquets, 241, 341
Croix Rouge Sovietique, 224
Crowds, 104, 111
Cruelty, 66–68, 93, 279
Cuba, 183, 205, 210–211, 215, 229, 235, 248. See also Havana
Cullen, Countee, 19
Culture, disintegration of, 136
Cunard, Nancy, 178
Customs revenue, 10
Cynicism, 100
Czekoslovakia, 207

Dagobert, Mme (In Mimola), 127
Dahomey, 216, 331
Dajabon, 181, 319
Dajon-Montéchristi, 182
Dakar, 137, 306
Daladier, Edouard, 207
Damas, Léon, xii
Damballah, 109, 109n, 112, 122, 130
Damiens, 60
Damned of the earth, 237
Dance, 35
Daniel (In Les Fantoches), 102, 105, 170
Daniel (In "Propos Sans Suite"), 73–74, 82–83, 85, 133, 282–283, 286–287
Dan-Maoua (In Mimola), 128, 304
"Danse du poète-clown, La" (Roumain), 21n, 32, 35–36, 38
    translation, 268
Dark. See Light and dark
Dartiguenave, Sudre, 10–11
Darwin, Charles, 3, 255
Davis, Harold, 8n
Death, 66
Decadents, 85, 85n, 86
    French, 85, 101
Décadent, Le, 101, 101n
Déclaration des Droits de l'Homme et du Citoyen, 67
    translation, 280
Declaration of Independence (Tonnerre), 44
"Défense de Paul Morand" (Roumain), 53–54
    excerpts, 53–54
    translation, 275
Dehumanization, 136
Délivrance, Délira (In Gouverneurs de la rosée), 230–233, 235, 237–240, 242–243, 337, 340
Democratic principles, 223

Denis, Lorimer, 126n
Département de l'Intérieur, 62, 62n, 76, 90, 144, 154, 155n
Department of Agriculture, 295
Department of the Interior. See Département de l'Interieur
Dervish, whirling, 35
Descartes, Rene, 162, 316
Desdemona (In "Langston Hughes"), 136, 306
Désilus (In La Montagne ensorcelée), 111–112, 114–121, 123, 129–138, 300–301
Despair, 29, 77, 102, 110, 187
Destinée de Carl Brouard, La, (Gaillard), 55, 55n, 57, 57n, 147
    excerpts, 55, 57
Detroit, 159
Devil, the, 124
Deville, Bruno (In "Le Champ du potier"), 158–159, 166, 169, 171
Deville, Julien (In "Le Champ du potier"), 159
Deville, Lucien (In "Le Champ du potier"), 171
Deville, Mme (In "Le Champ du potier"), 158, 164–165
Deville, Pauline (In "Le Champ du potier"), 157–161, 165–166, 170, 313
Dewey Square Hotel (New York), 141n
Dialectic, 197–198
Dialectical materialism, x, 103, 139–156, 167, 178, 208. See also Communism in Haiti; Marxist philosophy
Dialogue form, 39, 80
Dialogues de mes lampes (Saint-Aude), 222, 222n, 335
Diaquoi, Louis, 57
Diaspora of the black race, 136
Dictatorship, 93
Dignity, 178
Dimension et Limites de Jacques Roumain (Trouillot), 155n
"Dinner Reception to be Given Haitain by Writers and Artists," 206n
"Dirty Niggers" (Roumain), 325
"Discretion" (Laleau), 19
Dix Années de Lutte pour la Liberté: 1915–1925 (Sylvain), 8n
    excerpt, 7–8
Dominican government, 180, 182
Dominican Republic, 145, 166, 180, 180n, 181, 183–184, 217, 319
    president of, 184
Dorilas (In La Montagne ensorcelée), 109, 113, 122, 299

Doris, Jean (In "Le Champ du potier"),
    189, 235, 24., 314
Dorisca (In *Gouverneurs de la rosée*), 343
Dormeus (In *Gouverneurs de la rosée*),
    235
Dorneval (In *La Montagne ensorcelée*),
    109–112, 115, 117, 119–121, 123, 245,
    302
Drame de la terre, La (Cineas), 126
Drums, 135, 215. *See also* Tom-toms
Duplessy, Jean-Gille (In "Gouverneurs
    de la rosée"), 186–192, 243, 248,
    320, 323
Durand, Oswald, 17n, 102, 259
Dust, motif of, 234
Duvalier, François, 126n, 131n, 304
*Dynamo: A Journal of Revolutionary
    Poetry*, 155, 156n, 157n

Easter, 124
Eastern point of view, 48, 86
Eastern setting, 35
"Echappée" (Roumain), 21n, 24, 24n
    excerpts, 24, 30–31
    translation, 261, 265
Ecole Polytechnique, 5
Economics, 150
"Ecroulement du mythe nationaliste"
    (Comité Central du Parti
    Communiste Haïtien), 150–151
    excerpts, 150–151
"Elegia a Jacques Romain," 252
"Eloge à la 'Cruauté' de Christophe."
    See "Idées et Opinions—Eloge à la
    'Cruauté' de Christophe"
Eluard, Paul, 22, 40, 40n
Emilio (In "Propos Sans Suite"), 74, 77,
    84, 89, 105, 133, 203, 287
Emotion artistique, 41
Engels, Friedrich, 139, 159, 221, 314,
    331, 334
Engineering, 257
English government, 49–50, 274
English (language), 142
Enrique (In "Le Champ du potier"),
    160, 314
"Entre Nous: Jacques Roumain"
    (Vieux), 2n, 21, 253n
    excerpts, 2, 5–6, 38–39, 41–42
    translation, 256, 258, 269–270
Epaves, Les (Baudelaire), 41
Epic literature, 33–34, 44, 78, 168–169
Estienne, Irène (In *Les Fantoches*), 91,
    94, 96, 98–99, 101, 107, 165, 292

Estinval (In *Gouverneurs de la rosée*),
    241, 341
Etats-Unis. *See* United States of
    America
Ethnography, 126, 176
Ethnology, 213–223, 253
Europe, x, 7n, 8, 83, 175, 197, 204, 206,
    210–211, 213, 329
Europe, L', 235n
European literature, 5, 15, 20, 22
European tradition, 135, 197
Evans, F. E., 60
Exceptional man, the, 48
"Exiled Haitian poet at Guild Club
    December 13, 1940," 208n
Exoticism, 128, 187n
Eyeglass lenses, 42

Faculté d'Ethnologie, 216
"Faded Violets" (Roumain), 256. *See
    also* "Violettes fanées"
Fantoches. *See* Puppets
Fantoches, Les (Roumain), 68, 71, 73, 84,
    91–108, 116, 118, 128, 135, 140, 157,
    165–166, 171, 189, 204, 245, 247
    excerpts, 84–85, 92–95, 105, 107, 135
    translation, 209–297, 305
Fascism, 168n, 177–178, 183, 206
    Italian, 16
"Fatalisme religieux du paysan haïtien,
    Le" (Souffrant), 235n
Fate, 32
Fattu, Mlle (In *Les Fantoches*), 91,
    106–107, 165
Fauset, Jessie, 206
Fédération des Jeunesses Haïtiennes, 61
"Femmes Damnées" (Baudelaire), 86
    excerpt, 86
    translation, 288
Fetishism, 217
Feudalism, 168
Feuerbach, Ludwig, 220–221, 334
Fin-de-siècle, 85
Fire, symbolism of, 35–37
First Consul (Primier Consul), 45
Fitts, Dudley, 132, 132n
Fleurs du Mal (Baudelaire), 86
    excerpt, 86
    translation, 288
Fleury-Battier, Alcibiades, 44
Foisset, Père, 219–220, 332–334
Folklore, 125–127, 132, 140, 260
Fonds Rouge (In *Gouverneurs de la
    rosée*), 229–230, 233–234, 238
Fontaine, La, 47

Forbes Commission, 11–12, 61
Form, 23, 38–39
Fouché, Franck, 14n, 15n, 20
Fox, Ralph, 168n
"Fragment d'une confession"
    (Roumain), 75–78, 80–81
    excerpts, 75–79
    translation, 283–285, 288
France, 19, 94, 126, 136, 177, 205–206,
    210, 218, 292
Franco, 198, 209, 325
Freedom
    poetry of, 31
    of the press, 184
"Free Jacques Roumain: A letter from
    Langston Hughes" (Hughes), 156n,
    157
Freeman, Joseph, 168n
Free verse, 20
French clergy, 51, 53–54, 216–217
French culture, 5, 43–44, 126, 140
French government, 183
French (language), 122, 140, 141n, 186n,
    215, 223, 244
French legation, 9
French peasants, 130, 217
French press, 183
French race, 193
French Review, The, 244n
Frères de l'Instruction Chrétienne, 2
Frè Ti Dor, 128, 304
Fruit, 69, 84, 102, 104, 115, 281
"The Frustrated Poetry Renaissance,"
    208
Fun, 42

Gaillard, Roger, 8n, 55, 55n, 57, 57n,
    61n, 81, 89–90, 129, 147, 157, 177n,
    198, 242, 245, 276–277, 290, 325
Gandhi, Mahatma, 48–50, 50n, 63–64,
    64n, 65, 67–68, 273–274, 278
García Barcena, Rafael, 20
García Lorca, Federico, 179, 209
Garde d'Haïti, 10, 60, 154, 248. See also
    Gendarmerie d'Haïti
Garde D'Haïti, La (McCorcklin), 8n
Garoute, Louis, 7n
Garret, Naomi, 21n, 132n, 251n
Gauguin, Eugène Henri Paul, 69, 281
Gendarmerie d'Haïti, 10, 13. See also
    Garde d'Haïti
General Receiver, 10
Georges, Mme (In Mimola), 127–128, 304
Gérant-responsable, 44, 44n, 54, 59
German culture, 5

German (language), 5, 132n
German race, 193
Germany, 8, 184, 206
Gervilen (In Gouverneurs de la rosée),
    230, 239, 249
Gide, André, 178
Giono, Jean, 129–130, 166
"Giorgio de Chirico" (Eluard), 40n
Gloomy days and monotonous seas, 91
Gobineau, Joseph Arthur, 95
God, 122, 124, 220, 238
    will of, 49n
Gonave, La, 214
Gouraige, Ghislain, 17n, 127n, 198, 325
Gourde (Haitian monetary unit), 57, 57n
"Gouvernement de Sténio Vincent sous
    les mots d'ordre de 'Liberté et
    Nationalisme', Le" (Zamor), 153n
"Gouverneurs de la rosée" (Roumaine),
    69–70, 185, 185n, 186–187, 191, 244,
    246–247
    excerpts, 69–70, 187–192
    translation, 320–323
Gouverneurs de la rosée (Roumain), 56,
    69, 120, 157, 170, 176, 176n, 185,
    192, 227, 229–249, 253–254
    excerpts, 232–244
    translations, 339–343
Governing classes, 15
Grâce (In "Créole"), 137
Grâce (In La Montagne ensorcelée),
    109–116, 119, 122, 245, 298–299
Graduate School of Arts and Sciences at
    Columbia University, 209
Grandeur, 67–68
Greenwich Village, 168n
Greffe Correctionelle, XIIe Chambre, 184n,
    185n
Greffe de la Cour d'Appel, 185n
"Griefs de l'homme noir" (Roumain),
    193–195
    excerpts, 193–195
    translation, 323–324
Griots, Les, 214
Group I interviews, xi, 2n, 3–5, 6n, 16,
    18, 22, 42–43, 57–58, 62, 87, 129,
    133n, 140, 142, 145, 147, 147n,
    150–151, 157, 164, 167, 176n, 177n,
    178, 185, 195n, 196, 205–206,
    210–211, 223–226
    definition of, xi, 2n
    excerpts, 2–3, 87
    translations, 255
Group II interviews, xi, xin, 2n, 57,
    127n, 198, 213
    definition of, xi, 2n

Group II interviews (cont.)
  excerpt, 198
  translations, 325
Grünau. *See* Institut Grünau
Guérin, Daniel, 56n
Guérin, Elie, 54–56, 276–277
*Guide pour l'étude de la littérature
  haïtienne* (Fouché), 14n
  excerpt, 14–15
Guillén, Nicolás, 141n, 211, 211n,
  222–223, 252, 343
Guinea, 116, 132, 132n, 135–136, 202,
  235, 305–306, 328
"Guinea" (Roumain), 132n
"Guinée" (Roumain), 131–132, 132n,
  134–136, 251
  text, 135–316
  translation, 305
Guyenne, 218

Hafiz, Shamsuddin Mohammed, 3–4, 58
Haiti
  army of, 10, 45n
  art of, 7, 125
  communism in. *See* Communism in
    Haiti
  flag of, 43
  government of, 143
  House of Deputies of, 12n
  independance of, 10
  king of, 67
  legislature of, 10–12
  life-styles in, 14, 84, 106, 122, 125
  literary history of, 13, 127
  literature of, 14, 17, 20, 42, 44
  modes of being in, 14, 101
  monetary unit of, 57n
  poetry of, 20
  police of, 10
  president of, 10–12, 153–154, 302
  provisional president of, 12
  Senate of, 12n
  War of Independence of, 17, 17n
  youth of, 46–48, 54, 61, 87
Haitian American Sugar Company
  (HASCO), 146, 309
Haitian autonomy, 51
Haitian bourgeoisie, 142, 150
Haitian clergy, 51–53
Haitian climate, 24–25
Haitian heart, 44
Haitian independence, 93
Haitian intelligensia, 139
Haitianism, 126

Haïti-Journal, 22n, 63, 63n, 64, 64n, 65n,
  66, 66n, 68n, 70, 71n, 73, 93,
  131–132, 134–137, 141n, 145, 145n,
  146, 146n, 147n, 152n, 153, 154, 177,
  311–312
Haitian landscape, 51
Haitian legation in Paris, 144
Haitian masses, 133, 139, 150, 180
Haitian minister in Paris, 145
Haitian Nationalism, 6–7, 13, 36, 43–71,
  126, 133, 139, 143–144, 147, 150,
  176, 186, 197, 253, 311
"Haitian Novel, The" (Cook), 244n
"Haitian Scribe to be Honored—Jacques
  Roumain Guest at Big Banquet,"
  206n
Haitian self-image, 51
Haitian soul (*l'âme haïtienne*), 17, 20–21,
  126
Haitian spirit, 24–25
Haiti Under American Control, 1915–1930
  (Millspaugh), 8n
Hands, motif of, 29–30, 79, 124
"Happy New Year" (Hughes), 176n
Harlem, 137, 306
Harlem YWCA, 206
Hart, Henry, 167
HASCO. *See* Haitian American Sugar
  Company
Hate, 190
Havana, 210n, 211, 224, 251n, 330, 343
Hegel, Georg Wilhelm Friedrich, 197,
  220, 325
Heine, Heinrich, 3–5, 255
Helvé (In *La Montagne ensorcelée*), 121
Heraclitus, 219–220, 333
Herndon, Angelo, 195, 324
Hero, first true, 189
Hero, the
  concept of, 31–33, 48–49, 65, 68, 70,
    77–78, 80, 99, 114, 139, 165, 170,
    173, 189, 190
  cosmic, 77
  lonely and sensitive, 32, 77–78, 81, 99
  lost in space and in darkness, 31, 77,
    79
  romantic, 77
  as savior-martyr, 35–36, 230–249
  as sportsman, 34
  and victory, 33–34, 77
Heroes
  bourgeois, 82
  dead, 44, 46
  folk, 122
  national, 43
  proletarian, 169–170

"Héros Caché, Le" (Barun), 21
Heurtelou, Daniel, 15, 18
Hibbert, Fernand, 14, 62
Hibbert, Lucien, 177n, 317
Hibbert, Nicole, 62. *See also* Roumain, Nicole
Hicks, Granville, 167, 168n
High Commissioner. *See* American High Commissioner
Hindus, 48, 50
Hippolyte, Dominique, 19
Hirarion (In *Gouverneurs de la rosée*), 230, 235, 249
Hispaniola, 180n, 182
Histoire de la Littérature Haïtienne (Gouraige), 17n, 198
  excerpt, 198
  translation, 325
Histoire du Peuple Haitien (1492–1952) (Bellegarde), 8n, 180n
History, 103, 160, 169
Hitler, Adolph, 16n, 177, 182, 205, 207, 209
Holy Communion, 94, 124
Holy Land, 45
Holy See in Rome, 51
Homeland, defense of, 47
"Homme Contre un Empire—Mahatma Gandhi, Un" (Roumain), 48
  excerpt, 49–50
  translation, 273
Homme de couleur, L', 193, 193n
Homo Pekinensis. *See* Peking man
Hopelessness, 102
"Horizon . . . soleil" (Roumain), 21n, 27, 29, 39–40, 58
  excerpts, 27, 29
  translation, 262–264
Houngan, 215, 235
Howard University, xii
Hoy. See Noticias de Hoy
Hudicourt, Max, 14–15, 144, 144n, 147, 150, 153n, 156
Hughes, Langston, 85n, 131–132, 132n, 134, 136–138, 141, 155–156, 156n, 157n, 176n, 177n, 186n, 197–198, 206, 223n, 252, 252n, 308
Huitzilopochtli, 34, 95, 103, 266, 293
Humanité, L', 184n
Human nature, 247

Ibrahim (a pseudonym for Jacques Roumain), 58. *See also* "Mon Carnet" [Roumain]
Idealism, 47, 159, 171, 209

Idea of Decadence in French Literature: 1830–1900, The (Carter), 85n, 101n
"Idées et Opinions—Agissons!" (Roumain), 63, 63n
  excerpt, 63
  translation, 278
"Idées et Opinions—Eloge à la 'Cruauté' de Christophe" (Roumain), 66n, 68, 93
  excerpts, 66–68
  translation, 279–280
"Idées et Opinions—Mahatma Gandhi" (Roumain), 64n, 67
  excerpts, 64–65
  translation, 278
"Idées et Opinions—Un aspect du probleme haïtien" (Price-Mars), 64n
Ideology, 169, 221
Image-reversal, 134, 179
Imagery, 22–25, 31, 38, 81, 84, 115, 133–137
  dream, 173
Images
  of ennui, 28
  of impatience, 28
  of still, suspended time, 28–29
India, 48–50, 50n, 65, 203, 207, 329
Indian Nationalism, 48–50
Indigenism, 17, 17n, 20–21, 24, 109, 127n, 132, 134, 137, 259, 303
Indigenous Haitians, 102
Indios Steigen von Mixco Nieder: Sudamerikanische Freiheitsdichtungen, Die (Arendt), 132n
Indo-China, 207
Infinity, 25, 27–31
Innocent, Antoine, 122, 127–128, 128n, 303–304
"Insomnie" (Roumain), 21, 21n, 26, 29–30, 40, 79
  excerpt, 26, 29–30
  translation, 262, 264
Intellectuals, 77, 82, 101, 168, 168n, 170, 189
  leftist, 177
"Interview de M. Jacques Roumain," 61, 62n
"Introduction" (Cook and Hughes), 85n, 223n
"Introduction" (Freeman), 168n
"Introduction" (Roumain), 148–149, 152
  excerpt, 148–149
Introduction to Haiti (Cook), 42n
Institut de Paléontologie Humaine, 176
Institut d'Ethnologie, 176, 214, 216, 216n

Institut Grünau (Berne), 3n, 4, 4n, 5, 48, 255–256
Institution Saint Louis de Gonzague, xii, 2
Intuition, 25
Irony, 104
Irrationality, 99
"Is Poetry Dead?" (Roumain), 208, 208n, 209, 222
  excerpts, 208–209
Italy, 206
I Wonder as I Wander (Hughes), 176n, 177n

"Jacques Roumain" (Brutus), 88, 88n, 131, 253
  excerpts, 88, 131
  translation, 304–305
"Jacques Roumain interviewe a La Havane," 224n
  excerpts, 224
  translation, 335–336
"Jacques Roumain vivant" (Alexis), 223n
Jahn, Janheinz, 132, 132n
Jannet, (In *Colline*), 129–130
Jaume (In *Colline*), 129–130
Jean, Doris (In "Le Champ du potier"), 157, 159–160, 164, 166, 169–173
Jean (In "Propos Sans Suite"), 73–74, 286
Jean, Tonton (In *La Montagne ensorcelée*), 117, 300
"Je ne sais pas pourquoi tu penses" (Guillén), 222
"Je rêve que je rêve" (Roumain), 21n, 40, 58
Jesus, 199. *See also* Christ
"Jeune Haïti" (Roumain), 47
  excerpt, 47
  translation, 272, 273
"Jeune Littérature Haïtienne, La" (Sylvain), 20, 20n
  excerpt, 20
  translation, 260
"Jeunesse, A la" (Petit and Roumain), 47–48
  excerpt, 47–48
  translation, 273
Jews, 50, 169, 182, 184, 207, 274
John (In "Nouveau sermon nègre)", 200, 326
Jolibois Fils, Joseph 7, 45
Jordan River, 199, 326

Josaphat (In *Gouverneurs de la rosée*), 234, 316
Josaphat (In "Le Champ du potier"), 158, 161–162, 172
Joseph, Manuel Jean (In *Gouverneurs de la rosée*), 227, 229–242, 245–246, 248–249, 254, 337, 339–343
"Jouer aux billes, A" (Roumain), 21n, 25–26, 38
  excerpt, 25–26
  translation, 262
Judas Iscariot, 169n
"Jugement de MM. Elie Guérin, Georges J. Petit et Jacques Roumain, Le," 55–56
  excerpt, 56
  excerpts (quoting Roumain), 55–56
  translation, 276–277
Julien, Camille, 312
Juliot (White bishop), 55, 276
Juste, Fernande, 147–148
Justine (de Sade), 86
  excerpt, 86
  translation, 288

Khaddar, 50, 50n
Khayyam, Omar, 3–4, 58
Kierkegaarde, Sören, 162, 316
Ku Klux Klan, 194
Koran, The, 3
Krupp, 203

Laboring classes. *See* Workers
Labor meetings, 159
Labor unions, 194
Lafond (In *Les Fantoches*), 95
Laforest, Edmond, 14n, 257
Lagos, 136
Lala. *See* Mimola
Laleau, Léon, 14, 19, 181
Land, ownership of by foreigners, 11
Lange, Jeannette (In *Les Fantoches*), 91, 95–96, 100–101
"Langston Hughes" (Roumain), 131–132, 134, 136–138, 197
  excerpts, 136–137
  translation, 306–307
Lanoue, Le Substitut, 55–56, 276–277
Larivoire (In *Gouverneurs de la rosée*), 230, 234, 238–239
Las Casas, Bartolomeo de, 215
Latin America, x, 136n, 180
Laughter, mirthless, 83–84, 91

Laurelien (In *Gouverneurs de la rosée*), 230, 232, 235–237, 240, 245, 340
Laval Decree, 183–184
Lazaré, Chéri (In *La Montagne ensorcelée*), 110, 112, 115, 123, 302
League of American Writers, 208, 210
Lebinhin (white bishop), 55, 276
Lechaud (Roumain's attorney), 154, 312
Lecocq, Albert (In *Les Fantoches*), 91, 94, 107, 297
Lefevre (In *Les Fantoches*), 91–97, 99–100, 104–105, 107, 165, 170–171, 293, 296
Left Bank 145
Legba, 231, 233, 235
Legislative branch, reestablishment of, 63
Legislative elections, 59, 91
Leitmotiv, 232
Lemaire, Philéas, 54
Lenau, Nikolaus, 3, 255
Lenin, Nikolai, 143, 159, 176, 252, 308, 314
Léon (In *Mimola*), 127
Lesbianism, 41
Lescot, Elie, 148, 213, 217, 223–225, 335
"Lettre, La" (Chapter in *Les Fantoches* (Roumain)), 96–99
   excerpts, 96–98
Lhérisson, Justin, 122
Liautaud, André, 14–15
Liberation, 48, 51, 53, 63, 65, 167, 237
Light and dark, 26–29, 32, 78, 81, 91, 104, 134–135, 138, 173
Light-dark motif. *See* Light and dark
Ligue d'Action Constitutionnelle, 11
Ligue de la Jeunesse Patriote Haïtienne, 11, 54, 59–61, 61n
Literature
   black, xii
   Haitian, xii, 19
   indigenous, 19
   theory of, 38
"Literature—From Toussaint Louverture to Jacques Roumain" (Antoine), 42n, 251n
Loa, 127, 129, 230
Loan from United States, 10
Local color, 20, 128
Locke, Alain, 141n, 142, 142n, 206
Lopez, Antonio (In "Le Champ du potier"), 160, 314
Lost Generation, 77
Louisiana, 327
Louverture, Toussaint, 42n, 43, 93, 225

Love, 4, 29, 94, 98, 107, 110, 157, 168n, 169
   carnel, 58, 93, 241
Lovers, 39, 113–115
Lucien, Brother. *See* Lucien, Jean, Frère
Lucien, Jean, Frère, xii, 59
Lumière, La, 184n
Lyricism, 32, 34, 39, 78, 80–81, 120, 242–243

McCrocklin, James H., 8n, 13n
Madrid, 178–179
"Madrid" (Roumain), 178–180, 196, 227, 237
   excerpts, 179–180
   translation, 318
"Mahatma Gandhi". *See* "Idées et Opinions—Mahatma Gandhi" (Roumain)
Malaria, 157, 157n, 159–160
Mallarmé, Stéphane, 208–209, 222
Mamelles de Tirésias, Les (Apollinaire), 40n
Manger marrassa, 124
"Manifeste à la Jeunesse des écoles" (Roumain and Petit), 53
   excerpt, 53
Manifesto poetry, 45–48
Manuel (In *Gouverneurs de la rosée*), 341, 343. *See* Joseph, Manuel Jean
Manuscript sources, private, xi
Mapou tree, 109, 109n, 112, 130, 298
Marau, Aristide (In *Les Fantoches*), 92–93, 100, 105–106, 292, 296
Marguerite, Tante (In *Mimola*), 127–128
Mariani, 214
Marianna (In *Gouverneur de la rosée*), 234, 337
Marines. *See* United States Marine Corps
Maringouins, 117–118
Mario (In "Le Champ du potier"), 160, 314
Martial, André (In "Le Champ du potier"), 163–164, 166, 169, 171
Martial, Frédérick (In "Le Champ du potier"), 163, 171, 313–314
Martial, Pierre (In "Le Champ du potier"), 157–168, 163–166, 169–173, 189, 207, 232, 247, 311, 316
Martinique, 206
Martyr-messenger, poet as, 36
Marx, Karl, 139, 143–144, 159, 176, 308, 314
Marxist ethic, 167

Marxist novel, 189
Marxist philosophy, 139, 144, 147–149, 151, 160, 164, 208, 222, 237, 246
Massacre River, 319
Massacres
  in Dominica, 180–181, 184
  at the National Prison, 9
Masses, the 169. *See also* Haitian masses
Masters of the Dew (Roumain), 85n, 223n. *See also Gouverneurs de la rosée*
Mater dolorosa, 70, 243, 281
Materialism, regressive, 44
Matin, Le, 51, 154, 177n, 312, 317
Mayakousky, Vladimir, 209–210
Mayan culture, 3
Mayard (In *Les Fantoche*), 96
Medicine, 224, 224n
"Médicin rural ou la science au service du peuple, Le" (Roumain), 224
Medieval lyric genre, 39
"Meeting électoral, Le" (Chapter in *Les Fantoches* (Roumain)), 92
  excerpt, 94
"Meeting Se Tiendra Dimanche Matin, Le," 60
Meilleurs poètes et romanciers haitiens: pages choisies, Les (Gouraige), 127n
  translation, 303
Mercantilism, 44
Metaphors, 4, 25, 28, 31, 33, 36, 84, 115, 124, 179
Metaphysics, 118, 123–125, 160, 209, 221, 236
Metraux, Alfred, 214
Mexico, 33n, 181, 214, 223–226, 229
  chargé d'affaires to, 223
"Midi" (Roumain), 21n, 22–24, 24n, 134
  text, 23
  translation, 260
Militancy, 177
Military classes, 15
Milky Way, 31
Millieu, Emilienne, 153
Millieu, Léonina, 153, 153n, 154, 156
Millspaugh, Arthur Chester, 8n
Mimola (Lala) (In *Mimola*), 126–129, 304
Mimola, ou l'histoire d'une cassette (Innocent), 127, 127n, 128n, 129
  excerpts, 127–128
  translation, 304
Minister of the Interior, 148
"Mirage" (Garcia Barcena), 20, 21n, 29–30
  excerpt, 29–30
  translation, 264–265

"Miragôane" (Roumain), 21n, 24, 24n, 40, 134
  excerpt, 24
  translation, 261
Mirville (In "Gouverneurs de la rosée"), 186–188, 320
"MM Roumain, Pierre Paul, Cauvin sont-ils des assassins ou des conspirateurs?", 60
Mobilization, 169
Mohammed, 179
"Mon Ami Alcibiades" (Roumain), 73n, 76
  excerpt, 76–77
  translation, 284
"Mon Carnet" (JR) [Roumain], 40–41, 41n, 58, 86, 207
  excerpts, 40–41, 58–59, 86
  translation, 270, 277
Mondésir (Haitian priest), 55, 276
Monier, Christian (In "Le Champ du potier"), 157, 161–162, 169–173, 315–316
Monroe Doctrine, 8
Montagne ensorcelée, La (Roumain), 69, 71, 108–110, 113–115, 118, 120, 122, 124–126, 128–131, 140, 142, 157, 166, 172, 176, 181, 187, 241, 243–246, 305
  excerpts, 111–113, 115–117, 120–125, 227
  translation, 297–303
"Monte Carlo, Palace Hotel" (Amberger de Osa), 58
Montherlant, Henry de, 6, 256
Moral character, 48, 50
Moral courage, 64, 68
Morand, Paul, 53–54, 275
Moslems. *See* Muslims
Mothers, 69–70, 244
Motif symbolism, 33
"Mouvement communiste en Haïti étouffé dans l'œuf par le Gouvernement, Un" (Roumain), 140–141, 141n
  excerpt, 140–141
  translation, 307–308
"Mr. Jacques Roumain au Quartier-Général de la G. d'H.," 60
Mulattos, 151, 159
Mullen, Edward, 178n
Munro, Dana, 12
Musée del L'Homme, 176
Museums, 175–176, 214
Muslims, 49n, 50, 274
Mussolini, Benito, 16n, 177n
Mysticism, 49, 64, 129, 209
Myth, 25, 110, 119, 130

Narrative, 80
National consciousness, 53
National debt, 10
Nationalism. *See* Haitian Nationalism
Nationalist government, 15, 61
Nationalist groups, 11–12, 60–61
Nationalist leaders, 7, 12, 45
Nationalist poetry, 17n, 62, 133, 197
Nationalist writers, 14n
National Palace, 9
National Penitentiary, 144n, 147
National Prison, 9
Nature
    description of, 4, 23, 134, 245
    motif of man in, 116, 118, 129, 187–188
Navy. *See* United States Navy
"Nécessité de la Théorie" (Roumain),
    148
    excerpt, 148–149
    translation, 310–311
Negritude, 133–137, 179, 197, 202–203,
    226, 325
"Negro Speaks of Rivers, The"
    (Hughes), 137
Nehru, Jawaharlal, 209
*Neo-African Literature: A History of Black
    Writing* (Jahn), 132, 132n
    excerpt, 132
Neo-Marxist point of view, 198
Neo-Platonic imagery, 27
Neo-Romaticism, 17
New Masses, 160, 166–167, 208n, 222,
    314
New Masses group, 210
Newspaper Guild Club, 208
New Republic, 155
New York, city of, 141, 141n, 142n, 143,
    146, 152–153, 155, 159, 175, 206,
    208–211, 222, 232. *See also*
    Greenwich village
New York Age, 206n, 210n
New York Amsterdam News, 206n, 208n
New World, 199
Neitzsche, Friedrich, 3, 7n, 48–49, 139,
    255
Night, images of, 134–135
"Night in Haiti," 210
Nihilism, 4, 92
Noctambulation, 82–83, 91
"Noir" (Roumain), 21n, 29
    excerpt, 29
    translation, 264
Nonviolence, 48–49, 64–65
"Non-Violence, La" (Roumain), 49
    excerpt, 49–50
    translation, 273

"Noon" (Roumain), 260. *See also* "Midi"
"Notes pour servir à un manuel de
    parfait arriviste" (Roumain), 65,
    65n, 66, 68
    excerpts, 65–66
    translation, 278
"Notice Biographique," 176n
"Notice: Le Musée du Bureau
    d'Ethnologie" (Roumain), 214
    excerpt, 214
Noticias de Hoy, 211, 211n
Nous garderons le dieu (Brierre), 143,
    143n, 149
    excerpt, 143
    translation, 308
"Nouveau sermon nègre" (Roumain),
    195–196, 198–199
    excerpts, 199–200
    translation, 326
Nouvelle Ronde, La, 14–15, 15n, 18. *See
    also Ronde, La*
" 'Nouvelliste' Inconscient, Le"
    (Roumain), 52
    excerpt, 52
    translation, 275
Nouvelliste, Le, ixn, 7n, 52, 61n, 62n,
    144n, 145n, 147n, 152n, 155, 213n,
    214n, 216–217, 217n, 219, 222, 224n,
    255, 331–335
Novel, eighteenth-century European,
    128
Novel and the People, The (Fox), 168n
Novels. *See* Peasant novels *and*
    Roumain, Jacques: as novelist
"Nungesser et Coli" (Roumain), 21n, 34
    text, 34
    translation, 267

Obrero de Caribe, El, 146
Occide, 54, 275
Occupation. *See* American Occupation
Oeuvres Choisies (Romain), 223n
• Office of the registrar, Columbia
    University, letter from, 210n
Old Testament, 35
"Ombre des bougainvillers, A l' "
    (Chapter in *Les Fantoches*
    (Romain)), 94
Opposition, 7
Oppression, 2, 151, 175–211, 247
"Orage" (Roumain), 21, 21n, 22, 22n,
    25, 27, 38, 40
    excerpt, 25
    translation, 261

Organe officiel de la Ligue de la Jeunesse Patriote Haïtienne, 54. *See also Petit Impartial, Le*
Origines sociales de la littérature haïtienne, Les (Trouillot), 17n
Orozco, José, 225
"Orphée noir, L' " (Sartre), 196, 197n, 203, 203n
  excerpt, 197
  translation, 325
Orphic descent-into-hell, 21
Ossietsky, Carl von, 208
Ouanaminthe, 181, 319
"Outillage lithique des Ciboney d'Haiti, L' " (Roumain), 214–215
Oviedo y Valdés, Gonzalo Fernandez de, 215

Pagan rites, 103
Pain, 101
Palmette in the Light, The (Werleigh), 257. *See also Palmiste dans la lumière, Le*
Palmiste dans la lumière, Le (Werleigh), 14n
  translation, 257
Paola (In "Langston Hughes"), 136–306
Papal ambassador to Haiti, 217
Paradise, 122
Paris (France), 40n, 69, 85, 101, 144–145, 153, 156n, 176, 176n, 177–178, 180–181, 185, 193, 195, 195n, 204, 206, 211
Paris Exposition, 181
Parsis, 50, 274
Parti Communiste Haïtien (P.C.H.), 141–142, 149–152, 211, 311
Partisan Review, 167
"Parti Revolutionnaire Haïtien," 177n
Pascal, Blaise, 58
Passion, 199, 239
Passivity, 49, 111
Pastores, 154, 312
Pathetic fallacy, 24
Patriotic fervor, 133
Patriotic school of poetry, 17n
P.C.H. *See* Parti Communiste Haïtien
Peasant novels (*Romans paysans*), 71, 109–131, 133, 157, 173, 246
Peasants, 171, 180, 185, 188, 191, 196
Peasant women. *See* Women: peasant
Peasant workers, 10
Peking man, 162, 316
"Pélerinage" (Roumain), 68
Pequero, 145–147

Péralte, Charlemagne, 10–11, 43, 46, 46n, 68, 70, 180, 243, 281
"Péralte Crucifié" (Roumain), 46
  excerpt, 46
  translation, 272
Persia, 58
Perversion, 86
Pétion, Alexandre Sabès, 93, 100
Pètion-Ville, 214
Petit, Georges J., 43, 45, 48, 51, 53–57, 59, 59n, 61, 87n, 273–275, 277, 289
Petit Impartial, Journal de la Masse, Le, 42–44, 48, 49n, 51–57, 59, 59n, 62, 64–65, 73, 87n, 89, 103–104, 133, 177, 186, 207, 248, 271, 274–276, 289
Petty bourgeoisie, 151–152, 184. *See also* Bourgeoisie
"Peuple et l'Elite, Le" (Roumain), 44–45
  excerpt, 45
  translation, 271
Phalange, La, 219
Philodor, Jean-Baptiste (In *Les Fantoches*), 106, 106n
Philosophy, 172, 254
Picardy, 218
"Pièces Condamnées Tirées des Fleurs du Mal" (Baudelaire), 41
Pierre, 153
Pierre Paul, Antoine, 60–61, 61n
Piquion, René, 198, 198n, 325
Pittsburgh, 159
Placinette (In *La Montagne ensorcelée*) 109–110, 114–115, 117–119, 122–125, 129–130, 227, 298, 300, 302
Plasticity, 23, 116, 129, 179, 189, 241, 244–245
Platonic theory, 218
Pleasure, 42
Plot, 107, 111, 118
"Pluie" (Roumain), 21n, 22–23, 26, 28, 39
  text, 22–23
  excerpt, 26
  translation, 260, 262
"Poème" (Roumain), 131
"Poème de Jacques Roumain" (Roumain), 132, 137
Poèmes d'Haïti et de France (Roumer), 7n
Poèmes quisquéyens (Burr-Reynaud), 14n
"Poem for Jacques Roumain, A" (Hughes), 252, 252n
" 'Poesía Negra' in Latin America" (White), 33n, 136n
Poésie engagée, 39
Poet as martyr-messenger, 36
Poet-clown, 35–36

Poet-prophet, 89
Poetry, patriotic, 44
Poetry, 132n
Poetry of the Negro, The: 1746–1949
    (Hughes, Bontemps), 132n
Poetry of Haiti, The: 1782–1934
    (Underwood), 132n
Political organization, 150
Poor whites, 182, 184
Pope, the, 252, 331
Port-au-Prince, 1, 2, 4, 9–10, 24, 42, 51,
    54, 62, 68, 73–77, 91, 95, 97, 140,
    142n, 143, 146, 155–156, 169, 181,
    214, 216, 251, 295, 317
"Port-au-Prince–Cap-Haïtien"
    (Roumain), 68, 68n, 177n, 181, 243
    excerpts, 68–69
    translation, 280
"Portrait: Jacques Roumain" (Garoute),
    7n
"Portrait d'une paysanne rencontrée"
    (Roumain), 68–69, 281
Potter's field, 169n
Pouchkine, 194
Pradel, Seymour, 60
Pre-Columbian archeology, 3, 176
Pre-Columbian culture, 3, 6
"Préface à la vie d'un bureaucrate"
    (Roumain), 73n, 75, 80–81, 83–84,
    89–91, 164
    excerpt, 80–81, 83, 106
    translation, 283–285
"Préface de Jacques Roumain" (Saint
    Armand), 222n
    excerpts, 222
    translation, 335
Preintellectual knowledge, 25
"Préjugé de couleur et lutte de classe"
    (Comité Central du Parti
    Communiste Haïtien), 150–151
    excerpts, 151–152
"Prélude," 195–196, 226, 226n
    excerpt, 226
    translation, 336
Premier Consul. *See* First Consul
Président de la République. *See* Haiti:
    president of
Press, freedom of the, 184
Presse, La, 21, 27, 39–41, 53, 57, 59–60,
    60n, 61n, 62, 131n, 133n, 207, 262,
    270
Pre-Taino people, 215
Prêtre savane, 120, 120n, 235
Prey and the Shadow, The (Roumain),
    289, 290, 304. *See also La Proise et
    l'ombre*

Price-Mars, Jean, 19, 62, 64, 64n,
    125–126, 128, 175, 213–214, 216
Pride, race, 151
Prince, Gerald, xii
"Prochaine récolte en Haïti et les
    devoirs qui incombent aux
    Partisans de la C.S.L.A., La," 145
    excerpt in *L'Action Nationale*, 146
Proie et l'ombre, La (Roumain), 71, 73,
    73n, 81–82, 84–87, 87n, 88–91,
    98–99, 101–102, 105–106, 108–109,
    116, 131, 164, 166, 189, 247, 289
    excerpt, 85–86
    excerpt (from Vieux's preface), 86–87,
    106
    translation, 289, 296–297
Proletarian consciousness, 141
Proletarianism, 133, 170, 180
Proletarian literature, 166–167, 167n,
    168, 168n, 169–171
*Proletarian Literature in the United States:
    An Anthology* (Hicks), 168n
"Proletarian Novel, The" (Seaver), 167n
Proletariat, 140, 141n, 152, 171, 197, 325
Propaganda, 103, 166
Prophets, 25
*Propos de la campagne "anti-
    superstitieuse", A* (Roumain), 103,
    128, 216–217
    excerpts, 217–219
"Propos sans suite" (Roumain), 73–75,
    82–84, 105
    excerpts, 73–74, 82–84
    translation, 282, 286–288
Prosa de Prisa: Cronicas, 211n, 330
Prostitutes, 74, 82, 85–86, 136
Protestantism, 52, 275
"Puilboreau" (Roumain), 68
Puppets (*les fantoches*), 98–99, 105, 189
Puppets, The (Roumain), 388. *See also
    Les Fantoches*

Qualo (Haitian priest), 55, 276
"Quand bat le tam-tam" (Roumain),
    131, 134–135, 197
    text, 134
    translation, 305
Quisqueyan Poems (Burr-Reynaud), 258

Race, 150, 190, 198
"Rain" (Roumain), 260. *See also* "Pluie"
Race and Colour in Caribbean Literature
    (Coulthard), 196, 196n
    excerpt, 196

Race consciousness, 52–53, 95, 132–134, 141, 151, 293
Racial inferiority, feelings of, 53
Racism, 133n, 150–151, 169, 177–178, 325
Rape, 194
Ramakrishna, 48
Ravine-à-Couleuvres, 45, 271
R.D. *See* Réaction Démocratique, La
"R.D. et la lutte de classe, La" (Comité Central du Parti Communiste Haïtien), 152
"Réaction Démocratique, La (R.D.), 150, 152
"Rédaction du Soir, La" (Chapter in *Les Fantoches* (Roumain)), 94
excerpts, 94–95
"Réflexions" (JR) [Roumain?], 49n
Regands, 178, 180, 183–184, 184n, 185, 185n, 186, 187n
Relève, La, 88n, 289
Religion, 169, 180, 247
Religious practices, 103, 128
Rémy, Tristan, 140–141, 141n, 142, 155n, 164, 208
Renaissance, 5
Renaissance of Haitian Poetry, The (Garret), 21n, 132n, 251n
Renn, Ludwig, 225
"Répliques au Révérend Père Foisset" (Roumain), 103, 219–211, 237
excerpts, 219–221
translation, 332–334
Resurrection, 218
"Rêve de Georges Sylvain, Un" (Sylvain, Normil G.), 47
Revisionism, 150
Revolution, 141n, 160, 167, 168n, 169, 196–197, 203
poetry of, 31, 226
"Revolution and the Novel" (Hicks), 167
Revolutionary novel, 167
Revue Caraïbe, La, 109, 132
Revue de la Ligue de la Jeunesse Haïtienne, La, 14
Revue Indigène: Les Arts et le Vie, La, 2n, 6n, 13, 15, 17, 17n, 18, 18n, 19–20, 20n, 21, 25, 29–30, 34–35, 38, 40–44, 47, 53, 58, 73, 121, 132, 207, 248, 261–262, 264–265, 267–268, 271
Rey, Jeanne (In "Préface à la vie d'un bureaucrate"), 76, 165
Rey, Michel (In *Les Fantoches*), 91–92, 94, 100, 102–103, 106, 133, 165, 170, 290
Rey, Michel (In "Préface à la vie d'un bureaucrate"), 75–77, 80–81, 83–84, 89–91, 165, 170, 283, 288
Rhine (River), 179
Rhyme patterns, 39–40
Rhymes, using voiced and voiceless stops, 40
Rhythms, 20, 78, 80–81
abbreviated, 38
rigid, 39
rugged, 36–37
staccato, 38
Rire/sourire, motif of, 115. *See also* Laughter, bitter
Rissalvat al Tarohid, The, 3
Ritual killing, 119, 130
River, image of the flowing, 137
Rivera, Diego, 225
Rivet, Paul, 176
Rivière du Massacre, 181
Rolland, Romain, 178
Roman indigène, 125
Romans paysans. See Peasant novels
Ronde, La, 14n. *See also Nouvelle Ronde, La*
Rosalie, Tante (In *Mimola*), 127–128
Roumain, Auguste, 1
Roumain, Jacques
as adolescent, 4
as agronomy student, 6
as anthropologist, 103, 109, 123, 128, 209
appearance of, 42, 140
as archeologist, 176
arrest of, 54, 57, 60, 147, 147n, 152, 183
birth of, 1
Breton ancestry of, 133
as *chef de division*, 62, 90, 141, 144
daughter of, 210
death of, 157, 223–228, 251
and dialectical materialism, x, 103, 139–156, 167, 178, 208
as diplomat, ix, 223–225, 253
early youth of, 1–3, 7
as ethnographer, ix, 176, 213, 253
in exile, 175–211
father of, 44n
during first European period, 3–6
during first homecoming, 6–8, 22–23
generosity of, 140n
as Haitian Nationalist, 43–71
health of, 157, 157n
and humanism, x, 67, 131, 236
and idealism, 31
as journalist, ix, x, 43–71, 133, 177

as leader, 2–3, 5, 42
marriage of, 89
as melancholy youth, 5
mother-in-law of, 89
as novelist, ix, 69–71, 91–131, 229–249, 253
as poet, ix, 4–6, 16, 20–21, 21n, 22–42, 88, 91, 131–138, 140, 177–182, 198–204, 208, 253
as politician, ix, 43–71, 139–157, 175–211, 253
in prison, 42, 57, 60–61, 147, 155–157, 157n, 173, 175, 185
as professor, ix
and return from exile, 213–228
as revolutionary, ix, 139–173
and romanticism, ix, 4–6, 22–25, 31, 42, 77–78, 132
as short story writer, 16, 73–90, 177, 185, 185n, 186
as sociologist, ix
son of, 175, 210
as speaker, ix, x, 178
and symbolism, 22–23, 33
and surrealism, 6, 22, 25, 31, 33, 40, 132, 222
as translator, 20–21, 58
on trial, 55–57, 147, 152–155, 184–185, 205
wife of, 175, 210. See also Roumain, Nicole and Hibbert, Nicole
Roumain, Nicole, 210, 343. See also Hibbert, Nicole
Roumer, Emile, 7n, 18, 43, 89, 105, 156
Roy, Eugène, 11, 62
Ruling class, 194
Russell, General (American High Commissioner), 12, 133, 133n

Sacrements, 218
Sacrifice du tambour-assoto(r), Le (Roumain), 214–215
Sacrificial fire, 35–36
Sacrificial lamb, 35
Sacrificial victim, 35, 94
Sade, Marquis de, 86, 288
Sadism, 101
Saint-Amand, Edris, 222, 222n, 335
Saint-Aude, Clement Magliore, 222
Saint-Dizier, Pierre, 183–185
St. Martin, Gesner (In Les Fantoches), 96, 107
Saivre (In "La Veste"), 75, 77–78
Sajous, Marcellus, 147–148, 309–310
"Sales nègres" (Roumain), 31, 195–196,
198, 200, 202
excerpts, 200–201
translation, 326
Saline, La, 143, 154, 312
Salnave, Richard, 15, 17
Salvation, 32
Sam, Vilbrun Guillaume, 8–9, 61n
Santiague (In Les Fantoches), 91–96, 98–100, 102, 104, 104n, 105, 107, 133, 135, 138, 165, 170–171, 292, 294
Santo Domingo, 17n, 181, 319
Sartre, Jean-Paul, 196, 197n, 203, 203n, 325
Satire, 89, 165–166
Sauveur, (In Gouverneur de la rosée), 343
Savain, Pétion, 7n
Savoir-hero, 238, 243
Satyagraha (Gandhi), 67
"Savane désolée" (Roumain), 68
Scansion, twelve-syllable, 39
Scapegoat, 109
Schiller, Johann, 93, 291
Schopenhauer, Arthur, 3, 255
Scientific socialism. See Marxist philosophy
Sclerosis of liver, 226n
Scottsboro case, 155, 205, 329
Seaver, Edwin, 167n
Secretariat du Caribe (New York), 144n
Secret messages, 145
Seduction, 95–96, 101
Seghers, Anna, 225
Seine river, 40n, 136
Self-determination, 63
Senghor, Léopold Sédar, 179n, 197n
Sensuality, 69
Sentimentality, 128, 151
Serpents, 109, 109n, 119, 122
Service Technique d'Agriculture, 98
Setting, 4
Sicily, 203, 329
Silvani, Monseigneur, 217
Siqueiros, David, 225
Sky, motif of, 36, 81
Slavery, 67
Snake god. See Damballah
"Sobre Jacques Roumain" (Guillen), 211, 211n
excerpt, 211
translation, 330
Socialism, 144, 176, 178
Social justice, 3, 51, 151
Société des américanistes de Paris, 176
Soir, Le, 93–94, 103
Solidarity, 45, 47, 50, 53, 206, 229–249
Sonnet form, 40

Sorbonne, the, 176
Sorcery, 109, 119, 121, 123
Souffrant, Claude, 235n
Soul, concept of, 27, 218
Soul motif, 27–28
"Sous le Signe de la Solidarité
    Humaine" (Gouraige), 198
  excerpt, 198
South (Haiti), 146
South (U.S.), 13, 182, 319
South Africa, 201, 207, 327
Spain, 6, 6n, 7, 17n, 42, 177, 177n, 178,
    203, 211
  queen of, 33
Spaniards, 215
Spanish Civil War, 177–178, 180, 187n,
    198, 325
Spanish (language), 6
Spanish Loyalists, 177–178, 180
Spider, motif of, 124, 227
Spinoza, Benedictus de, 92, 291
Sports, 5–6, 34–35
Stalin, Joseph, 159–314
Stalingrad, 198, 325
State farm cooperatives, 150
Statement and resolution, 4
Stone Age, 193
Strikes, 168, 168n, 169
  at Damiens, 61, 63
  hunger, 147, 166
Style, 112–113, 119, 149, 171–172
Suicide, 75, 77, 80, 164, 171
Supernatural, 110, 114, 116, 124–125, 129
Superstition, 123, 128, 234, 237
"Surgi d'une natte de paille peinte"
    (Roumain), 21n, 26
  excerpt, 26
"Sur la liberté de l'écrivain" (Roumain),
    204, 204n, 205–206
  excerpts, 205
  translation, 329–330
"Sur le Chemin de Guinée" (Roumain),
    132n, 197
"Sur les superstitions," 216, 221, 237
"Surprise-Party chez Madame Lange"
    (Chapter in Les Fantoches
    (Roumain)), 95, 118
  excerpts, 96
Survival propaganda, 45
Switzerland, 3, 5, 7, 104, 256
Sylvain, Georges, 8n, 47, 259
Sylvain, Normil G., 17n, 18, 18n, 19–20,
    20n, 47, 259–260
Symbol, flower as a, 4
Symbolism, 104–105, 130, 134–135, 173,
    192, 241, 243

quasi-religious, 46, 192, 239
Syncretism, 218

Tafia, 42
Taino people, 215
Tartuffe, 106
Tendances d'une génération, Les (Denis,
    Duvalier, Bonhomme), 126n, 131,
    131n
  excerpt, 131
  translation, 304
Tension of forces unleashed, 39
"Terre et les Mort, La" (Roumain), 46
  excerpt, 46
  translation, 272
Terrorism, 153
Thaelmann, Ernst, 209
Third International, 147
Thoby-Marcelin, Philippe, 7n, 14, 15n,
    18, 20, 257, 258
"Three Negro Poets" (Lunard), 178n
  excerpt, 178
Threnody for Haiti (Laforest), 257. See
    also Thrène pour Haïti
Thrène pour Haïti (Laforest), 14n
  translation, 257
Timing, 111–113
"To Honor Toymain [sic] at 'Night in
    Haiti' Program," 210,
Tom-toms, 74
Tonnelle, 111, 111n, 137, 138, 297, 301,
    307
Tonnerre, Boisrond, 44
Tortue, La, 214
"Tragédie haïtienne, La" (Roumain),
    180–183, 185
  excerpts, 181–183, 185
  translation, 319–320
"Transmutation" of values, 66
"Travers la Littérature, A" (Duvalier),
    131n
Trinity, 230
Tropical atmosphere, 24–25
Trouée: Revue d'Intérêt Général, La, 13,
    15–18, 20–22, 24–25, 34, 43, 53, 73n,
    77, 260–261, 267
  excerpts, 16, 18
  translations, 258–259
Trouillot, Hénock, 17n, 132, 155n
Trujillo, Leonidas, 181–184
Tsar Noir (Morand), 53
Turgeau, 1–2, 106n

Under Secretary. See chef de Division
Underwood, Edna Worthley, 132n

Unemployment, 168n
Union organizers, 176
Union Patriotique, 11, 59–60
"Union Patriotique," 60
United Nations, 224
United States Marine Corps, 8–10,
    12–13, 73, 186, 247
United States Navy, 9
United States of America, 10–13, 64n,
    155, 167, 168n, 180, 182, 184, 193,
    205–211, 213, 278, 319, 323, 327
  Black American intellectual
    community, 142
  president of, 10
Université d'Haïti, 216
University of Pennsylvania, xii
Univers romanesque de Jacques Roumain,
    L' (Gaillard), 81n, 89, 129, 157, 242,
    245, 290
  excerpt, 90
  translation, 290, 341–342
Upanishads, The, 3
Urban fiction, 110, 113, 115, 133, 157
Utilitarianism, 43

Valencia, 178
Valery, Paul, 19, 209
Venceremos, 2
Venice, 136
"Veste, La" (Roumain), 20, 73n, 75–76,
    78
  excerpt, 78
  translation, 284
"Vie Littéraire, La" (Roumain), 57–58
Viergine (In "Créole"), 137
Vieux, Antonio, 2, 2n, 3, 3n, 5, 5n, 6,
    7n, 14, 15n, 17n, 18, 20–21, 21n,
    38–39, 41–42, 57, 86–87, 109, 133,
    253n, 256, 258, 269–270
Vilaire, Etzer, 62
Vincent, Sténio, 12, 62, 71, 143–145,
    145n, 153n, 156–157, 177n, 182–183,
    213, 317
Vincent government, 144–145, 145n,
    175, 182
"Violettes fanées" (Roumain), 4–5,
    22–23
  text, 4
  translation, 256
Virginity, 97
Virgin Mary, 231, 242
Virtuosity, literary, 39
"Vision d'outre-tombe" (Garcia
    Barcena), 20
Vital force, 37
Vivekananda, 48

Vodun, x, 109, 109n, 112, 116–118, 122,
    124, 127–129, 140, 215, 215n,
    216–218, 247, 301, 307, 331–332
Voix de la génération de l'occupation, La,
    7n
Voluntaires, Les, 178, 204, 204n, 329–330
Voodoo. See Vodun

"Waiting" (Roumain), 264
War, 67, 168n, 179–180, 206, 225. See also
    Spanish Civil War
War of Independence (Haitian), 43, 45n
Washington, D.C., 9, 141–142, 142n
Water, motif of, 192, 234–235, 241
Welfare of all people, 133
"Wenn der Tam Tam Schlagt"
    (Roumain), 132n
Werleigh, Christian, 14n, 257
Western point of view, 86, 199
West Indian ports, 159
Wharf-aux-Herbes, 74, 82, 154, 286, 312
"When the Tom-Tom Beats" (Roumain),
    132n
Whiskey, 42
White, Florence, 33n, 136n
White Race, 133–134, 190, 193, 321
Whites
  poor, 182, 184
  southern, 194
Whitman, Walt, 210
Witchcraft, 124
Women, 62, 69, 75, 84, 89, 97, 165,
    188–189
  black, 194
  bourgeois, 89, 101–102, 106
  middle-age, 89, 106–107
  peasant, 74, 91, 101–102, 104, 114–115,
    133, 137–138
  white, 194
  young, 89, 101, 107
Worker-organizer, 169
Workers, 168n, 169, 180, 194, 196
Workers, Haitian, 61, 143
Working class, 168n, 176
World War I, 34
World War II, 66, 198, 325
Wright, Richard, 206

Yankee brutality, 183
Youth of Haiti, 46–48, 54, 61, 87

Zamor, St Juste, 152–153, 153n
Zanzibar, 40n
Zombis, 117, 300
Zurich, 5–6, 8n, 257